D1314281

The Politics of
Minority Coalitions

The Politics of Minority Coalitions

Race, Ethnicity, and Shared Uncertainties

Edited by
WILBUR C. RICH

PRAEGER

Westport, Connecticut
London

Library of Congress Cataloging-in-Publication Data

The politics of minority coalitions : race, ethnicity, and shared
   uncertainties / edited by Wilbur C. Rich.
       p.   cm.
   Includes bibliographical references and index.
   ISBN 0–275–95488–9 (alk. paper).—ISBN 0–275–95489–7 (pbk. :
alk. paper)
       1. Minorities—United States—Political activity.   2. Coalition
   (Social sciences)   I. Rich, Wilbur C.
   E184.A1P65   1996
   323.1'1'0973—dc20   96–10428

British Library Cataloguing in Publication Data is available.

Library of Congress Catalog Card Number: 96–10428
ISBN: 0–275–95488–9
       0–275–95489–7 (pbk.)

First published in 1996

Praeger Publishers, 88 Post Road West, Westport, CT 06881
An imprint of Greenwood Publishing Group, Inc.

Printed in the United States of America

The paper used in this book complies with the
Permanent Paper Standard issued by the National
Information Standards Organization (Z39.48–1984).

10 9 8 7 6 5 4 3 2 1

Copyright Acknowledgments

The author and the publisher gratefully acknowledge permission to use the following:

Excerpts from *Can We All Get Along? Racial and Ethnic Minorities in American Politics* by Paula McClain
and Joseph Stewart, Jr. Copyright © 1995 by Westview Press. Reprinted by permission of Westview
Press.

Excerpts from "Surviving Democracy's Mistake: Japanese Americans and Executive Order 9066," by
Don T. Nakanishi. *Amerasia Journal* 19, no. 2 (1993): 7–35.

In memory of my father,
Savage Rich

Contents

Illustrations

FIGURE

Preface

In these turbulent days of second-guessing the nation's commitment to affirmative action, we need to ask ourselves, who are we and what have we become? We certainly are not the melting pot many hoped we would become before the turn of the century. We are no longer a black and white nation. We are a mosaic nation with people from around the world. Some of these people have suppressed their ethnicity, whereas others have publicly celebrated it. The recognition that we are a multicultural and multiracial nation has had a profound impact on politics in the United States.

A 1994 Wellesley College conference examined the long-term political implications of our status as a nation of multiple minorities. The preliminary indications were that the various groups are not assimilating but rather are moving toward separate minisocieties complete with separate languages, cultures, and enclaves. Even if society accepts the notion that cultural pluralism is consistent with democratic principles, the possibility of political hyperpluralism (with endless and nonproductive conflicts among groups) is daunting.

The conference provided an important opportunity for minority scholars to discuss possibilities for collaboration, networking, and coalition building. At present, few such opportunities exist for political scientists from different racial and ethnic groups to talk with each other. For them, social distancing is the norm. This book, which was generated from the conference, represents a comparative approach to race and ethnic relations, which should make the teaching of race and ethnic relations more inclusive.

Conference participants examine the political situations of their racial or ethnic groups in this book. Some chapters deal with the backgrounds of minority organizations, voting behavior issues, and coalition possibilities. Others examine the varieties of political accommodations assumed by these minorities. Still others address the lack of communication among these minorities and the consequences.

In addition to material presented at the conference, we have solicited two chapters that provide another perspective on intergroup relations. We hope that the reader accepts this book as the first installment of an ongoing discussion about coalition building among minorities.

Several colleagues at Wellesley College provided financial and other assistance for the conference. Although we cannot acknowledge them all here, we would like to mention a few: Diana Chapman Walsh, president of Wellesley College; Professor Joanne Berger-Sweeney, chair of the Committee on Lecture and Cultural Events; Professor Joel Krieger, chair of the Department of Political Science and Committee against Racism and Discrimination; and Professor Frances Malino, director of Jewish Studies. However, the views expressed in this book are those of the writers.

We also thank the staffs of the Public Affairs Department at Wellesley College for handling the publicity, Special Events and Conferences Department for organizing logistics, and the Audio-Visual Department for providing equipment for the conference.

Introduction

Wilbur C. Rich

America remains a polymorphic nation of cultural and political contradictions. We are a multicultural and polyglot nation dominated by a nineteenth-century unicultural Anglo-Saxon impulse. Our national inclination to discriminate against minorities of any type is reinforced by a variety of institutions and traditions. After years of protesting, outlawing discriminatory practices, and promoting racial and ethnic understanding, white America seems light years away from accepting nonwhites as political equals. Why? There is no single explanation. Political analysts spend their careers trying to explain the persistence of racial and ethnic antagonism in American life. None of the proffered explanations fully explains the inability of America to live up to its espoused political creed that all men are created equal and should be treated accordingly. In order for national politics to develop into a full democracy, it must incorporate all minorities. Without political incorporation, minorities will remain marginal in American political life and will not be able to enjoy the most important gift of American citizenship: freedom.

Before a group can be incorporated, it must have internal unity. Herein lies the dilemma for most except African Americans. Many disparate groups, which share racial features but differ in countries of origin, are lumped together into a single census group such as Hispanics or Asians. The prospect of all Asian and Hispanic groups agreeing on a single political goal is quite remote. Although Yen Le Espiritu (1992) in her book *Asian American Panethnicity* is optimistic about the prospects of an Asian coalition, there is little evidence to support her claims. Louis DeSipio's chapter in this book outlines barriers for a panethnic Latino identity. He highlights the cultural and socioeconomic differences among Hispanic groups. There are even more barriers when one talks about a pantribal identity for Native Americans (see Fleming's chapter). Lacking any common racial experience in America, minority groups remain separate. Each subgroup has sought a separate accommodation with the white majority (a vertical linkage), and in most cases groups have eschewed relationships with other minority groups (a horizontal linkage). This posture creates opportunities for mistrust and stereotyping. For example, some blacks believe that they do most of the protesting (shaking the tree) and that other minorities are "free riders" (picking up the fruit). Hispanics believe that hard work will allow them to prosper in America. Some Hispanics believe stereotypes that blacks do not want to work or are unwilling to work for low pay. Some Asians believe that entreprenuership is the secret to making it in America (see Cho and Kim's chapter). Asian Americans are puzzled by the lack of black-owned businesses in the black community. While some ethnic pretensions are harmless, others feed into long-standing stereotypes. The stereotypes about Arab Americans, caricatured in television and movies as bogeymen and terrorists, are examples of harmful stereotypes (see Mehdi's and Al-Qazzaz's chapters in this book). Stereotypes held among minority groups and those promoted by the white majority obviate chances for creating coalitions.

At the expense of underutilizing their collective political clout, minority groups continue to shun each other for at least four possible reasons. First, ethnocentrism creates an often unarticulated insularity among groups. Second, groups distrust each other and tend to maintain social distance. Third, there are differing assessments of group opportunities of assimilation (queuing). Fourth, minority groups now enjoy ad hoc alliances within the white majority group.

Defined by political and ethnic forces, minority groups hold a number of perceptions about themselves and their place in society. Some fear an anglicized political self, but others embrace the idea. Dario Moreno's chapter recounts how Cuban Americans distance themselves from other Hispanic groups by embracing white conservatives and the Republican party. Among minorities a strong sense of political efficacy is not universally shared. Rodolfo O. de la Garza makes this point when comparing African Americans and Latino Americans. A few groups have eschewed politics entirely. Increasingly, other minorities such as Asian Americans, Arab Americans, and Native Americans are being pressured by political parties, bureaucrats, and social scientists to think of themselves as political minorities.

The next few years will witness even more changes in American urban politics. There will be more Asian Americans and Arab Americans running for elective office. Conflicts and competition are inevitable, as each group seeks to maximize its own interests. Paula McClain's chapter analyzes the coming competition for elective office and political resources between African Americans and Hispanic Americans. As she points out, the political elites of both groups may coalesce, as they did in Los Angeles, but masses will continue to compete for jobs and housing. There are many questions regarding the current relationships among minorities which need to be addressed.

What factors other than size preclude effective political coalitions for these groups? Are there common themes in the disparate grievances of minority groups? Are rainbow coalitions possible without white liberals? What are the disincentives for creating minorities-only coalitions? Do minority groups have differential opportunities for assimilation? Will the informal queuing system for minorities preclude certain political communication? Will the inevitable competition for political office between blacks and Hispanics serve to make coalition building impossible? Will Asian American politicians create alliances with majority politicians at the expense of other minority groups? All of these questions arise because of the social distance between groups.

THEORIES OF SOCIAL DISTANCING

Robert Park (1924) is credited with the pioneering work on ethnic assimilation and social distance in which he defined social distance as an attitude or human feeling rather than a spatial concept. Parks believed he could measure the social distance between people. Conducting a nationwide survey, Borgardus (1967) developed the first scale to measure social distance. Reviewing the work of others concerning his scale and accumulated assumptions in social distance theory, Borgardus found that social distance decreased as people became more educated and established more contacts with other ethnic groups.

In this essay, social distance is a measure of avoidance among minorities based on group calculation of risks and benefits arising from contacts. Becoming political brings groups into intense involvement and conflicts with other groups. Therefore, some groups eschew politics and decide to remain marginalized in the political system. Dyer, Vedlitz, and Worchel (1989) found that blacks, Latinos, and Anglos maintain at least as much social distance from each other as Anglos maintain toward the two minorities. They postulate a matrix of relations among ethnic and racial minorities, according to five determinants of group political activism or acquiescence: group expectations, economic resources, group history, worldview (e.g., an old country–new country nexus), and leadership. In addition, groups can be classified according to their relative engagement in politics and their degree of visibility. Groups range from the politically engaged (blacks and Jews) to the politically alienated (Filipino Americans and mainland Japanese Americans). An array of ethnic groups exists along this continuum.

Moreover, groups can adopt either visible or invisible postures. High-visibility minorities (e.g., blacks and Latinos) are not only more numerous but also more politically organized. Low-visibility minorities, including some Asian groups, have a decidedly low political profile. Group profiles are subject to change. Forced to organize into political groups, some minorities such as Asians and Native Americans are becoming more visible as a result of recurring incidents. The chapters by Glenn Morris and Walter Fleming trace these developments among Native Americans. Yong Hyo Cho and Pan Suk Kim analyze how recent conflicts between Korean Americans and African Americans created conditions for alliances and more political cooperation. Don Nakanishi explores how mainland Japanese Americans can move beyond the tragedy of internment to more mainstream politics. These ethnic civic groups and political organizations, however, must maintain contact with black organizations beyond the active crisis period. Contact tends to prevent misunderstanding and internecine conflict. High-visibility minorities—blacks, Hispanics, and Jews—often seek to present their political preferences through political spokespersons. Low-visibility minorities such as Asian Americans have eschewed developing such spokespersons. Many in these latter groups have tenaciously held to their cultural and religious traditions, which reinforce enclaving and ethnic separateness.

Lana Stein's chapter on Jewish liberalism captures some of the group's historical plight that serves as the focal point for the literature of minority politics. Also included is Terri Fine's chapter on the changing political context of Jewish life in America. Whereas we have learned much about the politics of Hispanics from recent research on this group, there has not been a corresponding amount of work on Asian Americans. We still know little about the politics of Asian and Native Americans. For this reason we have classified them politically invisible. Their numbers are small, and there is no discernible group solidarity. In contrast, Arab Americans are very diverse, but international politics force them to see themselves as a monolithic minority group.

In this country visible minorities such as blacks, Hispanics, and Jews have frequently been required to produce political spokespersons. Many of these individuals are employed by associations to act as liaisons with other groups and to appear before the media. This is especially true for leaders of black associations, such as the NAACP and the Urban League, whose roles allow them to become national figures. In his chapter Martin Kilson discusses the developmental metamorphosis of black leadership. Kilson's comments about various political persona displayed by black leaders also hold true for Hispanic and Asian American leaders as they move into the mainstream of American politics. Although he concedes that the developmental cycle varies for different groups, there are always political and psychological problems when group leadership attempts to converge with the mainstream.

There is no Asian American equivalent of the Reverend Jesse Jackson. Yet many groups, such as Korean Americans and Chinese Americans, have tenaciously held onto their cultural and religious traditions which reinforce enclaving and ethnic separateness. They prefer to manage political interest in a private way.

These two dimensions outline a group orientation to political life in America. Presented in matrix form, the categories are as follows: engaged/high visibility, engaged/low visibility, and alienated/high visibility, alienated/low visibility (see table below).

Given the social distance among minorities and relative political visibility, what are the prospects for competition and conflict among them? More important, if all minorities are not at the same place in socioeconomic queue, then why cooperate?

Dimensions of Group Orientations

	High Visibility	Low Visibility
Engaged	Black Americans Jewish Americans	Arab Americans Korean Americans
Alienated	Hispanic Americans	Native Americans Chinese Americans Filipino Americans

THEORY OF QUEUE JUMPING

In an earlier discussion of the growing competition among minorities in public employment, I concluded that minorities are arranged in queues and that middle-class ethnic minorities with skills and credentials will become a ready-made recruitment pool. I asserted that the "children of this pool, armed with more job opportunities and education, will become better queue jumpers" (Rich 1989). Assuming that white insiders in public organizations decide who get which jobs, one expects decisions about ethnic outsiders to be made incrementally. The outside ethnic groups to be accepted will be the ones perceived as possessing the values closest to those of existing insiders. The second group may be those who aspire to those values. The queuing continues until all groups are given positions within the organization. For example, there are few Asian leaders of universities. Blacks have more higher education administrative experience than most Asians, but are less likely to be selected to lead a "white" university if there is a choice among minority groups. Selecting an Asian does not mean that barriers to university leadership are now erased for all Asians. One exception is not a harbinger of a queue rearrangement. I agree with the argument advanced by Hout (1986) that whites hire minorities who resemble them in education and attitudes. Employing a few members of a minority can create an impression of change, but the reality is that one queue jumper is not the doorperson for the minority community. Often the employment of one minority takes off the pressure to hire others.

In some employment centers certain minorities are preferred for queue jumping. That is, a conscious effort is made to place one minority ahead of schedule in occupational upgrading and social mobility. I like the term "preferred minority" because it shows how the white majority can arbitrarily grant privileges to a particular group without justification (Rich 1989). In such cases, individual members of this minority group are allowed to move up the occupational ladder faster than their collective groups can move. At first glance, it would appear that whites prefer those who are generally closer to them in facial appearances and behavior. A closer look reveals this has little to do with racial affinity. These white-like individuals are simply playing a token role in a stratagem. They are not the vanguard for their ethnic group.

Such queue preferences may signal more social acceptability, but not the end of job discrimination. For example, an Asian American could be hired as a scientist in a research group, but rarely would Asian Americans be hired in clerical positions in the same organization. There is still considerable resistance to seeing Asians in some types of jobs. Alternatively, black faces are fine in certain roles, but not in others. For example, blacks rather than Asians seem more acceptable as community relations and personnel specialists.

Professional blacks find themselves in very visible token roles, but not en-trenched in the organizational hierarchy. Few accumulate enough political power within their organizations to become effective mentors for other blacks. There are limits to what token minorities are allowed to do. Often minorities from different ethnic groups do not realize their common plight. There is usually little, if any, networking among the various minority groups. Organizations have traditionally manipulated position and resource scarcities to divert members from building coalitions. Individuals who form coalitions can do much more to control their social environments than those who remain isolated.

COALITION BUILDING IN THEORY AND PRACTICE

For purposes of this essay, I define coalition building as a process of creating a working relationship between ethnic or racial groups, which seeks to maximize political preferences. Participant groups agree to work together to achieve particular goals and, during periods of policy disagreements, to maintain a working relationship, defined as an agreement to communicate political intentions, actions, and expected outcomes to coalition partners. Besides communication, there must be an agreement to coordinate actions with each other and with the dominant groups. Accordingly, working relations require a strategy, a reward structure, and an organization to resolve disagreements. This coordinating organization exists solely to promote communication between groups and to provide a forum for debating topics of common interest. Given this definition, there are no formal coalitions among minorities. Why is this the case?

Caplow (1956) offers a theoretical model for coalition building. Using Simmel's sociological theories to build his power theory of coalitions, Caplow suggests that coalitions are reflections of relative resources controlled by political actors. For him coalitions contain dominant and subordinate members. Essentially, members of coalitions differ in strength. The strong member seeks to control the weaker one. In Caplow's triad, control over two parties is preferred to control over one. For example, in a triad of African Americans, Hispanics, and Asians, the African Americans, having a demographic advantage, voting strength, and visible leaders, will attempt to control the other members. For Caplow the internal dynamic of a triad is separate from the conditions leading to coalition building. In the precoalition stage, groups are free to bargain with each other regarding the conditions of their membership. Once the coalition is constructed, one group will attempt to control the others.

Later, Caplow (1959) created a typology of coalitions, arguing that "continuous coalitions" involve relations among groups in which one member permanently controls the internal dynamics of the triad. "Episodic coalitions" involve coalitions that distribute rewards to control the internal dynamics of the group. Loyalty to the coalition is assured with the distribution of incentives. "Terminal coalitions" are collaborating groups that dissolve after a single distribution of resources gained in the contest. In such cases, conflictual or competitive relationships develop between groups.

Coalitions are by nature unstable. Part of the reason is explored by Jerry Watts in Chapter 2. He argues that the black-Jewish coalition was a rhetorical construct, that is, it never was agreed to by the masses. If it ever existed, it was negotiated by political elites. Watts raises a series of questions about the origins and utility of this disjointed coalition. Generally speaking, we can say that coalition instability arises from a variety of activities inside and outside the political environment. Besides the possibility of side payments to groups influencing behavior, groups seldom bring equal amounts of political clout or resources to the coalition-building process. Hence, there are few opportunities to equalize the weight of coalition members, thus creating the conditions for instability.

It is difficult to equalize the contributions of coalition participants because they are constantly changing. Some minority groups have more education, more institutionalized associations, and greater financial resources. Pluralist theorists tell us that the accumulation of these resources or the solicitation of these resources accounts for why some groups consistently get their preferences enacted into law.

Besides resources, some minority groups have more internal solidarity than others (Carmichael and Hamilton 1967). This group solidarity may stem from a common language, racial features, or culture. Group solidarity can also be influenced by the political environment. Ironically, discrimination serves to reinforce group solidarity. Arati Rao's chapter on South Asian Americans makes this point well; however, the most glaring example is the role of de jure segregation laws in the South. These laws worked to deny blacks equal opportunities, but they also institutionalized racial solidarity among diverse groups of African Americans. In the North, racial segregation in housing performed the same function. These exclusionary practices are reinforced by social isolation.

Our political culture discourages ethnic solidarity among certain minority groups by offering the possibility of total assimilation if old cultural practices are discontinued. For example, a host culture may outlaw cultural practices of certain immigrants, such as family-arranged marriages, thereby making it difficult to maintain ethnic ties and formalized ethnic solidarity. Without these cultural linkages, individuals within the group will identify with the majority European group. In their chapters, Al-Qazzaz and Mehdi make a similar point about Arab Americans. Groups with European racial features are especially vulnerable to this tactic. The more successful and talented members can be raided away from the group so that the group is unable to create and sustain a leadership class (Rich 1989).

Throughout American history, the federal government has acted as a countervailing force when there is too much imbalance among competing groups. In the case of black Americans, the government acted, albeit slowly, to protect their right to vote in the South. Accordingly, the rule of southern politics changed. Through the 1965 Voting Rights Act, the political resources of black citizens were increased without decreasing the power of white citizens. The power of white segregationists to impose race-restricting laws was limited by the introduction of black voters. This change created more opportunities for building coalitions between blacks and progressive whites in the South. In this book, Rodolfo de la Garza shows how the Voting Rights Act also changed Mexican American politics and opportunities in the Southwest.

Following Caplow, I suggested that coalition politics will more likely occur if there are new organizations that allow extant minority associations to retain their organizational identities. This will maximize a variety of relations among groups of unequal size and resources. Conceding equality to all minority groups creates the possibility of conflicts between the smaller groups and the larger group. In other words, if Asians and Hispanics agree to grant each other equal status, it is still unlikely that coalition politics will occur. From his study of Los Angeles politics, Raphael Sonenshein (1993) concluded:

> While racial liberalism is necessary for the creation of a biracial coalition, it is not sufficient. Biracial coalitions between Blacks and white liberals are viable on ideological grounds, but they are not inevitable. Like most political coalitions, biracial coalitions are influenced by interest. The interests of white liberals may conflict with Black interests. Interest alliance, or at least the absence of interest conflict, is a condition required for strong biracial coalitions. (p. 10)

Although there are possibilities for coalition building based on ideology, such coalitions are the most vulnerable to side payments. Could a white Republican mayoral candidate split a biracial coalition by offering coalition sub-leaders more than they are receiving in their current arrangement? Sonenshein has correctly suggested that leadership ties and trust act to offset what I call "driveby pandering" of coalition members. Although Sonenshein's conclusions are based on observations of a black-white coalition, his point about mutual trust and respect is also key to forging successful coalitions among minorities.

NEW VOICES

There is a dearth of Asian and Latino Americans in mainstream politics. The chapters in Parts II and III suggest some reasons why this is the case. The interests of all minorities are served by more minorities being involved in politics and more communication among groups. In order to be active in mainstream politics, the less visible minorities must speak the language of politics. Speaking politically means more than articulating a political agenda, but also mastering the nuances of political language. Besides learning and mastering the language, less visible minority groups must reconcile their ethnic political group culture with the majority political culture. What is more important, new groups do not have to invent ways of entering mainstream politics, they can learn from the more visible minorities.

This decade should be remembered as a period when a variety of minority groups sought to speak to the country of their birth or adoption. Obviously the act of speaking is not without its perils. Usually new positive voices are welcomed, but dissonant ones are attacked. As a group exercises voice, the more other groups take notice (see Hirschman 1970). Taking notice means assessing a new group's potential as competitors or coalition partners. The window of opportunity is open. All minorities have an opportunity to speak truth to power.

The era of multiple advocacy brings with it new challenges and problems. Although all groups may have the right and obligation to speak, it is less likely each will be heard equally. Granted, each group has a special message, but overlapping and redundant messages are inevitable. To prevent a cacophony of voices, there must be more communication and coordination among minorities. Continuous communication is difficult, if not impossible, without some organizational structure. Within that structure a variety of ideological positions and interests can be accommodated. Even with this structure, there are limits to what Sonenshein calls the philanthropic model of coalition making in which some members are motivated by goodwill and altruism and others act as clients. No coalition can exist for a long period with such blatant paternalism. Equally, there are limits to ethnic exclusionary mobilization models. Gaining a complete understanding of each coalition member's interests, fears, and aspirations is the only way to make an alliance work.

REFERENCES

Borgardus, Emory. 1925. Social distance and its origins. *Sociology and Social Research* 9 (July–August): 216–225.

——— . 1933. A social distance scale. *Sociology and Social Research* 22 (May–June): 265–271.

——— . 1967. *A forty-year racial distance study*. Los Angeles: University of Southern California Press.

Caplow, Theodore. 1956. A theory of coalitions in the triad. *American Sociological Review* 19: 23–29.

——— . 1959. Further development of a theory of coalitions in the triad. *American Journal of Sociology* 64: 488–493.

Carmichael, Stokely and Charles V. Hamilton. 1967. *Black power: The politics of liberation in America*. New York: Random House.

Dyer, James, Arnold Vedlitz, and Stephen Worchel. 1989. Social distance among racial and ethnic groups in Texas: Some demographic correlates. *Social Science Quarterly* 70, no. 4 (September): 607–616.

Espiritu, Yen Le. 1992. *Asian American panethnicity*. Philadelphia: Temple University Press.

Hirschman, Albert O. 1970. *Exit, voice and loyalty*. Cambridge: Harvard University Press.

Hout, Micheal. 1986. Opportunities and the minority middle class: A comparison of blacks in the United States and Catholics in Northern Ireland. *American Sociological Review* 51 (April): 214–223.

Park, Robert. 1924. The concept of social distance. *Journal of Applied Sociology* 8 (July–August): 339–344.

Rich, Wilbur C. 1989. Minorities and the public service. *International Journal of Public Administration* 12, no. 4: 651–670.

Sonenshein, Raphael J. 1993. *Politics in black and white: Race and power in Los Angeles*. Princeton: Princeton University Press.

Thurow, Lester. 1969. *Poverty and discrimination*. Washington, DC: Brookings Institution.

Part I

African Americans
and the Coalitional Mood

1
An Anatomy
of the Black Political Class

Martin L. Kilson

The political classes of different American ethnic blocs exhibit during their metamorphosis three distinct but connected politicization personae or faces. These hypothesized politicization personae correlate closely with specific social status levels acquired by a given ethnic bloc as it progresses from its marginal status to a salient one in the American system, that is, as a given ethnic bloc traverses from weak social status to middle-level social status and finally to a position of relative parity.

Corresponding to these developmental social status rankings are the following three types of politicization personae: Type I—the alienation or protest persona; Type II—the ethnic bloc empowerment persona; and Type III—the systemic-convergence persona or the transethnic persona. The goal of Type III is to achieve multiethnic support for the ethnic bloc's politicians, enabling these political leaders to be recognized as peers to the majority bloc's leaders. Though each of these politicization personae can be viewed as operationally discrete, this does not mean that some facet of one type cannot coexist with another type. In general, it is not likely that each major ethnic bloc political class will manifest these politicization personae at precisely the same point in its development or with precisely the same political composition. Why is this so? For two reasons at least: first, the character of social status metamorphosis varies among American ethnic groups; and second, ethnic groups experience different degrees of bigotry and oppression during the changes in their status. The latter situation is particularly important in shaping the development of politicization personae of the black political class.

THE IRISH PATTERN: A CASE STUDY

A look at the development of the Irish politicization personae will sharpen our understanding of the generic dynamics relating to ethnic bloc politicization.

Between the 1870s and the 1930s, the Irish political class experienced the three types of politicization personae that I propose (Josephson and Josephson 1969). In regard to Type I, the Irish political class fashioned a protest persona that was mainly anti-WASP in content. It had a two-tier political composition: on one tier it was culture driven; on the second it was class driven. For example, the first tier was represented by militant pro-Celtic groups like the Fenian Brotherhood and Sinn Fein, which throughout the late nineteenth and well into the twentieth centuries were active in American politics as instruments of anti-British rebellious groups in Britain and Ireland. Even today a low-level (though real) manifestation of this earlier Irish protest persona is found in Irish American bourgeois and working-class support for the IRA, the terrorist militants in Britain and Ireland who seek to overturn Anglo-Protestant hegemony in Northern Ireland. On the second tier, the Irish protest persona during the early part of the twentieth century involved trade unionism, which was often militantly anticapitalist and sometimes prosocialist. But neither of these two strands of the Irish protest persona was very deep ideologically. Why? Partly because the Irish clergy and intellectuals favored the Americanization of the Irish working-class and bourgeois cultures. Also the majority of the Irish working class favored the moderate or pragmatic-activist sector of Irish trade unionism, and they supported George Meany of the American Federation of Labor.

The Type II political class persona (ethnic bloc empowerment) characterized the Irish political class during the same time that this political class exhibited a Type I persona—between 1870 and the 1940s. To put this another way, within the ranks of the emerging Irish American political class during this period, there was competition, so to speak, between Type I and Type II politicization persona. This competition is in fact a generic phenomenon within the political culture of American ethnic groups in general: no major American ethnic group has avoided some variant of this competition between Types I and II.

What happened to this competition in the Irish experience? Let me present just the skeletal attributes of the competition between Types I and II. First, the Type II persona vanquished the Type I persona. Second, in the Irish experience, the Type II victory over the protest persona among Irish politicians was a clean sweep. In other words, by the end of the 1920s most of the alienation or protest face of politics, the Type I persona, was attenuating and on the verge of dying out.

Moreover, this victory of the empowerment persona over the protest persona resulted in the early emergence of the third type: the convergence or transethnic persona. The fundamental feature of the Type III persona is that an ethnic bloc's political class—or rather some special members within it—increasingly fashions a political demeanor that legitimates it and enables its members, when they run for major offices, to gain recognition from voters outside the native ethnic bloc.

To a politically significant degree, the Irish American political class exhibited a viable transethnic persona by the first decade of the twentieth century. In 1910, Edward Wilson became the first Irish politician to convince a majority of non-Irish voters at the state level to elect him governor of Ohio. By 1915, Al

Smith became the second and ultimately the most famous convergence persona Irish politician to emerge. He was elected governor of New York and re-elected twice. After 1920, numerous Irish American politicians won elections as governors, senators, and congressmen from WASP-dominated districts. And, of course, in 1928 the first politician from the Irish bourgeoisie won the presidential nomination from a major political party: the Democrats nominated Governor Al Smith.

A Note on Other White Ethnic Blocs

Politicians in other white ethnic groups—Italians, Jews, and Poles, for example—present informative comparisons. An analysis of political class development reveals that some variant of the Type I persona characterized the Italian, Jewish, and Polish leaderships in the formative stage of their social mobility—the stage when the vast majority of the ethnic group is weakened by poverty or economic conditions. The group is primarily working class, with only a small middle class (under 20 percent). Among Jewish Americans, facets of the protest or Type I persona persisted even into the middle stage of social mobility, that is, when about 50 percent of the ethnic group has entered stable working- and middle-class positions in the society. For example, as the Jewish political class entered the Type II stage in the 1930s through a three-way ethnic alliance led by Mayor LaGuardia of New York, a Type I protest persona persisted in a segment of the Jewish leadership. This segment was composed of left-wing activists—intellectuals, unionists, and some elected politicians—associated with both socialist and communist elements in the United States during the 1930s and early 1940s (Bayor 1988).

The competition between Type I and Type II personae was resolved in favor of the Type II pattern by the late 1960s, thereby facilitating the transition to the convergence persona (Type III). This transition was characterized by a highly deferential tilt toward Americanistic conservative symbolism by a major segment of the Jewish leadership. The label "neoconservatism" was attached to a key segment of the Type III transition among Jewish Americans, which contributed significantly to the overall conservativization of American politics during the Reagan-Bush era.

Furthermore, as was the case with Coughlinism and McCarthyism in the Irish political class's formation of the convergence persona, the Jewish Type III transition cultivated an Americanistic establishmentarian put-down of vulnerable groups on the liberal side of the political spectrum—especially the black Americans' civil rights movement and the feminist movement.

DEVELOPMENTAL ATTRIBUTES OF THE BLACK POLITICAL CLASS

The evolution of the Type I persona in the black American political class has been similar to what I have schematically outlined for the Irish political class. But in substantive operational terms, the black pattern has been both the same and different. The differences are politically crucial when analyzing the black political class's development within the American system (Levine 1966).

First, if we look at the Type I politicization persona for the black political class, we see immediately that when compared to the Irish political class, the Type I pattern persists across three generations of black politicians. The Type I pattern began in the early 1900s among the 10–15 percent of the black American population living outside the authoritarian racist system in the South, that is, living in the North between, say, 1910 and 1960. Every big and middle-sized black urban community in the North had at least one (and sometimes several) political organizations led by Type I politicians—organizations like the NAACP, the National Urban League, the National Negro Bar Association, the National (Negro) Medical Association, and the National Negro Business League.

Functionally, the Type I politicization persona for the black political class from the early 1900s to the 1960s performed a unique constitutive and systemic task that the Irish Type I persona did not have to perform—namely, to incorporate blacks into the citizenship social contract. The Irish protest persona, by contrast, performed the task of articulating cultural and class interests of a subproletariat that was culturally alienated from WASP-hegemonic America but that had citizenship status by virtue of being white. Surmounting the ethnic illegitimacy attached to blackness was, then, a Sisyphian function of the black protest persona that no white ethnic bloc protest persona confronted (Roediger 1991).

One outcome of this situation was that the protest politicization associated with the Type I persona had a much broader base among black Americans than protest politicization had among white ethnic blocs, where it was usually limited to the leaders of the white working class and only a few from the middle class. Furthermore, the Type I persona among black leaders did not exhibit a short-run militancy, but instead spawned a protracted cultural militancy, owing to blacks' rigid racial-caste type of ethnic marginalization in American life, a range of ethnic marginalization not experienced by any white ethnic blocs.

Furthermore, there has been a unique leadership subplot or strand within the Type I protest persona that historians have called the black separatists or nationalists. For my purposes, this black nationalist category can be dated to the rise of Marcus Garvey's Universal Negro Improvement Association around 1918. Its lineal progeny is an important component in black political life today, as in the case of the Nation of Islam. In general, however, the mainstream sector of the black political class articulated the Type I persona in terms that were convergent with societal and cultural incorporation of blacks within American life. Therefore the mainstream black political class, in contrast to the black separatists, deployed the Type I protest persona as a weapon to guarantee citizenship or social contract incorporation.

There are two basic structural attributes that distinguish the black political class's Type I persona. First, as political class persona, it prevails almost three times longer than its counterpart in white ethnic blocs. Second, owing to the juridical and violence-riddled exclusion of blacks from citizenship contract incorporation—

political class's formation of the convergence persona—the Jewish Type III transition spawned a small but effective conservative segment. It seems that each major white-ethnic group's convergence persona entails some measure of an Americanistic deferential tilt toward establishmentarian systemic predilections in American political culture—a kind of political "tip-of-the-white-ethnic-hat" to the WASP-hegemonic aura within the American system. Whether the metamorphosis of the Type III convergence persona among the African American political class will also exhibit an Americanistic deferential tilt toward the WASP-hegemonic aura within American life remains to be seen.

Dilemmas of the Black Political Class Type II Persona

As already noted, though the ethnic bloc empowerment persona became available for white ethnic politicians while their communities were, in terms of social mobility, still within the weak social status stage, the Type II persona was not available, in effect, to the black political class until a period late in the middle-level social status developmental stage. This long lead time transition to the Type II persona produces important structural deficiencies for today's black political class.

In general, the development of the Type II persona of politicians among Irish, Italians, Polish, and Jewish Americans suggests that each ethnic bloc political class leveraged public resources in government offices (e.g., mayoralties, county commissions, state legislatures, governorships, federal legislatures) to consolidate or expand the developmental resources of the ethnic bloc bourgeoisie. This is what I call a bourgeois-consolidation policy allocation, and it seems to be a fundamental posture for the Type II persona of all major white ethnic blocs (Zink 1930). Furthermore, the bourgeois-consolidation process under the Type II persona has been the basis for interethnic electoral alliances since the early 1900s. As Clark (1973) has shown, the Irish political class in Philadelphia was masterful at creating and choreographing electoral alliances among white ethnic groups through an exchange of public policy resources that aided the bourgeois-consolidation process among white groups. And, with the huge expansion in allocations of public policy resources in the New Deal, white ethnic electoral and legislative alliances fashioned public policies that improved the economic status of both the white working class and poor whites (Buenker 1973).

What about the qualitative aspects of the Type II persona in the black political class? I suggest that this persona has developed in unique ways in regard to its public policy dimension. When compared to its counterparts in white ethnic blocs, which evolved in a milieu that John Buenker (1973) has aptly called the "era of urban liberalism and reform (1890–1950)," the black political class's Type II persona has evolved during the past thirty years amid conservatism in public policy. This is a far cry from the innovative public policies of the Wilson administration (1912–1921) and the Roosevelt and Truman administrations (1932–1952), and even the moderate Republican innovations in public policy under Eisenhower (1952–1960), which initiated the interstate highway system and subsidized agricultural production through price supports, soil banks, and federal assistance to technological innovation in farming. Federal supports, however, declined massively during the Nixon-Reagan-Bush years of fiscal conservatism, a period corresponding to the black political class's Type II development.

A problematic political legitimacy has surrounded this class's access to public policy resources from 1968 to the present. Even the Carter administration (1976–1980) could not significantly alter this dynamic; indeed, it did not generate a quantum-leap expansion of initiatives around blacks' policy needs. The result was that the black political class was limited to producing mainly policy benefits for the bourgeois-consolidation process among African Americans rather than programs to reduce joblessness and poverty.

Above all, the conservative limitations on these resources in the era of new conservatism since 1980 have had an impact on the black political class's ability to deliver viable education systems for black children from working-class and poor households, sections of the community that are seen as weak in terms of their political power. Of course, factors not directly linked to conservative policies—factors of social decay such as female-headed households, drugs, and crime—have figured in the subaverage education of working-class and poor blacks. Nevertheless, the ethnic bloc empowerment persona for the black political class has confronted many more obstacles to its enjoyment of public policy resources than the white ethnic politicians' metamorphosis through the Type II phase from the early 1900s to the 1950s. Erie (1988) uses the apt phrase "rainbow's end" to characterize the differentials between white ethnic blocs and the black political class as each evolved through the Type II phase, and he skillfully disentangles the political and ideological dimensions within the American system that shaped the policy-resource allocation differentials in these groups' experiences with the ethnic empowerment persona.

THE CLASS BASIS OF CLEAVAGES IN THE BLACK LEADERSHIP

At the core of the current intrablack leadership cleavage is the separatist or antiwhite variant of the protest persona—a black leadership style first fashioned by Marcus Garvey's Universal Negro Improvement Association during World War I and later honed into a cathartic politicization instrument by the Black Muslims or the Nation of Islam, first under Malcolm X and today under Minister Farrakhan. As contrasted with the pragmatic sector of mainstream black leadership, which employs the protest persona to enhance the quality of black incorporation in American society (such as the NAACP and the Reverend Jesse Jackson), the separatist or Afrocentrist leadership style emphasizes the sharpening of black-white fissures and schisms. The separatist leaders, moreover, are quite successful, as measured in part by Farrakhan's ability to attract approximately 20,000 black citizens to a public stadium in Baltimore or New York to hear him speak, at $20 per person. No pragmatic-sector figure among mainstream black leaders—not the head of the NAACP or the Urban League, or leading officeholder like former

Virginia Governor Douglas Wilder, not even the Reverend Jackson himself—can do the same.

Why has this intrablack leadership cleavage emerged? For many reasons, of course, but mainly because between the late 1960s and middle 1980s there arose an odd two-tier mobility dynamic among black Americans. On the top tier occurred the major forging of what might be called the New Black Bourgeoisie epoch. Starting in the mid-1960s and extending into the 1980s, a combination of buoyant national economy and black mobility pump-priming practices associated with the federal government's affirmative action policies expanded the black middle-class occupational ranks from 13 percent of employed blacks holding such occupations in the early 1960s to 45 percent by 1983. Another 20 percent of employed blacks from the 1960s to 1983 moved from weak working-class to strong or upper working-class jobs, which provided incomes that facilitated at least lower middle-class living standards (see Landry 1987). The cumulative effect on social structure of these two strands of job market advancement among African Americans from the mid-1960s to the mid-1980s translated into an unprecedented bourgeois penetration of white America by black America (Kilson 1983; Kilson and Cottingham 1993).

Alas, no sooner had the New Black Bourgeoisie epoch surfaced than it immediately faced the dilemma posed by the simultaneously evolving Lower-Class Black Crisis epoch, representing a veritable leadership vacuum over the issue of how to contain or reverse it. Continued growth of indices of societal decay among the black poor complicated the problem of this leadership vacuum. In addition there was fierce alienation felt by the black poor, males especially, who witnessed the brutality of white police forces in our cities and saw the legacy of white America's racism. This alienation played a major role in the riotous black insurrections that gripped major cities in the late 1960s and the early 1970s, for example, in Los Angeles (1965), Newark (1967), Detroit (1968), and Gary (1968).

Who, then, would fill this gigantic leadership vacuum? Among the possible leadership options, the pragmatists among the black intelligentsia, benefiting from the pump-priming mobility policies of the federal government, looked to be a major contender. And contend they did, producing the first full-fledged black American political class based on electoral politicization rather than mainly protest-type civil rights politicization. The growth of this class was protracted but substantive—from around 300 elected officials nationwide in 1963, to over 7,000 by 1989, to approximately 8,000 in 1993. When black administrators' office-holding and policy technicians-qua-advisers are added, the aggregate political class among blacks constitutes well over 30,000. The officeholding sector of the political class typically functions in or near urban communities where the vast majority of African Americans now reside, and though some officeholding blacks function at the federal level, they often perform tasks related to issues affecting urban communities.

But has this now full-fledged Type II black political class and its network of professionals within the new black bourgeoisie displayed a serious behavioral readiness to fill the leadership vacuum between the haves and have-nots in black

America? In general terms, the answer is No! They have not effectively attended to this leadership vacuum; they have not, that is, designed leadership strategies focused on that massive crisis of poverty and societal disarray—an increasingly internecine cycle of crime and violence—that has stunted modern mobility among 30–40 percent of black American households. The now full-fledged Type II black political class has done little more than replace the governmental posts once occupied by white ethnics with blacks.

It seems that the allocation of public policy benefits between the have-nots and the haves among African Americans over the past twenty-five years has been massively weighted toward the haves, that is, toward the upper working-class, the middle-class, and the upper bourgeois elements, who in aggregate constitute about 70 percent of black households. For example, black professionals who perform major city functions under black mayors or in urban regimes with major black political clout, have executed these city functions mainly in a bourgeois mobility-consolidating rather than in a lower-class outreach manner (Kilson, forthcoming). Emerging studies by urban analysts like Rich in Detroit and Gary and Cottingham in Newark bear out this assertion. Cottingham's research in Newark, in fact, shows that black teachers and education bureaucrats—along with their white peers— have used the billions of dollars in public budgets they administer mainly to enhance income and bourgeois perks, without creating an accountability system that requires them to train African American students to function well in the system (Cottingham forthcoming; McCaffery 1991).

Above all, this bourgeois-consolidating manipulation of city budgets virtually amounts to the black elite's thumbing its nose at the black poor and weak working class, whose activist role or street radicalism contributed to the break-throughs in national policy in the late 1960s, breakthroughs that grew out of the overall activism of the civil rights movement, including the Civil Rights Act of 1964, President Johnson's Affirmative Action Executive Orders and Rules in 1964–1965, the Equal Employment Opportunity Act of 1964, the Voting Rights Act of 1965, the Civil Rights Acts of 1967 and 1968, and sundry administrative rules attendant on these and other pieces of legislation that deepened and extended their sway. These breakthroughs laid the basis for the emergence of the black political class.

The Antisystemic-Oriented Black Poor

Keep in mind that these policy breakthroughs were linked to a volatile push from the bottom of the black lower stratum—a kind of street radicalism during the 1960s that was electorally harnessed by the new Type II political class in the 1970s. And since the 1980s there continues to be a push from the bottom, but it differs fundamentally from the earlier street radicalism in that it has not been electorally harnessed. Why has this incredible political vacuum proved so elusive? The reasons are many: some are systemic, tied to the new conservatism that has shaped public policy interventionism vis-à-vis our capitalist system's abandonment of the black poor; other reasons are linked to the new dynamics among the black elite.

If we perceive this political vacuum from the everyday perspective of "the 'hood," it is clear that the new black bourgeois sector that has emerged since the 1960s has not "paid its dues." Thus, "the 'hood" is aflame with disenchantment, anger, rage, and an overall normlessness that can be called anomie. In cities like Detroit, Baltimore, Washington, D.C., New York, and East St. Louis, nihilistic black youth revel in a maddening game of "knock-the-stick-off-my-shoulder" played today no longer with rolled-up hands called fists but with vicious automatic weapons.

Though now abandoned economically by our cynical, hyperplutocratic, and globally skewed American system, the black poor in general and black poor youth in particular will not let themselves be thrown away. Political analysts seldom ask why today's black poor should allow the hyperplutocratic American system to "discard" them. Does the governing elite possess a special edge in moral rectitude vis-à-vis nihilistic black and Hispanic youth in our cities? If the guide to the quality of moral and ethical rectitude among the power elite is the data on the S&L rip-off of nearly one-half trillion dollars of American citizens' wealth, then the answer to this query must be a resounding No! (see Stewart 1992; Bok 1993; Valentine 1994).

Black poor youth have taken the offensive by fashioning a two-tiered, high-risk economic system—the drug trade—outside the formal economic system. On the bottom tier we find the black poor. On the top tier is the drug trade—an economic market that, like most American markets, is controlled by whites both at the organizational level, especially with the large Mafia role, and at the financial level, where numerous banking structures participate illegally in the multibillion dollar laundering process. Though one would never know this from America's media, white Americans consume illegal drugs at a greater ratio than black Americans do, and this is even true for white youth at all class levels. Yet the focus of police interdiction of the drug trade and drug use is disproportionately centered on black urban communities. On the bottom tier, the focus has been on the expanding criminality—the muggings, burglaries, auto thefts, robberies, and homicides, that occur daily. Today the black crime rate is one of the top national issues.

What is the political meaning of this informal economic system available to the black poor? One thing it means is that today's black poor, unlike their counterparts of an earlier era, are no longer so deferential toward mainstream authority (and power), but now harass postindustrial Americans rather like the barbarians who harassed the Roman Empire. The Hispanic poor, who are also involved in the drug-driven economy, are equally involved in this harassment of the postindustrial and hyperplutocratic American system; the white poor are rapidly expanding their involvement as well. For the leaders of the black political class in particular, the black poor's role in harassing American life today constitutes a major dilemma. The black political class has not electorally harnessed the black poor segment. The political vacuum vis-à-vis the black poor persists.

Overcoming the Afrocentrist Cathartic Impact

There are at least two options that the black political class could deploy vis-à-vis the current leadership vacuum. First, it could employ political penetration, especially through the electoral process. Second, it could employ cathartic penetration, especially through the vast infrastructure of cultural agencies available to the new black bourgeoisie, for example, churches, voluntary and civic associations, and professional associations. Political penetration has not worked for reasons relating to deficiencies of Type II black politicization as well as to the structural deterioration of the black poor because of the decaying inner-city economies and the related societal disarray—situations that are unfriendly to viable politicization. Neither has cathartic penetration (the cultural authority mobilization) among the black poor been mastered by the black political class. Thus, the failure to provide leadership in these two spheres vis-à-vis the black poor is at the heart of the overall African American leadership schism.

Since the 1980s a major struggle for control has arisen among black leaders over the cathartic penetration option. This control has been seized by the separatists or Afrocentrists among black leaders. At least two strands among the Afrocentrist leaders are evident: the Afrocatechists who are sometimes based in universities and represented by separatist intellectuals like Professor Asante Molefi at Temple University; and those in the xenophobic sector, which is best represented by the Nation of Islam and Minister Farrakhan. The Afrocentrists exhibit a hands-on ghetto connectedness, a multilayered presence in "the 'hood," especially through Afrocatechist ties to black public and private schools where they work as curriculum advisers, administrators, and teachers.

What does the presence in the black community of several strands of Afrocentrists mean vis-à-vis the political metamorphosis of the black political class? First, insofar as the evolution of the Type II persona of black politicians into viable public policy clout requires a high electoralization of black voters, the growth of influence by Afrocentrists militates against this goal. Why? Because the Afrocentrist mode of ethnic-bloc mobilization is only tangentially related to electoral politics. Instead, the Afrocentrist mobilization centers on mythologizing history and life experiences, inspiring African Americans with a chosen people mystique, a people deserving of a millenarian salvation. This paradigm purports to be a more effective way of channeling the black poor (and even middle-class blacks) into modern development. As such, the Afrocentrist paradigm is not generically new, since, for example, the Mormon denomination among WASPs has successfully promoted a noble people mythology for attracting millions of adherents, and the Hasidim sect among traditionalist Jewish Americans has done the same. The question, then, is not whether the Afrocentrists are trying to invent the impossible, but rather whether they can pull it off among the black lower stratum.

This issue cannot be answered at present because there is not adequate data on the development of the several strands of the Afrocentrist black leadership. It is conceivable that a pragmatic disciplining of the Afrocatechist strand among Afrocentrists—the strand that emphasizes a kind of Afro-romantic socialization of black children through their schooling—might very well achieve viable development among the black lower stratum. Meanwhile, there remains the xenophobic sector of Afrocentrists, now dominated by the Nation of Islam and Minister Farrakhan, whose impact on African American realities is intensified by the anger-driven mobilization of a sense of black self-efficacy through bashing and scapegoating whites, especially Jewish Americans. Xenophobic bashing by Nation of Islam leaders has also been directed against Catholics, gays, and feminists. What does this mean for the mainstream black political class? Above all, it creates a highly counterproductive political milieu within which it must attempt to expand its public policy capability. Biracial alliances at both electoral and legislative levels are the key to expanding the black political class's clout. There is no way to ignore this. The xenophobic Afrocentrists inevitably complicate biracial alliance politics.

CLEAVAGE AND ALLIANCE CRISES: A NOTE ON BLACK-JEWISH DISCORD

The black political class has been as pragmatic in its overall politicization strategy during the evolution of its Type II persona, as different white ethnic groups have been at comparable developmental periods. The strategy of maximizing interethnic alliances at both the electoral and legislative levels has, therefore, been given a prominent agenda status in the past twenty-five years of Type II persona metamorphosis. Black mayors in several major cities like New York, Philadelphia, Chicago, Cleveland, and Atlanta, as well as black state legislators and other elected officials, have consistently cultivated interethnic or biracial alliances.

In general, however, white interest groups and voters have not yet found a cross-ethnic openness toward quality black candidates for major elected positions as white candidates have experienced. The explanation for this situation lies, of course, in the complex interplay among white voters' policy orientation on the one hand, and racial attitudes on the other, with most white voters opposing policy orientations that correspond with an activistic black civil rights agenda. Though blatant antiblack attitudes among whites are no longer widely held—at least as measured by public opinion surveys—a variety of social realities associated with black Americans (like the high rates of crime, teenage pregnancy, unwed mothers, poverty, and welfare) are perceived in strongly negative terms by a majority of whites. These are inevitably translated into at best a cautious posture toward biracial alliances and at worst a negative posture (Browning, Marshall, and Tabb 1990).

A good analytical subplot of the overall dilemma of interethnic alliances as they relate to whites and the black political class is provided by the alliance dynamics involving blacks and Jewish Americans. Between the late 1950s and the late 1960s, the activist or radicalizing phase of the civil rights movement witnessed what is commonly called a black-Jewish alliance. This alliance did not yet involve a mobilization of Jewish voters to support a Type II black political class since one did not exist in this period, though the old black-Jewish alliance did involve mobilizing Jewish votes for white politicians favorable to the civil rights agenda, as well as mobilizing Jewish individuals for activist roles and for financial support of civil rights organizations. However, the old black-Jewish alliance weakened and dissolved by the start of President Nixon's second term. The alliance was displaced by two simultaneous ideological metamorphoses among blacks and Jews. Among

Jews there was the steady evolution of a conservative voter sector—either Republican or conservative Democratic—with major Jewish intellectuals fashioning a new conservatism that de-emphasized public policy interventionism.

In this same period of the late 1960s an expansion of separatist militancy occurred among those civil rights elements to the left of the NAACP and the National Urban League, such as the Stokely Carmichael wing of the Student Non-Violent Coordinating Committee, separatist-minded teachers, and especially those influenced by Malcolm X. This growing separatist militancy was at the center of the conflict in the Oceanhill-Brownville School District dispute in 1968 in New York, when militant black teachers and community groups employed anti-Semitic appeals to mobilize in favor of the ousting of Jewish teachers and administrators.

This event reverberated throughout the civil rights movement, turning black-Jewish concord into discord that the fledgling Type II black political class in the 1970s could not contain. Now, in the 1990s, a well-developed Type II black political class recognizes that it cannot advance its public policy capability in areas important to the needs of black citizens, particularly those of poor blacks, unless it can expand biracial alliances at both the electoral and the legislative levels. At present, the antiwhite and anti-Semitic utterances common to xenophobic Afrocentrists have become the focus of a set of political maneuvers by the black political class. These maneuvers were initiated in the fall of 1993 at a conference of black leaders who designed a strategy for mobilizing black organizations to combat the rise of crime and violence in inner-city neighborhoods. Among the participating organizations was the Nation of Islam, with the NAACP being the host body.

Inevitably perhaps, the inclusion of the Nation of Islam in a new coalition of black organizations, at a period when the anti-Semitic posturing of figures like Farrakhan and Khalid Muhammad was escalating, has exacerbated black-Jewish discord. Why, then, did the black political class include the Nation of Islam in this effort? Because the black political class sought to forge interactions between the Nation of Islam and other groups with the hope that these interactions ultimately would reduce the Nation of Islam's antiwhite and anti-Semitic extremism. I think the strategy will work in the long run, but at present Jewish leaders have rejected the black leaders' anticrime and antiviolence mobilization out of hand.

Several leading Jewish intellectuals representing these elements published articles in January 1994 chastising the African American intelligentsia for what they viewed as softness toward anti-Semitism among blacks in general and in the Nation of Islam in particular. A. M. Rosenthal in the *New York Times* and Richard Cohen in the *Washington Post* wrote prominent articles, and full-page ads sponsored by the Anti-Defamation League appeared in major regional newspapers around the country. But these attacks are, I think, misplaced, analytically shallow, and sometimes lacking in good form, which is to say they lack elemental fairness. For one thing, the charge that the black intelligentsia has been soft on black extremists is factually wrong. Anyone close to the black intelligentsia cannot be unaware of its vigilance against black extremists, a vigilance that has prevented the export from the black American community of demented extremists to crisis areas in Africa like South Africa where they can wreak terrorist havoc. Black leaders like Leon

Sullivan, Jesse Jackson, Andrew Young, Julian Bond, and John Conyers have exerted crucial pressure, moral and organizational, against this dangerous escalation of extremist discourse among black American groups. Alas, a Jewish American organization, the late Rabbi Kahane's Kach movement, has engaged in the same irresponsible and dangerous shuttling of both extremists and financial resources for overseas activity (Fainaru 1994).

The Kach movement, based in Brooklyn and a number of suburbs, supplies an anti-Palestinian cadre to populate settler communities on the West Bank. Until an American member of the Kach movement massacred over thirty Palestinians while at prayer in Hebron, the establishmentarian Jewish American groups virtually ignored the terrorist extremists among Jewish Americans, preferring to focus on black extremists like the Nation of Islam. The African American intelligentsia in general has a good record at challenging and chastising black anti-Semitic and antiwhite extremists like Farrakhan, far better than Jewish American intellectuals have regarding Jewish extremists, or Irish Americans have vis-à-vis the IRA, whose funding resources come significantly from Irish American communities. Charges that the black intelligentsia is soft on black extremists—charges that do little more than exacerbate black-Jewish discord—are unwarranted.

Also, these charges lack elemental fairness and respect, for they do not grant the African American intelligentsia the same assumptions regarding devotion to upholding America's pluralist or antiextremist values that are typically granted to the white ethnic intelligentsias. The charge of softness toward black extremists posits an absurdly pristine leadership standard for the African American intelligentsia that is never expected of other ethnic intelligentsias or other leadership groups vis-à-vis extremists within their ranks. This standard would have us believe that every bigoted utterance by some zealous right-wing WASP or feminist or disciple of Rabbi Kahane is challenged immediately by the corresponding mainstream group of intellectuals. This unrealistic standard for managing extremist elements among different ethnic groups is presented to the African American intelligentsia but not to any other ethnic group's intelligentsia. This double standard unnecessarily inflames black-Jewish discord.

Another aspect of this double standard for black intellectuals has been a tendency of conservative Jews to distort the degree of political menace associated with anti-Semitic extremists like Farrakhan. Despicable though they are, black anti-Semites are small-fry extremists when compared, say, to the Aryan Nation, to Herbert Poinsett's anti-Semitic ranting on his television talk show in Tampa, and to Gerhard Lauck's Nebraska-based National Socialist German Workers Party (Overseas Organization). Lauck's group has become one of the largest publishers of hate literature in United States: its anti-Semitic magazine, New Order, is widely read, and the group is a major supplier of hate publications to Germany's rightist groups (Pertman 1994).

Of course, there are authentic political reasons within American political culture for challenging bona fide laxness on the part of ethnic leaders toward nativistic or bigoted extremists within the ranks of any given ethnic bloc. Nativistic and bigoted extremism in our system can be contained only by vigilant democratic challenges, and in general the Jewish American intelligentsia has understood this better than any other white ethnic group. I might add that the black American intelligentsia must be ranked beside the Jewish intelligentsia in their recognition of the importance of vigilant democratic challenges to extremism.

Overcoming Paternalism: A Critique of Jewish Conservatives

I want to underline the point that the current charges against the black intelligentsia of being soft on black extremism leveled by conservative Jewish intellectuals like A. M. Rosenthal, Robin Cohen, and Martin Peretz are both mistaken and analytically shallow. They are, in fact, a smoke screen for at least two conservative political purposes: (1) to strengthen the new conservatism's political agenda that establishmentarian Jewish intellectuals and organizations adhere to vis-à-vis blacks' public policy needs; and (2) to recall the era of black-Jewish coalitions during civil rights activism when those I call the Jewish establishmentarians often assumed a paternalistic demeanor toward blacks. The role of white-ally-as-gatekeeper-to-mainstream-power-structures is preferred by some Jewish conservatives who manipulate the public perception of the extremist character of blacks as a strategy for sustaining this paternalism. As a consequence, they help sustain black-Jewish discord. Why do I say this? Because the Type II metamorphosis of the black political class militates intrinsically against old paternalistic patterns between blacks and their white allies. Of course the Afrocentrist leaders cynically and shrewdly manipulate the old paternalistic black-Jewish paradigm.

What is politically crucial about the Type II stage of metamorphosis is that empowerment politicization demands that the ethnic political class—whether white, black, or Hispanic—be viewed as relatively sovereign in the definition of its political formation. The political class of the Irish, Italians, Jews, Poles, and other groups experienced this process at some point in their Type II metamorphosis (see Kantowicz 1975). Thus, today the black political class is experiencing this need for sovereign definition, which is exacerbated by the leadership cleavage between the pragmatic and the Afrocentrist sectors.

This need for sovereign definition was, therefore, at the center of the black political class's decision in the fall of 1993 to initiate an anticrime and antiviolence mobilization that included the Nation of Islam. Since Farrakhan and the xenophobic leaders of the Nation of Islam had been the wagging tail of the black political class for several years, the summit meeting might be called a checkmating response by the black political class which was long overdue. Though including the Nation of Islam created an odd-bedfellow or grab-bag coalition between pragmatic and Afrocentrist sectors, it is not uncommon in American political life to find antithetical groups joining forces for mutually beneficial goals.

Moreover, though establishmentarian Jewish groups have argued that this odd-bedfellow relationship between the black political class and the Nation of Islam is naïve on the part of the pragmatists, this charge is mistaken and uninformed. The black political class and its white allies in the Democratic party possess an important carrot-and-stick capability in relation to Farrakhan and the Nation of Islam. Today's Nation of Islam is increasingly dependent on public resources for much of its operating revenue, much of which is now derived through sizable contracts with federal housing projects in inner-city neighborhoods that involve the Nation of Islam (NOI) Security Agency in providing surveillance against drug trafficking and overall criminal activity. Such contracts in Pittsburgh, Chicago, Philadelphia, Los Angeles, and Baltimore amounted to over $2 million by 1993, and currently the NOI Security Agency is negotiating a $5 million contract with the Chicago Housing Authority (Holmes 1994).

Above all, the black political class is sophisticated in its understanding of the fact that odd-bedfellow coalitions are part of the pragmatic genius of American political culture, however disconcerting in moral terms. For example, the policy advances of the New Deal forged in a sea of odd-bedfellow coalitions were riddled with politicians and groups that also supported the Ku Klux Klan. Though bitter about these racist-tinged New Deal coalitions, the mainstream African American leadership like the NAACP, the National Urban League, and church leaders in the 1930s and 1940s did not fracture the political and electoral basis of the New Deal itself. Jewish critics of the black political class's associations with the Nation of Islam might well take a leaf from these New Deal precedents.

PROBLEMS OF TRANSITION TO THE CONVERGENCE PERSONA

The transition from the Type II persona of the black political class to the Type III convergence persona encounters two sets of problems. One set relates to what might be called the tenuous status legitimacy of the black political class as perceived by white voters. A second set of problems involves the schism between the pragmatists and the Afrocentrists, which has attained high national visibility through manipulation by conservative elements in American politics.

An interesting paradox surrounds the tenuous legitimacy problem of the black political class. At the electoral level the problematic legitimacy accorded black candidates remains a major constraint on a quantum-leap expansion of black officeholders elected by nonblack majority constituencies (offices such as state executive posts, county offices especially outside the South, and congressional offices). At the legislative level (state or federal), the seniority rule has enabled black politicians slowly but steadily to advance their political authoritativeness in a kind of "quiet" transition. This can be seen in Table 1.1.

Table 1.1 shows that, given the long tenure of black legislators, some black congresspersons have acquired a firm critical-minority presence. For example, in four committees at nearly 15 percent membership ratio, in four committees at between 19 and 23 percent membership ratio, and in three committees at between 33 and 47 percent black membership ratio. This new clout has translated into a "quiet" transition from Type II to Type III in the political class persona of blacks in Congress. Thus, despite what sometimes appears to be fierce discord between blacks and Jews, the most conservative Jewish organizations do not shun the black

Table 1.1
Black Congresspersons as a Percentage of Democrats on House Committees in the
103rd Congress

House Committees	Percentage	Numbers
Post Office	46.7	7 of 15
Public Works	17.9	7 of 39
Banking	23.3	7 of 30
Ways and Means	20.8	5 of 24
Small Business	33.3	9 of 24
Judiciary	19.0	4 of 21
Government Operations	40.0	10 of 25
Veterans Affairs	19.0	4 of 21
Education and Labor	14.8	4 of 27
Foreign Affairs	14.8	4 of 27
Appropriations	8.0	3 of 37
Energy and Commerce	14.8	4 of 27
Ethics	14.3	1 of 7

Source: Focus: Journal of the Joint Center for Political and Economic Studies 1993.

congresspersons on the Foreign Affairs Committee (nearly 15 percent) and the Appropriations Committee (8 percent black Democrats) when they seek annual support for the billions of dollars of U.S. aid, loans, and grants to the state of Israel. And the Congressional Black Caucus has one of the steadiest and strongest pro-Israel voting records among congressional voting blocs. Thus there is no doubt that in the eyes of Jewish organizations involved in foreign affairs, black legislators in Congress have full-fledged convergence political attributes. Yet voting records show that, with few exceptions, black candidates do not gain a significant proportion of the available Jewish voters' support, as contrasted with Irish or Italian candidates who have strong voting records on pro-Israel issues.

Though I have not yet investigated this matter fully, I am reasonably sure that this kind of white-voter hypocrisy toward the black political class (like the Jewish voters' contradictory interface with black congresspersons) is widespread. This response finds white voters claiming disproportionate public policy benefits but rendering to black political class a minimal exchange in votes (perhaps in monetary contributions, too). Further studies of this response are needed, especially of white constituencies who rely on public policy allocations for an important segment of their wherewithal or living standard, like the elderly, veterans, small businesses, and farmers.

The black political class has also made some gains in authoritativeness at the electoral level, with a few white voters behaving in a colorblind manner. Recently in medium-sized cities with two-thirds nonblack or white voters, a few black mayoral candidates have fashioned successfully a convergence demeanor, so to speak, unexpectedly claiming either a majority of white voters or a sizable minority of white voters in combination with a majority of votes from the black minority. This pattern occurred in Saginaw, Michigan in 1993 (40 percent black); in Pontiac, Michigan in 1993 (42 percent black); in Evanston, Illinois in 1993 (22 percent black); in Roanoke, Virginia in 1992 (24 percent black); in New Haven, Connecticut in 1993 (36 percent black); in Denver, Colorado in 1995 (13 percent black); and in Dayton, Ohio in 1993 (48 percent black). Though these and other black mayoral successes are important steps in facilitating the black political class's transition from the Type II to the Type III persona, they are nonetheless small steps. A quantum-leap metamorphosis of the black political class into the convergence politicization persona must await a veritable sea change in white neoracist perceptions of the black intelligentsia generally, in regard to entrusting this intelligentsia's political class with the sacred trust of officeholding.

This situation points out graphically, I think, the deep-rooted constraint of America's long-standing racial caste legacy on the mobility of African Americans from the margins of American society to relative parity. In contrast with the ethnicity legacy that shaped the marginalization of white ethnic groups such as the Irish, Jews, Italians, Poles, and Armenians, the important difference in regard to African Americans is that the American system's racial legacy was massively juridical, massively and viciously coercive, and neurotically emotional and psychocultural. Neurotic elements of America's racist legacy are alive and well today among both gentiles and Jews, and every black school child knows this intuitively, as does every black member of the new bourgeoisie or at least everyone save the black bourgeois converts to the new conservatism that gained prominence in the Reagan-Bush era. Major alterations in the hold of the neurotic psychocultural dimensions of the country's racist legacy on the worldview of white Americans are required before a quantum-leap metamorphosis from the Type II to Type III persona among the black political class can occur.

TAMING XENOPHOBIC AFROCENTRISTS

In a democratic polity like ours, xenophobic organizations that manipulate mean and vicious strategies to anoint one group or community through denigrating and scapegoating others will render themselves political pariahs. But this is an uneven process, with different constituencies accepting such characterization of a xenophobic organization or leader at different rates and with different intensity. Presently, most whites fully accept the characterization of Farrakhan and the Nation of Islam as political pariahs, but most blacks view Farrakhan as a quasipolitical pariah. Their image is what I would call a hybrid pariahization. Put another away, many blacks give Nation of Islam spokesmen an attentive ear but not an authoritative one. Owing to the country's long-standing racist denigration of black individuals and of blacks as a group or people—stripping millions of blacks of a viable self-esteem—black Americans today demand a catharsis, a chance to "feel whole," to "feel like somebody," as well as the concomitant need to release pent-up anger, disenchantment, and even rage.

The pragmatists among the black intelligentsia and the political class do not choreograph their leadership in a manner to satisfy this vast appetite for catharsis; the xenophobic Afrocentrists, however, do. A measure of Farrakhan's success in performing this function is found in a recent survey of black American attitudes (Yankelovich Partners 1994). The findings might be analyzed in terms of their political-cathartic and political-substantive dimensions. Let us consider the "political cathartic" response first. The results presented in Table 1.2 indicate that there is a strong political-cathartic nexus between black Americans and Farrakhan's political style. Farrakhan's political style satisfies deep cathartic needs that are associated with the long-standing racial caste pariahization of blacks in American life.

What about the political-substantive dimension? In this regard, blacks respond in ways that sometimes diverge sharply from responses along the political-cathartic dimension. Thus, when asked if they have generally favorable or unfavorable impressions of a given leader, blacks overwhelmingly chose Jesse Jackson, not Louis Farrakhan (86 to 48 percent), with Illinois Senator Carol Moseley Braun near to Farrakhan at 42 percent, and Ron Brown, secretary of commerce in the Clinton administration, at 38 percent. On another query that measures political-substantive perceptions, when asked to compare separatist black organizations like the Nation of Islam with the pragmatic-activist sector like the NAACP, the latter gained a 74 percent favorable response, compared to a 31 percent favorable response for the Nation of Islam. Finally, as shown in Table 1.3, when asked Who is the most important black leader today? a strong plurality of 34 percent of black respondents chose Jesse Jackson, compared to 9 percent for Farrakhan (Yankelovich Partners 1994).

Thus, it is clear that an important discrepancy exists now in how black Americans interact with the xenophobic Afrocentrist leaders as represented by Farrakhan and the Nation of Islam, favoring it along the emotional or political-cathartic dimension, not favoring it along the political-substantive dimension. They are willing to listen to the xenophobic Afrocentrists and gain an important emotion-salving release from persistent aspects of America's racist legacy, but they are not willing to vote for Afrocentrist candidates who run for election to city councils or to mayoralties, or even to join a xenophobic Afrocentrist organization and thereby lend their financial and other resources to its purposes. At present, the Nation of Islam's membership ranges only between 10,000 and 20,000 (out of 30 million blacks), while interestingly enough, blacks now make up 42 percent of the nearly 2.5 million Americans who practice standard or orthodox Islam.

Table 1.2
African Americans' Views of Louis Farrakhan

Does Minister Farrakhan . . .	Percentage of Blacks Responding Yes
Say things the country should hear?	70
Speak the truth?	63
Say things that are good for the black community?	63
Provide a role for black youth?	53

Source: Yankelovich Partners 1994.

The issue of taming the xenophobic dimensions of the Afrocentrist leadership within our democratic politics is, as noted earlier, a matter of crosscutting the ideological rigidity and militancy of this leadership with broader interest group linkages. This is typically a protracted process, one involving odd-bedfellow coalitions that can be morally distasteful and produce conflict, but that also can service the goal of taming xenophobic patterns. Mainstream African American leaders today have fashioned a crosscutting set of linkages with the Nation of Islam, and the prospects for successful outcomes in regard to the taming or reining-in of dysfunctional extremist features of the Nation of Islam are, I suggest, quite good. Owing to a new era of black middle-class political mobilization following the Million Man March—an event in which the black middle class exhibited fine skill at group solidarity mobilization along pragmatic lines—African American politics is entering what I call an Afro-activist phase.

By Afro-activist phase I mean a metamorphosis in black politics whereby a major focus will center on the task of fusing the leadership function of racial equalitarianization (the ending of persistent racist patterns in American life) with

Table 1.3
Who Is the Most Important Black Leader Today?

Black Leaders	Percentage of Respondents
Jesse Jackson	34.0
Martin Luther King, Jr.	9.0
Louis Farrakhan	9.0
Colin Powell	4.0
Malcolm X	3.0
Other	1.3
Not Sure	25.0

Source: Yankelovich Partners 1994.

the leadership function of black-community uplift. Though the task of fusing these two crucial functions of African American leadership has been attempted numerous times between the founding of the NAACP in 1910 and the rise of the viable black elected leadership over the past twenty-five years, it has never been adequately realized. The phenomenal success of the black professional and business elements (the bourgeoisie) in performing the dominant grass-roots organizational task during the Million Man March in October 1995, opens up a whole new sphere of politicization among blacks. This new development can be called the Afro-activist phase in black politics—a phase in which the task of fusing the equalitarianization and black-community uplift leadership functions will be executed, while grafted onto biracial alliance politics.

REFERENCES

Bayor, Norman. 1988. *Neighbors in conflict: Irish, Germans, Jews, and Italians of New York City, 1929–1941*. Urbana: University of Illinois Press.

Bok, Derek C. 1993. *Cost of talent*. New York: Free Press.

Browning, Rufus, Dale Rogers Marshall, and David Tabb. 1990. *Racial politics in American cities*. New York: Longman.

Buenker, John. 1973. *Urban liberalism and progressive reform*. New York: Scribners.

Clark, Dennis. 1973. *The Irish in Philadelphia*. Philadelphia: Temple University Press.

Cottingham, Clement. *Remaking black civil society in Newark, 1960s–1990s*. Forthcoming.

Erie, Steven. 1988. *Rainbow's end: Irish-Americans and the dilemmas of urban machine politics, 1840–1985*. Berkeley: University of California Press.

Fainaru, Steve. 1994. Jewish extremists rely on funds from U.S. sympathizers. *Boston Globe*, 14 March, sec. A1, 8.

Focus: Journal of the Joint Center for Political and Economic Studies. 1993. Political trends letter, 1 (September): 1–4.

Holmes, Steven. 1994. As Farrakhan group lands jobs from government, debate grows. *New York Times*, 4 March, 1, 18.

Josephson, Matthew, and Hannah Josephson. 1969. *Al Smith: Hero of the cities*. Boston: Houghton Mifflin.

Kantowicz, Edward. 1975. *Polish-American politics in Chicago, 1888–1940*. Chicago: University of Chicago Press.

Kilson, Martin. 1983. Black bourgeoisie revisited. *Dissent* 30 (summer): 85–96.

——— . *Politics of inclusion: Blacks in American political culture*. Forthcoming.

Kilson, Martin, and Clement Cottingham. 1993. La Politique d'affirmative action dans le système americain. *Hommes et Migrations* (February–March): 1162–63

Landry, Bart. 1987. *The new black middle class*. Berkeley: University of California Press.

Levine, Edward. 1966. *Irish and American politicians*. South Bend, IN: University of Notre Dame Press.

McCaffery, Peter. 1991. *When bosses ruled Philadelphia: Emergence of the Republican machine, 1867–1933*. Philadelphia: Pennsylvania State University Press.

Pertman, Adam. 1994. Nebraskan fueling German neo-Nazis. *Boston Globe*, 11 January, 1, 11.

Rich, Wilbur C. 1996. *Black mayors and school politics*. New York: Garland Press.

Roediger, David. 1991. *The wages of whiteness: Race and the making of the American working class*. London: Verso.

Stewart, James B. 1992. *Den of thieves*. New York: Simon and Schuster.

Valentine, Paul. 1994. Ex-fugitive S&L chief convicted. *Washington Post*, 2 April, 1C, 5C.

Yankelovich Partners. 1994. *Yankelovich partners survey*. February 16–17.

Zink, Harold. 1930. *City bosses in the United States*. Durham, NC: Duke University Press.

2
Blacks and Coalition Politics: A Theoretical Reconceptualization

Jerry Gafio Watts

During the 1984 primaries for the Democratic Party presidential nomination, Jesse Jackson made his infamous statement in which he referred to New York City as "Hymie Town." Since that day when candidate Jackson whispered those words into the ear of *Washington Post* reporter Milton Coleman, the American public has been bombarded with repeated claims that the black-Jewish coalition has been irreparably fractured (see Gates 1984). From that moment every indiscriminate conflict between blacks and Jews was placed on a continuum of a supposed escalation of black and Jewish dislike for each other (see *New Republic* 1991). These public announcements of the demise of the black-Jewish coalition gave rise to numerous conferences, op-ed pieces in national newspapers and even special editions of television news shows like *Nightline* and *Frontline*.

For his "Hymie Town" comment, Jackson was vociferously and justifiably criticized. In coming to Jackson's defense, Minister Louis Farrakhan only deepened the perceived cleavage between blacks and Jews by openly threatening the "traitorous" Coleman and the American Jewish community. Directing his anger toward Jews, Farrakhan warned, "If you harm this brother, in the name of Allah, that will be the last one you do harm" (Gates 1984). The black-Jewish coalition was thought to be in hopeless disarray.

THE BLACK-JEWISH COALITION

But just what was the substance of this supposed coalition? It seems that the idea of a special black-Jewish coalition developed as the result of a perceived and perhaps authentically disproportionate historical presence of American Jews within the various black political struggles for equality (cf. Kaufman 1988; Salzman, Back, and Sorin 1992). American Jews as diverse as Joel Spingarn of the NAACP and Jack Greenberg of the NAACP Legal Defense Fund had committed themselves to the black freedom struggle. The prominent Rabbi, Abraham Heschel, had demonstrated with Martin Luther King, Jr. Michael Schwerner and Andrew Goodman, two young Jewish CORE activists in pursuit of justice for blacks in Mississippi, had been murdered alongside black civil rights worker James Earl Chaney (Cagin and Dray 1988; Ditmer 1994). As a result of the heroic participation of these individuals and numerous others, Jews as a group may have become more publicly identified with the black struggle than any other single segment of white America.

Not as clear is the extent to which blacks have championed "Jewish issues." Certainly some black Americans have actively supported and participated in the struggle against anti-Semitism. It can be surmised that the black quest for civil rights became a crucial vehicle by which the devalued legal status of American Jews was also challenged. In its early stages, the black struggle may have provided some Jewish activists with a forum for contesting the devalued status of Jews in America.

The rhetoric signaling the demise of the black-Jewish coalition should not be taken at face value. It is not that black and Jewish interest groups are not in conflict over various issues at present. The rhetoric of demise should not be interpreted to mean that there was once a time when the broader masses of blacks thought of themselves as being in a special partnership with a majority of Jews or vice versa. In fact, the black-Jewish coalition was, to the extent that it has existed, a rhetorical construct at the mass level. Moreover, even in instances where there appeared to be some type of conscious partnership between the two groups, it was a negotiated affair between the progressive political elites of the two groups.

The case of the black-Jewish coalition raises three significant questions pertaining to the existence and substantive performance of American coalitions. First, how did such a "limited partnership" (between political elites) become publicly articulated as having been etched in the consciousness of the rank-and-file members of each ethnic group? Second, did the popular rhetoric that helped to sustain the idea of a mass based black-Jewish coalition actually influence individual members of the respective groups to think of themselves as partners in a coalition? Third, did this rhetorically premised belief in the existence of a black-Jewish partnership actually influence some individuals to engage in coalition activities? The latter two questions, although essential, are beyond the scope of this chapter. To answer them adequately, I would need survey information not only on black and Jewish beliefs concerning each other but also on the interactions between the two groups. I am not sure that such data even exists.

In answer to the first question, it should be immediately clear that the political elites from each group had a vested interest in marketing their coalition desires as having been ratified by the mass publics for whom they claimed to be representative. More precisely, given the elusiveness of ethnic identity and notions of ethnic representation, it is not an infrequent occurrence that he or she who speaks loudest from within the belly of the ethnic group ultimately determines popular perceptions of ethnic norms for that group. One speaks louder than one's intraethnic competitor by claiming to speak for more people than he or she does.

Ethnic Identity

This ability of the elites of an ethnic group to control the popular perceptions of their group depends in part on the authority granted to the leaders and their group by the broader culture. A publicly accepted ethnic self-definition for the entire ethnic group can occur only in the absence of widespread prejudice against the group. It is one of the ironies of American political culture that ethnic self-definition, which is premised upon the valorization of ethnic elite voices, presupposes the absence of widely held negative stigmas against the group (see Goffman 1986). The history of Jews and blacks in America only highlights this point (Stember 1966; Sklare 1967; Ringer 1967).

For generations both groups were publicly perceived (by non-Jews and non-blacks) as embodying social characteristics that none of the ethnically legitimate elites from each group ever espoused. During various periods of American history, anti-Semitism and antiblack racism were simply overwhelming in their ability to suppress the desires of the two groups to define themselves in a positive manner. Similar popular stigmatization of various white ethnic groups historically hindered their ability to control their ethnic image. Witness the cultural vices that the first and second generations of Irish American and Italian American political elites had to confront. Italian American elites had to resist vicious negative stigmas through-out the early generations of Italian immigration. During the early twentieth century, sections of American society perceived Italians as less than truly white. The point here is that blacks represent the worst-case scenario: they are the most stigmatized American ethnic group.

The mere existence of such rhetorical creatures as "Jewish leaders" or "black leaders" speaks to the ways that ethnicity is objectified for some social groupings in America. What is a "black leader" except someone who apparently has the ear of white Americans in regard to issues of high salience to blacks. Such leaders do not have to be certified by any democratic process, procedure, or institution that would insure their representativeness of the broader black populace (Reed 1986). Likewise, such leaders are bound, if at all, by weak constraints from within the ethnic group. In other words, there is no mechanism to insure ethnic (that is, popular) accountability. The problem of perceived representativeness in the ab-sence of procedures insuring accountability is crucial here, for it speaks to the resilient stigmatization of the affected ethnic groups. "Black leaders" or "Jewish leaders" do not historically need to be popularly certified by a procedure insuring their representativeness because blacks and Jews have historically been perceived as undifferentiated hordes. That is, the black community in America was thought by many whites to be ipso facto representable by any black person who claimed to do so. An indication of the lessening of stigmas against American Jews is that there are fewer "Jewish leaders" today than there were forty years ago. The attenuation of ethnic leaders (in the manner of Jewish leaders) is directly proportional to the degree of social inclusion experienced by members of the group.

Any claim that an individual seemingly by his very nature inherently represents other people who are physically or culturally similar is premised on the faulty notion that he or she shares a significant, unalterable core identity with the others. For a black to be viewed as inherently representative of all other blacks (or even an articulator of "the black point of view") assumes that there is some trait, undoubtedly, his or her blackness, that generates ontological similarity to all blacks and ontological difference from all whites (cf. Spelman 1988). In such instances, blackness becomes a reified construct that exists as a commodified possession in the being of all black people (Fuss 1989; Goldberg 1993; San Juan 1992; Omi and Winant 1994). Reified identities lie at the heart of racist determinations of group character traits. Likewise, reified identities lie at the heart of commonsense American notions of representation. This crucial fact lies at the very center of all discussions of black-Jewish coalitions.

The Problem of Imagined Communities

In the case of the supposed black-Jewish coalition, the reified identities of those who participated in coalition building between the two groups were appropriated by those members of both groups who had never actually participated in coalition-building activities. Using a reified vantage point, Andrew Goodman, the murdered CORE activist, becomes the collective contribution of all American Jews to the civil rights movement. Goodman ceases to be what he actually was, a dedicated and heroic individual. More precisely, the fact that an individual Jewish American helped blacks to confront racial subjugation at a specific moment became an indication of the way that all Jews felt and feel toward blacks. What "he" did becomes through ethnic reification what "we" did. "We" becomes a loaded term, a term indicating vicarious participation in events that one could only lay claim to through one's ethnic imagination and ascriptive birth rights. Now this is not a criticism of Jewish Americans but an example of how reified ethnic identities generate false senses of inclusion in social spaces that one has never occupied. Quite frankly, it is just as problematic for all blacks to claim that "we" were in the civil rights movement.

In a similar vein, the anti-Semitic articulations of Louis Farrakhan come to be seen as representative of the attitudes of many, most, or even all blacks, depending on who interprets the phenomenon. In the case of Farrakhan, the telltale of white negative stigmatization of black reification lies in the fact that the only way for a black to escape the Farrakhan taint is by publicly denouncing him. Individual white political leaders do not have to denounce publicly a white racist in order not to be tainted by his or her racism. Whites are perceived as sufficiently individual-ized. Instead, one racist white person speaks only for himself and those who have explicitly endorsed his views. There are no such entities as "white leaders," for white leaders would have to issue strong denouncements. A racist black speaks for all or most blacks unless otherwise proven not to be true.

Even if such an entity never really existed, the interesting phenomenon about the repeated invocation of the idea of a black-Jewish coalition is that at some point, the idea might begin to take root in the consciousness of blacks and Jews. However romantic and nostalgic, the idea of a past when blacks and Jews were supposedly linked in pursuit of the betterment of humankind can either generate a utopian vision of possibility or a disempowering vision of despair at how far we have fallen. In all likelihood, how we appropriate this myth of a harmonious past will depend on our general outlook and political intentions at the specific moment of appropriation. In effect, we witness the creation of a media-mediated coalition sensibility that has sporadic material embodiment. Yet, it can endure precisely because of the ways in which we have been socialized to consume the reified identities projected back onto us by the mass media. Similarly, many backs who did not participate in the civil rights movement now claim that "we marched in Selma." The point here is that popular usage of various ideas of political inclusion is only a fabrication that helps us to make a disorderly world seem orderly and in doing so to grant us a sense of efficacy that we have not truly earned. It is therefore of little surprise that Americans are riddled with memberships in "imagined communities" (Anderson 1983). These communities are not epiphenomenal but actually do influence political perceptions and determinations of self-worth, both of which impact public action.

This problem of imagined communities strikes at the heart of any attempt to assess accurately the existence of coalitions in the United States today. In many instances when we talk about coalitions we are actually speaking about coalitions between various imagined communities. For instance, any discussion of black-Jewish coalitions presupposes the existence and sanctity of a black community. But there is no such entity as the black community except in rhetorical practices. If there were such an entity, we could not possibly have the epidemic of black-on-black violence that dominates our large urban areas. Moreover, we would not see the utter indifference to the plight of the black poor that we see among large elements of our black middle class. The point here is that our analytical nomenclature is out of touch with the reality that it seeks to describe. Instead of admitting paradigmatic failure, political scientists too often participate in and give credence to a view of American life that is illusory. If I may be a bit precocious, I claim that this emperor has no clothes.

This problem of rendering imagined communities more real than they are seriously impacts the social construction of black America. For instance, when analysts say that a candidate carried the black vote, he or she is in effect silencing the coalitions that go into creating that "black vote," instead of describing how blacks from differing socioeconomic classes, regions, and genders colluded to support candidate X. The mere labeling of these voters as black supposedly renders their voting habits analytically comprehensible.

WHAT IS A COALITION?

The idea of a political coalition needs to be made more conceptually precise. To call any existent electoral configuration of different peoples (however defined) a coalition is to make the term too broad to be of any analytical utility. The mere fact that the mayor of Washington, D.C., Marion Barry, received a very large percentage of the vote of the black poor in southeast Washington, D.C. as well as

a large percentage of the vote of the white gay and lesbian community of the
Dupont Circle and Adams Morgan areas does not mean that there was a coalition
between the black poor and white gay and lesbian voters.

All too often, political scientists define a coalition as any configuration mobilized behind a specific candidate or a certain issue. The existence of such mislabeled
coalitions can supposedly be determined by mere after-the-fact assessments of the
vote. I do not view this as a valid notion of a coalition. A coalition requires some
degree of forethought. It requires the concerted intent on the part of individuals
and groups of individuals to link themselves together for reasons of pursuing an
end (a candidate's election or the projection of a certain issue) that could not in
all probability be attained if these disparate groups did not pool their resources. In
effect, the existence of a coalition presupposes strategic bargaining. In many crucial
respects my definition of coalition mirrors that of Barbara Hinckley (1981: 32),
who offers a sound description of a coalition:

> We should first exclude the number of studies that use the word coalition
> loosely to mean merely an aggregate, or collection, of separate political
> components. People speak of a candidate's "electoral coalition" or "ideologi-
> cal coalitions" when they mean merely groups that have found themselves,
> or have been arranged to be found, together. There is no consciousness of
> the group's part that they are involved in coalition formation, and at times
> not even consciousness of themselves as a group. . . . We restrict coalition
> studies to those in which actors join together to determine outcomes in
> mixed-motive situations: the actors are aware of themselves as actors in such
> a situation, of their mix of motives, and of their opportunity to determine a
> political result.

My conception of a coalition presupposes the presence of definable groups that
have as their membership criteria characteristics deemed rational within the parent
society and sufficiently salient among group members to generate conscious loyalties, and political elites who can speak for and bargain on behalf of these groups.
Spokespersons must have some mechanism to insure accountability and representativeness between themselves and those they speak for. In the United States
a political coalition is most often a formulation designed and mediated by elites.

Whether or not a coalition is successful ultimately depends on several factors
including the ability of the various political elites of the uniting factions to
discipline their constituencies. (Here, I am referring only to electoral coalitions,
not to movement coalitions.) In effect, the degree of power that the elites control
over their constituencies along with the size of their constituencies determines the
bargaining authority of the elites who, in some sense, steer the affected groups into
the coalition. This is important because the weakness of the black political
infrastructure at the national level precludes serious bargaining between black
political elites and the national Democratic Party apparatus. As in the case of
Clinton, the national candidate can simply ignore the public policy needs of a
constituency that he need not bargain for. Coalitions cannot be composed of

passive actors. The mere fact that American Jews and blacks both purchase Pepsi Cola does not allow us to define them as a coalition.

Types of Coalitions

There are two major ideal types of coalitions. For the sake of better terminology, I refer to one type as a disjointed coalition and the other as a shared core coalition.

Disjointed Coalitions

A disjointed coalition is one in which the participating groups or factions have a shared goal, and that goal is instrumental to the realization of more important specific goals that are not shared. Participants in these coalitions band together for strategic reasons in order to pursue or project their particularistic desires. There can be as many goals in such a coalition as there are participating groups. In such coalitions, groups band together because they do not believe that they have sufficient resources to articulate successfully their goals by themselves. Such groups may not have entered into the coalition had they singularly possessed sufficient resources to project their peculiar interests. The groups coming together to create a disjointed coalition need not endorse the specific agendas of the other members of the coalition—in fact, they may oppose them.

Disjointed coalitions most often are found in electoral politics. Unlike the after-the-fact arbitrary voting conglomerates that Barbara Hinckley (1981) correctly identified as noncoalitions, there is a rich history of electoral coalition building in the United States, where groups with distinctively differing agendas concertedly join forces in order to realize an end. Usually, disjointed electoral coalitions center on the election of an individual candidate or party that has made various specific promises to the disparate groups. A classic case of the disjointed electoral coalition might well be the New Deal coalition. In some variant, the New Deal coalition has dominated national Democratic Party politics for the last fifty years. The New Deal coalition consisted of Jewish Americans, Irish Catholics, Italian Americans, northern blacks, and southern whites (see Gamm 1989; Andersen 1979; Tindall 1967).

As the basis of the four electoral victories of Franklin D. Roosevelt, this coalition was particularly active during Roosevelt's final terms in office (Weiss 1983; Sitkoff 1978). Northern blacks voted for Roosevelt in large measure because he was seen as more responsive to their economic needs than the Republican presidential candidates. Moreover, Roosevelt was a master of symbolic racial appeals to blacks. In this sense, his wife, Eleanor, must be understood as his primary outreach to the black community.

The New Deal coalition is an excellent nucleus for the discussion of disparate coalitions precisely because it was predicated on blatant contradictions. To the extent that Roosevelt openly courted the southern white vote, which at the time was solidly Democratic, Roosevelt implicitly and explicitly endorsed black disenfranchisement in the South. Though there was a massive migration of southern blacks to northern industrial centers (1910–1950), the black population remained overwhelmingly southern during the years of the Roosevelt presidency. Northern blacks who voted for him had to wrestle with the fact that Roosevelt forthrightly supported white supremacy in the American South. Yet, northern blacks (and some southern blacks) did benefit from New Deal public works programs like those administered by the Work Progress Administration and the Civilian Conservation Corps. Northern black supporters of Roosevelt acted politically under a pragmatic utilitarian sensibility that dictated their support for Roosevelt and his mediocre record of concern for blacks as opposed to the less-than-meager offerings of the national Republican candidates. Yet in doing so, northern blacks colluded in the disenfranchisement of southern blacks.

Other crucial examples of disjointed coalitions were those coalitions which emerged in cities dominated by Irish Catholic political machines (see Erie 1988). Whether it was Chicago, New York, Boston, or Jersey City, blacks and white ethnic voters participated in machine-dominated elections in order to obtain various incremental goals. The machine was explicitly structured along competitive ethnic blocs. The ethnic groups that delivered the largest numbers of votes for the machine were supposedly rewarded with benefits that were directly targeted to the group (Gosnell 1935). Of course, the depth and resilience of white racism fundamentally altered these ground rules in regard to blacks (Hirsch 1983).

Grimshaw (1992) persuasively shows that the benefits accrued to black machine voters was far less than their importance in the election of the machine candidates. Grimshaw notes how during one mayoral election, Mayor Richard Daley, the machine boss, lost the majority of the white vote in Chicago, but won reelection because of overwhelming support in the black wards. Yet the benefits delivered to the black wards was far less even than that given to white wards that did not support the machine candidate. The lesson here is that the successful electoral coalition is quite distinct from the actual governing coalition. Because of white racism and the weak political infrastructure of black urban polities, black urban voters often play a much more crucial role in the election of a candidate than they do in the subsequent governing of the city.

Ethnic group supporters of political machines participated in a system of reward structures that gave primacy to the conditions of their local wards as opposed to the policy concerns of the city at large. In the case of Tammany Hall, the Democratic machine in New York City, a strategic trade-off was engineered by ethnic political elites. In return for the votes of the Irish Catholic masses, the Irish Catholic political elites were able to utilize the police and fire departments as Irish Catholic employment agencies. Tammany's trade-off to Jewish machine leaders for the support of Jewish voters was, in part, to give Jews jobs in the education system, primarily as school teachers.

The weakness of disjointed coalitions is that they structurally undermine notions of civic responsibility to the society at large. Disjointed coalitions tend to create political cultures and political incentive structures in which individuals and groups are encouraged to think primarily of themselves over and above the needs of the broader society. Political identities become defined in a narrow manner that ultimately undermines the ability of the individual or group to develop empathetic linkages to the world beyond. Disjointed machine electoral coalitions are inherently premised upon the willingness of voters to be ethnically insular in their focus and concerns.

Given the history of blacks in America, it is easy to see that any political structure or culture that tends to validate popular insularity is a structure and culture that is not going to be receptive to the social inclusion of black Americans. In effect, in already existing coalitions there is no incentive for anyone to develop an empathetic political concern for the plight of blacks. Such a concern would only dilute their ability to cordon off benefits for their own group. As such, racism itself has been quite functional to existent disjointed coalitions, for it functions as merely another factor encouraging parochialism in its members.

Shared Core Coalitions

A shared core coalition exists when various disparate groups come together because they support a common issue agenda. These coalitions are more difficult to generate than disjointed coalitions. First, in order for a shared core coalition to emerge, each of the participating sectors of the coalition must relinquish key aspects of their own specific agendas in pursuit of a universally shared agenda. In many instances, particularly within the electoral arena, these universally shared agendas are the lowest common denominator. On face value, arriving at a lowest common denominator may appear somewhat easy, but in fact it is quite difficult. After all, the elites who enter into this type of formation have to insure order and allegiance within their own ranks. That is, they have to convince their constituencies that this lower common denominator is all that can be acquired at present given the existent political contexts and the group's resources. This is difficult, for it may mean that nothing less than the renunciation of desired policy objectives has to be entertained and ultimately sanctioned. Many populaces will refuse to enter into this self-effacing contract. Many of those who do enter into the coalition do so without enthusiasm. Lowest common denominators are hard sells, and, if the lowest common denominator is insufficiently comprehensive, the coalition may never get off the ground.

Conversely, any attempt to reformulate the lowest common denominator into policy profiles that would capture the passions of the potential members of the electoral coalition runs the risk of being insular and thus insufficiently appealing to an adequately large number of voters. If the lowest common denominator is intensely held but inadequately encompassing to insure the allegiances of the potential members of the coalition, then the coalition will be insufficiently expansive and thus weak. Perhaps the best examples of insufficiently inclusive but intensely held shared core electoral coalitions are the coalitions that emerged around the presidential campaigns of Republican Barry Goldwater in 1964 and Democrat George McGovern in 1972. In effect, electoral campaigns that are passionately premised upon emphatic ideologies are usually shared core coalitions. Instead of universally held issue positions functioning as the lowest common denominators, the Goldwater and McGovern campaigns fashioned an attitude toward the role of government as their coalescing core. A shared ideology was therefore the lowest common denominator. In both instances, the candidacies generated tremendous enthusiasm among small groups of followers. This enthusiasm can appropriate the quality of a higher moral calling. As such it can become quasi-apocalyptic, that is, more concerned with ideological purity than with winning elections.

Post-Goldwater and post-McGovern candidates have had to learn that the intensity of one's following, particularly within the electoral arena, has little to do with one's success or failure. Given the fact that electoral success depends solely on the aggregate numbers of votes and not on the intensity of the feelings behind those votes, ideological intensity may well be a hindrance to one's electability, if such intensity arises at the cost of breadth of support.

Perhaps the best examples of shared core coalitions are those coalitions that arise as social movements. The civil rights movement was, for the most part, a shared core coalition. Individuals from various backgrounds, ethnicities, locations, came together in the movement to help better the sociopolitical, economic plight of blacks. Moreover, these individuals were, by and large, committed to utilizing a nonviolent praxis. More often than not, shared core coalitions emerge in response to a political crisis. It is the heightened sense of crisis that often allows diverse people to scuttle their parochial interests on behalf of something greater. It is this very same quality that makes movement-based shared core coalitions difficult to sustain over a long period of time. After all, one cannot remain in a long-standing crisis, for then the crisis is no longer a crisis but a normality.

Another shared core coalition arose in response to the United States involvement in the Vietnam War. The antiwar movement consisted of a group of distinct shared core coalitions, including the New Left. Yet many who participated in antiwar protest activities were not affiliated with the New Left (Breines 1982).

Given the higher degree of political energy necessary to sustain a shared core coalition, it is not surprising that they arise far less often than disjointed coalitions. Moreover, they require more intense discipline and far greater shared knowledge on the part of those participating. Yet on those rare occasions when the needs of blacks lie at the very center of a shared core coalition, then the pragmatic sacrificing of the black poor for the sake of consensus is significantly reduced.

At present, the black presence in disjointed electoral coalitions has become significantly problematic, the cost of including blacks openly in disjointed national campaigns has generated a backlash on the part of large numbers of the white electorate. The marginalization of the black vote and thus black Americans as a claimant group has intensified ever since the decline of the New Deal coalition as a majority coalition at the national level. The first sign of this decline occurred in 1948 when the Democratic Party took the risk of alienating the southern white Democratic vote by placing a civil rights plank in its party platform. As blacks became a more vocal element within the party structure, large numbers of white voters departed. The civil rights movement and the favorable response of a former segregationist senator turned integrationist president quickened the pace of the departure of the white South from the Democratic Party ranks during national elections. Though winning in an unprecedented landslide in 1964, Lyndon

Johnson, an incumbent Democratic president from the former Confederacy, lost six southern states to Republican Barry Goldwater. Simply put, Johnson's pro–civil rights actions alienated large numbers of the white Southern vote. From 1948 to the present, the majority of the black vote in a presidential election has coincided with the majority of the white vote only once (Johnson in 1964). This has meant that a winning coalition can capture the White House without the black vote. In fact, not having the black vote has become a semiotic statement of the candidate's willingness to champion the needs of various white communities. Given the nature and resilience of American racism, it is clear that large numbers of white Americans do not believe that they share any significant policy profiles with black Americans.

RACE AND ELECTORAL CAMPAIGNS

One of the major issues confronting black electoral strategists today is the growing perceptions within the broader white populace of blacks as an illegitimate claimant group. One of the shortcomings of racially and ethnically reified identities is that many whites have come to view socioeconomically marginal blacks as other than their social-civic brothers and sisters. Blacks are often seen as a foreign entity of some sort: inauthentic citizens. It was one of the ideological masterpieces of the Reagan administration and contemporary conservative political posturing to create an image of the black poor as wards of their ethnic group. The black poor came to be seen as the responsibility of the black non-poor (Watts 1990). In effect, they have ceased to be viewed as American citizens, that is, as persons who had linkages to the broader American community. This image and the resultant ideological discursive marginalization of the black poor—a marginalization that cast them outside the purview of social concern and empathy—are manifestations of a broader problem confronting black politics at present within the national electoral arena. Simply put, for whatever reasons, it appears that large numbers of white voters are not very concerned about the plight of blacks. That is, at the national level, it appears that a candidate's position on blacks is important to the majority of the white voting populace only if that candidate is imagined as appealing too much to the black vote. The white voting populace seems quite capable of voting for a candidate who appears to be not only indifferent but antagonistic to the peculiar needs of blacks. Remember Ronald Reagan!

Recognition of the decline in support among whites for specifically delineated public policy interventions on behalf of blacks has given rise to a growing body of literature that takes as its point of departure the belief that all one need do to circumvent the black-white racial cleavage is to package their policy imperatives differently (Reed and Bond 1991). At the forefront of this strategy is the sociologist William J. Wilson (1987). While these authors differ on the substantive policies they might advocate to address the needs of the black poor, all of them seem to believe that the most effective way to generate support for the peculiar needs of blacks in the eyes of whites is to mask policies that address black neediness behind policies that address everyone's perceived neediness. The supposed model for this type of policy initiative is social security which is imagined as having wide popular support because everyone is a beneficiary. Policies and programs that specifically benefit poor recipients, however, are viewed as much more vulnerable to public antipathy (for example, Aid to Families with Dependent Children).

The Wilsons of the world are, however, quite naïve about the workings of race and racism within the American political arena. First, they have not understood the sophisticated use of racial imagery that has been generated by the American Right. Simply put, the American Right has been able to stigmatize certain public policies and types of policies as inherently bearing the imprint of the unworthy needy and blacks. That is, blackness has now been associated with policy images themselves (Quadagno 1994). As such, in order to shy away from being too openly identified with racial character traits, the Wilsons and others would essentially have to scuttle certain policy options. This association of certain policies with blackness becomes quite apparent during many of the attempts by black candidates to gain electoral support within majority white constituencies. In some instances— Ed Brooke, Republican senator from Massachusetts; Tom Bradley, Democratic mayor of Los Angeles (Sonenshein 1993); and Doug Wilder, governor of Virginia (Yancey 1988; Edds 1990; Baker 1989)—the black candidate in search of broader legitimacy in the white community essentially had to de-ethnicize himself by articulating public policies that were not imagined as those typically associated with blacks.

Furthermore, there is little indication that the way to reduce racism and racial parochialism is to sidestep it by means of clever transracial appeals. In fact, the best way to service the needs of the black poor might well be to confront the parochialism of the white electorate, especially during moments of national economic crises when ethnic parochialism functions as a therapeutic outlet for social anxieties.

There is, however, another strain of political analyses of the emergence of a white populace that does not grant blacks a legitimate claimant status as blacks. This strain assumes that the ethnically-racially parochial white popular response is rational and that ultimately blacks should not exist as a claimant group. This response has been advocated by Fred Siegel, Shelby Steele, Thomas and Mary Edsall (1991), and Jim Sleeper (1990) among others. In effect, they believe that white ethnic and racial parochialism is the rational response of white ethnics who have been disrespected and attacked by blacks and their supposed white liberal backers. Such analyses presuppose that there was a racially cosmopolitan white working class that lost its sympathy for blacks as policies emerged that favored blacks at their expense. Of course, their arguments could not explain to us why white urban ethnic America created a neo-apartheid-like residential state in northern urban areas long before blacks became a viable pressure group. One need only read Arnold Hirsch's Making the Second Ghetto (1983) or Massey and Denton's American Apartheid: Segregation and the Making of the Underclass (1993) to grasp the phenomenal extent to which blacks have been historically confined to segregated residential areas.

Finally, there is a strain of the white populace that simply defines itself in negation to the existence and practices of blacks. This is a visceral response, one that is deep-seated and resilient. Huckfeldt and Kohfeld (1989: 184) concluded that

[t]he extent to which whites are willing to support the Democratic Party is directly related to the reliance of the party on black voters. As the Democratic coalition becomes blacker, whites become less willing to participate. This unwillingness is especially apparent among lower-class white voters, and thus we see a major factor underlying the decline of class in American politics: race is the wedge that disrupts lower-class coalitions.

Jesse Jackson as Symbol of Black Outsider Status

The election of Bill Clinton to the presidency is, for many analysts, ultimate proof that the Democratic Party has entered a new, postliberal era. A Democrat with ties to traditional Democratic Party constituencies that support an expanding welfare state (i.e., blacks, women, and Jews), Clinton also generated overtures to the moderate wing of American conservatism who believe that there are some social problems that are best solved by government nonintervention. Sitting astride two factions, Clinton has engaged in a balancing act of sorts. It is therefore not surprising that his cabinet includes liberals like Donna Shalala and Robert Reich and conservatives like Lloyd Bensten. In many respects, the hybrid nature of Clinton's administration reflects his successful campaign strategy: Clinton ran as a moderate Democrat, a man who has supposedly learned that liberalism does not have sufficient appeal to generate a majority of the popular vote.

Of all the major Democratic Party leaders, no one may have been more ambivalent about a Clinton victory than Jesse Jackson. We must certainly take Jackson at his word when he claimed that he was excited by the end of the Reagan-Bush era. Yet Jackson must have been somewhat nostalgic about his two previous runs for the Democratic endorsement.

Jackson had long contended that a national Democratic majority could be fashioned through an appeal to women, Latinos, blacks, Asian Americans, and liberal white males. Clinton believed that the key to revitalizing the Democratic Party lay in winning back white Reagan Democrats. Whereas Jackson is at home with Hightower of Texas, Wellstone of Minnesota, Dellums of California, and Conyers of Michigan, Clinton's cronies include Lieberman of Connecticut, Robb of Virginia, Nunn of Georgia, and Congressman John Lewis of Georgia.

During the primaries Clinton was not above using the racial image of Jesse Jackson as the staging area to create his "new Democrat" identity. Interestingly, Clinton attacked the image of Jackson despite the fact that Jackson was not a candidate. Unlike those white Democratic Party candidates of the recent past who appeared to many whites as having timidly shied away from confronting Jackson, Clinton tried to show them that he was unafraid of the black Baptist minister. In fact, he desired and sought a confrontation with Jackson. As a result he created a hyped-up media event assault on Jackson in order to generate the right image in the eyes of certain white voters and the news media—enter the Sister Souljah fiasco. Clinton attacked Jackson in a rather belated and cowardly manner. Later it was discovered that Jackson had in fact criticized Souljah, but no apology was forthcoming from Clinton. Jackson immediately saw that Clinton was intent on using him, but there was little he could do. Had Jackson been a candidate, Clinton might have never engaged in the assault, for the staying power of Jackson's anger and dismay could have unsettled his coalition. Since Jackson was not a candidate, he was incapable of quagmiring Clinton in a long fight in which Clinton would ultimately lose by having his image tarnished.

Unfortunately for Jackson, Sister Souljah saw the Clinton attack as her opportunity to generate name recognition within the marketplace. She viewed Clinton's attack on her as an attempt to silence her; consequently, she decided to lash back, but her outspokenness and the parochialism of her views only played into Clinton's hands, for she appeared irrational. Jackson, by default, became associated with her excess. Contrary to her intentions, Clinton's legitimacy rose with each of her attacks because she was considered illegitimate by the majority of the voters Clinton was seeking.

Clinton was the candidate of a post-liberal Democratic Party, a position that grants some degree of validity to the views of those white Americans who believe that the Democratic Party no longer speaks to their interests precisely because it appears too interested in representing black interests. In other words, Clinton and his cronies in the Democratic Leadership Council (DLC) are intent on creating an image of the Democratic Party that generates a preemptive strike against white backlash by justifying it. Even the moderate black governor of Virginia, Doug Wilder, an avowed Jackson foe, called the DLC a "white man's club." After all, the logic of the DLC, as embodied in Senator Chuck Robb of Virginia, was to twice fight to deny Wilder the nomination of the Virginia Democratic Party. Robb did not want Wilder to obtain the party's nomination for lieutenant governor or governor, and he worked under the assumption that a black candidate was intrinsically weaker (read less able to obtain white votes) than a white one. Certainly, Robb was technically correct, although his logic would have made black political figures beholden to the threat of white backlash. In effect, Robb's logic assumed the validity of white racism as a determinant of the electoral process. In some crucial sense, Bill Clinton's successful presidential electoral strategy made similar assumptions.

No single figure in either party has historically inspired the antagonism of the Democratic Leadership Council more than Jesse Jackson (except perhaps Ted Kennedy). Hoping to project a candidate for the party's presidential nomination who was sympathetic to the DLC, the DLC established the Super Tuesday Democratic primaries. The plan backfired in 1984 and 1988 as Jackson used multiple primary wins on Super Tuesday to establish his credibility as a viable vote getter. In 1992 the plan worked as Clinton rode the tide of Super Tuesday primary victories.

Despite the energy and enthusiasm generated by the Jackson campaigns of 1984 and 1988, Jackson has had to live with the fact that there are no lasting legacies to his two presidential electoral campaigns. In large measure the minimal impact of the Jackson presidential candidacies stemmed from Jackson's strategic misunderstanding of American electoral politics. Jackson actually believed that the number of votes that he obtained during the Democratic Party primaries should have granted him power within the elite circles of the party. Certainly, the party elite viewed Jackson as a problem that must be tenderly dealt with, but they did not see him as a member of their ranks. Jackson's miscalculation lay in misreading his constituency. He seemed to believe that he "controlled" the votes of his supporters in that they would indefinitely and in some disciplined fashion listen to his directions. What he did not understand is that his voting support was as situational and fluid as that of any other candidate. Jackson would have discovered this in 1992, had he chosen to enter the Democratic primaries. Many of his former black voting supporters would have abandoned him for a more viable opponent to incumbent President George Bush. Fortunately, some Jackson supporters among the black political elite informed him that they too would no longer "waste" their vote on his symbolic candidacy. It was therefore not surprising that he did not run; likewise, it was unsurprising that there was no large outcry from voters asking him to run.

Jackson could have been more successful at generating an enduring political presence among the party elite had he spent the time and energy helping to establish a pro-Jackson political infrastructure. During the 1984 and 1988 electoral bids, Jackson made symbolic gestures in this direction, although he did not substantively act. Many of his most active followers were less enthusiastic about his presidential runs than the possibility that his candidacy would help them to establish an ongoing Rainbow Coalition.

Like most charismatic figures, Jackson did not want to establish any type of organization that would subject his behavior and beliefs to rules, regulations, or institutionalized expectations. Simply put, charismatic leaders do not like the idea of being accountable to anyone (but God). As a result, they are usually incapable of recognizing the importance of establishing routinized organizational structures. For this reason few charismatic leaders are able to establish organizations that survive their demise or death. Black America is notorious for producing charismatic leaders who create organizations that crumble upon their death (for example, Elijah Muhammad and the Nation of Islam, Father Divine, Martin Luther King, Jr., and the Southern Christian Leadership Conference). Jackson would be no exception. In fact, Jackson might have been worse, for he did not even grasp how an organization could have helped his charismatic ambitions in the short run.

What is now going to happen to the range of issues that Jackson championed in the face of the election of a moderate-conservative Democratic president? New champions of these issues will emerge, now that Jackson has been so marginalized. In the aftermath of George Bush's defeat, however, many liberal American voters are feeling so thoroughly elated that they might not yet recognize the degree to which Clinton is authentically opposed to progressive politics.

Ironically, one real success of the Jackson campaign is that it helped to launch the national career of Ron Brown. One could not imagine Ron Brown as chairman of the Democratic National Committee without recognizing Jackson's important brokering role. Paradoxically, Jackson helped to broker into the national chair a figure who as a black was able to engineer the marginalization of Jackson without invoking protests of racism. After all, to the extent that Brown was black, he symbolically took the heat off the Democratic Party for isolating its most liberal and outspoken black, Jesse Jackson. In 1992, as Democratic Party chairman, Brown presided over a national campaign in which race was marginalized. Because a black man was the party chair, the criticism of the Democratic Party's racial politics was muted.

The problems concerning race in American society will not disappear. They have only become more entrenched because they have been neglected or ignored. To what extent does the running of a presidential campaign that marginalized race and discussions of racism create expectations within Clinton's electoral base that prevent him from tackling such issues once in office? If the white electorate demands of its candidates that they pretend that racism is no longer a major evil in America, are the successful candidates bound to govern according to this charade? The ultimate irony is that black Americans are linked to a disjointed coalition that once again views them as illegitimate claimants. The very coalition that might elect a sympathetic candidate is the very one that can win only if that candidate does not appear to be sympathetic.

REFERENCES

Andersen, Kristi. 1979. *The creation of a democratic majority, 1928–1936*. Chicago: University of Chicago Press.

Anderson, Benedict. 1983. *Imagined communities*. London: Verso.

Baker, Donald. 1989. *Wilder: Hold fast to dreams*. Cabin John, MD: Seven Locks Press.

Breines, Wini. 1982. *The great refusal: Community and organization in the New Left, 1962–1968*. South Hadley, MA: J. F. Bergin.

Cagin, Seth, and Philip Dray. 1988. *We are not afraid: The story of Goodman, Schwerner, and Chaney and the civil rights campaign for Mississippi*. New York: Macmillan.

Ditmer, John. 1994. *Local people: The struggle for civil rights in Mississippi*. Urbana: University of Illinois Press.

Edds, Margaret. 1990. *Claiming the dream: The victorious campaign of Douglas Wilder of Virginia*. Chapel Hill, NC: Algonquin Books.

Edsall, Thomas Byrne, and Mary Edsall. 1991. *Chain reaction: The impact of race, rights, and taxes on American politics*. New York: W. W. Norton.

Erie, Steven P. 1988. *Rainbow's end: Irish Americans and the Dilemmas of urban machine politics, 1840–1985*. Berkeley: University of California Press.

Fuss, Diana. 1989. *Essentially speaking: Feminism, nature, and difference*. New York: Routledge.

Gamm, Gerald H. 1989. *The making of New Deal Democrats: Voting behavior and realignment in Boston, 1920–1940*. Chicago: University of Chicago Press.

Gates, David. 1984. The Black Muslims: A divided flock. *Newsweek*, 9 April, 15–16.

Goffman, Erving. 1986. *Stigma*. New York: Simon and Schuster.

Goldberg, David Theo. 1993. *Racist culture: Philosophy and the politics of meaning*. Cambridge, MA: Blackwell.

Gosnell, Harold. 1935. *Negro politicians: The rise of Negro politics in Chicago*. Chicago: University of Chicago Press.

Greenberg, Jack. 1994. *Crusaders in the courts: How a dedicated band of lawyers fought for the civil rights revolution*. New York: Basic Books.

Grimshaw, William. 1992. *Bitter fruit: Black politics and the Chicago machine, 1931–1991*. Chicago: University of Chicago Press.

Hinckley, Barbara. 1981. *Coalitions and politics*. New York: Harcourt Brace Jovanovich.

Hirsch, Arnold. 1983. *Making the second ghetto: Race and housing in Chicago, 1940–1960*. Cambridge: Cambridge University Press.

Huckfeldt, Robert, and Carol Weitzel Kohfeld. 1989. *Race and the decline of class in American politics*. Urbana: University of Illinois Press.

Kaufman, Jonathan. 1988. *Broken alliance: The turbulent times between blacks and Jews in America*. New York: Scribners.

Massey, Douglas S., and Nancy A. Denton. 1993. *American apartheid: Segregation and the making of the underclass*. Cambridge, MA: Harvard University Press.

New Republic. 1991. Special issue: Hate story. 14 October, 21–31.

Omi, Michael, and Howard Winant. 1994. *Racial formation in the United States: From the 1960s to the 1990s*. 2d ed. New York: Routledge.

Quadagno, Jill. 1994. *The color of welfare: How racism undermined the war on poverty*. New York: Oxford University Press.

Reed, Adolph. 1986. *The Jesse Jackson phenomenon: The crisis of purpose in Afro-American politics*. New Haven, CT: Yale University Press.

Reed, Adolph, Jr., and Julian Bond. 1991. Equality: Why we can't wait. *Nation*, 9 December, 733–737.

Ringer, Benjamin B. 1967. *The edge of friendliness: A study of Jewish-gentile relations*. New York: Basic Books.

Salzman, Jack, Adina Back, and Gretchen Sullivan Sorin, eds. 1992. *Bridges and boundaries: African Americans and American Jews*. New York: George Braziller.

San Juan, E., Jr. 1992. *Articulations of power in ethnic and racial studies in the United States*. Atlantic Highlands, NJ: Humanities Press.

Sitkoff, Harvard. 1978. *A new deal for blacks*. New York: Oxford University Press.

Sklare, Marshall. 1967. *Jewish identity on the suburban frontier: A study of group survival in the open society*. New York: Basic Books.

Sleeper, Jim. 1990. *The closest of strangers: Liberalism and the politics of race in New York*. New York: W. W. Norton.

Sonenshein, Raphael J. 1993. *Politics in black and white: Race and power in Los Angeles*. Princeton: Princeton University Press.

Spelman, Elizabeth. 1988. *Inessential woman*. Boston: Beacon Press.

Stember, Charles Herbert. 1966. *Jews in the mind of America*. New York: Basic Books.

Tindall, George B. 1967. *The emergence of the new South: 1913–1945*. Baton Rouge: Louisiana State University Press.

Watts, Jerry. 1990. Racial discourse in an age of social Darwinism. *Democratic Left* (July–August): 3–7.

Weiss, Nancy. 1983. *Farewell to the party of Lincoln*. Princeton: Princeton University Press.

Wilson, William J. 1987. *The truly disadvantaged: The inner city, the underclass and public policy*. Chicago: University of Chicago Press.

Yancey, Dwayne. 1988. *When Hell froze over: The untold story of Doug Wilder: A black politician's rise to power in the South*. Roanoke, VA: Taylor Publishing.

3
Coalition and Competition: Patterns of Black-Latino Relations in Urban Politics

Paula D. McClain

Manifest changes continue to occur in the demographics of most major cities in the United States. Where we once referred to urban political dynamics in terms of whites versus blacks, now Latinos, increasing numbers of Asians, and to a lesser extent, Indians have been added to the equation. These demographic changes have not only altered the political·dynamics of urban politics, but also have created a new context for the relationships between racial minorities, which may take the form of coalitional, conflictual, or mutual nonrecognition. Several questions arise: Does shared racial minority group status provide the foundation for political coalitions between racial minorities? Does that shared status cause racial minorities to view each other with suspicion and distrust resulting in competitive behavior? Sonenshein (1993: 3) observes that the debate over biracial coalition politics in Los Angeles has been intense and enduring. The looming questions have always been: Should minorities go it alone and bargain with the larger society, or do they need to form alliances to counter their minority status? And if they make alliances, with whom should they link their fate?

This chapter focuses on the increasing tensions between two racial minority groups, blacks and Latinos, in urban politics. In addition, some aspects of coalitional and competitive behavior are explicated, and a brief case study of Los Angeles is presented.

INTERMINORITY GROUP RELATIONS

Eisinger (1976: 17–18) provides a useful framework for patterns of black-white race relationships. He argues that where differences arise among groups regarding political goals and outcomes the potential for conflict exists. Political coalitions, however, require that groups have similar goals, desire similar outcomes, and are willing to pursue their objectives in a collaborative and cooperative fashion. Coalitions, he argues, may be loosely or tightly organized, and cooperation may be tacit or explicit. Like coalitions, the form of competition between groups with differing goals will also vary. Competition may be pursued on an "enemies always" basis or on a "not permanent enemies" stance. Yet Eisinger (1976: 18) cautions that "similarity or dissimilarity of goals does not tell us much beyond the shape of the basic pressures that influence the establishment of intergroup political relationships."

Group competition, Blalock (1967) argues, accounts for some aspects of discrimination experienced by minorities. Individuals and groups accrue power and status in a variety of ways, thus, some power contests are understood as involving group against group. Competition exists, when two or more groups strive for the same finite objectives, so that the success of one implies a reduced probability that another will attain its goals. One could view group competition in terms of power contests that exist when there is rivalry and when groups have roots in different cultures. Furthermore, the greatest perceived competition may occur among near-equal groups. Blalock's framework, while addressed to majority-minority relations, is useful in examining relationships between minority groups if one recognizes that not only status differences but status similarities (near-equal groups) may become bases for conflict.

Coalition or Competition Politics?

The presence of multiple minorities in major metropolitan cities has led to the assumption that shared racial minority group status generates the potential for political coalitions among the various groups. (One of the assumptions of coalition theory is that the relationship between the various racial minority groups will be one of mutual respect and shared political goals and ideals). Yet, as Sonenshein (1993) reminds us, another assumption of coalition theory has been that black political assertiveness is incompatible with biracial political coalition between blacks and whites. Although referring to African Americans, Stokely Carmichael and Charles V. Hamilton (1967: 79–80) offer four bases on which viable biracial coalitions between whites and blacks can be formed, which may also apply to coalitions among blacks, Latinos, Asians, and Indians:

1. parties entering into a coalition must recognize their respective self-interests;
2. the belief that each party will benefit from a cooperative relationship with the other or others;
3. each party has its own independent power base and has control over its own decision making; and
4. all parties recognize that the coalition is formed with specific and identifiable goals in mind.

Accordingly, they stress that interests rather than ideology provide the most substantial basis for the most productive biracial coalitions. Arguing that "politics results from a conflict of interests, not of conscience," Carmichael and Hamilton (1967: 75) believe that whites, liberal or otherwise, would desert blacks if their own interests were threatened.

Sonenshein (1993: 7), however, suggests that the argument of interests versus ideology is at the heart of the debate over a theory of biracial coalitions. One side of the argument, represented by Carmichael and Hamilton among others, sees interests as the ties that bind biracial coalitions; these are, at best, short-lived tactical compromises between self-centered groups. On the other side, those who emphasize ideology argue that the essential character of biracial coalitions is common beliefs. This perspective of coalition theory holds that preexisting racial attitudes influence perception on racial issues and that these attitudes shape political actions; thus coalitions form not from objective self-interests but from shared ideology. The most likely coalition will be between groups close in ideology even when another union would be more advantageous.

The interests versus ideology distinction for biracial coalition is not as clearcut as it may appear. Sonenshein (1993) demonstrates that when black and liberal white, primarily Jewish, interests came into conflict in New York City, liberal sentiments were not sufficient to hold the coalition together. Nevertheless, he argues that while ideology alone may not hold coalitions together, biracial or interracial coalitions are unlikely to form at all without a shared ideology.

There are numerous instances of coalitions between blacks and Latinos. Common concerns during the 1960s, such as poverty, formed the foundation for unions between blacks and Latinos, especially Mexican Americans (Estrada et al. 1981), and there is clear evidence of coalition building between blacks and Latinos (see, e.g., Browning, Marshall, and Tabb 1984, 1990; Henry and Muñoz 1991; Sonenshein 1993). Sonenshein (1993) demonstrates that in Los Angeles over the past two decades, the mechanism for minority political incorporation has been a tightly knit coalition of African Americans and liberal whites, primarily Jews, with subsidiary support from Latinos and Asians.

The coalitions between blacks and Latinos, however, began to break apart when policies designed to promote equal access and equity for different groups were sometimes in conflict. Falcon (1988: 178), for example, notes that blacks were concerned that bilingual education would shift resources from the push for desegregation; accordingly, they did not support bilingual education. Latinos perceived that blacks support the English Only movement, employer sanctions, and opposed the extension of coverage to Latinos in amendments to the Voting Rights Act (National Council of La Raza 1990). Furthermore, Latinos began to question whether affirmative action had benefited them to the same extent as blacks, since they perceived blacks to have secured more municipal jobs than had Latinos (Cohen 1982; Falcon 1988).

Sonenshein (1990) also observes that the coalition between blacks and liberal whites in Los Angeles was beginning to show signs of strain during the last years of Mayor Bradley's administration "both because of divergent economic interests among the principal partners and because of increasing demands on the part of Asians and Latinos. Both of these latter minority groups differ significantly from blacks and whites in terms of ideology and interests" (Henry and Muñoz 1991: 329).

A 1993 *Los Angeles Times* survey of southern California residents found that of the groups mentioned—whites, blacks, Asians, and Latinos—blacks identified whites as being the most prejudiced (65 percent) and perceived Asians as being the next most prejudiced (45 percent), an increase from the 19 percent of blacks who expressed this feeling in a similar 1989 survey. Moreover, blacks believed that Asians (39 percent), far more than whites (29 percent), were getting more economic power than was good for southern California (UCLA Asian American Studies Center 1993: 5). When pressed to be specific about which group of Asians was perceived as causing problems, a quarter of both blacks and Latinos, 26 and 25 percent respectively, felt all Asians were causing problems. However, 19 percent of blacks identified Koreans as the source of problems, while a similar percentage of Latinos mentioned Vietnamese. For the most part, blacks did not view Latinos as prejudiced (11 percent) nor as getting more economic power than was good for the area (16 percent). These results are supportive of Henry and Muñoz's inference that "blacks and Latinos are the most likely coalition partners followed by Asians and Anglos in that order" (1991: 330). Uhlaner (1991) found affinities between blacks and Latinos, as compared to whites and Asians. As Sonenshein (1993: 263) reminds us, indicators such as these "provide an invaluable taste of reality for those who hypothesize the easy formation of coalitions of minorities."

There is also the possibility of competition arising among the various groups when blacks, Latinos, and Asians each have different goals, when there is distrust or suspicion among the three groups, or when the size of one group is such that it becomes unnecessary to form coalitions with other minority groups to gain political success (McClain 1993; McClain and Karnig 1990; Falcon 1988; Warren, Corbett, and Stack 1990; Meier and Stewart 1990). There is increasing evidence that in many communities blacks compete for scarce jobs, adequate housing, and government services (Falcon 1988; MacManus and Cassell 1982; Oliver and Johnson 1984; Johnson and Oliver 1989; Welch, Karnig, and Eribes 1983; Mollenkopf 1990). Moreover, some survey data suggests a growing hostility and distrust among the three groups (Oliver and Johnson 1984; Johnson and Oliver 1989), with a majority of Mexican Americans not in favor of building coalitions with blacks (see also Ambrecht and Pachon 1974; Browning, Marshall, and Tabb 1984; Grebler, Moore, and Guzman 1970; and Henry 1980).

McClain and Karnig (1990) and McClain (1993) in a 1980 study of all forty-nine United States cities greater than 25,000 in population containing at least 10 percent black and 10 percent Latinos found that analyses of socioeconomic data—income, education, employment, and percent nonpoverty—revealed no harmful competition in general between blacks and Latinos. The results supported a positive covariation relationship: where any group (black, Latino, white) prospered with respect to education, income, employment, and nonpoverty, the other groups did significantly better as well. Political outcome data—percent elected to city council seats, proportionality of council representation, black or Latino mayor—presented a somewhat different picture.

When either blacks or Latinos gained politically, they did so at the expense of whites. Political competition between blacks and Latinos was evident only when controls for white political outcomes were introduced. This relationship suggests that as black and Latino political successes increased, political competition between blacks and Latinos may be triggered, especially as fewer whites reside in minority-dominated cities.

Evidence also indicated that competition did appear to occur as the size of the black population increased, with negative consequences for Latinos, particularly on several socioeconomic measures. Increases in the Latino proportion of a city's population, however, did not appear related to competition harmful to blacks. Moreover, in a small sample of cities in which blacks were a plurality or majority, Latinos seemed to fare less well socioeconomically and, in particular, politically.

In the area of municipal employment, black and Latino municipal outcomes co-vary negatively with white municipal employment outcomes. These figures indicate a degree of competition for municipal jobs: blacks or Latinos gain at the expense of non-Latino whites. Evidence also indicates that competition in municipal employment does appear to occur as the size of the black work force increases and that this increase does have consequences for Latinos. The most significant predictor of limits to Latino municipal employment opportunities is the black percentage of the work force. As the black share increases, Latino opportunities decline. The Latino work force percentage, however, does not appear to have the same effect on black municipal opportunities. Furthermore, in a small sample of cities in which blacks are a plurality or majority, Latinos seem to fare less well in municipal employment outcomes, whereas in cities where Latinos are a plurality or majority, the consequence to black municipal employment is not consistent. Clear evidence that blacks suffer deleterious effects in municipal employment outcomes exists in only one city. It should be noted, however, that the latter suppositions are based on simple means and are therefore subject to over-interpretation. Nevertheless, the findings are suggestive and are supportive of the fact that increases in the size of the black work force have negative consequences for Latino municipal employment opportunities. At the same time, the findings highlight the masking effect that occurs in aggregate analyses of the effect of Latino dominance on black municipal employment outcomes in a small set of cities.

While these findings are limited in scope, they intimate a changing dynamic in the urban political landscape—the emergence of potential patterns of interminority group competition. In the future, the increasing presence of one group can have negative consequences for the political representation and political rewards of the other group. Moreover, it is highly possible that the dynamics of the relationship between blacks and Latinos will differ in cities depending on the size of one group relative to the other group. As one group begins to constitute the population majority, although continuing to view themselves as a minority, they may begin to function as a dominant majority, receiving a disproportionate share of the political rewards.

While the foregoing results indicate increasing competition between blacks and Latinos in certain urban areas, recognize that both coalitional and competitive behaviors can occur in the same city, but between different strata of individuals within each group. For example, elites could engage in political coalition building, while working- and lower-class persons see their interaction with other racial groups as competition for jobs, housing, and city services. Los Angeles illustrates this dual pattern of interaction. Moreover, it is a city in which blacks, Latinos, and Asians are represented in sufficient numbers for their political behaviors to have consequences for city politics.

LOS ANGELES

Los Angeles is a sprawling city which is prototypical of turn of the century western nonpartisan reform cities. Sonenshein (1993), whose work is the primary source for this section, has described it as an entrepreneurial city in which electoral politics are organized so that business interests play a significant role and urban bureaucracies are structured so as not to be dominated by either elected officials or local business interests. Moreover, the nonpartisan tradition of California city politics guarantees that political party organizations play a minimal role in Los Angeles city politics. (For a very good analysis of the political history and current state of racial politics in Los Angeles, see Sonenshein 1993).

Despite the conservative reform structure of Los Angeles, voters in 1925 approved a district electoral system for city council members, which provided an opening, albeit a small one, for minority participation in city politics. The political culture, however, was hostile to minority representation and even in substantial minority councilmanic districts, it was difficult for blacks and Latinos to get elected. In 1960, all three city council districts with sizable black populations were represented by whites. In 1949, Latinos had slightly more success electing one representative, Edward Roybal. In later years, the city leaders used gerrymandering to ensure that blacks and Latinos were unable to elect minority representatives to the city council.

As inhospitable as the Los Angeles political culture and structure were to blacks, Latinos, and Asians, Sonenshein (1993: 35) argues that the very nature of the system provides the foundation for multiethnic politics in the city: "Modern Los Angeles had never been a melting pot; everybody who differed from the white conservative model was excluded. Therefore, a Los Angeles-style melting pot had to be created politically." Minority exclusion provided the basis for coalition politics between blacks, Latinos, and Asians.

Coalition Politics

Beginning in 1960, blacks pressed to gain elective representation on the Los Angeles city council from the three council districts with sizable black populations: the eighth, ninth, and tenth. Success was achieved in the 1963 municipal elections when blacks won all three seats with Thomas Bradley winning the seat in the tenth district. Bradley's campaign for the tenth district seat is identified as the beginning of a multiracial coalition in Los Angeles politics. Liberal whites, especially Jews, blacks, Asians, and Latinos, particularly Edward Roybal, were instrumental in getting Bradley elected. The multiracial coalition forged in 1963 and fortified through a series of events over a decade, eventually propelled Bradley into the mayor's office in 1973.

In the wake of the changes occurring in the United States, and on the heels of the election of Richard Hatcher (Gary, Indiana) and Carl Stokes (Cleveland, Ohio) in 1967 as black mayors of major cities, Councilman Tom Bradley decided to become a candidate for mayor in the 1969 election. The specter of the Watts riot and racial polarization in the nation as well as in Los Angeles, overshadowed the race between Bradley and incumbent mayor Sam Yorty. Bradley hoped to build on the biracial coalition that won his tenth district seat to win the mayor's office, but 1969 proved not to be the year.

In the primary, Bradley led the packed field with 42 percent of the vote, just 8 percentage points short of winning the mayor's office outright. Yorty came in a distant second with 26 percent of the vote. Consequently, Bradley and Yorty moved into the general election. Bradley's primary campaign assumed a common ideological bond between blacks, Jews, liberal gentiles, and Mexican Americans. To a certain extent, it worked in the primary; however, in the general election where Bradley had to increase his level of white support, Yorty was able to exploit the weaknesses in Bradley's coalition strategy.

Yorty set about to impede a coalition by recalling the conflict between blacks and Jews in the Ocean Hill–Brownsville school conflict in New York City in 1968. He told middle-class Latinos that Bradley would ignore their needs since he pitched his campaign to poorer Latinos. Yorty also directly exploited white fears of having a black mayor by running ads in the real estate section of San Fernando Valley newspapers showing Bradley's picture with the caption "Will Your City Be Safe with This Man?" (Sonenshein 1993: 91). In addition, Yorty stoked the embers of the conflict between Bradley and the Los Angeles Police Department (LAPD), who saw Bradley, despite his previous police career, as an enemy of the department because of his criticisms of the department and its procedures.

In the general election, the three-way coalition between blacks, liberal whites, and Latinos did not come together as well as Bradley had expected. Yorty won the race with 53 percent of the vote to Bradley's 47 percent. Black support for Bradley was high and Jewish support moderate, but two-thirds of Latinos turned to Yorty, as did a similar percentage of whites (Sonenshein 1993: 93–94). Despite the loss in 1969, the experience set the stage for Bradley's run for and election to the office in 1973.

With a more professional and reorganized campaign organization, Bradley emerged from a three-way primary contest in 1973 in first place with Sam Yorty second, and Jesse Unruh, an unexpected Democratic challenger, who cut into Bradley's black and Jewish support, in third place. Once again, Bradley and Yorty faced each other in the 1973 general election. Yorty attempted to use similar tactics in the 1973 race that he used in 1969, but was not as successful. The LAPD also campaigned heavily against Bradley threatening that if he were elected there would be mass resignations in the department. Despite these attempts, Bradley easily defeated Yorty with 54 percent of the vote. Bradley's victory was achieved with "high Black turnout, solid Jewish support, an increasing Latino base, and little countermobilization by conservative whites" (Sonenshein 1993: 108). There was evidence of an emerging black-Latino coalition, but one that was class based. Upper-class and middle-class Latinos did not appear to be amenable to coalitions with blacks, but lower-class and lower-income Latinos were politically aligning with similarly situated blacks, as well as with upper- and middle-class blacks. Bradley's win exhibited the depth and strength of multiracial coalition politics in Los Angeles—a coalition that would consolidate power, bring Asian Americans into its fold, and control city hall from 1973 to 1992, when Bradley stepped down as mayor, although the breakup and decline of the coalition began in 1985. The loss of Michael Woo, Democratic Asian American member of the city council and member of Bradley's coalition, to Richard Riordan, Republican millionaire businessman, in the 1992 race for mayor signaled the final demise of the multiracial coalition that had governed Los Angeles for two decades.

Competition

At the same time as the formation of the Bradley multiracial coalition, there were tensions between black, Latino, and Asian elites over the ability of Latinos and Asians to elect representatives to the city council while blacks solidified their control of three of the fifteen city council seats. During councilmanic reapportionment activities in 1985 and 1986, Bradley vetoed a plan that would have eliminated the only Asian American district in order to create a Latino district. However, the unexpected death of a sitting council member provided the opening to reapportion districts in a manner that satisfied all parties of Bradley's coalition. As a result, by 1986, two Latino members and one Asian American served along with three blacks on the fifteen-member Los Angeles city council.

Tensions arose as well among lower-income blacks, Latinos, and Asians. James Johnson and Melvin Oliver (1989) detail the increasing economic and housing market competition among blacks, Latinos, and Asians in Los Angeles. The economy of Los Angeles suffered through restructuring after the loss of industry jobs from the city. Los Angeles lost an estimated 70,000 heavy manufacturing jobs as a result of plant closings. Because of their concentration in the heavy-manufacturing sector, blacks experienced tremendous job loss "as a result of plant closings, automation and the development of flexible production systems, and the movement of industrial firms to Third World countries in search of cheap labor" (Johnson and Oliver 1989: 451). In addition, between 1970 and 1980, poor Latino and Asian immigrants moved into the formerly all-black South Central area of Los Angeles. Johnson and Oliver observe that Latino immigrants were unable to find housing in the Latino barrio, East Los Angeles, and began to settle in increasing numbers in black South Central.

Sharing residential space is not the only incursion blacks in South Central perceive. Asian immigrants, especially Koreans, have become involved in entrepreneurial activities in black areas, opening businesses of all types. In Los

Angeles, Koreans have penetrated the small-business market in South Central. Relations between Korean shop owners and black customers have been filled with tension. Johnson and Oliver (1989: 457) suggest that disadvantaged blacks see the Korean merchants as "foreigners" who charge high prices, refuse to invest in the community in which they do business, refuse to hire blacks, and are rude and discourteous in their treatment of black customers. The killing of a black teenager by a Korean store owner and the proprietor's light sentence for manslaughter in 1991 served only to intensify the conflict. This antipathy between blacks and Koreans culminated in the targeting of Korean businesses by blacks and Latinos in 1992 during the Los Angeles riots. Johnson and Oliver (1989: 455) observe that the basic bone of contention, especially between blacks and members of immigrant minority groups, is the issue of jobs. Given their deteriorating position in the American urban economy, there is a growing perception among inner-city blacks that the new immigration has hurt them economically.

Yet, the conflict is also over housing and social amenities. Blacks in South Central are concerned that the influx of immigrants into their neighborhoods has a displacement effect. They charge that landlords, preferring to rent to Latinos or Asians because of the presence of multiple wage earners in those families, force black families out. Consequently, blacks are forced to move outside the Los Angeles metropolitan area to areas with lower housing costs. Additionally, blacks view Latino and Asian immigrants as "free riders" on the social services and benefits that blacks feel the immigrants have not fought to achieve through protest and activism in Los Angeles (Johnson and Oliver 1989: 456).

While Los Angeles has provided a case study for this discussion of racial minority group coalition or competition politics, elements of these patterns of interaction can be found in other cities. Los Angeles is a special case because it is a western nonpartisan city where political parties play a limited role in local politics. In cities where political parties are strong and actively involved in city politics, a different dynamic of coalition politics is likely to be present. The increasing tensions between blacks, Latinos, and Asians in urban politics, however, seems to be present in many cities regardless of governmental structure and partisan activities. While the competition between whites and various racial minority groups in urban politics is still a reality in many cities, the increasing competition between blacks, Latinos, and Asians will continue to grow as the white presence in many urban centers decreases.

REFERENCES

Ambrecht, Beliana C., and Larry P. Pachon. 1974. Ethnic political mobilization in a Mexican American community: An exploratory study of East Los Angeles, 1965–1972. *Western Political Quarterly* 27 (September): 500–519.

Blalock, Herbert M. 1967. *Toward a theory of minority-group relations.* New York: John Wiley and Sons.

Browning, Rufus P., Dale Rogers Marshall, and David H. Tabb. 1984. *Protest is not enough.* Berkeley: University of California Press.

Browning, Rufus P., Dale Rogers Marshall, and David H. Tabb. eds. 1990. *Racial politics in American cities*. New York: Longman.

Carmichael, Stokely, and Charles V. Hamilton. 1967. *Black power: The politics of liberation in America*. New York: Random House.

Cohen, Gaynor. 1982. Alliance and conflict among Mexican Americans. *Ethnic and Racial Studies* 5 (April): 175–195.

Eisinger, Peter K. 1976. *Patterns of interracial politics: Conflict and cooperation in the city*. New York: Academic Press.

Estrada, Leobardo, F. Chris Garcia, Reynaldo F. Marcias, and Lionel Maldonado. 1981. Chicanos in the United States: A history of exploitation and resistance. *Daedalus* 110 (spring): 103–132.

Falcon, Angelo. 1988. Black and Latino politics in New York City. In *Latinos in the political system*, edited by F. Chris Garcia. South Bend, IN: Notre Dame University Press.

Grebler, Leo, Joan Moore, and Ralph Guzman. 1970. *The Mexican American people*. New York: Free Press.

Henry, Charles P. 1980. Black and Chicano coalitions: Possibilities and problems. *Western Journal of Black Studies* 4 (winter): 222–232.

Henry, Charles P., and Carlos Muñoz, Jr. 1991. Ideological and interest linkages in California rainbow politics. In *Racial and ethnic politics in California*, edited by Byran O. Jackson and Michael B. Preston. Berkeley: Institute of Governmental Studies.

Johnson, James H. Jr., and Melvin L. Oliver. 1989. Interethnic minority conflict in urban America: The effects of economic and social dislocations. *Urban Geography* 10 (September–October): 449–463.

MacManus, Susan, and Carol Cassel. 1982. Mexican Americans in city politics: Participation, representation, and policy preferences. *Urban Interest* 4 (spring): 57–69.

McClain, Paula D. 1993. The changing dynamics of urban politics: Black and Hispanic municipal employment—Is there competition? *Journal of Politics* 55 (May): 399–414.

McClain, Paula D., and Albert K. Karnig. 1990. Black and Hispanic socioeconomic and political competition. *American Political Science Review* 84 (June): 535–545.

McClain, Paula D., and Joseph Stewart, Jr. 1995. Can we all get along? Racial and ethnic minorities in American politics. Boulder, CO: Westview Press.

Meier, Kenneth J., and Joseph Stewart. 1990. Interracial competition in large urban school district: Elections and public policy. Paper presented at the annual meeting of the American Political Science Association.

Mollenkopf, John H. 1990. New York: The great anomaly. In *Racial Politics in American cities*, edited by Rufus P. Browning, Dale Rogers Marshall, and David H. Tabb. New York: Longman.

National Council of La Raza. 1990. Background papers for black-Latino dialogue. Unpublished paper.

Oliver, Melvin L., and James H. Johnson, Jr. 1984. Inter-ethnic conflict in an urban ghetto: The case of blacks and Latinos in Los Angeles. In *Research in Social Movements Conflicts and Change* 6: 57–94.

Sonenshein, Raphael J. 1990. Biracial coalition politics in Los Angeles. In *Racial Politics in American cities*, edited by Rufus P. Browning, Dale Rogers Marshall, and David H. Tabb. New York: Longman.

———. 1993. *Politics in black and white: Race and power in Los Angeles*. Princeton: Princeton University Press.

UCLA Asian American Studies Center. 1993. *Crosscurrents* 1 (fall–winter): 5.

Uhlaner, Carole J. 1991. Perceived prejudice and the coalition prospects of blacks, Latinos, and Asian Americans. In *Ethnic and racial politics in California*, edited by Byran O. Jackson and Michael B. Preston. Berkeley: Institute of Governmental Studies.

Warren, Christopher L., John G. Corbett, and John F. Stack, Jr. 1990. Hispanic ascendancy and tripartite politics in Miami. In *Racial politics in American cities*, edited by Rufus P. Browning, Dale Rogers Marshall, and David H. Tabb. New York: Longman.

Welch, Susan, Albert K. Karnig, and Richard A. Eribes. 1983. Changes in Hispanic local employment in the Southwest. *Western Political Quarterly* 36 (December): 660–673.

Part II

Asian Americans:
Conflicts and Political Self

4
Korean-Black Conflicts and Street Level Politics

Yong Hyo Cho and Pan Suk Kim

The Korean American community in South Central Los Angeles recently faced a deadly crisis in the riots of 1992. The outburst of violence and destruction followed the announcement of the not guilty verdict in the Rodney King case on 29 April 1992 and resulted in 51 deaths, 1,419 injuries, 4,536 fires, 4,393 arrests, and $550 million in estimated property damage to approximately 1,600 businesses (McEnrue 1993: 18). Three of the 51 dead were Asian, even though Asians and those of Asian descent constitute less than 0.5 percent of the population in South Central Los Angeles. Estimates of the property damage vary slightly: according to Chang (1993a: 3–4), for example, the original estimate was around $750 million, about 2,300 Korean businesses suffered considerable or total loss, and the total damage sustained by Korean Americans is estimated to be around $400 million. Nakano (1993: 168) gave roughly the same estimate as Chang. Chin (1992: 1) reported that 1,839 Korean-owned businesses were burned or looted, accounting for almost half of the city's total property damage.

A major factor in this conflict is the African American community's distrust of police officers, reinforced by the video of California State Highway police savagely beating Rodney King. Another factor is the uneasy coexistence of Korean merchants and African American residents in South Central Los Angeles. Before the 1992 riots, very little was done to improve communication and dialogue between the two groups, and they were left largely to their own devices to resolve their mutual problems. In addition, the media often sensationalizes stories about blacks and Koreans, when, in fact, violent crime between these two ethnic groups constitutes only a small fraction of total crime in the inner city. Selective reporting exacerbates ethnic conflicts, while diverting attention from other, more serious problems that plague both the African American community (Aubry 1993: 154) and the Korean community.

This chapter discusses implications of the uneasy race relations that exist between these two communities. Generally, researchers agree that the Los Angeles civil unrest is America's first major multiethnic riot, revealing the complexity of interracial relations in American cities today (Chang 1993a). The incident is a wake-up call to all ethnic communities. What are the implications of living in a multiethnic society? Is there a need for a stronger Korean American leadership class in light of increasing conflicts with blacks? What does it mean to be a Korean American in urban America? In the following discussion, we present a Korean perspective on civil unrest throughout America, with particular emphasis on the Korean-black conflict in Los Angeles.

KOREANS IN THE UNITED STATES

Large-scale Asian immigration to the United States began during the 1850s (only forty-six Chinese immigrants were counted in 1820–1850), although some Chinese were noted to have settled in Pennsylvania as early as 1785 (Daniels 1988: 9; Barringer, Gardner, and Levin 1993: 24). When the kingdom of Hawaii signed a reciprocity treaty with the United States permitting Hawaii to export sugar duty-free to a previously tariff protected American market, large numbers of Chinese emigrated from China to Hawaii (Patterson 1988: 3). Just before the fabled Gold Rush of 1849, the trans-Pacific immigrants from China came to San Francisco (Kitano and Daniels 1988: 19). Poorly paid and grossly mistreated, they labored on the Union Pacific railroad that joined the eastern states to the West Coast.

The first large numbers of Japanese immigrants came to the independent kingdom of Hawaii as indentured laborers. After the United States annexed Hawaii in 1898, many of them moved to the West Coast (Kitano and Daniels 1988: 52). For Koreans, Hyung-chan Kim sees that the Jemulpo Treaty of 1882 opened diplomatic relations with the United States. However, the wars in northeast Asia acted as the catalyst for the initial Korean immigration (Kim 1970: 65–83).

According to Patterson (1988: 9), the first wave of Korean immigrants arrived in Hawaii as laborers in 1903, although a small number of merchants, political exiles, and students came to the United States as early as 1883. The first record of Koreans disembarking in Hawaii (they must pass through Hawaii on the way to the mainland) is that of the arrival in May 1896 of two men with the surname Kum (a variant of Kim), who listed their occupations as merchants (Patterson 1988: 9). By 1905, 7,266 Koreans had arrived in Hawaii, with another 1,033 immigrating to Mexico (Barringer and Cho 1989: 5; Kitano and Daniels 1988: 107). Later, substantially larger numbers of students, political refugees, and merchants entered the United States. After 1924, the year of the Oriental Exclusion Act, there were no substantial Korean immigrants to the United States until the end of World War II. In addition to the highly restrictive immigration law, when Korea was seized by Japan in 1910, the Japanese prevented Korea's citizens from leaving the country. Thus, the number of Koreans in the United States remained static for nearly half a century. The second wave of immigration took place after the Korean War

(1950–1953). During and after that war, emigration to the United States increased, consisting mostly of a small number of business people, students, professionals, and brides of American servicemen stationed in Korea (Barringer and Cho 1989: 6). The third wave of immigration was in response to the Immigration and Naturalization Act of 1965, a landmark legislation that opened the gate for Asian emigration to the United States (Kitano and Daniels 1988: 110–11). After the mid-1960s, Korean immigration doubled from 9,521 in 1960–1964 to 18,469 in 1965–1969 (Barringer and Cho 1989: 7), and since then, Korean immigration has increased sharply, leveling off at about 30,000 per year in the 1980s. The 1990 census reports approximately 798,000 Koreans in the United States (Table 4.1).

Table 4.1
Race and Origin of the United States Population: 1890 and 1990 (numbers in thousands)

Race and Origin	1890		1990		
	Number	Percent	Number	Percent	Change
All persons	225,545	100.0	248,709	100.0	9.0
Asian and Pacific Islander	3,500	1.5	7,273	2.9	107.8
Japanese	700	0.3	847	0.3	0.9
Chinese	806	0.4	1,645	0.7	104.1
Korean	35	0.2	798	0.3	125.3
Filipino	774	0.3	1,406	0.6	81.6
Asian Indian	361	0.2	815	0.3	125.6
Vietnamese	261	0.1	614	0.2	134.8
Hawaiian	166	0.1	211	0.1	26.5
Samoan	41	0.0	62	0.0	50.1
Guamanian	32	0.0	49	0.0	53.4
Other	n/a	n/a	821	0.3	n/a
Hispanic other	14,603	6.4	22,354	9.0	53.4
African American	26,495	11.7	29,986	12.1	13.2
White	188,371	83.1	199,686	80.3	6.0

Source: U.S. Bureau of the Census 1991.

KOREANS IN LOS ANGELES

The Los Angeles metropolitan area has the highest concentration of Koreans in the United States. The Koreans who settled in Los Angeles are perceived to have advanced better than blacks economically and numerically. In fact, the African American population has declined in size and in economic status (Stewart 1993; Yu, Phillips, and Yang 1982: 165–183). In Los Angeles, African Americans and Hispanic Americans trail Korean Americans in both education and economic gains. The median family income for African Americans, Hispanics, and Korean Americans in 1989 was $14,930, $15,531, and $20,147, respectively. Today, approximately eight million people reside in Los Angeles County, and close to 3.5 million live in the City of Los Angeles (U.S. Bureau of the Census 1990). In 1970, the population was 71 percent white. By 1980, African Americans, Latinos, and Asians together made up the majority (51.1 percent) of the total population (UCLA Ethnic Studies Center 1987). By 1990, the largest ethnic group in the city consisted of 1,391,411 Hispanics or those of Hispanic origin. The second largest ethnic group, of African descent, numbered 487,674, followed by 341,807 Asians, of whom 72,970 are Korean Americans. The remaining 1,841,182 of the city's population are whites (U.S. Bureau of the Census 1990). Table 4.2 presents these statistics in terms of percentages.

In 1980, the number of African Americans in South Central Los Angeles almost equaled those of whites and Latinos in the same area, but the 1990 census found that both white and African American groups had declined. The demographic statistics of South Central Los Angeles suggest that what was once perceived as a primarily African American area is now becoming a Latino community—a transformation resulting from the influx of economic and political refugees from both Central and South America. Navarro (1993) predicts that Latinos will become an indisputable majority ethnic group in the Los Angeles area by the year 2000. Even in Koreatown, Latinos outnumber Koreans by 48 to 3 percent (Navarro 1993: 72).

In general, the mass media portrayed the 1992 Los Angeles eruption as one of primarily African American and Asian American violence. This faulty impression suggested that Latinos were involved only peripherally in the violence; however, approximately one third of those killed were Latino, and many Latino-owned businesses were destroyed (Ramos and Wilkinson 1992).

The number of Korean-owned small businesses in African American neighborhoods increased rapidly during the 1980s. Since the mid-1970s, Korean immigrants have begun to fill the void created by the departure of Jewish merchants and the relocation of large retailers to the suburbs. Unable to find jobs because of a lack of English proficiency and other market barriers, recent immigrants have opened grocery and liquor stores, vegetable stands, gas stations, laundry shops, indoor swap meets, and carryout shops. For most, these were their first businesses, and they found the choice attractive, not only because the shops in the black neighborhoods were relatively inexpensive to purchase or rent (Nakano 1993: 168), but also because they offered the opportunity for entire families to participate. The influx of Korean merchants into black neighborhoods, however, has resulted in increased

Table 4.2
Changes in Los Angeles Area Population, 1980–1990

Race/Ethnicity	Year	South-Central Los Angeles	City of Los Angeles	Los Angeles County
White	1980	31.8	47.9	52.9
	1990	21.9	37.4	40.8
African	1980	29.4	17.0	12.6
American	1990	24.5	13.9	21.9
Latino	1980	31.1	27.5	27.6
	1990	46.0	39.9	37.8
Blacks of	1980	31.1	27.5	27.6
Hispanic origin	1990	9.1	1.0	0.7
Korean	1980	1.1	1.1	0.8
	1990	2.1	2.1	1.6
Chinese	1980	1.4	1.5	1.3
	1990	1.7	1.9	2.8
Japanese	1980	2.1	1.7	1.6
	1990	1.6	1.3	1.5
Filipino	1980	1.4	1.5	1.3
	1990	2.0	2.5	2.5

Source: Navarro 1993: 70–71; Anderson et al. 1992: 8.

complaints, tensions, resentment, and, unfortunately, violent confrontations as manifested by such highly publicized conflicts as the boycotting of the Red Apple, a Korean-owned grocery, in Brooklyn in 1990 and the shooting of fifteen-year-old Latasha Harlins by a Korean merchant, Soon Ja Du, in South Central Los Angeles in 1991. These two nationally publicized cases have come to symbolize the fractured relationships between African Americans and Korean Americans (see Taylor 1992).

THEORETICAL CONSIDERATIONS

Historically, the United States population has grown through successive waves of immigration, with Asians making up the most recent. The issue of black-Korean relations should be considered in a broad context because tension between ethnic or racial groups is not unique to the Koreans or blacks or to the Los Angeles area. Rather, it is a problem that exists between many ethnic and racial groups over most of America. Accordingly, this issue may be viewed from historical perspectives as a problem associated with the adaptation of immigrants to host countries.

Immigrants face a multitude of problems such as cultural and linguistic differences, changes in roles, and conflict in norms and values. These problems are more pronounced for Koreans and Asian immigrants than the European immigrants due to the sharper differences in the cultures. For Korean immigrants, occupational adjustment generally means downward mobility, and their life is largely segregated from mainstream American society. Many own and operate small businesses, work long hours, and overuse family and relatives. Many of these small business owners have college degrees and professional or managerial experience, but their difficulties with English have forced them to abandon dreams for a professional career. They usually start out by taking menial work and, by scrupulous self-denial, save enough money to buy a convenience mart or small store. Their skills and education may not be relevant to their integration into the workplace, indicating the split labor market they face (Kitano and Daniels 1988: 113).

Koreans and African Americans cite institutional racism and other oppressive cultural conditions for contributing to interethnic tension and hostility in American society (Stewart 1993: 35). Some of these racial and ethnic inequalities include the class structure of American society and its unequal opportunities, as well as institutional racism, urban economics, and public policies. Cultural factors are sociopersonal values, attitudes toward education, family relationships, and psychological inclinations (Webster 1992: 176).

Steinberg (1981) and Cheng and Bonacich (1984) point out that education, one of the preferred routes to social mobility by immigrants, does not appear to have been a requisite with first generation Europeans in the nineteenth century or with Asians in the early twentieth century. Rather, by finding economic niches in the host society, these newcomers gained economic security first, then through education assured their children's mobility to become professionals. The failure of educational institutions to accommodate the needs of racial minorities has been one of the chief criticisms of the structuralists, who argue that the exploitation and continued segregation of ethnic and racial minorities perpetuate ethnic differentiation rather than assimilation. The relative socioeconomic positions of whites, blacks, and Hispanics support the validity of the structuralist argument (Barringer, Gardner, and Levin 1993: 11–12).

In many respects, Asians and blacks have suffered from prejudice more than any other ethnic group. In 1790, Congress excluded both blacks and Asians from citizenship by denying naturalization to anyone who was not a "free white person." Blacks, but not Asians, became citizens in 1870, when Congress authorized the naturalization of "aliens of African nativity and persons of African descent." Most blacks in the country were brought here by force and robbed of their freedom, their identity, and their culture. To succeed in today's society, blacks must overcome severe restrictions. In U.S. history, the pecking order of socioeconomic status of racial and ethnic groups is established by the chronological order of their immigration to this country, although blacks are excluded from this rule as a result of systematic discrimination against them. Even the most illustrious black Americans, despite their extraordinary personal achievements, cannot escape from this discrimination.

Using a Marxist framework, many social scientists seek to shed light on the causes of violence in terms of class struggle (Reich 1981) or structural deficiencies of the system (Johnson 1964). The internal colonial theory (Blauner 1972: 90) views black ghettos as internal colonies of white America, where whites dominate and control the economic, political, and cultural lives of blacks. The ethnic succession theory (Gans 1973: 218; Aldrich 1975: 327) attempts to explain why African Americans have failed, whereas European Americans have succeeded. According to the successionist view, conflict or competition between ethnic groups is the inevitable consequence of their striving to achieve success in America. According to Sowell (1980) and Chang (1991: 169–178), all immigrant groups experience discrimination, but some of them are able to overcome these barriers and move up the economic ladder more quickly. Chang (1991) argues that a major weakness of the successionist theory is that it ignores the historical perspective of race relations in America.

Other scholars (Gurr 1970; Davies 1968; Navarro 1993) contend that violent eruptions result from relative deprivation (RD), along with a frustration-aggression framework. Relative deprivation refers to the gap between what people have and what they think they should have (Navarro 1993: 74) or a perceived discrepancy between people's value expectations (i.e., the goods and conditions of life to which people believe they are rightfully entitled) and their value capabilities (the goods and conditions they think they are capable of attaining or maintaining) (Gurr 1970). Thus, aggressive behaviors are the by-product of discrepancy between expectations and actualities (Gurr 1970: 13). RD fosters popular discontent, which in turn engenders social volatility. Yet the pervasiveness of frustration alone is not sufficient to detonate violence (Navarro 1993: 74). Some violence is triggered by so-called accelerators, such as economic crises (Johnson 1964). The climate of discontent is also a product of race and ethnic degradation such as racism, nativism, prejudice toward people of color, and scapegoating immigrants for social and economic problems.

Figure 4.1 presents a model of racial violence based on some of these theoretical perspectives. This model may be appropriate to explain the violence of South Central Los Angeles, but no attempt is made here to argue the case. However, it must be noted that this model easily fits with the Los Angeles riots and many other urban riots experienced in American cities since the middle 1960s.

Figure 4.1
Framework for Violent Behavior

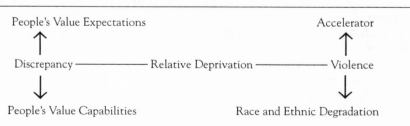

Navarro argues that the Los Angeles riots were predictable, even inevitable, considering the impoverished socioeconomic conditions and deteriorating race relations of the South Central Los Angeles area, which comprises economically impoverished enclaves plagued by high unemployment and underemployment, crime, poor housing, and other social problems. The pervasiveness of poverty was a precondition for popular frustration and anger (Pastor 1993: 6). Furthermore, the spark that ignited the fire was the unexpected verdict in the trial of the police officers charged with assaulting Rodney King.

In the case of African Americans, quality of life diminished under Mayor Bradley's administration. In 1990, two years before the Los Angeles riots, Byran Jackson (1990: 175) had predicted civil unrest similar to the Watts riots:

African-American communities are plagued by gang warfare, poor housing conditions, lack of jobs, poor schools, and drug problems. Politically, many would argue that a few black political appointments are not enough for the African-American vote in Los Angeles. However, lacking an alternative to Bradley, African-American voters have given their support to the Bradley regime out of "symbolic" pride. Currently, while there are many African-American organizations engaged in politics in Los Angeles, the larger African-American community has not been able to organize in such a way as to exact substantive policy concessions from the Bradley regime. However, symbols do erode, and the future may bring violent outbursts in the city similar to the Watts riots.

A Korean Perspective: An Old Problem or Something New?

It is commonly argued that the sources of tensions, hostilities, and violence are rooted in the changing ethnic, cultural, and racial makeup, leading to fierce competition for employment, housing, and economic development among groups (Stewart 1993: 24). Aubry (1993: 150) believes that the so-called black-Korean problem reflects "the pent-up frustration" of both communities. As ethnic successionists explain the pattern of demographic changes in urban neighborhoods, for example, Aldrich and Reiss (1976) and Elazar and Friedman (1976), the Korean merchants in the 1980s and 1990s have simply replaced the Jewish merchants in African American neighborhoods and the Korean-African American conflict is nothing more than the old problem of the Jewish-African American conflict. According to this view, ethnic succession seems to be the inevitable order in a multiethnic society, and subsequent competition for goods and services is associated with conflicts between different groups. Baldwin (1970: 4) presents the line of thinking this way: "Jews and Koreans have 'taken over businesses' in African-American neighborhoods. Jews and Koreans 'exploit African-Americans' for their own economic benefits. African-Americans react to Jews as whites, as perforce part of the white majority, even if they were perceived to be different within that majority."

Ella Stewart (1993) provides some causes of interethnic tensions in both African Americans' view of Korean American proprietors and Korean Americans' attitude toward their African American patrons. According to Stewart's study, African Americans complain about being watched and lack of respect shown toward patrons. Also African Americans ask why Korean store owners do not hire black employees. African Americans perceive that Korean merchants are not really part of the community and do not contribute to or participate in community-based organizations.

To answer these questions satisfactorily would require a deep inquiry into cultural values held by both Korean Americans and African Americans. First, many Korean merchants cannot afford to hire anyone because many Korean-owned businesses are mom-and-pop stores and must depend upon family labor in order to generate profits. Second, Korean immigrant merchants believe that it is easier to work with Latino immigrants in terms of their status as immigrants and because of common barriers like language. Third, some Korean merchants complain that nonimmigrant workers such as African Americans often demand higher wages than they can afford. Fourth, the Korean-African American conflict is also exacerbated by America's current economic problems. Asian Americans feel that there are ties between the rise of anti-Asian bigotry and violence and the increase in America's trade deficit with Asian nations. Finally, it is not as if Korean Americans are far more economically powerful than black Americans. Even though household incomes were close to the national average, extended and intact families meant that Koreans in 1980 had a per capita income of only $5,544, which is closer to the $4,545 for blacks than the $7,808 for whites. The average small store brings in no more money than a good union factory job. The fact is that Koreans are more often self-employed than any other ethnic group, and their willingness to work very hard for very little money gives them a competitive advantage in inner-city neighborhoods where supermarkets or anyone else fear to tread (Hu 1992: 14).

In addition, Korean-owned stores have a high ownership turnover rate compared to Jewish-owned stores in African American neighborhoods. Since the primary motive for Koreans to open small businesses in African American neighborhoods is to make a substantial sum of money in the shortest possible time, they tend to resell their stores if the price is right (Chang 1993c: 14). Thus, they are less likely to establish personal ties with African American customers because it takes at least a few years to establish an understanding of their business environments and neighborhoods. However, Jewish merchants in African American neighborhoods maintain a paternalistic relationship with African American customers because many have lived in the neighborhoods and participated in community activities.

Also, African Americans complain that Korean proprietors made patrons feel unwelcome at their place of business by not smiling or greeting patrons. However, it is not easy to smile or greet patrons in a potentially unsafe environment. In 1991, Korean entrepreneurs in South Central Los Angeles ran a chance of one in 250 of being killed while pursuing their business activities—about the same odds that a U.S. soldier had during a tour of duty in the Vietnam War. Many Korean merchants in inner cities have difficulty because "outside" merchants catch particular resentment from local residents who often perceive them as opportunistic and successful at the community's expense (Aubry 1993: 150). Moreover, residents in South Central Los Angeles are tired of being put upon by continuing social and economic inequities, and many are increasingly inclined to lash out at the most visible and convenient targets. In these circumstances, it is convenient for Korean merchants to become scapegoats for the many ills facing the African American community (Aubry 1993: 155). The majority of Korean immigrants are newcomers who arrived in America after the passage of the 1965 Immigration Act, mostly in the 1970s and 1980s. Some newcomers are unaware of the historical significance of the civil rights movement.

One variation on Rodney King's question—"How do we get along with each other?"—applies to members of every ethnic group in America. To pretend that racism does not exist in America not only insults the intelligence of those who are victims of racism and discrimination, but, worse, suggests a state of denial and ignorance on the part of those who question its existence. Thus, the question "How do we get along with each other?" may necessarily need to include "How do we get along with each other in the presence of institutional racism and discrimination?" (Stewart 1993: 42).

It is a fallacy to compare Korean immigrants of the 1990s with Jewish merchants of the 1960s. Korean Americans still suffer from political, social, and cultural subordination in American society. It is essential to differentiate Jewish American success from that of Korean immigrants as they struggle with their status of marginality and powerlessness (Chang 1993c: 17).

Researchers such as Chang (1993c: 12) view the Jewish and African American relationship as a vertical one, whereas the Korean-African American relationship is a relatively horizontal one. Jewish-African American relations, on the one hand, resemble the traditional economic, political, and social subordination of African Americans. The Korean American-African American relationship, on the other hand, is more horizontal because Korean Americans seem to have some economic advantages while African Americans have far more political and social-cultural advantages. If this is true, it can be argued that the Korean-African American relationship is potentially more explosive because members of each group view themselves as "at least equal to or better than the other." African Americans fear a shift in political power, and newly arrived Latinos further diminish scarce resources at other minorities' expense.

Although its applicability is uncertain, Chang (1991: 172) suggests that Bonacich's combined model of the internal colonial and middleman theories provides a unique perspective in understanding the Korean-black conflict within the context of American capitalism. Interestingly, Bonacich (1987) modified the internal colonial model and the middleman minority theory and argued that immigrant entrepreneurs are oppressed in addition to being the oppressors. According to Bonacich (1987: 455), middleman minorities concentrated in retail and service-oriented industries serve as buffers between the dominant and subordinate populations. In addition, ethnic ties do play a vital role in business development. Bonacich argues further that immigrant entrepreneurs are not only exploited by

American capitalism, but are also involved in the oppression of the underclass. Immigrants are subject to discrimination because of their cultural and physical differences as well as their legal status. This model contributes useful theoretical research on the role of immigrant entrepreneurs in American society by combining the two factors of race (internal colonial model) and class (middleman minority).

KOREAN-BLACK ALLIANCE BUILDING

All ethnic communities generally agree that they want to get along, but the critical question is how to get there. In the wake of the Los Angeles riots of 1992, myriad new needs were created: short-term disaster relief assistance, long-term policy and regulatory change in the areas of planning, zoning, finance, and social services for limited-English-speaking communities, and the demand for litigation to address fundamental legal issues in both the civil and criminal arenas. Under this circumstance, African American-Korean community relations are not the only issue demanding attention in the riot-torn city.

Despite a fumbling start, the manner in which New York City handled the Red Apple incident provides a useful precedent in rebuilding the African American–Korean community relationship following a serious conflict. Mayor Dinkins waited eight months to visit the grocery store and refused to help enforce a court order to keep boycotters fifty feet from the store. He underestimated the seriousness of the hostility between black customers and Korean merchants, as well as the importance of his duty to intervene. He learned from his errors. The mayor's office improved communication with both blacks and Koreans, and the two communities began to talk to each other in earnest, partly at the mayor's urging. In 1990 and 1991, the city helped organize goodwill missions to Korea—one by black ministers and another by a cross-section of local community leaders. This provided a far better understanding of the cultural background of recent Korean immigrants. The trip by the community leaders, in turn, led to the formation of the Ethnic Committee for Racial Harmony and Outreach (ECHO), which promotes dialogues between Koreans and African Americans and other ethnic groups. ECHO raised funds for scholarships and sponsored 100 minority students for intercultural studies in Seoul. Meanwhile, the city's Human Rights Commission has provided sensitivity training to Korean merchants and the African American community on how to prevent tension and what to do when problems occur.

In Los Angeles, the Black-Korean Alliance (BKA) was formed, with the assistance of the Los Angeles County Human Relations Commission, to improve relations between the Korean and the African American communities after four Korean merchants were killed in robberies during April 1986. The BKA sponsored activities and events, such as joint church services, education forums, joint cultural events, and seminars on crime prevention and community economic development. However, Elaine Kim (1993: 17) argues that it was not successful in cooling black-Korean conflicts in Los Angeles: "The BKA was unable to prevent the killing of a dozen more Korean merchants in Southern California between 1990 and the Los Angeles Riots." According to her observation, the BKA had neither its own meeting place nor a telephone. Grassroots participation was not extensive, and the BKA never received political or financial support from the public or private sectors, but only the good intentions of the individuals involved.

The deadly conflicts between blacks and Koreans have renewed the critical need to build a black-Korean alliance. Churches of both the African American and the Korean communities can play a useful role in this alliance. One of the special characteristics of the Korean immigration has been the role of the Christian churches (Kitano and Daniels 1988: 113). The churches played several roles for the earlier immigrants in Hawaii. Some of them were active in the Korean independence movement and helped to maintain cultural traditions by sponsoring language schools and serving as social centers. The Christian churches continue to play an active role in the present Korean community. In southern California, the number of Korean churches has increased from 11 in 1965 to 215 in 1979 to about 1,000 in the early 1990s (Hurh and Kim 1984: 182–190). The Korean Christian churches provide for many needs such as religious involvement, an identity, a resource for newly arrived immigrants, a place for meeting people, and a place for prayer, as well as a place to seek peace of mind. It seems that the Korean churches are central to the Korean community.

However, there are some ideological differences between Korean and African American churches. Dearman (1982: 165–183) found that more than 90 percent of Korean churches in Los Angeles belong to fundamentalist, conservative, or evangelical sects and, most of all, they are nonpolitical. Out of the sixty-five ministers who responded to the questionnaire, only one minister classified himself as a liberal. African American churches are the leaders of community action in social and political arenas, addressing the most critical issues for the African American community such as racial oppression, discrimination, and injustice of all kinds, as exemplified by the role that the Southern Christian Leadership Conference played in the civil rights movement in this country. Even theologically conservative African American churches still promote political activism and encourage their members to participate in voting drives or protest movements. African American churches continue their involvement with the general welfare of the African American community today. In contrast, the Korean immigrant churches tend to be almost completely inactive in the social, economic, and political concerns of the Korean community, offering little promise for change in the foreseeable future.

In addition to building a Korean-black alliance, Koreans are beginning to deliver their own voices to the municipal authorities. Through the efforts of the volunteers working with the Asian Pacific American Bar Association, the Korean Association, the Korean Chamber of Commerce, and other Asian organizations, there have been some developments in the way the city, the police, and the prosecutor's office are providing service to the Asian community. For example, in the wake of a series of violent crimes in Washington, D.C., merchants of Asian descent, Asian community members and political activists met with Mayor Sharon

P. Kelly, Police Chief Fred Thomas, and other authorities in the U.S. attorney's office. Mayor Kelly appointed Kathleen Hom, a third-generation Chinese American, as her assistant for Asian and Pacific Islander affairs. Chief Thomas established a permanent Asian liaison office with Korean-speaking police officers, who provide communication with and access to the Korean merchants. The chief also mandated that each police district chief in their respective districts would meet with Asian and Korean community workers to discuss police initiatives such as translating safety brochures into Korean and other Asian languages, crime prevention surveys of stores, more foot and driving patrols, more stakeouts, and electronic surveillance (Oh 1994).

POLITICAL PARTICIPATION

While the mass media continues to praise Asian Americans as high achievers in education, businesses, and professions, seldom are Asian Americans included among the potential players in mainstream politics. Perhaps such lack of attention stems from the small Asian population and scarce data on Asian American electoral behavior. Scholarly attention to minority politics first focused almost exclusively on African Americans. Cole (1974) and Karnig (1976) pioneered the effort to look at African American representation on city councils. MacManus (1978) soon expanded the scope of inquiry to Hispanics.

Interestingly, Asian Americans, the fastest-growing minority group with a unique economic status, have not been studied much (Alozie 1992) and have just begun to receive scholarly attention. To this date, Asian Americans in general, and Korean Americans in particular, have remained an invisible and inaudible minority politically. By and large, they have not yet learned the American political game and how to play it. More importantly, Asian Americans have not regarded politics or public service as preferred professional and career pursuits. The low probability to succeed in the political arena due to the small number of Asian voters has obviously been a discouraging influence. Thus, there are a small number of elected officials among Asians at all levels of government and an even smaller number of Koreans. However, in 1991, a number of Korean candidates won elections, the most publicized case being Jay Kim, who was elected to the U.S. House of Representatives from Orange County, California. Others include one elected to the state senate in Oregon, one each to the state houses of representatives in Washington, Florida, and Hawaii, and one to the city council in Seattle. These Koreans exemplify their own personal success, not the political achievements of the Korean community as a whole, whose efforts in both campaign fund contributions and the number of votes delivered for these candidates were far too small to claim credit for the victories. Therefore, it is valid to argue that Koreans have not yet established an electoral power base.

According to Alozie's study, Asians' ability to gain council seats is affected by the percentage of Asians in the total population, median family income relative to whites', level of education, the size of the city council, and the electoral structure of council seats held by blacks and Hispanics. Nevertheless, the fact remains that the elected Asian mayors and appointed top administrators in American cities are extremely small in number as shown in Table 4.3.

The number of Asians in Table 4.3 is comparable with the number of Native Americans. These findings do not differ greatly from what has been observed for blacks and Hispanics, but Alozie asserts that the percentage of Asian population may not be as important as the percentage of black population in explaining discrepancies in Asian representation because African Americans form a more potent political force than Asian Americans do. The Asian population contains a considerable proportion of new immigrants, many of whom may not qualify or may not have the confidence to participate in the political process, as a result of the "liability-of-newness syndrome." Moreover, the Asian population contains a fair amount of heterogeneity, so the differing nationalities constituting the group may not vote in an election as a cohesive bloc as blacks often do (Alozie 1992: 97–98).

African Americans have been the dominant force in leading the civil rights struggle to great success, and naturally they have gained more political power and privileges than Asian Americans during the past twenty years. Mayors of the two largest cities in California (Los Angeles and Oakland) have been African Americans. There are many state assemblymen, city councilmen, and other politicians who represent African American communities in California and other parts of the United States. It is noteworthy that the new Clinton administration appointed four African American cabinet members while selecting no Asian Americans for high-ranking federal positions.

The great migration of African Americans from the South to the North, beginning in the 1920s, transformed African Americans from a basically rural population into an overwhelmingly urban one. The urbanization and concentration of African Americans in north central cities created an emerging political power in that region. The Voting Rights Act of 1965 and its enforcement substantially ended disenfranchisement throughout the nation. In 1941, there

Table 4.3
Key Municipal Officials by Race and Ethnicity

Position	Date	Asian	White	Black	Native American	Hispanic
Elected mayor	1985	25	6,448	117	20	37
or president	1991	11	6,578	144	19	103
Chief appointed	1985	20	9	49	13	27
administrative	1991	4,427	4,797	64	10	96
office or manager						
Assistand manager	1985	5	1,067	41	5	10
or CAO	1991	6	1,386	71	6	43

Source: International City/County Management Association 1992: 201; International City Management Association 1986: 302.

were three black elected officials, mainly in the North. By 1965, the number had grown to 280. Following the Voting Rights Act, the number increased to nearly 1,000 in 1968 (Gomes and Williams 1992: 53). The increase of elected African American officials over the past two decades is impressive, although it falls far short of the ideal of equitable representation as reported in Table 4.4. While African Americans comprise 12.2 percent of the nation's total population, they still hold fewer than 1.5 percent of its elective offices. In addition, the annual rate of growth for African American elected officials has declined. For example, the number of African American elected officials increased by 26.6 percent from 1970 to 1971, but the number rose only 5.8 percent from 1988 to 1989 (Gomes and Williams 1992: 54–55).

CONCLUSION

In general, every member of society should do his or her fair share to promote goodwill and understanding among all peoples. Members in both African American and Korean American communities should show common courtesy and respect for their neighbors, should value and treat each person as a unique human being with a unique history and culture, who deserves fundamental rights, and should show respect for the others' differences while searching for the one thread of commonality that can promote positive communication and understanding among all people (Stewart 1993: 46). In the absence of a well-conceived plan for addressing interethnic problems, emotion-driven actions will predictably result in further provoking violent incidents. It is imperative to start interethnic coalition building now. Each group should fairly participate in the formation of multiethnic coalitions predicated on the inclusion of all groups who share a common interest in building and maintaining a relationship for mutual accommodation and, better yet, cooperation. Korean Americans and African Americans must shift their

Table 4.4
Number of African American Elected Officials in Selected Categories, 1970–1989

Year	Members of Congress	State Senators	State Reps	County Officials	Mayors	City Council Members	School Board Members	Total
1970	10	31	137	92	48	552	362	1,469
1975	18	53	223	305	135	1,237	894	3,503
1980	17	70	247	451	182	1,809	1,149	4,912
1985	2	90	302	611	286	2,189	1,368	6,056
1989	24	101	315	696	299	2,882	1,537	7,226

Source: Joint Center for Political and Economic Studies 1989; Gomes and Williams 1992: 55.

attention from blaming each other to concentrating on achievable objectives based on mutual interests for survival and prosperity.

Until Korean Americans develop their own community organizations that can be effective in dealing with interracial issues and socioeconomic and political issues affecting the community, the responsibility for bringing about interracial dialogue and harmony lies heavily with government institutions such as the Human Relations Commission and with local political officials.

The Korean American community must first build social, economic, church, and political organizations to address the internal needs of the community as well as those beyond. Most of the existing organizations do not meet these needs, chiefly because the established organizations are controlled by first-generation leaders who are either unable to relate with the external world or are hostile to extending its interests externally. The best established and financed organizations, churches, exemplify this type of Korean organization.

There are economic organizations such as local chambers of commerce and trade organizations for laundry owners, grocers, service station owners, and roofing and contracting businesses. These economic organizations are usually not interested in social and political issues, nor are they equipped to be involved with them.

Professional organizations exist for Korean American accountants, lawyers, scientists, and engineers, but these groups are largely apolitical. A number of social service organizations serve the elderly and other needy individuals in the Korean American community, but these organizations are often led by American-born, American-educated figures. At this time, it seems that these social service organizations and some of the professional organizations, particularly organizations of lawyers, offer the best hope to meet the need for the community organizations. The East Bay Korean Service Center, an Oakland-based organization led by a young lawyer, Ann Park, is an example. Although the primary mission of the center is to provide social services to needy Korean Americans, its leadership helped mediate a conflict between a shopkeeper and a black student in Berkeley, California. The organizations of Korean lawyers have the potential to provide leadership in representing the interests of the Korean American community in relation to groups such as black community groups. The Korean churches may also change as the church members and their pastors change. As the American-born and American-educated pastors replace the first-generation pastors, their ideology and social outlook will likely embrace the social and political responsibility of the churches.

It is going to take time for the Koreans to acquire the organizational capacity and political skills necessary for them to find their niche, socially, economically, and politically, in this multiethnic and multicultural society. But we predict that they will make this transition more quickly than anyone might imagine possible.

REFERENCES

Aldrich, Howard. 1975. Ecological succession in racially changing neighborhoods: A review of literature. *Urban Affairs Quarterly* 10, no. 3: 327–348.

Aldrich, Howard, and A. Reiss. 1976. Continuities in the study of ecological succession: Changes in the race composition of neighborhoods and their businessmen. *American Journal of Sociology* 81: 846–866.

Alozie, Nicholas O. 1992. The election of Asians to city councils. *Social Science Quarterly* 73, no. 1: 90–100.

Anderson, Stuart, Adrain Dove, Armando Navarro, Ralph Rossum, and Robert S. Walters. 1992. *An atlas of South Central Los Angeles*. Claremont, CA: Rose Institute of Local and State Government.

Aubry, Larry. 1993. Black–Korean American relations: An insider's view. *Amerasia Journal* 19: 149–156.

Baldwin, James. 1970. Negroes are anti-Semitic because they're anti-white. In *Black anti-Semitism and Jewish racism*, edited by Nat Hentoff. New York: Schocken.

Barringer, Herbert R., and Sung-Nam Cho. 1989. *Koreans in the United States: A fact book*. Honolulu: Center for Korean Studies at the University of Hawaii.

Barringer, Herbert R., Robert W. Gardner, and Michael J Levin. 1993. *Asians and Pacific Islanders in the United States*. New York: Russell Sage Foundation.

Blauner, Robert. 1972. *Racial oppression in America*. New York: Harper and Row.

Bonacich, Edna. 1987. Making it in America: A social evaluation. *Sociological Perspectives* 30, no. 4: 446–466.

Chang, Edward T. 1991. New urban crisis: Intra-Third World conflict. In *Asian Americans: Comparative and global perspectives*, edited by Shirley Hune, Hyung-chan Kim, Stephen S. Fugita, and Amny Ling. Pullman: Washington State University Press.

———. 1993a. The Los Angeles riots: A Korean American perspective. *Korean and Korean American Studies Bulletin* 4 (summer–fall): 3–13.

———. 1993b. From Chicago to Los Angeles: Changing the site of race relations. *Amerasia Journal* 19: 1–3.

———. 1993c. Jewish and Korean merchants in African American neighborhoods: A comparative perspective. *Amerasia Journal* 19: 5–22.

Cheng, Lucie, and Edna Bonacich, eds. 1984. *Labor immigration under capitalism*. Berkeley: University of California Press.

Chin, Steven. 1992. Innocence lost: L.A.'s Koreans fight to be heard. *San Francisco Examiner*, 9 May, 1.

Cole, Leonard. 1974 . Electing blacks to municipal office: Structural and social determinants. *Urban Affairs Quarterly* 8: 17–39.

Daniels, Roger. 1988. *Asian America: Chinese and Japanese in the United States since 1850*. Seattle: University of Washington Press.

Davies, James C. 1968. The J-curve of rising and declining as a cause of some great revolutions and a contained rebellion. In *The politics of violence: Revolution in the modern world*, edited by Carl Leiden and Karl Schmitt. Englewood Cliffs, NJ: Prentice-Hall.

Dearman, Marion. 1982. Structure and function of religion in the Los Angeles Korean community: Some aspects. In *Koreans in the Los Angeles: Prospects and promises*, edited by Eui-Young Yu, Earl H. Phillips, and Eun Sik Yang, 165–183. Los Angeles: Center for Korean-American and Korean Studies of California State University.

Elazar, Daniel, and Murray Friedman. 1976. *Moving up: Ethnic succession in America*. New York: Institute on Pluralism and Group Identity.

Gans, J. H. 1973. Negro-Jewish conflict in New York. In *Ethnic conflicts and power: A cross-national perspective*, edited by D. E. Gelfland and R. D. Lee. New York: Wiley.

Gomes, Ralph C., and Linda F. Williams, eds. 1992. *From exclusion to inclusion: The long struggle for African American political power.* New York: Greenwood.

Gurr, Ted Robert. 1970. *Why men rebel.* Princeton: Princeton University Press.

Hu, Arthur. 1992. An Asian take on L.A.: Us and them. *New Republic,* 1 June, 13–14.

Hurh, Won Moo, and Kwang Chung Kim. 1984. *Korean immigrants in America.* Cranbury, NJ: Fairleigh Dickinson University Press.

International City/County Management Association. 1992. *The Municipal Year Book 1992.* Washington, DC: International City/County Management Association.

International City Management Association. 1986. *The Municipal Year Book 1986.* Washington, DC: International City Management Association.

Jackson, Byran. 1990. Black political power in the city of Los Angeles: An analysis of Mayor Tom Bradley's electoral success. In *Black Electoral Politics,* edited by Lucius J. Barker. New Brunswick: Transaction Publishers.

Johnson, Chalmers. 1964. *Revolution and the social system.* Palo Alto, CA: Stanford University Press.

Joint Center for Political and Economic Studies. 1989. *Black elected officials: A national roster.* Washington, DC: Joint Center for Political and Economic Studies.

Karnig, Albert. 1976. Black representation on city council. *Urban Affairs Quarterly* 11: 223–242.

Kim, Elaine H. 1993. Home is where the han is: A Korean American perspective on the Los Angeles upheavals. *Social Justice* 20 (spring): 1–21.

Kim, Hyung-chan. 1970. Korean community organizations in America: Their characteristics and problems. In *The Korean diaspora,* edited by Hyung-chan Kim. Santa Barbara, CA: Clio Press.

Kitano, Harry H. L., and Roger Daniels. 1988. *Asian Americans: Emerging minorities.* Englewood Cliffs, NJ: Prentice-Hall.

MacManus, Susan. 1978. City council election procedures and minority representation. *Social Science Quarterly* 59: 153–161.

McEnrue, Mary P. 1993. Managing diversity: Los Angeles, before and after the riots. *Organizational Dynamics* (winter): 18–28.

Nakano, Erich. 1993. Building common ground: The liquor store controversy. *Amerasia Journal* 19: 167–170.

Navarro, Armando. 1993. The South Central Los Angeles eruption: A Latino perspective. *Amerasia Journal* 19: 69–86.

New York Times. 1992. Bridges between blacks and Koreans, 18 May, 16.

Oh, Y. Kris. 1994. Interview. Washington, DC, 10 February 1994.

Pastor, Manuel. 1993. *Latinos and the Los Angeles uprising: The economic context.* Claremont, CA: Tomás Rivera Center.

Patterson, Wayne. 1988. *The Korean frontier in America: Immigration to Hawaii, 1896–1910.* Honolulu: University of Hawaii Press.

Ramos, George, and Tracy Wilkinson. 1992. Unrest widens rift in diverse Latino population. *Los Angeles Times,* 8 May, A1, A4.

Reich, Michael. 1981. *Racial inequality: A political-economic analysis.* Princeton: Princeton University Press.

Sowell, Thomas. 1980. *Ethnic America: A history.* New York: Basic Books.

Steinberg, Stephen. 1981. *The ethnic myth: Race, ethnicity, and class in America.* New York: Atheneum.

Stewart, Ella. 1993. Communications between African Americans and Korean Americans: Before and after the Los Angeles riots. *Amerasia Journal* 19: 23–54.

Taylor, Jared. 1992. *Paved with good intentions: The failure of race relations in contemporary America*. New York: Carroll and Graf Publishers.

UCLA Ethnic Studies Center. 1987. *Ethnic groups in Los Angeles: Quality of life indicators*. Los Angeles: Ethnic Studies Center of the University of California at Los Angeles.

U.S. Bureau of the Census. 1990. *1990 Census of population, general population characteristics*. Washington, DC: Government Printing Office.

——— . 1991. U.S. *Department of Commerce News, 1990*. New York: U.S. and Foreign Trade Commercial Trade Administration. Bulletin CB91-125, 12 June.

Webster, Yehudi O. 1992. *The racialization of America*. New York: St. Martin's.

Yu, Eui-Young, Earl H. Phillips, and Eun Sik Yang, eds. 1982. *Koreans in Los Angeles: Prospects and promises*. Los Angeles: Center for Korean-American and Korean Studies of the California State University.

5
Beyond Redress:
The Future of Japanese American
Politics on the Mainland

Don Toshiaki Nakanishi

> As time passes, it becomes more and more plain that our wartime treatment of the Japanese and Japanese-Americans on the West Coast was a tragic and dangerous mistake. That mistake is a threat to society, and to all men. Its motivation and its impact on our system of law deny every value of democracy.
> —Rostow, 1945: 193

On February 19, 1942, ten weeks after the Pearl Harbor attack, President Franklin D. Roosevelt signed Executive Order 9066, which gave to the Secretary of War and the military commanders to whom he delegated authority, the power to exclude any and all persons, citizens and aliens, from designated areas in order to provide security against sabotage, espionage and fifth column activity. Shortly thereafter, all American citizens of Japanese descent were prohibited from living, working or traveling on the West Coast of the United States. The same prohibition applied to the generation of Japanese immigrants who, pursuant to federal law and despite long residence in the United States, were not permitted to become American citizens. . . .

This policy of exclusion, removal and detention was executed against 120,000 people without individual review, and exclusion was continued virtually without regard for their demonstrated loyalty to the United States. . . . All of this was done despite the fact that not a single documented act of espionage, sabotage or fifth column activity was committed by an American citizen of Japanese ancestry or by a resident Japanese alien on the West Coast. . . .

The personal injustice of excluding, removing and detaining loyal American citizens is manifest. Such events are extraordinary and unique in American history. For every citizen and for American public life, they pose haunting questions about our country and its past.

> —Commission on Wartime Relocation
> and Internment of Citizens 1982: 2–3

In 1992, on the fiftieth anniversary of the World War II internment of 120,000 Japanese Americans, a number of activities were organized across the nation to draw attention to this "extraordinary and unique" event in our country's past. Days of remembrance ceremonies, exhibitions, conferences, and other events were held to enhance the public's understanding of not only what happened to the Japanese Americans during the war, but also why it happened, so that such a "tragic and dangerous mistake" never happens again.

For the Japanese American population, these commemorative activities carried additional symbolic and real meanings. For some organizers of these events, the fiftieth anniversary represented a major milestone in Japanese American history: apparently the last opportunity for those who had been incarcerated to share their deeply private memories and feelings about their wartime experiences, perhaps for the first time, with their children and grandchildren. For others, these events provided a timely occasion for finally addressing issues that had long remained controversial within the Japanese American community like those dealing with the "no-no" boys and their families (so named because of their negative responses to two controversial questions on the loyalty questionnaire required to be answered by Japanese Americans upon their internment in U.S. concentration camps at the onset of WWII), who were labeled as disloyal and ultimately imprisoned for the duration of the war at Tule Lake (Okada 1957). For still others, these activities were intended to signal the start of a new era for Japanese Americans—the so-called post–redress and reparations period—which would feature new visions, agendas, and organizational vehicles for guiding and leading the Japanese American community in the decade of the 1990s and beyond. In this respect, the commemorative activities provided a convenient, yet compelling, opportunity for the generations of Japanese Americans who were born after the internment to define their group identities on their own terms and to pursue a community leadership agenda in which internment-related issues were not prominent. For example, a statement in the program of the conference "The Future of the Nikkei Community" held in Los Angeles, in October 1992, offered this perspective on the internment:

On the fiftieth anniversary of the signing of Executive Order 9066 and the internment of our parents and grandparents, there is an obligation to look back and understand the importance of our ancestor's experiences on our heritage. However, we must also realize that there is a need to go beyond this now *familiar history* and take a hard look at where we are now, as Sansei and Yonsei (third- and fourth-generation Japanese Americans) of America. History lies not only behind, but ahead, and the role we choose to take is upon us. [Emphasis added]

Indeed, after fifty years, only a minority of living Japanese Americans can claim to have directly experienced the internment. By 1992, fewer than one in ten members of the Japanese American population were actual survivors of the wartime incarceration.

Although commemorative activities, particularly those that mark the fiftieth or one-hundredth anniversary of a major historical event, may be commonplace, there was far more involved in the internment-related activities of 1992 than simply looking back at a disastrous past. These activities were the continuation of a profound process of developing a new collective response by Japanese Americans to the internment. Since the late 1960s, Japanese Americans have departed from their decades-old silence and repression of the tragedy, and have come to identify with the internment in a highly visible, sustained, and multifaceted manner. Throughout the 1970s and 1980s, the internment was the dominant political issue for the Japanese Americans. The discussions eventually resulted in what was once thought to be an unthinkable political victory: on 10 August 1988 President Ronald Reagan signed the Civil Liberties Act of 1988, which provided for a formal national apology and a one-time payment of $20,000 to each surviving Japanese American who had been interned during the war. Although in hindsight it might appear that the resurrection of the memories and unresolved issues of the internment and the mobilization around its extensive agenda of unfinished business were inevitable, this process of reawakening was not automatic, predictable, or linear. Indeed, there were many seemingly plausible and logical reasons why Japanese Americans should have continued to repress and to remain silent about their wartime tragedy rather than elevating it to the most visible rung of their community agenda. In 1967, for example, on the symbolically rich twenty-fifth anniversary of Executive Order 9066, hardly any commemorative activities were organized, especially by the Japanese American community. A weekend workshop on the internment undertaken by the UCLA Extension Department was one of the few activities held anywhere in the nation to mark the occasion. If one had attempted to forecast the future saliency of the internment for Japanese Americans from the observable empirical reality of 1967, one would probably have predicted a form of historical amnesia by the time of the fiftieth anniversary in 1992.

This discussion provides an alternative to the customary manner of treating the internment as past history, as a voluminous body of literature has done (see, for example, Grodzins 1949; Girdner and Loftis 1969; Daniels 1971; Bosworth 1976; Weglyn 1976; Irons 1983). Rather, it examines the interaction of structural and psychological factors that led Japanese Americans to engage in an arduous, controversial, and largely unexpected process of coming to grips with the internment. My reasons for exploring this phenomenon are several. First, the internment experience is one of the few major events in Asian Pacific American history which are familiar to most scholars and many members of the general public; accordingly, it receives at least some attention in current American textbooks, studies on American race relations, and commentaries on individual legal rights and democratic principles. Although there remain lingering myths about its wartime necessity (Weglyn 1976; Commission on Wartime Relocation and Internment of Citizens 1982; Irons 1983), few dispute the interpretation that racism was at least one of its major underlying causes or that the removal and imprisonment of 120,000 individuals for upward of four years is an extraordinary action. Like other significant events in the group histories of American racial minorities, however, the internment is usually viewed as a distant and past tragedy, which will probably never happen again, and which, more importantly, has no enduring impact on or significance for the group or its members. It is largely considered to be a topic for historiographic investigation, or classroom discussion on American history. It serves as another benchmark for illustrating the severity of America's past racial oppression, or in a more optimistic vein, as a frame of reference for assessing the progress which the society has made in improving its race relations.

The resurrection of the internment by Japanese Americans, though, suggests that these common notions of past racial victimization may be limited. They may be based more on simplistic value judgments about the resiliency of individuals and groups to come to grips with such events rather than on in-depth empirical investigations. The following analysis provides an alternative and more rigorous treatment of the longitudinal significance of such events by drawing on data collected from multiple methodological approaches (cf. Nakanishi 1978). It gains its analytic insights from studies on survivors of major historical disasters like the Holocaust and the atomic bombing of Hiroshima, a body of literature that was earlier applied to and then largely dismissed in relation to understanding the behavior of African Americans *during* slavery (Degler 1976). However, the empirical findings and theoretical generalizations from these works on the behavior of individuals *after* these disastrous episodes suggest that the latent collective response of Japanese Americans to their internment experience, although unpredictable, should not be viewed as puzzling or unique. By analyzing the Japanese American case, perhaps we will not prematurely turn the page on past instances of racial victimization, but instead empirically ascertain their enduring significance for both the group and the larger society.

Another reason for analyzing the resurrection of the internment is that it reveals the shortcomings and ramifications of the popular view that Japanese Americans—and by extension, other Asian Pacific Americans—are a successful or model minority. This perspective was promulgated first by journalists and then by numerous scholars during and after the mid-1960s, a period of profound societal racial strife (Peterson 1966; Makaroff 1967; Varon 1967; Bell 1985). As Chun (1980: 1) writes, this view "created a glowing image of a population that, despite past discrimination, had succeeded in becoming a hard-working, uncomplaining minority deserving to serve as a model for other minorities." Its critics, however, have argued that this interpretation has been used invidiously to pit Asian Pacific Americans against other groups by placing them on a symbolic pedestal for others to emulate. More substantively, these critics argue that the perspective rests on an inadequate and normative analysis of selective aggregate-level census indicators and glosses over persistent and new forms of prejudice and discrimination faced by Asian Pacific Americans (Suzuki 1977; Chun 1980). And like some scholars who have challenged sociologist William Wilson (1978) on the emerging black middle class, these critics argue that the attainment of specific achievement levels by particular sectors of the Asian Pacific American population cannot be interpreted to mean that equality of opportunity and societal acceptance have been gained and that problems of institutional access, political representation, psychological well-being, or racial prejudice have been fully resolved. However, if this widely held view of Japanese Americans as a model minority represents a laudatory—indeed long sought—affirmation of societal acceptance, why would the group resurrect, visibly identify with, and seek reparations for an event that remained controversial and emotion laden even after many decades? Why would they engage in highly public activities, which would appear to jeopardize a uniquely positive stereotype of a racial group in American society? More substantively, why would a group which has been portrayed as docile, eschewing public attention in politics for private economic achievement, suddenly take center stage on a seemingly no-win issue dealing with past racial victimization and keep it firmly atop the group's agenda for over two decades?

This is the second puzzling aspect of the latent collective response of Japanese Americans relative to their internment experience. This seemingly unprecedented action cannot be explained by the model minority thesis or conventional perspectives on race relations. It also provides another example of how research in race relations—in this case the studies that used and promoted the model minority perspective—can have significant, although perhaps largely unanticipated, consequences for both public policy deliberations and group actions. The rise and continued promotion of this perspective in both journalistic and academic circles coincided with the resurrection of the internment. It served, on the one hand, as a major constraint for Japanese American organizations in seeking government and public recognition for the victimization that they experienced as a result of their wartime incarceration. On the other hand, it was one of the crucial elements of a dialectical process that influenced the direction, momentum, and scope of the process of reawakening. This discussion also seeks to illustrate the need to investigate seemingly group-specific topics within an explicitly multiracial framework. Probing the resurrection of the internment in this manner provides glimpses of a variety of largely overlooked areas of convergence and divergence between the contemporary and historical experiences of Japanese Americans and other American racial minorities with American political and social institutions. It therefore suggests a range of opportunities for coalition building among different racial and ethnic groups, as well as the potential for intergroup conflicts.

Examining the resurrection of the internment may also provide guidance in understanding and anticipating both the present and the future directions of Japanese American politics, especially in the mainland states. In recent years, for example, there has been speculation that the successful movement to gain redress represented the last hurrah for Japanese Americans, whose rise in American politics during the past two decades coincided with their decline in terms of their numerical representation among Asian Pacific Americans. For example, in 1970, when internment-related issues and activities were initiated, Japanese Americans were the largest Asian Pacific American group, representing over a third of all Asian Pacific Americans in the country. By 1980, however, both Chinese Americans (812,178) and Filipino Americans (781,894) surpassed Japanese Americans (716,331). Other Asian Pacific groups like Asian Indian Americans (387,223), Korean Americans (357,393), and Vietnamese Americans (245,025) grew rapidly through immigration. By 1990, both

Chinese American (1,645,472) and Filipino American (1,406,770) groups had grown to be nearly twice as large as the Japanese American (847,562) group, who experienced relatively little emigration from Japan and a gradually declining birth rate, and accounted for less than 10 percent of the entire Asian Pacific American population. The other three major Asian Pacific American groups—Asian Indian Americans (815,447), Korean Americans (798,849), and Vietnamese Americans (614,547)—also recorded substantial population gains by 1990. By the year 2000, it is projected that Japanese Americans will fall further down the population scale, with practically all other major Asian Pacific American groups outnumbering them, and Filipino Americans will replace Chinese Americans as the largest Asian Pacific American ethnic group (LEAP and UCLA Asian American Studies Center 1993). However, can this demographic scenario adequately anticipate the future role and significance of Japanese Americans in advancing their own group interests in American politics, as well as those that they share with other Asian Pacific American groups? I believe an examination of the process by which Japanese Americans resurrected the internment provides an important and largely overlooked frame of reference for considering the potential impact of these demographic factors on future Japanese American politics.

RESURRECTING THE INTERNMENT

> I had nearly outgrown the shame and guilt and the sense of unworthiness. This visit, this pilgrimage, made comprehensible, finally, the traces that remained and would always remain, like a needle. That hollow ache I carried during the early months of internment had shrunk, over the years, to a tiny sliver of suspicion about the very person I was. It had grown so small sometimes I'd forget it was there. Months might pass before something would remind me. When I first read, in the summer of 1972, about the pressure Japan's economy was putting on American business and how a union in New York City had printed up posters of an American flag with MADE IN JAPAN written across it, then that needle began to jab. I heard Mama's soft, weary voice from 1945 say, "It's all starting over." I knew it wouldn't. Yet neither would I have been surprised to find the FBI at my door again. I would resist it much more than my parents did, but deep within me something had been prepared for that. Manzanar (concentration camp) would always live in my nervous system, a needle with Mama's voice. (Houston and Houston 1973: p. 140)

Since the late 1960s, after a prolonged and collectively shared period of silence, Japanese Americans began to confront their World War II internment experience. Although such a late response to a past tragedy may not be unprecedented, it hardly follows a predictable itinerary. Survivors of other major disasters often exhibit a complex tug-of-war between remembering and forgetting their previous experiences. Yet it is not possible to forecast when and how the struggle of underlying psychological forces such as guilt, shame, repression, and vulnerability will be contested and resolved (see, for example, Niederland 1962, 1972; Lifton 1969; Erikson 1976; Wolfenstein 1957; Janis 1971).

The unpredictability of this reawakening stems, to a large extent, from the fact that surviving through and after a tragic event is a unique experience for each group of survivors. Each survival experience not only carries a distinct imprint from its disastrous episode, but also evolves from a different constellation of external factors—real or symbolic, historical or current—which serve to differentiate one group of survivors from another. For example, reading about a poster "of an American flag with MADE IN JAPAN written across it" may have triggered memories of the Internment for Nisei (second-generation Japanese American) writer Jeanne Wakatsuki Houston, but probably would not have had the same meaning for other survivors such as the Hiroshima *hibakusha* (survivors of the atomic bombings of Hiroshima and Nagasaki). As Lifton (1969: 485) observes, however, "mass-media reports of people dying from A-bomb disease, and reports of nuclear weapons testing; as well as the annual August 6th ceremony, the sight of the A-Bomb Dome, [and] war or war-like behavior anywhere in the world" do serve to generate recollections of the Hiroshima explosion for its survivors. Although the underlying process, which Lifton called symbolic reactivation, may be comparable for survivors of both the internment and Hiroshima, the specific stimuli that would bring memories and related symbolism to the surface are not the same and would probably vary in their frequency of appearance. Indeed, different groups of survivors may exhibit similar forms of postdisaster behavior, but each approaches the dilemma of survival from group-specific perspectives.

The resurrection of the internment by Japanese Americans probably could not have been foreseen. For over two decades after the successful passage of the Evacuation Claims Act in 1948, which allowed Japanese Americans to file claims "for damages to or loss of real or personal property . . . that is a reasonable or natural consequence of the evacuation" (Hosokawa 1969; Chuman 1976), the Japanese American community rarely engaged in formal organized activities dealing specifically with the internment experience. There were no pilgrimages to the former concentration camps; no legislative campaigns to rescind Executive Order 9066; no organizations that sought to educate the general public about the injustices and losses suffered by Japanese Americans during the war. Instead, when references were made to the internment, especially by the Japanese American Citizens League (JACL) during the late 1940s and early 1950s when successfully overturning a number of long-standing anti-alien and anti-Japanese laws (Chuman 1976), they functioned almost exclusively as tools of advocacy and public relations. They were used, in large measure, to show other Americans that Japanese Americans were loyal and patriotic (Hosokawa 1969). Two frequently used themes—that no acts of sabotage were committed by Japanese Americans during the war and that Japanese American soldiers provided "proof in blood" of their loyalty to America—served to buttress the view that the internment was wrong; yet it provided Japanese Americans with unexpected opportunities to demonstrate their worth as American citizens.

The internment came to symbolize a test of character for Japanese Americans, particularly the Nisei. Although the test may have been unnecessary and unconstitutional, the Nisei passed it with flying colors. They deserved recognition as full-fledged and equal American citizens, much as did World War II veterans of other racial and ethnic minorities at the time. However, in promoting this specific interpretation of the internment, very little was revealed about how the event adversely affected Japanese Americans, especially the first generation, alien Issei. Japanese Americans, to be sure, were portrayed as victims, but little was said about their victimization. Although one might fault Nisei leaders, as well as a number of scholars who wrote about the internment, for promulgating this narrow assimilationist view of the event, there is good reason to believe that both the American public and Japanese Americans were not ready for full discourse on the subject.

The avoidance of a number of unresolved issues for nearly two decades at the collective level mirrored an analogous process of repression and denial at the individual level for most Japanese Americans. It was not uncommon, for example, for third-generation, Sansei, children who grew up during the 1950s and 1960s to acquire only the most superficial facts about their elders' internment experience, such as the names and locations of the concentration camps. They gained little understanding of the personal and group impact of being abruptly removed from homes and incarcerated in desolate locales; of the decisions by many to volunteer for military service or by others to seek repatriation to Japan; or the extent of racial hatred and wartime hysteria. The late Amy Ishii, a founder of the Manzanar Committee, a group that began in 1969 to plan annual pilgrimages to the Manzanar concentration camp in California and to offer public education forums on the internment, commented about the difficulties of sharing the internment experience with Sansei:

> Women, if they've ever been raped, don't go around talking about it, you know, "I was a victim of rape," or anything like that. This is exactly the kind of feeling that we as evacuees, victims of circumstance, had at the time of the evacuation. A lot of Nisei and Issei are actually ashamed of the fact that they were in a concentration camp. You just don't talk about having been a victim of rape, and I think this is where our mental block is; therefore, it is very hard for the young people to go to their parents and ask them "Have you had this experience?" (Hansen and Mitson 1974: 14)

The Title II Campaign

Although the bulk of literature on the internment appeared during the twenty-year period following the war, very little found its way into American textbooks or the mass media (Okamura 1978). Most works treated the event as past history. Many discussed the broader constitutional significance of removing and incarcerating Japanese Americans, but none applied those historical lessons to an analysis of the McCarthy era's Internal Security Act of 1950, with its Title II provisions for the establishment of detention camps at locations such as Tule Lake, which was used during the internment. The first work to draw parallels between the internment and Title II was *Concentration Camps USA* by Charles Allen, Jr., which appeared in 1966. At the same time, unlike the body of literary works and personal accounts written by survivors of the Nazi death camps, only a handful of books about the internment were written by Japanese Americans during the two decades after the war (see Okamura 1978; Okada 1957; Weglyn 1976).

Far from being a cataclysmic event, the resurrection of the internment represented a gradual process of reawakening, influenced by an unexpected series of events and by individuals outside the Japanese American community. First, the black power movement had a broad effect on Japanese Americans and other minority groups, especially in terms of their group identities and perceived status in the society. The late Harold Isaacs (1975) provided the most eloquent interpretation of the rippling effect of this dynamic societal reexamination:

This crisis of "black" and "American" identity would by itself be crisis enough. But its effects in these years was to shake up all the other groups in the society located in various stations along the road from being "out" to being "in." It brought on change in the perception and self-perception of the "group" that had always been seen by all the others as "in"—the white Protestants of northern European origins who had been seen as the dominant majority "group" of the society and, who now began to be loosely and commonly lumped together under the pejorative label "Wasp." In other mostly nonwhite groups—the Mexican-Americans and other Spanish-speaking groups, the American Indians, the Chinese-Americans and Japanese-Americans—something of the black pattern began to be reproduced, with radical fringe groups appearing and reflecting—and momentarily speaking for—the much more widely felt and deeply laid feelings of whole populations that their status in the society and their image of themselves had to change. (pp. 20–21)

It was within this context of multiple group redefinition that the terms Asian American and later Asian Pacific American were born and eventually gained popular usage to reflect the commonality of experiences and the need to seek unity among the diverse Asian ethnic populations in the society (Uyematsu 1971: 9–13).

This climate of redefinition also spurred interest, especially among Asian American college students, in their history. The internment was intensely examined because it powerfully illustrated the common history of racial oppression that Asian Americans shared with other racial minorities. It also was a significant, yet psychologically repressed, experience in the lives of their parents and grandparents. Most Sansei had been sheltered from knowing about the traumatic aspects of the internment and had not been taught about the event. Indeed, the Sansei, who are the "heirs" of the internment (Epstein 1977; Bergman and Jucovy 1982; Nagata 1990), played a crucial role not only in resurrecting the event from its buried past, but also in demonstrating its relevance to the contemporary Japanese American community and to the general American public. In ways highly private and highly public, the Sansei would not allow the older generations to forget the internment.

Second, African American leaders such as Martin Luther King, Jr., Stokeley Carmichael, and H. Rap Brown voiced their concerns about the existence and potential use of concentration camps in the United States during 1967 and 1968 (Brown 1969; Okamura 1974). They spoke in the aftermath of ghetto riots and antiwar demonstrations and focused on the provisions of Title II of the 1950 Internal Security Act, "statutorily legislated in 1950 by reference to the World War II concentration camp experience of resident Japanese," and created the legal apparatus for "establishing concentration camps into which people might be put without benefit of trial, but merely by executive fiat . . . simply by an assumption . . . that an individual might be thinking about engaging in espionage or sabotage" (Okamura 1974: 73).

The nationwide uproar over Title II by African American activists and civil libertarians, as well as the various calls for its repeal, initially had an impact on a small—essentially Sansei and leftist-oriented—sector of the Japanese American community. Indeed, the top leadership of the JACL, which was the only national civil rights group for Japanese Americans, was initially opposed to using its resources for what was perceived to be a no-win legislative pursuit. Concern over the issue, though, broadened as individuals like Raymond Okamura and groups like the Asian American Political Alliance organized substantial grassroots support within the Japanese American community to propel a diverse cross-section of Japanese American groups, especially the JACL, into a major four-year campaign for the repeal of Title II (Okamura 1974). Title II eventually "became a viable issue which large segments of the Japanese American community could identify" (Kanno 1974: 107). And as the late Edison Uno (1974) wrote:

It sparked the imagination of Japanese Americans throughout the United States who utilized the Title II issue to enlighten and sensitize politicians, public media, educators, and the general public about the gross injustices of mass incarceration—in the past or future. What other group in our country could legitimately seek to repeal such a reprehensible law as Title II? Once we realized that we should no longer suffer the pain and agony of false guilt, we accepted our experience as part of our Japanese American heritage, that part of our history which involved a struggle for survival against tremendous odds which would test the character and spirit of each of us. (p. 110)

The Title II repeal campaign was the first major organized activity that Japanese Americans undertook in relation to the internment after two decades of silence, and unexpectedly demonstrated the potential for politically mobilizing the group. It had its origins in the black movement and was, in many respects, dedicated to showing solidarity with that movement. Okamura (1974: 76) writes that "[we] felt it was imperative for Japanese Americans to assume the leadership in order to promote Third World unity. Japanese Americans had been the passive beneficiaries of the Black civil rights movement, and this campaign was the perfect issue by which Japanese Americans could make a contribution to the overall struggle for justice in the United States."

The Title II campaign was the first of many contributions that Japanese Americans made to prevent another internment from happening to them or other Americans. Coupled with both the initiation of annual pilgrimages to Manzanar concentration camp in December 1969 and the general atmosphere of group redefinition, the movement "sparked the imagination" of Japanese Americans into considering other unfinished business of their internment experience, as well as sustaining and broadening the process of reawakening. The successful repeal of Title II provided Japanese Americans with not only a sense of the efficacy of pursuing other internment-related activities, but also a new and powerful symbolic message that the internment was beginning to be recognized as wrong and deplorable by a growing number of American citizens, politicians, organizations, and the media. Although some academic works had acknowledged that the internment should not have happened, Japanese Americans were still plagued by the historical legacy of the event and its close affiliation with the horrors of Pearl Harbor and World War II in the minds of many Americans. For example, a 1967 public opinion poll commissioned by the JACL provided a glimpse of this legacy when it was revealed that "80 percent of Californians approved evacuation in 1942, and a quarter century later, 48 percent still did" (Hosokawa 1969). The JACL's initial reluctance to join the Title II repeal movement probably stemmed from this and other more intuitive assessments of the American public's sentiments about the internment. This assessment reinforced its long-standing policy of avoiding activities, especially those dealing with the internment, which might undermine the acceptance of Japanese Americans and unexpectedly foment another round of backlash and prejudice, which had long plagued the group (TenBroek, Barnhart, Matson 1968).

To be sure, the Title II movement did not convince all Americans that the internment was wrong or that it represented an "extraordinary and unique" departure from democratic norms and practices. But it did serve to acquaint more Americans than ever before about the event and to allow Japanese Americans to begin to confront the myths surrounding their internment experience. By accentuating the link between Title II and the internment, Japanese Americans made Title II the first of a series of challenges to the wisdom and necessity of the internment rather than solely a contemporary public policy issue (Nakanishi 1978). Moreover, the repeal of Title II served to broaden the support and appeal of subsequent internment-related activities within the Japanese American community. After the issue was embraced by the JACL, as well as a number of religious, civil rights, and media organizations, resurrecting the internment was no longer perceived as an exclusively Sansei or leftist cause. It was embraced both politically and psychologically by diverse sectors of the Japanese American community.

THE PAST AS PRESENT

The resurrection of the internment during the late 1960s signaled the beginning of a new collective response. By identifying with it in both a highly publicized

manner such as the Title II campaign and a more intensely private and commemorative fashion like the Manzanar pilgrimage, Japanese Americans made a symbolic
statement that the internment should no longer be treated as forgotten by either
other Americans or Japanese Americans. Indeed, the slogan of the Title II campaign, "It happened once, can it happen again?, was as much directed toward
Japanese Americans as toward the general public. Far from being a faddish
phenomenon, the resurrection of the event served as the starting point for an
intense and controversial period of political actions, creative activities, and reexamination of the internment, which continued all the way to the fiftieth-year
anniversary activities in 1992.

Since the late 1960s, the internment was the preeminent issue for Japanese
American communities and organizations across the nation. Numerous public
forums and days of remembrance activities were held annually from Seattle to New
York. Pilgrimages to nearly all the former concentration camps were organized. An
extraordinary array of literary works, textbooks, theatrical productions, and motion
pictures, in which Japanese Americans occupy center stage, were developed, and
the Amerasia Journal devoted over fifty pages of one issue (Amerasia Journal, 1981)
to testimonies given at the hearings of the Commission on Wartime Relocation
and Internment of Civilians. Moreover, Japanese American organizations vigorously pressed for even greater public and government recognition that the internment not only was wrong and unjust, but also had a damaging impact on Japanese
Americans both individually and as a group. Since the early 1980s, for example,
former Japanese American civil service employees, who were summarily termi-
nated from their jobs as a result of Executive Order 9066, have gained back pay
and civil service credit from cities such as Los Angeles, Seattle, and San Francisco,
as well as from the state governments of California and Washington (Pacific Citizen
1983). More significantly, Japanese Americans and other Asian American organizations launched major legislative and legal campaigns to gain redress and monetary reparations for losses and damages from the internment experience and filed
successful coram nobis lawsuits in relation to the three major Supreme Court
decisions that tested the constitutionality of the evacuation and internment orders:
Korematsu vs. U.S., Hirabayashi vs. U.S., and Yasui vs. U.S. (Irons 1983, 1989;
Minami 1991). Over the course of the past two decades, more and more Japanese
Americans from all walks of life—celebrated World War II veterans or "no-no
boys," professionals, working men and women, English-speaking or Japanese-
speaking individuals—began the arduous task of working through their personal
internment experiences (e.g., Lane 1964; Janis 1971) and have openly discussed
the consequences of their wartime victimization (Nakanishi 1978).

The resurfacing of these memories was most dramatically exhibited during the
public hearings held in 1981 by the Commission on Wartime Relocation and
Internment of Civilians. Some Japanese American groups like the Chicago-based
National Coalition for Japanese American Reparations bitterly opposed this
so-called commission strategy as being an unnecessarily cautious legislative compromise and subsequently filed a separate class action lawsuit to sue the federal
government for their wartime incarceration. (In May 1988, the U.S. Court of

Appeals for the Federal Circuit dismissed the class action lawsuit, *Hohri vs. United States*, on the grounds that the statute of limitations had expired. Later that year, the Supreme Court refused to review the decision [see Hohri 1988].) There was no question, however, that the public hearings eventually captured the attention of more Japanese Americans and received greater media attention than any previous internment-related activity: "[M]ore than 750 witnesses: evacuees, former government officials, public figures, interested citizens, and historians and other professionals who have studied the subjects of commission inquiry" testified before packed audiences throughout the nation (Commission on Wartime Relocation and Internment of Civilians 1982: vii).

Although some of the testimonies dealt with well-researched topics like the internment's legal significance (TenBroek, Barnhart, Matson 1968; Rostow 1962; Takasugi 1974; Irons 1983), a number of aspects of the internment finally surfaced during the hearings. For example, earlier works had shown that the wartime incarceration had an all-encompassing economic impact on Japanese Americans involving not only personal losses of property, income, and savings, but also the structural destruction of a viable ethnically based economy (Fugita and O'Brien 1980: 260–274). The hearings extended scholarly understanding of these economic consequences through personal accounts of displacement from professions, farming, or fishing, and through analyses of the short- and long-term losses of being forced abruptly to sell businesses and property. Various scholars also charged that the Federal Reserve Bank's figure of $400 million in property losses at the time of the internment was underestimated, and they argued that total economic losses were at least three or four times greater. One researcher, Larry Boss, presented evidence that economic damages, excluding personal income, exceeded $6 billion if an annual inflation rate of 6 percent were applied to the original losses (Commission on Wartime Relocation and Internment of Civilians 1982). Similarly, the hearings not only reaffirmed the findings of earlier works on the social disorganization of the Japanese American family unit in adapting to the abnormal situation of life in concentration camps (Broom and Kitsuse 1973; Kitano 1976), but also revealed the largely hidden, long-range changes in family relations in readjusting to life after the camps. And finally, testimonies were given on rarely examined medical problems directly related to detention, the possible collusion between JACL leaders and government officials on the decision to remove Japanese Americans from the western states, and the enduring impact of the internment on both those who survived and subsequent generations. After considering these testimonies, as well as an unprecedented collection of government documents obtained through the Freedom of Information Act, the commission, in its final report, *Personal Justice Denied*, concluded that "Executive Order 9066 was not justified by military necessity and the decisions that followed from it—exclusion, detention, the ending of detention, and the ending of exclusion—were not founded upon military considerations. The broad historical causes that shaped the decisions were race prejudice, war hysteria, and a failure of political leadership" (1982: 35).

The report also urged Congress and the president to implement the following five recommendations to redress injustices to Japanese Americans during the war:

(1) issue a resolution recognizing "that a grave injustice was done" and offer a formal apology, (2) pardon individuals like Korematsu, Hirabayashi, and Matsui who were wrongly convicted of violating curfew and detention measures, (3) "direct the Executive agencies to which Japanese Americans may apply for the restitution of positions, status, or entitlements lost in whole or in part because of acts or events between December 1941 and 1945"; (4) establish a special education and research fund to encourage studies and public education projects on the internment; and finally (5) appropriate $1.5 billion in order to provide "a one-time per capita compensatory payment of $20,000 to each of the approximately 60,000 surviving Japanese Americans who were incarcerated during World War II" (1982: 40). Several bills, which were based on these recommendations, were introduced in the House and Senate after the issuance of the report and, after an extensive grass-roots and legislative campaign, led to passage of the Civil Liberties Act of 1988 and its formal signing by President Reagan on 10 August 1988 (Daniels, Taylor, Kitano 1991; Hohri 1988; and Tateishi 1991).

THE POLITICS OF THE PAST IN THE PRESENT

The recent resurrection of the internment has spawned an extraordinary level of organized activity by Japanese Americans; however, it would be simplistic to conclude that this prolonged re-encounter with the tragedy can be viewed as a noncontroversial act of group self-determination. Like other survival experiences, a unique set of circumstances both within and external to the Japanese American community has dialectically influenced the direction, momentum, and scope of this process. The resurrection coincided with the promulgation of Japanese Americans as the model minority, having faced insurmountable racial and economic barriers but having achieved high levels of socioeconomic and academic success. Peterson (1966: 1) offers this bold and heroic pronouncement:

> Barely more than twenty years after the end of the war-time camps, this is a minority that has risen above even prejudiced criticism. By any criterion that we choose, the Japanese Americans are better than any other group in our society, including native-born whites. They have established this remarkable record moreover, by their own almost totally unaided effort. Every attempt to hamper their progress resulted only in enhancing their determination to succeed. Even in a country whose patron saint is the Horatio Alger hero there is no parallel to this success story.

That the experience tested the character of Japanese Americans continuously, worked at loggerheads with their efforts not only to grapple, individually and collectively, with the unfinished business of the internment but also to redefine their group status in American society.

Like earlier interpretations, the success story thesis treated the internment as past history. Although Japanese Americans were recognized as victims, their victimization was seen as having no lasting adverse consequences for the group or its individual members. Instead, they were now viewed as a model minority that others, especially other racial minorities, should emulate in overcoming their racial subordination. If Japanese Americans could succeed despite their long history of racial persecution, then other groups could do the same without special government, legal, or private intervention. The thesis indeed provided an ironic twist to the classic blaming-the-victim perspective in race relations research.

More important, this thesis had a direct impact on the process of resurrecting the internment at the individual and collective level. The glowing image of postwar Japanese American progress and societal acceptance, which originated during the height of the civil rights movement, provided many Japanese Americans with a self-fulfilling justification for not psychologically departing from their long-standing repression and avoidance of the internment experience. As a result, many opposed early and even current internment-related activities, which might subvert this positive group image and work against a renewed sense of self-esteem. It provided many Japanese Americans with a defensive rationale to let bygones be bygones and led many to settle psychologically on the view, which S. I. Hayakawa consistently argued as a syndicated columnist and as a U.S. senator during the 1970s and early 1980s, that the internment was a "blessing in disguise" (Tachiki et al. 1971). The model minority perspective also served to undermine the legitimacy of many group-level internment activities, which were interpreted as mere reflections of contemporary American fads rather than latent collective responses to a disastrous, shared experience as the renewed interest in the Holocaust, for example, is oftentimes portrayed (Himmelfarb, 1971). If the internment were not viewed as having an enduring impact on Japanese Americans, then the pilgrimages to former concentration camps and literary works on the internment, as well as the varied ways in which young Japanese Americans sought to learn more about their elders' wartime victimization, could be summarily dismissed as further examples of ethnic revival, which merely mimicked broader popular moods (Daniels 1971). Finally, the success story thesis served as one of the major counterarguments against monetary reparations for Japanese Americans in legislative deliberations. If Japanese Americans were so well off today, the argument went, then why pay them for something which happened so long ago? Some even argued that if Japanese Americans were given reparations, then what would prevent African Americans, Chicanos, Native Americans, and other groups from making similar claims for past and present victimization and suffering?

Despite many ramifications of the success story thesis, other developments propelled the process of resurrection. Throughout the 1970s and the 1980s the impact of Japan's trade policies on the weakening American economy generated anti-Japanese sentiments heard in the persistent references to Pearl Harbor, the widespread use of the term Japs, the campaign for boycotts of Japanese consumer products by the auto industry, and the whale preservation movement. Although they may not have been aimed directly at Japanese Americans, these sentiments are imbued with group-specific meaning, and they originate in the internment and other historical periods of anti-Japanese hatred when distinctions were not drawn between Japanese Americans and the government and people of Japan (Nakanishi 1978).

The reappearance of these signals during the 1970s and 1980s was not necessarily perceived as a prelude to another internment, in the way that such symbolic
elements have been observed among survivors of other major traumatic episodes
(Lifton 1969; Erikson 1976). Nonetheless, they underscored the necessity for
Japanese Americans to go beyond the Title II campaign, to confront the myths
about their incarceration, and to be politically vigilant about even remote resem-
blances to their wartime experiences. For example, during an early phase of
resurrecting the internment, Japanese American organizations lodged formal protests against President Carter and his transition team when it was learned that a
prominent Japanese American wartime veteran, who was being considered for the
ambassadorship to Japan, was questioned about his political loyalties. Carter's staff
wondered whether he could unequivocally represent American interests in tough
bargaining with Japanese representatives. Japanese Americans also recognized the
virulent chauvinism in calls made during the Iranian hostage crisis for the mass
roundup and deportation of all Iranian students because of their presumed ties to
the Ayatollah. Indeed, Japanese Americans were among the few groups who
protested the FBI interviews of Arab American leaders, in a manner reminiscent
of those interrogations after Pearl Harbor was bombed.

Japanese American and other Asian American groups have organized to combat
racially motivated acts of violence against Asians. For example, they launched a
grass-roots campaign to overturn the light sentences given to two unemployed
Detroit auto workers who killed a Chinese American named Vincent Chin in 1982
(the men thought Chin was Japanese, and therefore someone who had taken away
their jobs). In addition, the president's commission on the internment renewed
the efforts of Japanese American organizations to educate the public about this
racism. Although newspaper editorials called for redress, a number of commentaries and letters vehemently opposed the commission's recommendations for monetary reparations by drawing the groundless and yet highly emotional connection
between the internment and Japan's wartime atrocities in Asia, especially its
treatment of American prisoners of war (*Pacific Citizen* 1983).

The group's process toward recognizing the internment evolved in this struggle
between real and symbolic forces of acceptance and threat, forces that prolonged
the individual's internal struggle between remembering and forgetting. They also
shaped a collective response, at once defensive and assertive. Like other survival
experiences, these forces, on the one hand, prevented Japanese Americans from
resurrecting the internment in a sociopolitical context free of constraints. On the
other hand, they provided Japanese Americans with new opportunities to articulate their response to this victimization. Aside from these external factors, however, major internal developments in the political representation of Japanese
Americans helped shape this reawakening.

Japanese Americans and American Politics

Since the mid-1970s, a dramatic increase has occurred in the political involvement of Asian Pacific Americans, especially in electoral politics and protest

activities (Nakanishi 1986, 1991: 25–54). Although Japanese Americans have a rich political history, in no previous era have they equaled the recent levels of political participation. In contrast to earlier periods, the 1970s and 1980s witnessed the election and appointment of more mainland Japanese Americans to public office than in all previous years combined. At the same time, many Japanese Americans took up a number of causes, like the legal defense of Iva Ikuko Toguri D'Aquino (Tokyo Rose), which had long been viewed as social taboos (Uyeda 1978; Duus 1979). They were also spokespersons for several pan-Asian Pacific American groups and social movements (Nakanishi 1991: 25–54). Despite their numerical decline from representing slightly over one in three Asian Pacific Americans in 1970 to one in ten Asian Pacific Americans in 1990, Japanese Americans, as well as Chinese Americans, strongly influenced the leadership agenda of the Asian Pacific American population (Nakanishi 1993b).

To be sure, this change was affected by the overall increase in political participation by all racial minorities, especially African Americans, since the mid-1960s. With respect to internment-related issues, this heightened political involvement provided Japanese Americans with more political resources, both internal and external, than were available during the Title II repeal campaign. For example, Japanese American organizations like the JACL, which had previously channeled legislative concerns such as Title II through the long-standing Hawaiian Japanese American congressional delegation of U.S. Senators Daniel Inouye and Sparky Matsunaga, clearly benefited from the election of mainland Japanese American politicians. They came to view two California congressmen, Norman Mineta and Robert Matsui—and to a much lesser extent former U.S. Senator S. I. Hayakawa of California—as their principal legislative liaisons for issues like the creation of the president's fact-finding commission. In contrast to the Hawaiian legislators, however, none of the three mainland officials represented sizable Japanese American constituencies.

At the same time, other Japanese American organizations, especially those which opposed JACL's strategies, found their own legislative allies among non-Japanese American politicians who benefited from the electoral support of local Japanese American voters. Former congressman and now Washington Governor Michael Lowry of Seattle, for example, introduced the first Japanese American reparations bill in the House in 1979 shortly after his election, because he sought to recognize the Japanese American electoral support in his victory, and because he was personally committed to the reparations issue.

Internment-related efforts benefited from young attorneys and their community-based organizations like the Asian Law Caucus of Oakland, which were chiefly responsible for filing the successful *coram nobis* lawsuits. The continued resurrection of the internment had its own effect on the increased political involvement of Japanese Americans, dominating their organizations' agendas since the mid-1970s. These issues not only provided long-standing groups like the JACL with a renewed purpose for existing, but also spurred the creation of new organizations and the elevation of new community leaders whose principal raison d'être has been pursuing the unfinished business of the internment. Similarly, efforts to mobilize community-wide support for an array of political issues, such as opposing redevelopment projects in many local Japanese American communities by Japan-based corporations, were often couched in political symbolism relating to the internment (Gee 1976). Most important, a growing number of Japanese American leaders of diverse ideological persuasions came to believe that, aside from broader external causes such as racism and war hysteria, the internment occurred because Japanese Americans were politically naïve, lacked sufficient political representation, and were politically passive (Nakanishi 1978). As a result, many Japanese Americans saw their political participation, either electoral involvement or protest activities, as having deep significance in advancing their interests and in preventing the recurrence of such an unspeakable event.

BEYOND REDRESS: THE FUTURE OF JAPANESE AMERICAN POLITICS ON THE MAINLAND

Santayana may have been right when he argued that those who do not learn from history are condemned to repeat it. However, what should be learned from the past and how the past should be applied to the present are not always obvious. By resurrecting the internment since the late 1960s, Japanese Americans made both a concrete and a symbolic statement that their World War II experiences must not be forgotten and that they had to develop a collective response to this victimization. In making this declaration, it was far from apparent what actions, if any, Japanese Americans would undertake, what insights, interpretations, or lessons they would derive from it. The internment, like other crimes in history, does not automatically yield its lessons for its survivors, nor does it provide specific guidance on what to do with them. In some instances, such as the Title II repeal movement, circumstances may provide a specific sociopolitical context for approaching the past. In most instances, however, the linkages between past and present are probably not as direct, intuitive, or compelling (Jervis 1976). As the Japanese American case illustrates, numerous obstacles can prevent or delay survivors from seeing a link and, more important, from sustaining it once it is finally recognized.

The response of Japanese Americans to the internment suggests that we should modify our outlooks on the past. As in most works on the subject, we tend to treat major events in the experiences of American minority groups as past history, relegated largely to historiographic inquiries, but rarely viewed as having contemporary relevance. We seek to discover immediate causes and effects rather than to probe consequences for the minority group (Lifton 1969). By treating events in this limited fashion, we place an overly optimistic interpretation on the resiliency of individuals to reassemble their lives after such episodes.

The resurrection of the internment also underscores the necessity for seeking greater convergence in race relations research. The perspective offered here of treating survival experiences dialectically, and considering the interplay of individual and group processes is intended to be a contribution to this search for convergence. It seeks to extend our understanding of survival experiences beyond individual-level, clinical observations, which have dominated the literature (Wolfenstein 1957; Niederland 1962, 1972; Lifton 1969; Epstein 1977; Bergman and Jucovy 1982). Instead, it gains its analytic insights from works like Kai Erikson's pioneering study, *Everything in Its Path* (1976), which explored both the immediate individual and immediate collective consequences of a disastrous flood which struck a Pennsylvania mining town. By examining the resurrection of the internment, we better understand survival experiences, as well as the prolonged latency of individual and collective responses to such episodes—insights that are not merely psychological in nature, but cultural and political as well.

REFERENCES

Allen, Charles, Jr. 1966. *Concentration camps, USA*. New York: Marzani and Munzelli.

Amerasia Journal. 1981. Rite of passage: The commission hearings 1981, 8, no. 2: 53–101.

Bell, David A. 1985. The triumph of Asian Americans. *New Republic*, 15–22 July: 24–31.

Bergman, Martin S., and Milton E. Jucovy, eds. 1982. *Generations of the Holocaust*. New York: Basic Books.

Bosworth, Allan P. 1976. *America's concentration camps*. New York: W. W. Norton.

Broom, Leonard, and John Kitsuse. 1973. *The managed casualty: The Japanese American family in World War II*. Berkeley: University of California Press.

Brown, H. Rap. 1969. *Die nigger die!* New York: Dial Press.

Chuman, Frank. 1976. *The bamboo people: Japanese Americans and the law*. Albany, NY: Delmar Publishers.

Chun, Ki-Taek. 1980. The myth of Asian American success and its educational ramifications. *IRCD Bulletin* 15: 1–12.

Commission on Wartime Relocation and Internment of Citizens. 1982. *Personal justice denied*. Washington, DC: Commission on Wartime Relocation and Internment of Citizens.

Commission on Wartime Relocation and Internment of Civilians: Selected testimonies from the Los Angeles and San Francisco hearings. 1918. *Amerasia Journal*, 8 (summer): 53–105.

Daniels, Roger. 1971. *Concentration camps USA: Japanese Americans and World War II*. Hinsdale, IL: Dryden Press.

Daniels, Roger, Sandra C. Taylor, and Harry H. L. Kitano, eds. 1991. *Japanese Americans: From relocation to redress*. Rev. ed. Seattle: University of Washington Press.

Degler, Carl N. 1976. Why historians change their minds. *Pacific Historical Review*, 45, no. 2: 167–184.

Duus, Masayo. 1979. *Tokyo Rose: Orphan of the Pacific*. Tokyo: Kodansha International.

Epstein, Helen. 1977. Heirs of the Holocaust. *New York Times Magazine*, 19 June: 12–15.

Erikson, Kai. 1976. *Everything in its path*. New York: Simon and Schuster.

Fugita, Stephen, and David O'Brien. 1980. *Economics, ideology, and ethnicity*. Vol. 2 of *Asian Americans*, edited by Russell Endo, Stanley Sue, and Nathaniel Wagner. Palo Alto: Science and Behavior.

The future of the Nikkei community. 1992. Conference held in Los Angeles, CA, October.

Gee, Emma, ed. 1978. *Counterpoint: Perspectives on Asian America*. Los Angeles: UCLA Asian American Studies Center.

Girdner, Audrie, and Anne Loftis. 1969. *The great betrayal*. New York: Macmillan.

Grodzins, Morton. 1949. *Americans betrayed*. Chicago: University of Chicago Press.

Hansen, Arthur, and Betty Mitson, eds. 1974. *Voices long silent*. Fullerton: Japanese American Oral History Project, California State University.

Himmelfarb, Milton. 1971. Never again! *Commentary* 52 (August): 73–76.

Hohri, William. 1988. *Repairing America*. Pullman: Washington State University Press.

Hosokawa, Bill. 1969. *Nisei: The quiet American*. New York: William Morrow.

Houston, Jeanne Wakatsuki, and James D. Houston. 1973. *Farewell to Manzanar*. San Francisco: Houghton Mifflin.

Irons, Peter. 1983. *Justice at war*. New York: Oxford University Press.

———, ed. 1989. *Justice delayed*. Middletown, CT: Wesleyan University Press.

Isaacs, Harold. 1975. *Idols of the tribe*. New York: Harper and Row.

Janis, Irving. 1971. *Stress and frustration*. New York: Harcourt, Brace, and Jovanovich.

Jervis, Robert. 1976. *Perception and misperception in international politics*. Princeton: Princeton University Press.

Kanno, Hiroshi. 1974. Broader implications of the campaign to Title II. *Amerasia Journal* 2 (fall): 105–108.

Kitano, Harry. 1976. *Japanese Americans*. Englewood Cliffs, NJ: Prentice-Hall.

Lane, Robert. 1964. *Political ideology*. New York: Free Press.

LEAP and UCLA Asian American Studies Center. 1993. *The State of Asian Pacific America: Policy Issues to the Year 2020*. Los Angeles: LEAP and UCLA Asian American Studies Center.

Lifton, Robert. 1969. *Death in life: Survivors of Hiroshima*. New York: Vintage Books.

Makaroff, Julian. 1967. America's other racial minority: Japanese Americans. *Contemporary Review* 210: 310–314.

Minami, Dale. 1991. Coram nobis and redress. In *Japanese Americans: From relocation to redress*. Rev. ed. Edited by Roger Daniels, Sandra C. Taylor, and Harry H. L. Kitano, 200–202. Seattle: University of Washington Press.

Nagata, Donna. 1990. The Japanese American internment: Transgenerational consequences of traumatic stress. *Journal of Traumatic Stress* 3 (January): 47–69.

Nakanishi, Don T. 1978. Can it happen again? The enduring impact of the Holocaust and evacuation on the political thinking of American Jewish and Japanese American leaders. Ph.D. diss., Harvard University.

———. 1986. Asian American politics: An agenda for research. *Amerasia Journal* 12, no. 2: 1–27.

———. 1991. The next swing vote? Asian Pacific Americans and California politics. In *Racial and ethnic politics in California*, edited by Byran O. Jackson and Michael Preston. Berkeley: Institute of Governmental Studies, University of California.

———. 1993a. Surviving Democracy's Mistake: Japanese Americans and Executive Order 9066. *Amerasia Journal* 19, no. 2: 7–35.

———. 1993b. Transforming Asian Pacific America: The challenge of growth and diversity of Asian Pacific migrants and citizens in the United States. Paper presented at the conference Asian Pacific Migration Affecting Australia: Temporary, Long-Term and Permanent Movements of People. Darwin, Australia. September.

Niederland, William G. 1962. Psychiatric consequences of persecution. *American Journal of Psychotherapy* 26 (July): 191–203.

———. 1972. Clinical observations on the survivor syndrome. In *The emotional stress of war, violence, and peace*, edited by Rolland S. Parker. Pittsburgh: Stanwix House.

Okada, John. 1957. *No-no boy*. Rutland, VT: Charles E. Tuttle.

Okamura, Raymond. 1974. Campaign to repeal the emergency detention act. *Amerasia Journal* 2 (fall): 71–111.

————. 1978. The concentration camp experience from a Japanese American perspective and review of Michi Weglyn's *Years of Infamy*. In *Counterpoint*, edited by Emma Gee, 27–30. Los Angeles: UCLA Asian American Studies Center.

Pacific Citizen. 1983. Newspaper published by the Japanese American Citizens League.

Peterson, William. 1966. Success story: Japanese American style. *New York Times Magazine*, 9 January, 20ff.

Przeworski, Adam, and Henry Teune. 1970. *The logic of comparative social inquiry*. New York: Wiley-Interscience.

Rostow, Eugene. 1945. Our worst wartime mistake. *Harper's* 191 (September): 193–200.

————. 1962. *The sovereign prerogative*. New Haven: Yale University Press.

Suzuki, Bob. 1977. Education and the socialization of Asian Americans: A revisionist analysis of the "model minority" thesis. *Amerasia Journal* 4: 23–51.

Tachiki, Amy, Eddie Wong, Franklin Odo with Buck Wong, eds. 1971. *Roots*. Los Angeles: UCLA Asian American Studies Center.

Takasugi, Robert. 1974. Legal analysis of Title II. *Amerasia Journal* 2 (fall): 95–104.

Tateishi, John. 1991. The Japanese American citizens league and the struggle for redress. In *Japanese Americans: From relocation to redress*. Rev. ed. Edited by Roger Daniels, Sandra C. Taylor, and Harry H. L. Kitano, 191–195. Seattle: University of Washington Press.

TenBroek, Jacobus, Edward N. Barnhart, and Floyd Matson. 1968. *Prejudice, war, and the Constitution*. Berkeley: University of California Press.

Uno, Edison. 1974. Therapeutic and educational benefits. *Amerasia Journal* 2 (fall): 109–111.

Uyeda, Clifford. 1978. The pardoning of Tokyo Rose: A report on the restoration of American citizenship for Iva Ikuko Toguri. *Amerasia Journal* 5: 69–94.

Uyematsu, Amy. 1971. The emergence of yellow power in America. In *Roots*, edited by Amy Tachiki, Eddie Wong, Franklin Odo with Buck Wong, 9–13. Los Angeles: UCLA Asian American Studies Center.

Varon, Barbara. 1967. The Japanese Americans: Comparative occupational status, 1960 and 1950. *Demography* 4: 809–819.

Weglyn, Michi. 1976. *Years of infamy*. New York: William Morrow.

Wilson, William. 1978. *The declining significance of race*. Chicago: University of Chicago Press.

Wolfenstein, Martha. 1957. *Disaster: A psychological essay*. Glencoe, IL: Free Press.

6
Bridges Across Continents:
South Asians in the United States

Arati Rao

South Asians in the United States historically have played important roles in constructing the boundaries of outsider and insider, foreigner and citizen, sojourner and resident. Although the term "South Asian" denotes the geographical area south of the northern Himalayan mountain ranges, South Asian identity is a unifying political garb not easily worn by the extraordinarily diverse peoples from Bangladesh, Bhutan, India, the Maldives, Nepal, Pakistan, and Sri Lanka (U.S. Bureau of the Census 1990). Because this term has emerged only recently in response to political exigencies in American society, it is likely to become more prevalent as South Asian communities become increasingly politicized.

Recent immigrants, particularly South Asians who arrived after the 1965 Immigration Reform and Control Act, value the possibility of success in the workplace, the culturally central institutions of the family and the community, and the general public's response to their presence in the United States. Unlike the earlier farmer immigrants whose numbers and status were kept low by discriminatory legislation, the post-1965 immigrants from South Asia have achieved a relatively high degree of economic success which influences their participation in "high" politics, particularly in the campaigns of both major parties, fundraising, and lobbying for domestic programs as well as foreign policy affecting South Asia.

The 1980s, however, saw the emergence of other kinds of South Asian Americans: the American children born of post-1965 immigrants and less educated immigrants in low-paying service sector jobs. The young South Asian Americans contribute to a new configuration of class and immigrant history and practice a more grass-roots-oriented activism, which includes coalition building with other minority groups on the basis of shared oppression. The climate of hostility and violence in the United States against visibly different people, combined with anger against recent immigrant populations and envy of their economic success, has prompted vulnerable South Asian Americans to reassess political strategy in favor of broader coalitions with similarly targeted groups, particularly other Asian American communities, in organizations such as the New York-based Coalition Against Anti-Asian Violence (CAAV).

SOUTH ASIANS TODAY

Statistics from the Census Bureau (1990) show that South Asians constitute the economically most successful ethnic group in the United States today. Historically, however, the general impact of their presence on the larger American society has always outweighed their numbers. From the early 1900s to the end of World War II, the total number of South Asians or East Indians, as they were called, rarely exceeded 6,000. In that period, they remained geographically concentrated in the western states, notably Washington and California. For much of that time, they remained a predominantly male working-class population in whose name a small group of educated urban Indians struggled for legal justice and social respect.

In the two decades following the 1965 Immigration Act, immigration numbers leaped dramatically, and census data from 1990 shows a national Indian immigrant population of about 815,000 and a Pakistani population of roughly 81,000. South Asians constitute roughly 11 percent of the total Asian population of 7,274,000 in the category of Asians and Pacific Islanders (Statistical Abstracts 1994; Dutta 1982; Chandrasekhar 1982; Peterson 1985). As many as 75 percent of the South Asians in the country today were born outside the United States. Given their numerically higher representation and concomitant greater presence in research data, I focus on Indian Americans in this chapter as a significant, though not exhaustive, example of South Asian experience. South Asians continue to experience the evil legacy of color-based hatred of the Other. The frequent physical and verbal attacks on South Asians, their personal experience of the glass ceiling in the workplace, and their suffering at the hands of organized gang terrorism in states like New Jersey have caused many South Asians to rally around their group identity. The ambiguous nature of their self-identification—caught between cultures, countries, indeed, worlds—has given way to a confident use of economic status and organizational skills in political participation. The latest generation of South Asian Americans has taken innovative turns in coalition building and political participation, which suggest a radically new direction for future American citizens of South Asian origin, and call for a fresh understanding of politics itself.

Discrimination and Violence Against South Asians

South Asians face multilevel discrimination in different contexts. The most articulate are among the professional classes, who continue to experience the glass ceiling. Some note that they can advance only where their merit is measured without prejudice, thus, the preponderance of Indians in technical rather than managerial or administrative positions. Strategies to combat white-collar discrimination take the form of lawsuits or formal complaints to professional associations and government authorities. Turbaned Sikh men remain vulnerable to the same religious and cultural discrimination which the early immigrants encountered. For example, a turban-wearing Sikh was fired four days after being hired by the New York City Transit Authority on account of the policy requiring hard hats to be worn by car inspectors. The fired employee's response was to file suit against the Transit Authority (*News India-Times* 1995: 26).

Discriminatory treatment is not experienced by the professional classes alone (see Gibson 1988). In 1987, local anger against all Indians erupted in New Jersey when gangs, calling themselves "Dotbusters," systematically attacked South Asians. In a letter published in a local newspaper in Jersey City, home to about 15,000 Indians at the time, the Dotbusters wrote, "We will go to any extreme to get Indians to move out of Jersey City. If I'm walking down the street and I see a Hindu and the setting is right, I will just hit him or her. We plan some of our more extreme attacks such as breaking windows, breaking car windows and crashing family parties. We use the phone book to look up the name Patel. Have you seen how many there are?" In September that year, a young man, Navroz Mody, was beaten to death by youths who chanted, "Hindu, Hindu" (Takaki 1989: 481).

Today, South Asians are increasingly verbally and physically harassed in public places. The attacks come from a variety of ethnic and racial groups. For example, in 1994, three teenagers accosted a twenty-five-year-old Indian immigrant in Queens, said that they "did not like Indian people," beat him up, and burned his face with a cigarette. Local Indian and Pakistani merchants told a reporter that youths harassed them frequently "because we are different" (*New York Times* 1994: 43). In addition to personal attacks and stone throwing, South Asian places of worship continue to be targeted for vandalism and burglary (Fenton 1988). The perception of a common threat has real uniting power among otherwise disparate groups. The particular cultural practices which mark a South Asian for racist attack, such as physical appearance or clothing or religious accouterments, make it difficult to perceive one's predicament as grounds for coalition with other victims of harassment. This is a primary area where coalition building can be more forcefully addressed; unfortunately, violence is a great leveler of distinction.

Conflicts and Coalitions

In the face of concrete discouragements to remaining in the United States, South Asians since the early part of this century have found ways to straddle both countries and, indeed, both continents: one country left behind with some idea of return after acquiring wealth in the United States; the other country itself unsure about rewarding nonwhite immigrants with citizenship and the right to belong. In occupying this liminal space in America, South Asians have had to retain both fictions, of sojourner and of citizen, awaiting the day when American law and society would change and give them full access to America. Because legal change occurred only thirty years ago with the 1965 Immigration Act, South Asians continue to bridge Asia and America in real and symbolic ways.

In material terms, South Asians participate fully in American economy and society. From this home base, they nurture family and business connections in their country of origin and often take their children back for holidays. In addition, fresh emigrants from South Asia continue to enter the United States under current immigration laws, furthering this pattern of connection between the old and new worlds, moving between Asia and America across the familiar bridges of departure, residence, and return.

In symbolic terms, however, the recent nature of their entry into America, along with the anti-immigrant and racist trends which target South Asian Americans, have encouraged the sense that one is not fully welcome, that one is assumed to have a home elsewhere to which one is expected to return, that one's enthusiastic embrace of the American Dream is no guarantee of acceptance. Discrimination in the workplace, ignorance in media portrayals, hatred on the streets, and unresponsiveness from government officialdom to complaints have resulted in the emerging awareness among Americans of South Asian descent that acceptance is not accorded on merit but has to be fought for.

Part of the American Dream for immigrant populations is the aspiration to attain the status of the social and economic elite: well-off whites. It is not until nonwhite immigrants encounter obstacles that they start the painful soul-searching: What does it take for a successful professional to understand that economic prosperity is no protection against hostility and anger? What are the costs and benefits of going against the current of complicity with hegemonic elites to form coalitions with non-South Asian communities? How can we confront our own racism, often imperceptibly sown already in our country of origin, but always encouraged to grow in the racially-charged climate of the United States? There comes a point when tending one's own garden is not enough, when one is forced by political realities to look for common ground in the larger surrounding society.

Three levels of coalition must be addressed. First, the disparate groups from South Asia must construct a unity that they did not need or would never have considered in their home countries. Accordingly, a common bond now may be forged in the United States between an Indian and a Pakistani, neither of whom had had reason to travel to the other's country while residing in South Asia. In America, these equally advantaged and disadvantaged immigrant professionals look at American society through similar lenses, reify their cultural practices, and retain a keen interest in a South Asia in which they very likely will not retire (although they talk about it often).

Building on this first stage of a partially imposed, partially embraced, unifying "South Asianness," South Asians then can join the many ethnicities under the umbrella term "Asian" to generate political alliances with other Asian groups. Subsequently, they identify common issues with non-Asian minority groups, such as African Americans and Latinos. The last step has been taken by younger American-born South Asians who do not use the bridge across the continents with the frequency of their parents' generation: these Americans are here to stay. (The bridge may be used again by their own children, in the established pattern of returning to roots in alternating generations.) Their self-perception of their Americanness brooks no suggestion that they go back to where they came from: their sights are set on the struggle for justice and respect from fellow Americans.

Their youth and early awareness of discrimination and racism makes liaisons with other ethnic minorities more possible; their class diversity makes them more willing to seek alliances with others rather than rely on a fantasy of the invulnerability in wealth.

In order to understand the strains of politicization among South Asians, we first need to learn their unique history in the United States. Despite the small numbers and limited economic advancement of the first immigrant Indians in the early twentieth century (prior to Indian independence from British rule and the creation of Pakistan in 1947, they were generally known as Indians), their presence triggered serious debates in the United States which shook key pillars of American society, notably the meaning of "American," the definition of citizenship, and concepts like freedom, democracy, pluralism, and assimilation. As shown below the obstacles to acquiring a stable identity kept Indians apart from other Asian groups, as well as from the rest of America. Even the 1946 Luce-Celler Act, which revoked the 1923 denial of citizenship to Indians, did not mean much to South Asians until 1965.

EARLY HISTORY OF SOUTH ASIANS IN NORTH AMERICA

The South Asian presence in the United States has a long but forgotten history, which even South Asians are not familiar with. A colonial diary of 1790 reports the presence of a man from Madras in Salem, Massachusetts, and over half a century later, local sources write of six Indians attending the 1851 Fourth of July festivities in Salem. California in 1849 saw Indians in its Gold Rush as well as in its ports as visiting merchants. Not until the turn of the century did immigrants, most from the northern Indian agricultural region of Punjab, begin to arrive in North America, having been recruited to work in the lumber industries of British Columbia, Canada, and the Canadian Pacific Railway Lines.

Racist anger in local Canadian populations prompted exclusionary measures from the government. Indeed, when Indians who met all the onerous requirements of Canadian law arrived in Vancouver harbor in 1914 on the ship *Komagata Maru*, they were fired upon and not allowed to land. The Indians soon looked southward, "hoping for a better reception, a less rigorous climate, more congenial employment and higher wages" (Chandrasekhar 1944: 141).

These Indians encountered in the United States racist profiles of Asians identified with Chinese immigrants. The racial exclusions of immigration law were reinforced by domestic laws on intergroup marriage, property ownership, land rights, legal personhood, and education. Still, they stayed, hoping to make money and return to India. In addition to racist legislation, they suffered racial attacks as early as 1907, when white workers invaded an Indian community in Bellingham, Washington, and drove seven hundred Indians across the border to Canada. This violence was, ironically, directed against a woefully small Indian presence: at this time the population of Indians in the United States did not exceed 6,000. As Chandrasekhar (1944: 138) observes, Indians were "a microscopic minority in the population." They seldom lived in communities exceeding thirty men, but their appearance and language marked them as different. Brown (1982: 41–47; see also Leonard, 1982: 30) suggests that "the overwhelming majority" was Sikh, turbaned and therefore easily targeted.

Despite popular rage, the law was not clear on the racial status of Indians. Their legal story is framed by the 1790 law reserving naturalization to one racial group: "any alien, being a free white person, who shall have resided within the limits and under the jurisdiction of the United States for the term of two years, may be admitted to become a citizen thereof" (Debates and Proceedings 1834). The impact of this law is inestimable: not until the mid-twentieth century did race lose its centrality in the criteria for immigration in the United States.

Are Indians "White"? The Supreme (Court) Challenge

South Asians constitute the only immigrant group whose very definition was questioned almost immediately after its arrival. Without doubt, the American government's reliance on the hopelessly indeterminate classification system arising out of late nineteenth-century "scientific" classification of the world's "races" faced its most serious challenge from Indians (cf. Appiah 1992). It took three major Supreme Court decisions spread over three decades to decide the perplexing question: Were Indians "Caucasians" and therefore "white," and consequently free to become naturalized citizens under the 1790 law?

This ambiguity had two major consequences for Indians. First, the differences between and within communities in their native lands (such as caste, language, religion, and region) now were subsumed under an artificial and imposed unity of identity: Indian. This concept challenged legal race classifications of white as well as Asian and Oriental. Second, particular groups like the Indians learned to use this imposed unity to negotiate the boundaries of these categories in order to exempt themselves from the exclusionary principles. Thus, a dialectical process of Indian self-identification emerged over the decades, with the government's racial call receiving a reifying response from its targeted immigrant group. Accordingly, Indians used a variety of identity-based strategies at different historical moments, to gain recognition. They claimed a common Aryan ancestry with Europeans to claim "whiteness"; they retained Indianness but refused Asianness; they rebuffed race in favor of religion, caste, or ethnicity as their primary identification; they referred to international standards like the Atlantic Charter to claim universal human rights over group differences.

The first two Supreme Court decisions on the question of Indian whiteness— Balsara in 1910 and Mazumdar in 1913—held that since Indians were scientifically classified as Caucasian in race, naturalization as whites was allowed (U.S. vs. Balsara, 1910, 180 Fed. 694; see also U.S. vs. Akhay Kumar Mazumdar, 1913, 207 Fed. 115). However, the 1923 Thind decision dramatically reversed this conclusion in a ruling which dismissed "Caucasian" as "a conventional word of much flexibility," and redefined "white" in terms of popular perception of skin color rather than scientific categorization (U.S. vs. Bhagat Singh Thind, 1923, 261 U.S. 204–215).

As Helweg and Helweg (1990: 54) observe, "It was a time of complete confusion of biology, geography, and culture, and situations were interpreted to suit the mood of the public and authorities at the time." The Supreme Court's *Ozawa* decision in 1922 had relied on the synonymity of "Caucasian" and "white" in ruling against Japanese eligibility for citizenship. Thus, *Ozawa* buttressed the security of one Asian group (Indians) with the legal exclusion of another Asian group (Japanese) (*Takao Ozawa vs. United States*, 1922, 260 U.S. 178). The *Thind* decision the following year, however, taught Indians that all nonwhite groups, including themselves, were vulnerable to exclusion.

In the *Thind* opinion, Justice Sutherland (himself a naturalized American citizen via England and Canada) denied the scientific basis for "white persons" and rejected Mr. Bhagat Singh Thind's ethnological claim of historical common Aryan ancestry with Europeans because "the average man knows perfectly well that there are unmistakable differences between them today." Even the framers of the 1790 law had relied on "the words of familiar speech" to refer to those immigrants who were "bone of their bone and flesh of their flesh." The law's reference to free white persons was "to be interpreted in accordance with the understanding of the common man."

The common man—and woman—had already expressed their understanding of racial distinctions in publications and action. Agnes Foster Buchanan asserted in 1908 that, unlike the "suppliant" Chinese and the "stealthy" Japanese laborers, the new "full-blooded Aryan" entrant from India was "a brother of our own race." And yet, since the frugal, family-less Indian men economically undercut white labor, Buchanan concluded by urging the State Department to inform Indians that "while the earth is large enough for us all, there is no one part of it that will comfortably accommodate both branches of the Aryan family" (1908: 308–313). Herman Scheffauer warned of the new peril to the United States, this "dark, mystic race" with a turbaned "face of finer features" which rose like a chimera out of the Pacific, bringing "a new and anxious question" (1910: 616–618).

In this charged climate, *Thind* had far-reaching consequences for Indians in the United States as well as for future immigrants. Finding the discrimination and exclusion unbearable, about 3,000 Indians returned to India between 1920 and 1940. Along with Mr. Thind, scores of naturalized Indians had their citizenship retroactively revoked by the government with the approval of the Departments of State, Justice, and Labor. Although these revocations were successfully overturned in higher courts, the basic issue of eligibility remained unresolved.

The 1965 Immigration Act, with its benign view of family unification, was central to the emergence of the resident, and not sojourner, South Asian. Earlier, Indian immigrants had been belittled by white Americans because they had no families and lived in male communal housing, but there were reasons for this lonely life. Early Indian immigrants were overwhelmingly men. Many had mortgaged their Indian farms for the trip, believed they would return home to their wives and children after making their fortune. In any event, within a few years of their arrival, the 1917 Immigration Act prohibited the entry of wives from home. Indian men who wished to marry white women became subject to antimiscegenation laws, particularly in California (where the laws remained on the books until 1950). At times, they traveled from California to get married in states like Arizona, where the laws were enforced in varying degrees. Some Indian men in California married Mexican women, over half of whom were immigrants themselves. According to one authority, there were fewer than thirty Indian women in California until 1930, when the Indian immigrant male-female ratio was calculated as 1,572 men per 100 women (Taylor and Vasey 1936: 291; see also Leonard 1982: 67).

Within weeks of *Thind*, the California state government began proceedings to nullify Indian land purchases under its 1913 Alien Land Law. During the Depression, Indians were turned away from federal relief programs because they were aliens ineligible for citizenship. Throughout, labor organizations like the American Federation of Labor were at the forefront of opposition to changes in naturalization laws, testifying before Congress in tones of dire prophecy regarding the fate of white working-class America. The Indian working man, however, was caught in limbo: unable to return to India and not permitted to sink roots in America.

DEMOCRACY AND EXCLUSION

The small educated student body among the early immigrants used American notions of democracy and self-determination to further the cause of India's freedom from the British Raj, and to fight the exclusion of Indians from American citizenship. Their small numbers and colonial predicament focused the spotlight on their own situation; they did not look to forge alliances with other excluded groups. The United States government, however, responded readily to pressure from Britain by suppressing Indian publications and attacking Indian organizations for violating neutrality laws during World War I.

However, when the United States joined World War II, the Nazi ideology of racial hierarchies and annihilation generated compelling arguments for racial equality from the Indian communities in the country. Writing from his office in the Department of Oriental Studies at the University of Pennsylvania, Chandrasekhar (1944: 142) warned, "If the United States is to successfully combat such dangerous ideas, it can ill afford to practice racial discrimination in its relations with Asiatic countries. The immigration policy of this country now excludes nearly a quarter of the human race. America cannot afford to say that she wants the people of India to fight on her side and at the same time maintain that she will not have them among her immigrant groups."

The call to justice and fair play with which Chandrasekhar concluded his article was met by the government's pragmatic consideration of the war effort. The government eventually decided that the potential success of Japanese propaganda and military strategy in South Asia required a preemptive counterweight from America, and the support of Indians to the Allied cause was deemed important. The efforts of various Indian lobbies paid off with the favorable Luce-Celler Act a year after the war ended, which established a tiny annual immigration quota of 100 Indians. So even this did not significantly increase their numbers: over the following eighteen years, 12,000 Indians entered the country. Still, as Hess (1982:

32) observes, "had not immigration and naturalization laws changed in 1946, the East Indian community would almost certainly have eroded significantly perhaps to the point of extinction."

By now, Indians in America had formed organizations and lobbying alliances among themselves. The first Asian to be elected to Congress was an Indian, Dalip Singh Saund, who came to the United States as a student in 1920 (Saund 1960). Elected president of the Indian Association of America in 1942, he directed war bond drives among Indians, hoping to earn the trust and confidence of patriotic white America. When President Truman signed the Luce-Celler Act in 1946, Saund applied for naturalization immediately. There were about 1,500 Indians in the United States at the time.

In November 1956, campaigning from the 29th Congressional District, Saund won his Democratic seat in the U.S. House of Representatives. In the 85th Congress, the freshman congressman was appointed right away to the prestigious Foreign Affairs Committee, and promoted the United States foreign aid program to Asia in a tour of the Far East and Middle East in 1957. In India, he addressed a joint session of both houses of Parliament, an honor reserved usually for a visiting head of state. He served three terms in Congress until a stroke incapacitated him during his bid for a fourth term. He died in 1973. Among his survivors was his son, Dalip Singh Saund, Jr., a veteran of the Korean War. Congressman Saund often used to say, "My guideposts were two of the most beloved men in history, Abraham Lincoln and Mahatma Gandhi."

The 1965 Immigration Act and After

Until 1965, South Asians received no encouragement to become "American." While numerous interpretations continue to be generated as to what this term means, for South Asians the prerequisites for their Americanness were precisely those rights and privileges that were denied them, directly or by consequence of denials of rights to other similarly situated groups. Helweg and Helweg (1990: 57) see the same themes playing through Indian immigrant lives over the decades to the present day: "the fight for rights in the new country, continued concern for India, and the desire to excel in America."

The watershed 1965 Immigration Reform and Control Act abolished the national origins system in favor of hemispheric quotas, allowed all nationalities equal right to apply for immigration, and gave preferential treatment to professionals and relatives of U.S. citizens and residents. Great Britain, the traditional goal for immigrating South Asians, already had passed its restrictive and racism-informed 1962 Parliamentary Act: "America's doors were opening and Britain's were closing" (Helweg and Helweg 1990: 60). Highly educated and talented South Asians now left home—amid rancorous debates about the brain drain—to fulfill their economic and career ambitions in the United States. They brought their families and settled down as permanent residents in their new country.

South Asians also entered the United States from non-Asian countries. When Great Britain passed legal restrictions on nonwhite immigration in 1962, Asians from Kenya used their British passports to enter the United States under the immigration quota for Britain. Ten years later, President Amin of Uganda ordered a mass overnight expulsion of Asians from his country in August 1972. Some came to the United States, using their business skills to sink new economic roots, much as the characters do in Mira Nair's *Mississippi Masala*, a film that portrays the experiences of one Ugandan Indian family engaged in running a motel in small-town America (cf. *Asian Week* 1986).

ECONOMIC PARTICIPATION AND MINORITY STATUS

Like other Asian groups, Indians made significant contributions to the national economy from the very start, working in the meanest farm and factory jobs without status or legitimacy in America. But after 1965, the arrival of many of India's educated and social elite signified a dramatic shift in the Indian experience. Economic success was not always immediate but very possible. The absence of the comfortable home and accepting environment left behind was now offset by professional and economic advancement—a tradeoff that continues to be reassessed ever since the hard times in the U.S. economy in the 1970s, which resulted in layoffs in industries like aerospace, where Indian engineers were often the first to be let go.

As early as 1975, Indians sought economic help from civil rights legislation. A 1975 memo from the director of the Office of Federal Contract Compliance which stated that persons of Indian descent were to be "regarded as white" generated differing views among Indian community leaders, who wished to publicize this racial discrimination but differed on how best to do it. The Association of Indians in America said to the U.S. Civil Rights Commission that year:

> The language of the Civil Rights Act clearly intends to protect those individuals who might be disadvantaged on the basis of appearance. It is undeniable that Indians are different in appearance; they are equally dark-skinned as other non-white individuals and are, therefore, subject to the same prejudices. . . . While it is commonly believed that the majority of Indians working in this country are well-educated and employed in jobs of a professional nature, their profiles are not at all unlike those of Korean and Japanese immigrants. (Takaki 1989: 446–447)

In contrast, the India League of America in Chicago argued against claiming minority status with the warning: "If employers find it possible to fill some kind of minority 'quota' by reporting high-level Indo-American employees, while continuing to discriminate against the truly disadvantaged minorities, we may find many Americans turning against us" (quoted in Takaki 1989: 446–447).

In 1982, the National Association of Americans of Asian Indian Descent got the Small Business Administration to recognize them as a socially disadvantaged minority group. Although the fight for minority status raised the same complex issues, the community clearly recognized that this status now rendered them eligible to compete with other minority businesses for government contracts.

These instances reveal a fundamental ambivalence among even the most vocal and politically engaged Indians about their location in the United States. On the one hand, they have benefited from prior advantages as well as struggled to receive the fruits of hard work and commitment. On the other hand, their experiences of discrimination despite this success forces them to consider themselves as disadvantaged. The coexistence of these two perceptions has produced a sense of separateness from other groups in society, which often invite equally ambivalent responses from the society at large.

In 1980, changes in census categories testified to other ambivalences that generated another self-protective move. In 1976, the government sponsored a meeting between representatives of all Asian Americans and Pacific Islanders to discuss the 1980 census categories. As a result of these deliberations, the census bureau agreed to add the category "Asian Indian" to the 1980 census, thereby enabling Indians to move out of the "White/Caucasian" and "Other" categories. Here, the overwhelming numerical representation of Indians among all South Asian groups resulted in another paradox: the insistence on "Indian" rather than "South Asian" in an environment where all South Asians are equally targeted for discrimination regardless of particular country of origin. The triumph of Indian lobbyists is one of nationalists lobbying for the simple majority rather than for a political principle: all the more regrettable in a situation where political bridge building and strategic unity, rather than nationalism should have prevailed (cf. Dutta 1982: 77).

Rich Indians, Poor Indians

The model minority fantasy among nonminority groups obscures the reality that all societies, including immigrant groups, are riven with differences. Scholars of all backgrounds focus the spotlight on the most visible kinds of prosperity, leaving whole areas of their realities, particularly gender and class inequalities, in darkness. For example, Saran (1980) calls the post-1965 Indians "elite ethnics." Leonard (1982: 186) writes: "They are members of the most affluent, highly placed Asian immigrant group in the United States." A Center for Immigration Studies report released in Washington, D.C., in 1994 found Indian Americans the highest-paid group of immigrant professionals, in part because of the large numbers in the medical profession. Two-thirds of all Indian professionals had advanced degrees, and over 90 percent had diplomas. The success of Indian professionals was heightened by the background statistics on other groups: Asian-born professionals had the highest median income, followed by white foreign-born, Chinese, and Japanese professionals. Mexicans were the lowest paid foreign-born professionals (Bouvier and Simcox 1994).

Yet an unreleased study completed by the U.S. Commission on Civil Rights in the 1980s found that American-born Indians had the highest level of poverty, over 20 percent, five times higher than that for any other group (Helweg and Helweg 1990: 188–189). Other research data from 1990 shows that the increased success of mid- and upper-level professionals conceals low income as well as poverty levels.

The reader of Table 6.1 should keep in mind that precisely because the Asian Indian population does not exceed 800,000, the percentage of Indians living at the poverty level ought to be all the more avoidable. Similarly, the public perception of Indians as uniformly affluent, despite their small numbers, is more informative of the public's willingness to homogenize Indians, than any universal Indian prosperity.

Poverty in the Indian community can be explained on many grounds. Alongside the increase in nonprofessional immigrants following the 1965 Immigration Act, family reunification rules continue to bring persons who are not members of the professional classes. Further, the increase in numbers of South Asians across America has resulted in increased exploitation of the underprivileged, outside the community as well as within. For example, restaurant workers, domestic workers, cleaning staff, and small business employees remain pitifully underpaid, ill-treated, without job benefits, and without hope of improvement of their condition (*India Today* 1995, 31 January: 76b–c). Often, South Asians enter low-income areas of economic participation for lack of capital and alternatives. For example, almost half of the roughly 350 newsstands in New York City are licensed to Indians or Pakistanis. Many remain open twenty hours a day. The typical South Asian newsstand owner works twelve hours a day in all weather and takes home $450 a week; he and his co-workers (often family members of either sex) are under constant threat of mugging, robbery, and harassment (*India Today* 1994, 30 Sep-

Table 6.1
Household Income and Poverty Levels by Ethnicity, 1990

Ethnicity	Median Income	% Income less than $10,000	% Income greater than $10,000	Below Poverty*
Chinese	$37,600	15	19	14
Filipino	$43,000	6	18	7
Japanese	$42,800	9	19	7
Asian Indian	$43,000	8	22	10
Korean	$30,300	17	11	15
Vietnamese	$31,300	16	11	25
Southeast Asian	$18,300	26	4	46
Other Asian	$32,000	15	12	17
Pacific Islander	$32,900	13	10	20

* Poverty rate is based on the proportion of the population that resides in a family with an income below the offical poverty line.

Source: Compiled from 1990 1% Public Use Microdata Sample taken from Ong and Hee 1994.

tember: 68e). South Asians are increasingly visible as taxi drivers in New York City, as indicated by the Taxi and Limousine Commission's most recent survey of new applicants for licenses in 1992: 43 percent were South Asian. Counting South Asian cab drivers already on the job, Vivek Bald estimates in his film *Taxivala/Auto-biography* that up to 60 percent of New York's taxi operators are South Asian.

Changes in United States government regulations continue to shape afresh the smaller South Asian communities, particularly their economic condition. For example, the State Department in 1995 expanded quotas for countries that were not traditional immigrant sources, allotting Bangladesh 3,850 visas for 1995. In their turn, these new immigrants are bound to apply for visas for family members. However, their economic well-being depends on the responsiveness of the Bangladeshi community's resources as well as the U.S. economy to the needs of this increased population. In New York, the American Bangladesh Friendship Association complained that no Bangladeshi-owned businesses had received contracts from Republican Mayor Giuliani's administration, unlike the preceding Democratic administration. The association's president warned, "We don't need welfare and will not go on welfare, but unless someone steps in to help with job and language training and helps them settle in, things will be a big mess" (*New York Times* 1995).

POLITICAL PARTICIPATION

Those who entered the United States immediately after 1965 were already in possession of the qualities necessary for a certain degree of immediate economic success in the United States: education, professionalism, personal confidence, and a sense of social worth. Similar adult South Asians continue to enter and contribute to the United States as successful professionals. However, the hidden South Asians today include the poor as well as the American born, thereby throwing into confusion the erroneous popular belief that all South Asians are prosperous recent immigrants.

Like most people, South Asians are primarily interested in the well-being of their immediate circle of family and friends. Family plays a central role in South Asian cultures, encompassing a wider range of relatives than the dominant American notion of the nuclear family. However, the linguistic, regional, and religious affinities that gave the first post-1965 immigrants a sense of community and belonging in a strange land have given way to a complex and changing set of personal ties. The longer an immigrant group remains and the greater its sense of security, the looser become the traditional bonds of kinship and community. Thus, well-off Indians actively engage in political lobbying and participation at the highest levels. We also find poorer and more recent immigrants whose lack of language and economic advancement keeps them working for low wages among their own kind, or taking ill-paid jobs requiring little training or knowledge of English in the service sector, without participation or representation at any political level.

The politicization of South Asians may seem at first glance to be moving at a slow pace, but closer examination will show the giant strides they have taken in the three short decades since 1965. In the 1980s, President Reagan's reiteration of the model minority description of Asians drew the ire of South Asians. They joined forces with other Asian groups to demand recognition for their contributions and to publicize their experiences of far from model treatment from the larger society. By the 1988 elections, Indians also had learned the power of financial contributions to political candidates. In California and New York (states with the largest number of Indian residents), Indians contributed generously to the campaigns of Senator Alan Cranston (D) and Congressman Stephen Solarz (D).

Politics in countries of origin spill over into South Asians' politicking in America. In addition to the Sikh separatist movement's demand for their own state of Khalistan, the Indo-Pakistani conflict over the status of the Himalayan region of Kashmir, and Tamil separatism in Sri Lanka have energized South Asian groups to become more politically active. Many right-wing Hindu political parties in India, such as the Bharatiya Janata Party (BJP) and the Vishwa Hindu Parishad (VHP or World Hindu Council), have support among the Indian American community. Overseas Friends of the Bharatiya Janata Party (OFBJP), which has branches in almost every state in the United States, and the VHP of America, have sent money to buy bricks for a Hindu temple to be constructed on the site of the sixteenth-century Babri mosque in Ayodhya, India, after the mosque's demolition (*Business Today* 1993: 57–59). This demolition was undertaken by a mob in December 1992, sparking off rioting and significant loss of life all over India in an orgy of right-wing fanaticism from which the country will take a long time to recover.

Antifundamentalist groups of South Asian Americans undertook vigorous campaigning after the Ayodhya tragedy, such as the *Coalition Against Communalism (CAC) and Concerned South Asians (CSA)*. These activists signify a radical change in South Asian Americans' understanding of themselves as South Asians and Americans, who can use their resources in the United States without relinquishing their connections with their ethnic country of origin. They use the Internet to engage in spirited debate about political projects, publish newsletters, and mount letter-writing and fund-raising campaigns. On university campuses South Asians continue the work through study groups and conferences.

Since the 1988 presidential election, Indians have held important organizational and fundraising positions in both major political parties, even though one study reports that only 20 percent of Asian Indians were registered voters in 1988 (*India Today* 1989: 86–88). Today, South Asians themselves hold political office with the newfound security of permanent residence in America. For example, Joy Cherian, an Indian American, served as a commissioner on the U.S. Equal Employment Opportunity Commission under the Bush administration. Following the 1994 elections, Maryland governor-elect Parris Glendening put twelve Indian Americans on his transition team, including the treasurer of the Glendening for governor campaign. South Asian organizations in California like Coalition 2001 and *Narika* (for battered South Asian women) mounted an unsuccessful struggle against Proposition 187.

Indian Americans running for public office do not appeal to parochial constituencies. Their assimilation into the American mainstream is testified to by their constituencies, which tend to be white-dominated when they are not partly mixed. While this indicates the candidate's desire to be judged on merit alone rather than on parochial loyalty, it does make political unity among Indian Americans themselves difficult. This must not be mistakenly viewed as Indian Americans' disinclination to aggregate their community power through numbers. Rather, it is indicative of the pattern of dispersed settlement of Indian Americans, who do not congregate in particular parts of a city, or even a particular region of the country. True, there are a few states of predictably high concentration, but this is open to change whenever the economic demographics of the country change and immigrants seeking economic success move and settle accordingly. Where enclaves have arisen, as in Queens, New York, and New Jersey, South Asian immigrants rarely let community ties get in the way of economic advancement. By and large, the well-off majority is as mobile, if not more so, as most white Americans of their class and education levels (see Table 6.2).

Prosperous Indian Americans lobby Congress on issues important to India: expanded economic relations, separating human rights from trade issues, reviewing controls on export of technology, removing labor or environmental conditions from trade agreements, and containing regional nuclear proliferation. Recent lobbying on issues important to Indians in America has focused on the spouse reunification bill supported by Senator Ted Kennedy. Under current conditions, the wait for South Asians to join their spouses in America can be as long as ten years (India Today 1994, 15 August: 48b-c). The dramatic gains of the 1965 act have been sabotaged by bureaucratic delays and suspicion: a dreadfully hard blow to South Asians in America and the home country alike.

It is revealing that South Asian American lobbyists target Congresspersons for their stand on issues pertaining to the home countries in South Asia, more than for their position on matters pertaining to South Asian Americans, the most politically involved of whom are affluent professionals. In early 1994, the Indian government hired a Washington lobbying firm to improve access to Capitol Hill (New India-Times 1994: 1). Along with Indian American community organizations, the firm lobbied critics of India, like Dan Burton (Rep., Indiana), Robert Toricelli (Dem., New Jersey), and Dana Rohrabacher (Rep., California), as well as supporters of India, like Sherrod Brown (Dem., Ohio), Jim McDermott (Dem., Washington), and Bob Andrews (Dem., New Jersey).

Although Indian Americans lobbied vigorously for the nomination of Stephen Solarz to the post of ambassador to India, the Clinton administration took a year before it appointed a career diplomat to the post—a delay that the community took hard. However, South Asia does command a certain response from the administration. Energy Secretary Hazel O'Leary, Defense Secretary William Perry, and Treasury Secretary Lloyd Bentsen visited India and Pakistan in 1994 and 1995. Hillary Clinton's trip to the region around the same time with her daughter Chelsea was designed to focus attention on the status of women.

The economic prosperity of Indian Americans bridges many gaps in Indo–US. relations. Indians abroad repatriate hundreds of millions of dollars annually (Helweg and Helweg 1990: 213–216). In 1986, the government of India relaxed

Table 6.2
Residence Patterns of Indians in the United States

State	1974–75	Percent	1980	Percent	1990 (projected)
California	8,406	11	57,989	16	119,548
Florida			9,138	2	22,078
Illinois	8,622	11	35,711	10	74,876
Maryland	2,971	4	13,705	4	27,576
Massachusetts	2,249	3	8,387	2	17,886
Michigan	3,561	5	14,680	4	53,770
New Jersey	8,411	11	29,507	8	61,368
New York	15,471	20	60,511	16	135,272
Ohio	3,572	5	13,105	4	27,104
Pennsylvania	4,385	6	15,212	4	34,460
Texas	2,700	3	22,226	6	46,790
Virginia			8,483	2	18,092
Total	75,847	100	361,544	100	797,318

Note: Blanks denote no data available.

Source: Adapted from Helweg and Helweg 1990: 265–266.

currency restrictions to encourage nonresident Indians (NRIs) to invest in their home country and set up collaborative business and technological ventures. Over the past three years, the economic restructuring program of the World Bank in India has encouraged NRIs to extend their investments in India. Several Indian American corporate leaders accompanied Secretary of Commerce Ron Brown on his February 1995 trip to India, a mission that generated $7 billion in contracts, mostly in the power and energy fields.

Political participation has educated Indian Americans. The rejection earlier immigrants felt when they arrived in the United States has given way to legal acceptance and economic advancement. The ability to stay and rear families in the United States was acquired very recently. The legitimate stake in America had been withheld from them for so long that Indians are having to learn about America as they rear their children here. Many of the post-1965 South Asian immigrants retain the sojourner mentality toward America although most of them will not go back to their country of origin. Indians with children continue to take their families back to their home country to inculcate in the next generation a sense of roots and cultural continuity. Like many other immigrant groups, they reify their cultures and traditions in desperate attempts to indoctrinate the next generation, trying to slow down, if they cannot halt, the tide of inevitable Americanization. Many Indian parents apply traditional notions of family honor, respectability, culture, and gender roles to their American children, fearing for their future as products of uncertainty: neither fully accepted in America nor fully familiar with their country of origin. The struggle to hold on to both home fronts, which shaped earlier Indian immigrant experience, continues to structure the dreams and fears of the post-1965 communities.

Redefining Politics: The New Generation

The most dramatic turn in South Asian life and politics in America is the younger generation's interest in collaboration, networking, and coalition building. These young Americans, most of whose parents came after the 1965 Immigration Act, see their future in the United States. In their education, social life, career objectives, and personal goals, they differ from their parents' generation. This new generation is inextricably connected to the American world of popular culture, individualism, and social engagement in which they were reared. Although conflicts with the older generation do emerge in the home, this new generation exemplifies the incorporation of many cultures without losing a sense of personal cohesion and identity. They are not as bound by distinctions of ethnicity, subcaste, language, and region as the older generation. They share American lives and American culture with one another.

Whatever one's economic status, the transmission of traditional cultural beliefs and practices to one's children, who are not South Asian but American, has resulted in a complex relationship for both generations with their South Asian country of origin. Children generally acquire the characteristics of the communities in which they are reared. Accordingly, the few areas of high concentration of South Asians in areas like Queens, New York, and parts of New Jersey, with shops, restaurants, and places of worship catering to their traditional practices, produce children who are in touch with their community practices. However, the larger American society in which these children also function has proven to be more powerful in its call than parental admonitions regarding dress, dating, and popular culture. When these children attain adulthood, their lives tend to take more cosmopolitan and American turns.

South Asians in the United States take advantage of their numbers (roughly one million) for quick communication and easy targeting of interested compatriots in organizing around socially relevant issues in local groups. Some groups have country-wide networks, such as India Alert, which disseminates human rights information and organizes letter-writing campaigns. Groups like South Asians Against AIDS (SAAA) in New York establish liaisons with similar groups in other countries, like Naaz of Great Britain. Others, like the Coalition Against Anti-Asian Violence (CAAV) in New York, extend the boundaries of their political concerns to address a broad range of discriminatory treatment against Asians in

America. Various groups address women's particular concerns, such as *SAKHI* (female friend) for South Asian Women and *Manavi* (woman) in the northeast, and *Narika* (woman) on the west coast. Gay rights groups have become active in pressing for their civil rights all over the country, including South Asian Lesbian and Gay Association (SALGA) in New York, Shamakami in San Francisco, and *Trikone* (triangle) in San Jose, California.

The most important consequence of this grass-roots mobilization among South Asian communities is that the "high" politics of the formal political arena of elections, fundraising, and campaign management is not the last word on political participation. This new, socially aware, and energetic political activism has expanded conventional understandings of political participation to include a wide range of concerns: issues of local interest in specific communities which are placed before local politicians and city councils; immigration issues which affect South Asians regardless of their geographical location; political and economic issues in South Asian countries on which America can have an impact, such as Kashmir, and bilateral trade; and international issues like AIDS, ill treatment, and discrimination. This is inclusive politics, democratic in the most literal sense of the word.

Despite strenuous efforts, South Asians have only just begun to make an impact on national politics. Until now, their particular history of recent immigration and post-1965 economic success has kept what political engagement there is at the level of formal or high politics. Consequently, they entered the coalition game rather late and are still building common bases among their extremely diverse membership. The general public's emphasis on their professional advancement and economic prosperity obscures the complexity of South Asians' existence in America. South Asians and the larger society both forget that recognition does not occur in a vacuum; they and the larger society are mutually constitutive. Race-based views prevalent in society, intellectually bankrupt though they are, continue to block complete acceptance of their presence in America. The escalation of immigrant bashing in the country also has taken its toll on the community's hard-won sense of belonging. South Asian political activity only recently has begun moving away from a reactive mode to counterdiscriminatory treatment, toward an autonomous assertion of presence and political interest.

This newfound independence is now being pushed forward to the next stage: to find ways in which common ground can be established between South Asians and non-South Asian groups. As the first woman of color to be executive director of the National Gay and Lesbian Task Force, Indian-born Urvashi Vaid puts it regarding the gay movement today, "We are seeing the limits of identity-based politics. Identity is very important: I am an Indian and I am never going to disown that identity. But organising around identity has gotten us into single-issue politics and we've not been able to come together to build an electoral majority" (*India Today* 1995, 15 January: 68b-e).

Building that electoral majority remains the political goal for all minorities as they forge new lives in the United States. To this rethinking of political strategy must be added the emergence of a new sense of self. In the words of anthropologist James Clifford (1988: 10–11), identity is "mixed, relational, and inventive. . . . A sense of difference or distinctness can never be located solely in the continuity of a culture or tradition. Identity is conjunctural, not essential." For South Asians who cross and recross the bridging space between Asia and North America, their inventive engagement with the United States surely will, one day, convince the world and themselves that this is truly their home.

REFERENCES

Appiah, Kwame Anthony. 1992. *In my father's house*. New York: Oxford University Press.

Asian Week. 1986. Indians discuss assimilation. 10 October.

Brown, Emily. 1982. Revolution in India: Made in America. *Population Review* 25, nos. 1–2: 41–47.

Bouvier, Leon F., and David Simcox. 1994. *Foreign born professionals in the United States*. Washington, DC: Center for Immigration Studies.

Buchanan, Agnes Foster. 1908. The West and the Hindu invasion. *Overland Monthly and Out West Magazine* 54, no. 4 (April): 308–313.

Business Today (New Delhi). 1993. The saffron vision 2000, 22 July–6 August, 57–59.

Chandrasekhar, S. 1944. Indian immigration in America. *Far Eastern Survey* 13 (26 July): 15, 141.

——— . 1982. Some statistics on Asian Indian immigrants to the United States of America. In *From India to America: A brief history of immigration: Problems of discrimination, admission and assimilation*, edited by S. Chandrasekhar, 86–92. La Jolla, CA: Population Review.

Clifford, James. 1988. *The predicament of culture*. Cambridge, MA: Harvard University Press.

Debates and Proceedings in the Congress of the United States, 1789–1791. 2 vols. Washington, DC: 1834 vol. 1, 998, 1284; vol. 2, 1148–1156, 1162, 2264.

Dutta, Manoranjan. 1982. Asian Indian Americans: Search for an economic profile. In *From India to America: A brief history of immigration: Problems of discrimination, admission and assimilation*, edited by S. Chandrasekhar, 76–85. La Jolla, CA: Population Review.

Fenton, John Y. 1988. *Transplanting religious traditions: Asian Indians in America*. New York: Praeger.

Gibson, Margaret. 1988. *Accommodation without assimilation: Sikh immigrants in an American high school*. Ithaca, NY: Cornell University Press.

Helweg, Arthur W., and Usha M. Helweg. 1990. *An immigrant success story: East Indians in America*. Philadelphia: University of Pennsylvania Press.

Hess, Gary. 1982. The Asian Indian immigrants in the United States: The early phase, 1900–1965. *Population Review* 25: 32.

India Today. 1989. Indian Americans: The lobbying game. 30 September, 86–88.

——— . 1994. Separated by law. 15 August, 48b–c.

——— . 1994. Good morning, New York. 30 September, 68e.

——— . 1995. Mainstream movers. 15 January, 68b–e.

——— . 1995. Bonded in America, 31 January, 76b–c.

Leonard, Karen. 1982. Marriage and family life among early Asian Indian immigrants. In *From India to America: A brief history of immigration: Problems of discrimination, admission and assimilation*, edited by S. Chandrasekhar, 67–75. La Jolla, CA: Population Review.

——— . 1992. *Making ethnic choices: California's Punjabi Mexican Americans*. Philadelphia: Temple University Press.

New York Times. 1994. Indian immigrant's face is burned with a cigarette, 20 February.

——— . 1995. A small melting pot, in danger of overflowing, 22 January.

News India-Times. 1994. Lobbying efforts cost $70,000 a month, 16 December, 1.

——— . 1995. Sikh files suit against MTA, 6 January, 26.

Ong, Paul, and Suzanne J. Hee. 1994. Economic diversity. In *The state of Asian Pacific America: Economic diversity, issues, and policies*, edited by Paul Ong. Los Angeles: LEAP Asian Pacific American Public Policy Institute and UCLA Asian American Studies Center.

Peterson, William. 1985. Who's what: 1790–1980. *Wilson Quarterly* (summer): 97–120.

Saran, Parmatma. 1980. New ethics: The case of the East Indians in New York City. In *Sourcebook on the new immigration*, edited by Roy Simon Bryce-Laporte. New Brunswick, NJ: Transaction Books.

Saund, Dalip S. 1960. *Congressman from India*. New York: Dutton.

Scheffauer, Herman. 1910. The tide of turbans. *Forum* 43 (June): 616–618.

Statistical Abstracts of the United States. 1994. Washington, DC: U.S. Department of Commerce, Economic and Statistics Administration, Bureau of the Census, Data User Sevices Division.

Takaki, Ronald. 1989. *Strangers from a different shore*. Boston: Little Brown.

Taylor, Paul S., and Tom Vasey. 1936. Historical background of California farm labor. *Rural Sociology* 1: 291.

U.S. Bureau of the Census. 1990. *1990 census of population, general population characteristics*. Washington, DC: Government Printing Office.

7
Exclusion and Fragmentation in Ethnic Politics: Chinese Americans in Urban Politics

L. Ling-chi Wang

Ethnicity has long been an important basis of political mobilization and empowerment in urban politics. Two distinct paths to ethnic political empowerment can be identified: (1) ward-based machine politics for white ethnics in big cities of major industrial northern states and (2) since World War II, the mobilization around civil rights and welfare issues for African Americans in northern cities and southern states.

In both cases, ethnic solidarity provides the basis of mobilization. European immigrants in large cities organized voting blocs in ethnic neighborhoods to consolidate political power and, more important, to gain access to patronage through civil service jobs and lucrative public contracts. Through this same machinery, city leaders and party bosses among white immigrant groups emerged, some of whom became national political figures. Their success and entrenchment in big city politics, however, turned them into obstacles for political outsiders: African Americans, Hispanic Americans, Asian Americans, women, gays, and lesbians.

Black solidarity, however, was shaped largely by the legacy of slavery. In their long struggle for racial equality and economic justice, African Americans mobilized for civil rights, welfare, and economic benefits. Since the Voting Rights Act of 1965, African Americans have gained substantial political power in black-dominated cities and in some of the southern states. Through direct confrontations and negotiated accommodations, they have secured power-sharing and token concessions from the white establishment. In the process, perhaps as much as one third of African Americans have achieved middle-class status through jobs and business contracts in both public and private sectors, and some even succeeded in making inroads into executive positions in city halls in major cities and in select corporate sectors.

The Asian American political experience has been quite different from those of white immigrants and African Americans. While ethnic solidarity has also been the basis of Asian American political mobilization since the 1970s, especially in raising campaign funds, the aim, style, and outcome of such mobilization have been quite different from that of the other two groups. Their presence in the American political landscape, to date, has been invisible. Not only have they not gained collective political strength, but they have not been able to derive political benefits from their participation in terms of public jobs, appointments, contracts, or recognition of their community's concerns.

In fact, for Asian Americans to be successful in electoral politics, they must win the confidence and support of white voters by presenting themselves as nonthreatening, nonethnic candidates, the antithesis of ethnic solidarity. While white ethnic candidates routinely present themselves as candidates representing citywide interests and while all racial groups and African American candidates openly and forcefully speak of representing black interests, Asian American candidates must go out of their way to prove to the voters, especially the white ethnics, that, aside from their skin color, they represent no Asian American interest. In other words, in return for white votes, Asian candidates, like former Lieutenant Governor S. B. Woo of Delaware, former U.S. Senator S. I. Hayakawa, and Secretary of State March Fong Eu of California, must carry "their agenda" instead of Chinese Americans' or Asian Americans' agenda. Even after their elections, politicians like Representative Norman Mineta of San Jose and Representative Robert Matsui of Sacramento, must remain vigilant, allowing no overt sign of over-representing Asian American interests or constituency. In short, denying one's ethnicity is a precondition for gaining legitimacy and acceptance by white voters and winning elections, a precondition not required of white ethnic and African American candidates. The process, in effect, permits Asian Americans only surface representation in politics and strips them of any substantive representation, even if they come from areas of high Asian concentration.

The glaring difference between Asian American and other ethnic group leaders can be attributed, in part, to their relative numerical weakness. According to the 1990 census, the total Asian American population was only slightly above 3 percent of the total U.S. population. However, numbers and percentages alone cannot explain this peculiar phenomenon. The 3 percent is concentrated in four major states and in a few metropolitan areas like San Francisco, Los Angeles, San Jose, and New York. In fact, one third of San Francisco is Asian. Yet Asian Americans remain invisible and powerless there.

I begin with a sketch of the historic structure of dual domination under which Asian Americans lived and how the first indigenous political movement, which surfaced in the late 1960s under the influence of the black civil rights movement, sought to liberate them from the structure. Using San Francisco as a case study, this discussion is followed by an analysis of the realignment of the Chinese American community, following the massive influx of immigrants since the 1970s and how, within the Chinese American community, division by class and nativity marginalizes the first indigenous political movement and how the liberal Democratic establishment exploits the division to subvert the Chinese American quest for political empowerment in the city of San Francisco. It is hardly a story of political success. It is a story that must be told and understood if Chinese Americans and Asian Americans are to overcome political exclusion and achieve political equality.

THE STRUCTURE OF DUAL DOMINATION

Unlike white immigrants and African Americans since the Civil War, Asian immigrants were systematically disenfranchised until after World War II because, by legislative and judicial decisions, they were excluded from citizenship and the democratic process. Numerically far smaller than European Americans and African Americans, Chinese Americans, Japanese Americans, Korean Americans, and Filipino Americans posed no political threat to the entrenched power, even after they were granted the right of naturalization after the war. They were routinely denied political and civil rights. Not until the late 1960s did they begin to mobilize for equal participation, benefiting from the fruit of the civil rights struggle of African Americans.

Two key elements shaped the formation of Asian American communities before World War II: the racist policies toward Asian immigrants in the United States and the abiding American imperialistic interests in East Asian countries from which Asians in the United States came. Racism guided not just our domestic and foreign policies, but also the creation of ostracized Asian ghettos in which respective Asian governments and their diplomatic representatives were permitted to exercise extraterritorial rule in total disregard of the laws of the United States and to control key community institutions like schools, mass media, and social organizations. With the exception of the Japanese American community, this phenomenon persisted and, in some cases, was reinforced throughout the Cold War. Vestiges of this legacy of extraterritorial domination are still found in Asian American communities.

The intersection of foreign and domestic politics in the Asian American communities created a unique structure of dual domination under which Asians in the United States were compelled to live. On the one hand, institutionalized racism systematically excluded Asian Americans from participation in mainstream American society. On the other hand, the extraterritorial domination of respective East Asian governments was condoned, if not encouraged at times, by the U.S. government. Asians were treated as aliens confined to urban ghettos, governed invariably in each by an elite merchant class legitimized by the U.S. government and reinforced by the omnipresent diplomatic representatives in all community affairs. Social institutions, motherland cultures, life-styles, and political factionalism in respective Asian countries were reproduced, modified, and institutionalized in the ghettos. Conflict over homeland partisan disputes—like the chronic dispute between the Manchu regime and various factions of reformers at the turn of the century and between the nationalists and communists in China throughout the twentieth century—kept the community deeply divided, draining scarce financial resources and political energy from each community and leaving behind a legacy of preoccupation with motherland politics and deep political cleavage. These urban ghettos were, in effect, treated as colonial settlements abroad by Asian governments, subject to the same laws and policies in respective motherlands, even if they were in conflict with the U.S. Constitution, and as subservient colonies within the United States by the mainstream society. During the Cold War, the extraterritorial domination intensified as military dictators in Taiwan, South Korea, and the Philippines, fully backed by the U.S. government, extended their repressive arms into Asian American communities in an effort to secure their political loyalty and to suppress political dissent.

For Asians born, reared, and educated in these urban ghettos before World War II, available career options were basically: (1) second-class citizenship in the United States or (2) an uncertain future in Asian countries. Those who chose to remain in the United States were compelled to disavow their ethnic identity, become fully assimilated, and abandon cultural and social ties within their communities. In essence, culture denial was the prerequisite for being accepted into the mainstream, inflicting a lasting obsession for acceptance among Asian Americans to this date. It is against this backdrop of dual domination that we must understand the emergence of the first political movement in the Asian American communities in the late 1960s and the disenfranchisement, even at this date, of Asian Americans, despite significant advances in education, employment, and business.

THE RISE OF ASIAN AMERICAN POLITICAL CONSCIOUSNESS

The African American civil rights movement inspired a new era of ethnic pride, political consciousness, and political mobilization among predominantly American-born, college-age Asians and created unprecedented opportunities in education, the arts, employment, business, and housing hitherto denied Asian Americans. (Whether they know it or not, Asian Americans are beneficiaries of the civil rights and welfare gains made by African Americans and are deeply indebted to the articulations and expressions of multiculturalism of African Americans.)

The movement, led by young Asian Americans, represented a significant departure with the past because it rejected both the racist model of forced assimilation and the political and cultural domination of Asian countries from which their ancestors came. They also rejected second-class citizenship and the option of returning to the Asian countries from which their parents originally came. Instead, they demanded liberation from the structure of dual domination. Toward this end, they simultaneously fought battles on two fronts: racial oppression and extraterritorial domination. In the struggle against racial oppression, the movement advanced two new notions: "Asian American" and "Third World solidarity." The former promoted pan-Asian solidarity among Chinese Americans, Japanese Americans, Korean Americans, and Filipino Americans as a viable means toward achieving political empowerment. As a politically constructed notion, Asian American was based on a vague racial and geographic origin in Asia, a shared historical experience of exclusion in the United States, and above all, the need for numerical strength in the body politic. But it was also a notion not readily accepted by older Asian Americans then and by the immigrants arriving from different Asian countries since. The latter placed Asian Americans in solidarity with African Americans, Chicano/Latino Americans, and Native Americans in their collective struggle for racial equality and economic justice. In so doing, the young Asian Americans made a deliberate decision to follow the African American path toward empowerment, including the use of African American political styles, organizations, and agenda. The notion of Third World solidarity, like the notion of pan-Asian ethnicity, was never fully understood in the communities, thus calling into question the breadth and depth of the emerging movement in the community and causing old, submerged cleavage within the community to open further. This lack of understanding had a profoundly adverse effect on their self-understanding as a minority that had suffered discrimination and complicated their positions on issues like affirmative action, immigration, and bilingualism.

In the struggle to free Asian American communities from extraterritorial domination, the second battle front, they also clashed with the community establishment and representatives of Asian governments. Unlike the African American movement, young Asian Americans had to struggle to free their communities from the political domination or extraterritorial rule of the U.S.-supported dictatorial governments of South Korea, Taiwan, and the Philippines. Quite simply, they wanted no political, economic, and cultural interference from foreign governments, and they wanted Americans to see them for what they were, rather than alien representatives of some distant Asian countries. Their effort was immediately red-baited by the establishment throughout the Cold War era, and they received neither sympathy nor support from the U.S. government; instead, they invited suspicion, surveillance, and harassment from the Federal Bureau of Investigation and other U.S. law enforcement agencies.

In their struggle to liberate themselves from the structure of dual domination, young Asian Americans found themselves increasingly isolated from many segments of the community and in open conflict with the conservative ruling community elites. Their political support bases in the communities, their claim of legitimacy, shrank. Even their legitimate efforts to rid the community of racial oppression and foreign domination were frequently discredited in the foreign-controlled community press, causing them to clash frequently with the elites, sometimes violently.

As the new kids on the block demanding equality and political empowerment in American cities, they also encountered strong resistance from well-entrenched power structures and institutions, controlled by either white ethnics or by a coalition of white ethnics and African American leaders. City halls openly questioned the motivation and legitimacy of young Asian Americans and routinely sided with the community establishment, knowing full well that the young Asian Americans had little or no support from the establishment and neither made generous political contributions nor delivered Asian American voters whose numbers, in their eyes, were negligible.

FRAGMENTATION OF THE CHINESE AMERICAN COMMUNITY

Chinese Americans emerged gradually from being an invisible minority living under the structure of dual domination after World War II to become, by the late 1960s, a visible minority with two conflicting public images, corresponding roughly to two self-defined, but opposing visions of Chinese Americans: (1) a docile, accommodating model minority and (2) an angry, contentious minority, demanding equality and justice for the poor and powerless. Numbering now about 2 million nationwide or less than 1 percent of the total U.S. population, Chinese Americans have become quite visible because nearly all of them are now concentrated in a few major urban areas and because their successes as well as their failures have become the focus of media and political attention.

While Chinese Americans have been predominantly an urban population since the late nineteenth century and their community has long been divided between the merchant elites and the working class, the convergence of two postwar historic events, the Cold War and the civil rights movement, have greatly deepened the division in the community by class, nativity, and residential location, giving rise to not just conflicting classes and images, but also conflicting visions. The sources of this open split can be traced to the changes in U.S. immigration laws and Cold War policies, as well as to the arrival of diverse Chinese immigrants from China, Taiwan, Hong Kong, and Southeast Asian countries. The division has had serious political and social consequences as Chinese Americans from opposing camps seek political empowerment in cities with deeply entrenched white ethnic power structures.

Three successive, overlapping waves of Chinese immigrants during the Cold War period contributed to the community's fragmentation and conflict. The first wave can be characterized as an intellectual migration that began in 1949. Even though Chinese were still excluded from immigration by the small annual quota of 105 before 1965, the liberal policy toward the admission of foreign students allowed thousands of bright, motivated Chinese students to enter research universities in the United States. From 1949 to 1989, no fewer than 250,000 of the brightest Chinese students received advanced degrees in science and technology. Through loopholes in immigration laws, they were eagerly recruited by the military-industrial complex, most notably those in electronics and aerospace. In general, they settled down not in the historic Chinatowns, but in new middle-class suburbs near industrial or research centers like the Silicon Valley, Los Angeles, and Orange County in southern California, and the NASA Center near Houston. Likewise, affluent pockets of Chinese American professionals can be found in large metropolitan areas like Boston, New York, Chicago, and Seattle. Many became leading scientists and top engineers in the United States, giving rise to the false impression that the prewar oppressed Chinese working class had finally pulled themselves up by their own bootstraps. This is, in fact, where the misleading model minority stereotype originated. These highly touted intellectuals, in fact, have little—politically, economically, and socially—in common with the direct descendants of the prewar Chinese communities in big cities.

The second wave of Chinese immigrants arrived after the racist quota law was repealed in 1965, setting the stage for family union and further brain drain. Thousands came in each year to be reunited with their loved ones. Chinatowns across the nation expanded. Generally, most of the new arrivals settled in cities with well-established, but largely disenfranchised Chinese American communities where they became the new urban working class. Others became small entrepreneurs. Speaking little English, they worked long hours in restaurants, grocery stores, gift shops, garment factories, laundries, and service industries. Old Chinatowns expanded rapidly and in some, such as San Francisco and New York, new Chinatowns were founded in other city neighborhoods. It was on behalf of the old-timers and the new immigrant population that the young Chinese Americans fought for racial equality and fair distribution of public resources and services. The well-educated immigrants in the second wave, fewer in number, joined the ranks of rising Chinese American professional and technical personnel in the middle-class suburbs.

The third wave of Chinese immigrants, numbering close to a million since the early 1970s, is more diverse in terms of geographic origin, linguistic differences, and class background, thereby contributing further to the division already present in Chinese American communities. They were immigrants fleeing either political instability or political repression. The United States-China détente in 1972 and the U.S. decision to disengage gradually from the Vietnam War signaled the abandonment of the policy of containment of China by military means throughout Asia: no longer would the United States support militarily the dictatorial regimes from South Korea to Indochina. Political upheavals reverberated throughout East and Southeast Asia, as repression deepened in countries led by the likes of U.S.-supported Chiang Kai-shek in Taiwan, Park Chung Hee in South Korea, Ferdinand Marcos in the Philippines, Suharto in Indonesia, General Nguyen Van Thieu in Vietnam, and Lon Nol in Cambodia. The results were political instability and a massive exodus of people and capital to the United States.

The third wave included two types of immigrants. The upper- and middle-class Chinese from Taiwan and Southeast Asia were among the first to seek long-term security for themselves, their businesses, and children by emigrating to the United States. They were joined by tens of thousands of ethnic Chinese from Vietnam and Cambodia who instantly became impoverished refugees and "boat people," as Vietnam implemented its anti-Chinese or ethnic cleansing policies in 1978. The rich acquired homes in middle-class neighborhoods in cities and in suburbs, such as Monterey Park, Mountain View, and Foster City in California; they made investments in real estate, businesses, and industries, while the poor settled in run-down neighborhoods in cities with well-established Chinese American communities. The interests of these two types of immigrants coincide at times, but usually they are at odds with each other. Over issues like housing and employment, where their relations are frequently those of landlord-tenant or management-labor, their views are far from congenial.

Absorbing these three waves of immigrants, the Chinese American community expanded rapidly even as it became fragmented. By the late 1970s and early 1980s, the Chinese American community can be seen roughly as two distinct communities separated by class, nativity, place of residence, and historical experience, each with its own needs, lifestyle, value orientation, and aspiration. They may have the same racial origin and may have encountered the same kind of racism in the United States, but they have very little in common. Half of the Chinese American population is relatively affluent, well protected by the civil rights laws of the 1960s, while the other half is poor, limited in its knowledge of English, and very much in need of help in education, housing, health, and job training. Sometimes they are seen as successful minorities and other times, as welfare dependent, resource draining, and worse, prone to organized crime. Neither reflects the diversity and complexity of the vastly transformed old Chinese America.

The militant path chosen by young Chinese Americans in the late 1960s and early 1970s, as noted above, was not understood and supported by the established order within the Chinese American community, which wanted only to retain the status quo and be left alone by the indifferent, racist society. To the newly arrived immigrants from Asia, many of whom were fleeing from the repressive regimes in East Asia and had no understanding of racial oppression and the notion of pan-Asian ethnicity, the civil rights agenda of young Asian Americans was just as alien and incomprehensible. To the affluent Chinese immigrants, the message was meaningless because they found their newly adopted country to be generous and fair, unaware of the civil rights struggles and gains made prior to their arrival. The result was the growing isolation of activist Chinese Americans from the increasingly immigrant-dominated Chinese American community and a widening gap and conflict between Chinese Americans and other racial minorities.

While the number of Chinese Americans increased dramatically in major metropolitan areas across the United States, the increase did not result in a comparable increase in their political strength along the respective trajectories of European immigrants and African Americans, as young Chinese American activists had hoped. Instead, Chinese Americans remained disenfranchised and powerless. In fact, the growing number of Chinese in the United States and their visible concentration in certain urban neighborhoods, occupations, and small businesses, aided by the model minority stereotype, have been deeply resented by some European Americans and African Americans, giving rise to widespread anti-Asian sentiment and the growing number of incidents of anti-Asian violence and murder. Their collective political response is to exclude the Chinese American community.

At this critical juncture, Chinese America finds itself fragmented and without effective leadership. The new immigrants are too preoccupied with adjusting to their new environment. The old Chinatown leadership, represented by district and family associations, has been impotent and ineffective, while the younger leadership, represented by the Asian American movement, has been marginalized and rendered irrelevant by shifting demographics. What is left of the visionary and bold political movement of the late 1960s and early 1970s are mostly professional Asian American organizations of lawyers, doctors, teachers, accountants, engineers, and entrepreneurs devoted not so much to broad community problems and issues, but to narrow professional interests and advancement.

The proliferation of anti-Asian racism since the 1980s should have heightened ethnic solidarity and aroused collective response. It did not. Instead, Asians, now dominated by new immigrants, have become more divided by national origin, culture, language, and historical experience. Reverting to the prewar era, most Asians seem to identify themselves by national origin. Notions of pan-Asian ethnicity and of Third World solidarity that inspired young Asian Americans to participate in electoral politics in the late 1960s have become irrelevant in political discourse, if not totally ignored. Tragically, they have become notions to be talked about, not acted upon in the Chinese American community. The 1992 Los Angeles riots exposed the true state of affairs of the Asian American political movement when the Korean American community found itself victimized, deserted not just by the city and state governments, but also by other Asian American groups. Reflecting their class status, some affluent Asian Americans even openly consider programs in affirmative action to be discriminatory toward their interests.

Chinese Americans in San Francisco

Today, the fragmentation of the Chinese American community in the United States is clearer than ever. It is not only evenly divided between the suburban and the urban, between the native born and foreign born, between the Cantonese and non-Cantonese speakers, but also between the working class and the professional class, between those born in China and those born outside of China, between male and female, between rich and poor. How this division affects their political participation in urban politics can be seen best in San Francisco, the city with the highest percentage of Chinese American population (about 20 percent) and the oldest Chinatown in the United States.

Chinese Americans have been in San Francisco since the Gold Rush, have endured some of the worst natural disasters and anti-Chinese violence in the United States, have been the leaders of social, cultural, and political life for Chinese throughout the United States, and more recently, have become a signifi-cant economic force in a city that wants to be seen as a gateway to and the leader in the Pacific Rim. San Francisco, with a population now of slightly over 700,000, is also the city in which Asian American students from the University of Califor-nia–Berkeley and San Francisco State began the first community activist project in Chinatown in the summer of 1968 and from which the movement toward political empowerment was launched.

Yet after twenty-six years of political mobilization, Chinese Americans—and for that matter, Asian Americans—remain politically invisible and powerless in this city, despite the fact that they constitute one third of its population. Of the eleven members on the Board of Supervisors, only one is Asian American. Thomas Hsieh, a conservative Chinese American, was elected after seven other Chinese American candidates (George Chinn, Gordon Lau, Ben Tom, Garrett Chan, Ben Hom, and Pius Lee) had tried and failed in the previous twenty years. No Chinese American has represented the city in both houses in the state legislature or in both chambers of the U.S. Congress and none can be expected in the foreseeable future.

Only token Chinese Americans, usually in lesser positions, are found on the mayor's staff, in managerial positions in the civil service system, on the city's commissions and boards, on the benches of municipal and superior courts, and in the management of the city's public schools and community college systems. Lucrative city contracts and concessions are rarely awarded to Chinese American businesses, and Chinese Americans are short-changed in vital public services and distribution of public resources. In the corporate world, they fare no better.

History and numerical strength have little impact on their political presence in the city. Chinese Americans do not seem to follow either the white immigrant or African American political trajectory. Repeated demands for equality by newly emerged younger groups, notably the Chinese American Democratic Club (CADC) and Chinese for Affirmative Action (CAA), have fallen on deaf ears. Neither their numerical strength, as in San Francisco and Monterey Park, nor their concerted push for equal representation seems to have made a dent on the political establishment. In fact, the white ethnic power structure—represented by the dominant liberal Democratic Burton machine and less powerful conservative Democrats represented by followers of former mayors George Christopher, Joseph Alioto, Dianne Feinstein, and Frank Jordan—is determined to maintain its privilege and power by cloning their own successors from within, by fragmenting the Chinese American population through gerrymandering of political districts, and by pitting Chinese American factions against each other with token appointments or small political favors, making sure no independent Chinese American leaders undermine their domination at local, state, and national levels. Although the two wings of the Democratic establishment may be divided, they have been united in keeping the Chinese American and Asian American newcomers from sharing a power in the city. Ironically, the liberal Burton machine has been most successful in keeping its loyal Chinese American constituency out of power. No Chinese Americans have been groomed for candidacy to elected offices, and among those who ran for public offices, none has received, to date, any significant financial support from either Democrats or Republicans. No Chinese American has been in the inner circle of any elected official or in any decision-making process in candidate selection of either party.

In effect, the city has been perpetuating the exclusion of Chinese Americans during the last twenty-six years. In response to demands for equal participation and inclusion, the political establishment has granted only token representation in city government, only admitting Chinese Americans into positions of lesser power, such as school boards and lesser city boards and commissions. The degree of toleration for Chinese American political leaders in the political establishment is inversely proportional to their degree of identification with the needs and concerns of the Chinese American community. To be accepted into the fringe of the political establishment, Chinese Americans are required to present themselves as nonethnic to the non-Chinese to get endorsements and votes and as ethnic to receive political contributions from Chinese Americans, prove themselves as loyal and compliant to the Burton machine, take stands on issues not offensive or threatening to the dominant white interests, and support candidates and issues dear to the establishment, even if they are not in the best interests of the Chinese American community.

Most insidious is the establishment's clever manipulation of the community to enrich their campaign treasuries. Since the mid-1970s, the political establishment in San Francisco has discovered a gold mine among well-heeled Chinese American immigrants whose sole interest is not in community welfare or empowerment but in personal recognition and pet projects like real estate development, zoning variances, permits for business, professional services, or the Taiwan lobby. In other words, they have no party loyalty, political ambition, or community interest: they are precisely the kind of contributors favored most by politicians who fear potential challengers or demands for accountability to the community. Through these fat cats, politicians of both parties and of all stripes have not only raised huge amounts of campaign funds for themselves, but also managed to marginalize, if not suppress, the movement to empower the community. To my knowledge, Chinese Americans are the only group in the United States that has failed to convert money into collective political power and community advancement.

Several reasons can be identified to explain the dismal showing of Chinese Americans in their quest for equal political representation in a city dominated by the liberal Democrats. First is the legacy of political exclusion: the denial of citizenship to Chinese immigrants and thus their right to participate in the democratic process. There is no tradition of political participation in the community. Chinese Americans simply do not participate at the rate commensurate with their population strength. Of the 400,000 registered voters in San Francisco, about 10 percent are Chinese Americans. Generations of exclusion and overt discrimination have rendered all Chinese Americans outsiders and made their participation in the same political institutions that persecuted them difficult, if not impossible.

Second, the exclusionary policy and the continuing practice of racial discrimination against the Chinese, unfortunately, tend to reinforce not just the well-established tradition of nonparticipation, but also the traditional Chinese aversion to and low regard for politicians and government officials, and hence, Chinese American reluctance to become registered voters and to become involved in electoral politics. As democracy becomes equated with only big money, political participation appears to become more costly and less relevant and effective, and as corruption and scandals occur endlessly in all three branches and at all levels of the government, more and more Chinese Americans cease to see any purpose in participating in the electoral process. Not only are Chinese Americans not becoming registered voters, those who are registered are turning away from both Democratic and Republican parties by declining to state their party affiliation and worse yet, less than 50 percent of Chinese American registered voters bother to vote on election day. This trend is significant in a city overwhelmingly Democratic and a clear indication that Chinese Americans now perceive no difference between the two parties and see no point in casting their ballots. Cynicism and distrust of government officials in China is greatly reinforced in the Chinese American community. This pathetic track record, well known to politicians, has become a license for them to raise political funds from the community and to ignore Chinese American concerns.

Third, since the majority of the Chinese American population is of immigrant background and noncitizen, many are also limited English speakers and are too busy trying to make a living for their families. Participation in the electoral process is low on their list of priorities. To many, government is irrelevant, if not corrupt, and voting has become a meaningless gesture. This is apparently an informed decision because they do have access to no less than ten Chinese-language dailies and a dozen weeklies, not to mention the Chinese language radio and television stations. Some of the immigrants, of course, are still ineligible for naturalization, but others who have become eligible do not even see any purpose in becoming citizens.

Last, the political establishment in San Francisco seeks to exploit the division within the Chinese American community. Politicians routinely promote the division to undermine ethnic solidarity and to prevent strong political leaders from emerging. They solicit contributions from competing forces, pitting them against each other for personal favors. The only leaders they will support are the ones willing to follow their marching orders and to perpetuate their privileged status and power.

In both public and private sectors, Chinese Americans either do not exist or do not count. They are outsiders, not foreigners. They are ignored by many large corporations and written off by both the Republicans and the Democrats. By and large, they are relegated to the sideline, watching the parade of African Americans, women, disabled Americans, Hispanic Americans, and gays and lesbians marching toward political empowerment and climbing the corporate ladders.

CONCLUSIONS

Unlike European immigrants and African Americans, ethnicity has not been the basis of political mobilization and empowerment for Chinese Americans. In spite of their deep roots in cities like San Francisco, New York, and Los Angeles, and their growing numerical strength and economic power in these cities, Chinese Americans remain deeply divided and politically powerless. Under the manipulation of the white ethnic establishment, ethnicity has been an asset only for political fundraising from Chinese Americans and a liability for building a political base and consolidating political power. From the San Francisco example, the entrenched white Democratic establishment is determined to keep Chinese Americans excluded and to hang on, presumably as long as possible, to the power, privilege, and benefit it enjoys, willing only to share its power partially with compliant Chinese Americans and with more militant and better organized African American and gay communities, if for no other reason than to keep Chinese Americans out of the power structure.

Many historical, economic, and political factors have undermined the Chinese American quest for political unity and empowerment. Among the major factors, first, is the absence of ethnic solidarity. Division by class, nativity, and preoccupation with partisan politics in China and Taiwan has effectively deterred Chinese ethnic solidarity and allowed the political establishment in the mainstream to exploit these divisions to its advantage. Second, the struggle for liberation from the structure of dual domination intensifies the conflict within the community, alienates many segments of the community, and substantially erodes the political base upon which the empowerment movement seeks to build and expand. Third, the racist double standards, compelling Chinese American leaders to deny their ethnicity in return for political support and acceptance, used by the media and the political establishment to judge Chinese Americans interested in public service and political career, effectively deprive the Chinese American community from developing strong, community-based political leaders and organizations. These factors have effectively prevented Chinese Americans from achieving ethnic solidarity and empowerment, along either the trajectory of European immigrants or African Americans.

To the white ethnic establishment and by extension, the dominant society, Chinese Americans are still aliens, decidedly not an integral part of San Francisco or of the larger society. Chinese Americans in San Francisco are to be tolerated as long as they remain useful and nonthreatening to the dominant interests. They are to be kept at a distance and excluded from the center of power by all means necessary: preventing Chinese Americans from the electoral process; perpetuating their disenfranchisement by political manipulation and bureaucratic means; granting them only token representation by appointing only compliant Chinese Americans to minor or harmless posts; limiting their access to vital public resources and services; failing to support independent Chinese American candidates; promoting division within the Chinese American community; and, most important of all, creating friction and suspicion among Chinese Americans, African Americans, Latino Americans, gays, lesbians, and other Asian Americans—in short, exploiting division within the community and across racial groups within the city to keep white political power and privilege intact and Chinese Americans weak and excluded.

The strategy, thus far, has been quite effective in various cities, including San Francisco. But it is not likely to last long. First, demographic and economic trends favor Chinese American political empowerment in San Francisco and other cities in the long run. Second, there is a growing awareness in the community that Chinese Americans are being shortchanged and being systematically excluded from equal and meaningful political participation in city politics. The day this awareness is transformed into a political movement will be the day when Chinese Americans finally conquer the frontier of political exclusion. Third, with the passage of time, the political factionalism within the community will subside as Chinese Americans become less involved in the Taiwan-mainland split and less concerned over the old-new immigrant, Cantonese-Mandarin, and American-born–foreign-born conflicts. Their shared interest in and commitment to maintaining strong family ties, acquiring high quality education for their children, and promoting an environment conducive to economic stability and prosperity will take priority over intragroup or intraethnic conflict, making themselves less vulnerable to the divide-and-conquer strategy and more willing to fight for inclusion in city politics. Furthermore, the Asian American vision of multiculturalism, racial equality, and economic justice of the late 1960s and earlier 1970s is slowly resurfacing in civic affairs and appears to be poised to play a leading role in creating a city whose politics and policies are based on multiracial democracy and distributive justice. Promoting voter education and establishing new political organizations are the first order of business. Just as important is the development of new political leadership committed to inclusionary rather than exclusionary politics which, unfortunately have been the hallmark of the city of St. Francis to date. Hopefully, out of their experience of exclusion, Chinese Americans will soon engage in a new kind of politics, the politics of inclusion.

Part III

Latinos and the
Challenge of Politics

8
Cuban Americans in Miami Politics: Understanding the Cuban Model

Dario Moreno

The Cuban community in Miami is now entering its fourth decade in exile. During the last thirty years, Cubans have dominated the cultural, economic, and political life of Miami, transforming it from a middle-sized tourist center to a modern metropolis for business, politics, literature, and art. The arrival of the Cubans gave Miami the human skills and hemispheric connections necessary to exploit its natural advantage and to emerge as the capital of the Caribbean Basin.

This transformation allowed Cuban Americans to enjoy remarkable economic success in contrast to other immigrant and minority groups (Portes 1982: 91–111). Studies of the Cuban experience in the United States, with few exceptions, have been preoccupied with how Cubans have "made it" economically (Grenier 1992: 134). While Cuban Americans' economic success has attracted a great deal of attention, there has been a paucity of research on Cuban political empowerment.

The rapid growth of Cuban political power in the United States has been extraordinary. In one generation Cuban Americans have elected three congressmen, won nine Florida state house seats, three Florida state senate seats, the mayoralties of Miami, Coral Gables, Hialeah, and other communities in both Florida and in northern New Jersey. In metropolitan Miami (Dade County), Latinos have consolidated their status as the core electoral constituency. Hispanics have also strengthened their local political position due to a federal court ruling that overturned the Dade County's at-large election system. This prevented Hispanics and blacks from electing their "preferred candidates." In state politics, Cuban Republican legislators from Dade County have emerged as important swing votes in the enactment or defeat of major policies. On the issue of reapportionment, Cuban Republicans dramatically modified the Democratic majority's plans for congressional and state legislative district lines. South Florida's Latin voters demonstrated that in close statewide contests, their bloc vote can alter the outcome. Both George Bush in the 1992 presidential contest and Connie Mack in the 1988 Senate race squeaked past Democratic opponents due to the overwhelming support of Cubans.

Nationally, the election of three Cuban Americans to the U.S. House (two from South Florida and one from New Jersey), combined with the ongoing lobbying efforts of such groups as the Cuban American National Foundation and the Valladares Foundation, has helped shape federal policy toward Cuba. For example, the Cuban American National Foundation was able to win U.S. congressional approval of Radio and T.V. Marti and the Cuban Democracy Act, which tightens U.S. economic sanctions against Cuba. More generally, Cuban Americans have emerged as a group whose support is actively courted by a growing number of politicians from presidential candidates to members of Congress. Most important, the community has asserted its political clout, and its influence is recognized by powerful groups.

THE CUBAN EXPERIENCE IN THEORETICAL PERSPECTIVE

These political accomplishments occurred in a general context of Hispanic ascendancy in Miami's culture and business. In the 1980s Miami moved from being a tripartite city (whites, blacks, and Hispanics) to becoming a largely Hispanic city. Moreover, all political, demographic, and social indicators suggest that the 1990s will see more dramatic political gains for Cubans.

The political and socioeconomic success of the Hispanic population in Dade County raises an important question for Latino politics: Is the Cuban model of political and economic empowerment unique to the Miami population, or can it be replicated by other Latino and minority populations? The Cuban American political experience does not fit neatly into the current literature on minority politics. For example, in their study of the condition of Latinos and blacks in ten northern California cities, Browning, Marshall, and Tabb (1984) argue that minorities must participate in governing coalitions in order to exert influence on policy. Incorporation is crucial, that is, minority participation in a predominantly liberal (Democratic) coalition in city government. Such incorporation is itself dependent on electoral mobilization. The authors conclude that policy responsiveness is largely determined by levels of participation in coalitions (Browning et al. 1984: 21), and in a later book they identify a range of possibilities for minority incorporation: "At the lower end, we have no minority representation; then some representation, but on a council—an equal or leading role in a dominant coalition that is strongly committed to minority interests. The higher levels of political incorporation are likely to afford substantial influence or control over policy" (Browning et al. 1990: 9).

The conditions Cuban Americans faced in Dade County was substantially different from the experience that blacks and Chicanos faced in northern California. Their political empowerment has occurred despite the fact that Cuban Americans do not participate in electoral coalitions. Cubans have won elections only when Hispanics constitute a majority of the electorate and a super majority of the district's population. Moreover, Cubans have not allied themselves with liberal Democrats. When Cubans do participate in coalitions, they join conservative Republicans. The Cuban alliance with Republicans can be partly attributed to the fact that the Republican party has been historically the underutilized party in Florida. As with many of the immigrant groups who came to the United States in the late 1800s, the party of opportunity frequently is that party which is the weakest in the region. Like the Irish in Boston who seized control of the Democratic party's local machinery in the face of Yankee Republicanism, the Cubans have become dominant in Dade County's Republican party, providing an entrée for Cuban political activists and candidates. In the late 1970s, facing significantly less competition for party nominations, Cuban Americans as Republicans offered opposition in what had formerly been one-party contests.

The pattern articulated by more radical theories of minority politics also does not fit the Cuban model. Scholars point out that mainstream political scientists' views of minority politics are flawed because they do not acknowledge the historical situation of blacks and Hispanics (Garcia and de la Garza 1977; Morris 1975). Blacks and Hispanics have been treated as conquered peoples—blacks were an enslaved people, whereas Chicanos were defeated in the U.S. conquest of the Southwest in the Mexican War. Scholars contend that the long-term consequences of these historical conditions have been more important for Latinos and blacks. In order to explain the lowly sociopolitical status of blacks and Latinos, critical scholars modified theories of classic colonialism to the situation of American minorities (Hero 1992: 7). According to Garcia and de la Garza (1977: 63), an essential feature of internal colonialism is a "situation where one group of people dominate or exploit another, and, generally the relations occur between culturally different groups."

The internal colonialism model suggests that the minority group entered the dominant society involuntarily, that is, through a forced process. Blacks and Latinos, therefore, are not immigrants as are other ethnic groups. The present disadvantaged position of minorities is in large part the result of severe oppression. As Hero (1992: 18) argues, the oppression continues, although it is no longer overt and may no longer be directly supported by formal government policy. Indeed, the unique historical conditions of Latinos have created a two-tiered pluralism in the U.S. political system. Two-tiered pluralism describes the political situation for Latinos and other minorities in which equality is largely formal or procedural, but not substantive. Hero argues that this formal and marginalized inclusion exists in most facets of the political process.

The Cuban political experience in the United States does not fit the internal colonialism model. As Shorris (1992: 333) writes, "Cubans identify with the conquerors, not the conquered, the subject, not the object." As recent arrivals in the United States, Cubans have not suffered the historical discrimination and oppression described by the internal colonialism model. Moreover, as political exiles, they entered the United States voluntarily, not in a forced process as did African Americans and many Latinos. The unique historical experience of the Cuban community in Miami has led many scholars to conclude that the minority model, used in Mexican American and African American studies, is not appropriate for Cubans. Hero (1992: 27) suggests that the traditional pluralist model might be better suited for Cubans than his two-tiered pluralism theory. Others argue that the Cuban American model for political incorporation more closely resembles that of ethnic groups such as the Irish and the Italian.

Although the internal colonialism model overstates the level of discrimination, the traditional pluralist approach understates both formal and informal discrimination against Cuban Americans. Cubans face discrimination because of their racial backgrounds, language, and national origin. Even the most privileged white Cuban immigrants of 1961 confronted racism in the United States. In Miami in the early 1960s, it was common to find signs posted in apartment buildings that read "No Pets, No Kids, No Cubans" (Torres 1986). During the 1960s and 1970s, local Anglo politicians urged that new Cuban refugees be relocated outside of Dade County in an effort to prevent their political empowerment. Public resentment against Cuban Americans is reflected in a 1993 USA Today-CNN-Gallup poll which found that only 19 percent of the respondents believed that immigration from Cuba has benefited the United States (Sharp 1993).

Cubans have suffered much discrimination because of prejudice surrounding the issue of language. Dade County is the birthplace of the English Only movement, and during the 1980s hundreds of employment discrimination complaints filed with the Equal Employment Opportunity Commission (EEOC) involved language.

In part because of this discrimination and the deterioration of minorities' quality of life, the Cuban community faces many social problems. Although the average income for Cubans is higher than for other Hispanics, it is still significantly lower than the average income for a white family. Cuban families also suffer from one of the highest divorce rates in the country, and single females who head households have inadequate child care and do not receive equal pay for equal work. Of all Hispanics, Cubans as a group have the oldest average age. Lack of adequate medical care, inflation, and an increasingly hostile environment toward those who do not speak English combines to make life in the United States difficult for elderly Cubans.

The stereotype of the Cuban community in America as living in "golden exile" is vastly exaggerated. In trying to understand the role of Cuban Americans in the political system, it is useful to remember that they form a stigmatized class, that is, they are vulnerable to the same types of discrimination as other Hispanics and blacks although they do not suffer from the historical legacy of slavery or conquest. The Cuban model is thus a unique mixture of official privilege and official discrimination.

Another major factor contributing to the uniqueness of the Cuban model are the generous federal benefits which Cuban refugees received. First, the United States granted Cuban immigrants special status, allowing them to enter the United States without the restrictions imposed on other groups. The Cuban Adjustment Act of 1966 gives automatic residency to any Cuban who comes to the United States, be it a tourist who overstays his visa or someone who sneaks in, after only a year and a day after arriving in the United States. People fleeing any other country, even other communist countries, must submit clear proof that they are persecuted. For Cubans, escape is usually enough to guarantee permanent resettlement in the United States. No other group has benefited from such an exception for so long. The act also allows Cubans to apply for federal assistance (Supplemental Security Income [SSI], Food Stamps, Medicaid, etc.) immediately after becoming legal residents. More than 500,000 persons emigrated to the United States under the Cuban Adjustment Act (Perez 1992: 85). Moreover, the U.S. government invested over $1 billion in assistance for Cuban resettlement in the United States through the Cuban Refugee Program (Boswell 1994: 31).

The Cuban American strategy for overcoming the stigma of discrimination is also unique. The critical factor in explaining the political empowerment of Cuban Americans is geopolitical. The interaction of Cuban talent and ambition with the opportunity provided by Miami's political and economic underdevelopment allowed Cubans to overcome the obstacles created by the city's Anglo establishment. When they arrived in the United States, Cubans faced a weak and fragmented political establishment. Miami before the Cubans comprised poor blacks, sun-seeking retirees, newly arrived farmers from other parts of the South, and Jews from the Northeast.

The population of Miami had little connection with the rest of Florida and little in common among themselves, except perhaps the love of sun and sand. The weakness of the Miami power establishment was reflected in the struggle to create a strong county government. It was not until 1957 that the Metro Charter creating unified government in the county was approved by a mere 1,784 votes and only after bitter opposition from the jealously independent incorporated cities. The fight pitted downtown business and civic interests, which saw a pressing need for coordinated authority, against local residents bent on protecting their own interests. The lack of loyalties among the diverse population of Dade and the lack of a municipal identity beyond that of tourist resort made the city far more permeable to outside influences than other cities in the United States (Portes and Stepick 1993: 80–88).

The weakness and fragmentation of the Miami power elite provided an opportunity for the arriving Cubans, most of whom came from the upper and middle strata of Cuban society. As Portes and Stepick (1993: 88) point out, "The first exiles encountered a social and political order that, if not entirely amorphous, was a far cry from the consolidated power structures in places further north, and therefore far more permeable. As the *Miami Herald* and its allies struggle to build a serious city out of the assemblage of theme parks, the entire Cuban bourgeoisie arrived on the doorstep."

Through an examination of the conditions that prevailed in Miami—specifically, patterns of migration, socioeconomic conditions, and the existence of a self-sustained Cuban enclave—we can begin to understand how the Cubans took advantage of these geopolitical conditions to incorporate themselves into the American political system. It was the interaction of Cuban migration and the city of Miami that produced the Cuban success story.

THE CUBAN ENCLAVE

The Cuban community in Dade traces its modern roots to Fidel Castro's revolutionary victory on 1 January 1959. Castro initiated a process of revolutionary change that, in its rapidity and pervasiveness, alienated large sectors of the Cuban population (Fagen, Brody, and O'Leary 1968: 100–101). An exodus from the island was underway by 1960, and the principal destination was Miami. During the ensuing thirty years, more than 750,000 Cuban refugees arrived in the United States, most passing through Miami. By 1990, the census bureau put the number of Cubans living in the United States at 1,140,000. Most Cuban Americans settled in Miami or returned to the city after first settling in the North, and thus over half (561,868) of the Cuban American population lives in the Miami area. Miami now ranks third in the nation, behind Los Angeles and New York, in the size of its Hispanic population. When one considers that Miami has a substantially smaller overall population than either of these other two cities and that almost all of the Hispanic population has settled in the city since 1960, it is of little surprise that Miami has undergone the single most dramatic ethnic transformation of any major American city in this century.

According to the 1990 census, well over 60 percent of all Hispanics living in Florida reside in Dade County. The 1990 census shows that about 51 percent of the population of Dade County is Hispanic, a dramatic increase in the Latin population over the last ten years (see Table 8.1). It is estimated that during the 1980s over 300,000 Latin Americans moved into Dade County. At the beginning of the decade, the Mariel boat lift brought in 125,000 Cuban refugees, most of whom were poorer than the Cubans who had come earlier. Around the same time 70,000 Nicaraguans fleeing the Sandinista regime and civil war arrived. Colombians, Peruvians, Hondurans, Guatemalans—each escaping turmoil in their countries—soon followed, melding into Dade's flourishing Hispanic community and taking advantage of the economic space created by Cuban Americans during the 1980s. The total Hispanic population of Dade County is 953,407 of which about 55 percent is Cuban American (Table 8.2).

Cuban Americans are concentrated not only in Miami, but also in well-defined areas within Dade County, which has distinctive neighborhood settlement patterns. The traditional concentration of Hispanics is the Little Havana section, where

Table 8.1
Dade County Population by Ethnic Group

Group	Population	Percentage
Non-Hispanic Whites	585,607	32.21
Hispanics	953,407	51.22
Blacks	369,621	16.57

Source: U.S. Census Bureau 1993.

Table 8.2
Total Hispanic Population of Dade County

Group	Population
Cubans	561,868
Nicaraguans	72,244
Puerto Ricans	68,634
Colombians	53,582
Dominicans	23,475
Mexicans	23,193
Hondurans	18,102
Peruvians	16,452
Guatemalans	8,242
Others	101,908

Source: U.S. Census Bureau 1993.

Cuban refugees first settled in the early 1960s. Most of the 239,400 Cubans in Miami live in Little Havana, which is 70–90 percent Hispanic. The most rapid Hispanic growth (Cubans, Nicaraguans, and South Americans) is taking place in Sweetwater, Village Green, Westchester, and West Kendall (all in the western part of Dade), where Hispanics make up over 70 percent of the population. The third area of Hispanic, mostly Cuban, concentration is the northwest section of the county, which comprises the cities of Hialeah, Miami Springs, and their surrounding neighborhoods. These areas range from 55 to 85 percent Hispanic. In addition there is a sizable Hispanic, mostly Mexican, farm workers' community in the Homestead area.

These settlement patterns have facilitated the development of the Cuban enclave in Miami, with highly differentiated entrepreneurial activity (Perez 1992: 90–91). Portes and Bach (1985: 203) define an ethnic enclave as "a distinctive economic formation, characterized by the spatial concentration of immigrants who organize a variety of enterprises to serve their own ethnic market and the general population." They argue that the two fundamental conditions necessary for an economic enclave exist in Cuban Miami: (1) the presence of immigrants with sufficient capital either brought from Cuba or accumulated in the United States to create new opportunities for economic growth and (2) an extensive division of labor. Unlike other minorities, the Cuban middle class developed an elaborate network of successful small enterprises rather than relying on the public sector for upward mobility. These enterprises served as a source of employment for ensuing waves of Cuban immigrants.

Rieff (1987: 74) captured the dynamic of Cuban exile economics when he wrote that "the first wave of immigrants (those who came to Miami in the first year after the revolution) founded the businesses that employed the second wave (those who came to Miami between the mid-1960s and the mid-1970s); in turn both groups employed the third wave."

The proliferation of small businesses, primarily serving Latin tastes, is the foundation of Cuban economic and political power in Miami, which ranks first in terms of the number of Hispanic-owned businesses relative to the size of the Latin population (O'Hare 1987: 33). Miami has an estimated 55,712 Hispanic-owned businesses. Some 7,700 of minority firms were large enough to have paid workers, and those employed 34,504 people (Philips 1991). These Hispanic-owned firms in the enclave also generated nearly $3.8 billion in receipts in 1987 or about 15 percent of all receipts generated by Hispanic-owned firms in the United States (U.S. Census Bureau 1993: 28). Among Hispanics, Cubans have by far the highest business ownership rate: 63 businesses for every 1,000 Cuban Americans. This rate is more than three times that of Mexicans (19) and nearly six times that of Puerto Ricans (11) (Boswell 1994: 28).

The high rate of business ownership among Cubans results from the selective migration of former business owners and better-educated adults after the Cuban Revolution, as well as the heavy concentration of Cubans in the Miami area, which had a booming economy during the 1980s. That large, prosperous ethnic enclave provides Miami's Cubans with a potent small-business incubator. Cubans have also been successful in the founding of larger corporations. With about 5 percent of the country's Hispanic population, Miami has almost one-third of the largest Hispanic-owned businesses in the United States. Thirty-one of the top 100 Hispanic businesses in the United States are located in Dade County. Bacardi Imports of Miami, with total 1987 sales in excess of $500 million, is the nation's most profitable Hispanic-owned business. The Cuban presence and their economic successes have also attracted Latin American tourists and capital, and resulted in scores of multinational corporations locating their Latin American offices in Miami.

Perez (1992: 91) points out that the strong and diversified entrepreneurial activity is responsible for the enclave's most important overall feature: institutional completeness. Cubans in Miami can, if they wish, live out their lives within the ethnic community, the wide range of sales and services, including professional services, available within the community makes possible its completeness. There are 30 Latin-owned banks, 1,500 Latin lawyers, 8 Spanish-language radio stations, 2 Spanish-language TV stations (Hollman 1987a). Cubans can work in a Cuban-owned business, shop in a Cuban supermarket, visit a Cuban doctor or dentist, eat at Cuban restaurants, and avoid all interaction with the dominant society. Clearly, the success of Cubans in Miami was, to begin with at least, almost independent of that of the larger community.

Language-Based Discrimination

The existence of the enclave also serves to insulate Cuban Americans from the effects of language-based discrimination. The Cuban enclave has become a community where Spanish-speaking immigrants settled without fear of being at a serious disadvantage because of the language barrier. The 1990 census showed that Spanish has replaced English in Dade as the language most often spoken at home. Fifty percent of those surveyed in 1990 said they spoke Spanish at home, compared to 43 percent who spoke English. Moreover, the number of Dade county residents speaking Spanish at home was up from the 1980 census, which had 43 percent of the residents of Dade County speaking a language other than English at home.

The fear of language-based discrimination has served to unite Dade's Hispanic communities. English Only initiatives, at both the county and state levels, seem to be specifically aimed at Miami's Latin population and indicate an anti-Spanish backlash. In November 1980, Dade County voters approved an ordinance prohibiting the use of any language other than English in county business. This ordinance overturned a metro ordinance that had established Dade County as "officially bilingual." The petition drive and resultant referendum turned into a name-calling contest between Hispanic and non-Hispanic communities. A poll taken at the time of the referendum indicated that nearly half of those voting for the ordinance did so in order to express their "protest" and "frustration" with Dade's Latinos, not because they thought the ordinance was a good idea.

The relative prosperity of the Cuban community and their large numbers in cohesive and contiguous neighborhoods have safeguarded the Cuban American community to a large extent from the prejudice and discrimination that has plagued other Latin groups in the United States. For many in the Cuban community, Miami is essentially a Cuban city; indeed, only in Havana itself is the Cuban population so numerous. This image of Hispanics making Miami uniquely "theirs" is reflected in a survey which showed that Anglos in Miami feel as much or more discrimination than Hispanics.

The Cuban American community has also taken the lead in defending the right of the Spanish-speaking minority (majority) in Dade County through the development of its own antidiscrimination institutions and through quick reactions to discriminatory behavior. The Spanish American League Against Discrimination (SALAD) is particularly noteworthy for its vigilance. Spontaneous citizen action also plays a significant role. For example, in the aftermath of the passage of Proposition 11, a supermarket clerk was suspended for speaking Spanish in front of customers. The Hispanic community's reaction was swift and effective. The store in which the incident occurred received over twenty bomb threats; picket lines were set up, and the powerful Spanish-speaking radio stations began organizing a boycott of the supermarket chain. Less than forty-eight hours after the incident, the company announced that the clerk would be reinstated, the offending manager transferred out of Dade County, and a public apology issued to their Spanish-speaking customers. Afterward, the chain conducted an extensive campaign in the Spanish-speaking media to regain their share of the Hispanic market. The Hispanic communities' vigilance against language-based discrimination was reactivated when news broke in April 1992 that a personnel agency refused to refer people with Spanish accents to job openings at a Miami bank.

TRIPARTITE POLITICS

The rising dominance of the Cuban American community in Miami has created tension between Hispanics and non-Hispanic groups in Dade. As Rieff (1987: 145) suggests, "It is difficult to live in someone else's capital city, particularly if you were there first." This raises the most troublesome problem of living in Miami: in-terethnic relations. As Portes and Stepick (1993: xii) point out, "the regrouped Cuban bourgeoisie not only redefined the character of the city, but also prompted other ethnic communities—native blacks and whites included—to cast their identities in sharper relief."

Dade County is profoundly divided by the competing interests of three distinct and separate ethnic groups. The black, Hispanic, and non-Hispanic white com-munities all have different social and economic interests. The division of Dade along ethnic lines has made Miami one of the contemporary symbols of racial upheaval in America; the deep ethnic tensions are illustrated by the four race riots in the 1980s. These cleavages have led to the development of tripartite politics in Miami: that is, ethnic factors dominate over all others in Dade politics, as indicated by the fact that blacks, Hispanics, and non-Hispanic whites each live in compact and contiguous neighborhoods, are politically cohesive, vote in blocs, and are politically polarized from each other.

The Hispanic-Anglo conflict has its roots in the replacement of the old, weak Anglo establishment with the exiled Cuban bourgeoisie. This tension between Hispanic and Anglo is often manifested in terms of the language issue. Non-Hispanics believe that Cubans, unwilling to learn English, seek to impose Spanish and their culture on native Americans. These feelings are reinforced by the nature of the large Cuban enclave in which Spanish is the lingua franca of commercial interaction. Enos Schera, a leader of the Citizens of Dade United, which led the fight for the 1980 English Only initiative, expressed Anglo reaction when he said that "Miami is a pressure cooker and they [Cubans] are hell-bent on making Americans learn Spanish. I have nothing against the Cubans, [but] the Cubans come here and don't learn our language. The message is 'When in Rome, you do as the Cubans.' It's total insanity. It's as though we are the foreigners" (DeQuine 1990: 1A).

Anti-Cuban feelings reached a high point in 1980 during the Mariel boat lift as the spectacle of 125,000 Cuban refugees arriving in Miami distressed the already besieged non-Hispanic communities. The drama of thousands of Miami Cubans chartering boats to rescue their family from the Castro regime created the percep-tion that Miami was being overwhelmed by a flood of Hispanics. Adding to the anxiety of the non-Hispanic community was the claim by the Castro government that over 45 percent of the new arrivals had criminal backgrounds. Castro claimed that the refugees from Mariel were "the scum of the country—antisocial, homo-sexuals, drug addicts, and gamblers, who are welcome to leave Cuba if any country will have them" (Portes and Stepick 1993: 21). The *Miami Herald* dutifully parroted the concerns of civic leaders and repeatedly castigated Cuban Americans for their eagerness to rescue relatives left in Cuba and shrilly echoed Castro's charac-terization of the new refugees (Portes and Stepick 1993: 23).

The reaction of the *Herald* to the Mariel boat lift backfired. It reinforced the deep cleavages between Cubans and the rest of the city and created a legacy of distrust between the Cuban community and the city's principal newspaper. This tension was also reflected in the feud between the president of the Cuban American National Foundation, Jorge Mas Canosa, and the publisher of the *Herald*, David Lawrence, over the *Herald's* editorial policy.

Moreover, Mariel destroyed the image of Cubans in the United States and, in passing, destroyed the image of Miami itself. According to an article in the *St. Petersburg Times* (Hollman 1987b), the lingering effects of Mariel were reflected when radio talk show host Taffy McCallum asked Anglos to call in with nice things to say about Hispanics. No Anglos did. Nasty things? That was another story. "They brought all the crime, all the crooks," charged one woman, becoming more and more enraged about Hispanics as she spoke. "They . . . They . . . They're animals."

In response to the growing Cuban presence in Miami, many Anglos simply left for whiter pastures in the North. "White flight," proclaimed newspaper headlines and radio talk show hosts. Non-Hispanic whites have, indeed, moved north: to suburbs in Broward County, retirement villages in Palm Beach, Orlando, or Tampa. In contrast to blacks and Hispanics, the non-Hispanic white population is rapidly declining, falling from about 80 percent of the county total in 1960, to less than 33 percent in 1990 (see Table 8.1). Non-Hispanic whites have left because they fear crime, are searching for opportunity, and can afford more house for the dollar someplace else. Or because they can't speak the language anymore. "It's quite clear among those who live in this place and follow what goes on that some non-Hispanic whites have moved out of Dade County because none of their neighbors speaks English," says University of Miami geographer Ira Sheskin. "Where people feel problems is when they walk into a store . . . and feel like they're in a foreign country" (Hollman 1987a).

Despite their decreasing numbers, non-Hispanic whites were able to retain considerable political power until 1992 by maintaining control of Dade's delegation to both Washington, D.C. and Tallahassee. Although they represent less than one-third of the county's population, non-Hispanic whites until the 1992 reapportionment comprised ten out of the twenty members of the Dade delegation to the state house, controlled three out of the seven state senate seats, and held three out of the four seats to the U.S. Congress. Fresh wounds were opened between the emerging Cuban elite and the old political establishment during the bitter struggle over redistricting in Florida. Cuban politicians successfully argued in court and in the legislature for greater Hispanic representation based on the Voting Rights Act. The liberal political establishment initially rejected this claim by arguing that Cubans were not minorities because of their socioeconomic status and thus not entitled to protection under the Voting Rights Act. "The Cubans have ridden on the backs of Mexicans and Puerto Ricans to claim privileges which, as the only middle-class émigrés of any size that we have had in this country, they don't need," said Jack Gordon, a state senator from Miami Beach, who chaired the Florida State senate reapportionment committee (Rother 1992). This feeble and ultimately unsuccessful attempt by the Anglo political establishment to hold on to power served only to deepen the rift between the old guard and the emerging Cuban community.

Black Miamians are often the odd men out in the contest between the emerging Cubans and the Anglo establishment for political hegemony. African Americans are the most disadvantaged of the three major ethnic groups in Dade County. According to estimates by the Dade County Planning Department, only one percent of local businesses belong to blacks. The average median family income for blacks was $20,209, in contrast to $23,446 for Hispanics (Cubans, the most affluent of Latinos, averaged $26,770), whereas whites enjoyed the highest at $35,977. Blacks are also more likely to feel the effects of discrimination. According to one poll, 34 percent of Miami's black community said that they or someone they know faced discrimination in seeking a job or promotion (see Table 8.3). Education for blacks is also far below the standard for Hispanics and non-Hispanic whites. According to the Dade County Public Schools, six out of the seven senior high schools designated as deficient in 1990 because of low test scores were predominately black. Black dropout rates were the highest at 8.9 percent, compared to 7.2 percent for Hispanic students and 5.5 percent for whites (Dade County School Board 1991: 62).

Moreover, Miami is still a segregated city. The gulf between African Americans and other Miamians, as well as the effects of lingering racism, was clearly revealed in a 1987 poll which showed that 42 percent of the Anglos and 45 percent of the Hispanics live in neighborhoods where there are no blacks. Blacks in Miami tend

Table 8.3
South Florida Racial and Ethnic Attitudes

People who said that they or someone they know has faced discrimination in seeking a job or promotions.

Group	Percent Facing Discrimination
Anglos	14
Blacks	34
Hispanics	13

People who said that another group would discriminate against them.

Group	Percent Facing Discrimination
Anglos blaming Hispanics	30
Hispanics blaming Anglos	28
Blacks blaming Hispanics	32
Blacks blaming Anglos	40

Source: Miami Herald 1989.

to live in fairly confined neighborhoods, segregated from both Cubans and Anglos. Black settlement patterns have had a profoundly negative effect on political mobilization. Historically, due to both the legacy of Southern racism and the conscious placement of some black neighborhoods in the unincorporated areas of the county, blacks traditionally played an insignificant role in local politics. Although Miami has always had a substantial black population, and while there has been some black resettlement in other Dade municipalities (especially Opa Locka and Florida City), over 60 percent of black Miamians live in unincorporated sections of the county. The extent to which this settlement pattern undermines black influence in local government and complicates grass-roots organizing, stands as a formidable barrier to political mobilization. These factors, along with the at-large county (until 1993) and Miami elections, combine in compounding the obstacles faced by blacks in shaping public policy in Dade.

Miami's black community has erupted in violence four times during the 1980s. The black neighborhood of Liberty City experienced one of the most violent riots of the century in May 1980, and Overtown experienced several nights of disorder in December 1982, in the spring of 1984, and again in January 1989. The immediate causes for these riots were the shootings by Miami police of black residents, but on a deeper level these disturbances indicate the degree of frustration that the black community feels for several reasons: the small number of black officers on the police force, the violence against black citizens, the absence of black-owned businesses—indeed, poverty, unemployment, ethnic tensions, and powerlessness in general.

With the boycott of the Miami tourism and hospitality industry in 1990, the black community adopted a more sophisticated tactic to express its grievances against the non-Latin white and Hispanic elites. The event that instigated this black movement was the less than dignified treatment given the African National Congress (ANC) leader, Nelson Mandela, when he addressed a labor conference in south Florida in June 1990. Winnie and Nelson Mandela were not officially greeted or honored by any elected official in Dade County—a response to Mandela's recognition of Fidel Castro and Yasser Arafat, both of whom supported the ANC's anti-apartheid struggle. The protesters of Boycott Miami-Coalition for Progress went far beyond formal protest; they attacked the economic lifeline of Miami, the tourism industry, hoping to redress the grievances of the African American community. The boycott, which according to Greater Miami Convention and Visitor Bureau (GMCVB) cost as much as $50 million in revenues, reflected the widely held view in the black community that Cubans and Anglos need to stop ignoring blacks. Robert L. Steinback, a black columnist for the *Miami Herald*, held that the outcome would determine the city's future: "Miami will in fact evolve into a hopelessly fractured city if the black community is not given clear reassurance that it is a welcome and vital part of the economic, political, and social environment in south Florida" (Sewell 1990: 1A). W. T. Smith, the leader of the boycott, agrees: "What you're seeing is the kind of friction that is necessary to mold together three communities who really have not had much time or interest in working together. Let's face it, it's going to be the Cubans' town. They have a tremendous stake in seeing that Miami becomes a bright and shining example" (Sewell 1990).

POLITICAL COHESIVENESS

Not only do Cuban Americans live in compact and contiguous neighborhoods, but they also display a remarkable level of political cohesiveness (see Table 8.4). The anticommunist ideology of the Miami exile community has attracted national and international attention. The clearly articulated goal of the Cuban community is the overthrow of Fidel Castro in Cuba and the establishment of a democratic government. All Cuban American elected officials and all mainline Cuban American organizations believe that compromise and dialogue with the Castro regime are impossible. Cuban Americans oppose by a four-to-one margin the establishment of diplomatic relations with their homeland. Anticommunism and anti-Castroism are givens in the Miami Cuban community (Perez 1992).

Table 8.4
Cuban Americans' Attitudes Toward Foreign Policy on Cuba

	Percent in Agreement	
Issue	1993	1991
Favor current U.S. policy (no diplomatic relations and no trade) toward Cuba	80	80
Favor tightening the U.S. trade embargo	85	86
Favor military action by the exile community against Cuba	73	76
Favor a U.S. invasion of Cuba	60	63
Favor U.S. support for and internal rebellion to overthrow the Castro government	77	75
Favor increased international economic pressure on Cuba	87	85
Favor negotiations with the Cuban government to allow family members to travel to the United States	77	75
Favor negotiations with the Cuban government to allow regular telephone communications with the island	52	62
Favor starting negotiations with the Cuban government to facilitate a transition to a democracy	56	62
Favor a national dialogue between the exile community, the Cuban government, and Cuban dissidents	43	41

Source: Florida International University 1991–1993.

This anticommunism has been underscored by a series of public flaps in the Cuban community over the right of Cubans and non-Cubans to dissent from this anti-Castro consensus. America's Watch (1992: 2) issued a report condemning the exile community for its lack of tolerance toward views that do not conform to the predominant ideology of uncompromising hostility to the Castro regime. The report concluded that "many anti-Castro Miami Cubans have a good deal in common with the regime they loathe. Freedom of expression suffers, much as it does in other countries of Latin America—or anywhere in the world—where violence rules."

One of the most infamous incidents of intolerance occurred in 1986 when 2,000 angry Hispanics, mostly Cuban, attacked 200 anti-Contra demonstrators at Miami's Torch of Friendship monument. The Cubans pelted the anti-Contra rally with eggs, rocks, and an occasional glass bottle, forcing Miami riot police to bus the smaller group of demonstrators out of the area. The event attracted numerous public officials, the vast majority of whom sided with the counterdemonstrators. A Cuban radio station broadcast live from the site. The mayor of Miami added to the political tension by referring to Marxist groups in the anti-Contra rally and telling the mostly Cuban crowd that "[u]nfortunately they have a right to be on the other side of the street" (Stack and Warren 1990: 629).

However, the anticommunism issue has by no means been limited to confrontations over substantive foreign policy questions. Frequently, symbolic politics and otherwise nonpolitical events become the forums for such conflict. Anticommunist fervor has been a regular part of municipal government deliberations, campaigns for local office, and cultural events. Plays by Cuban-born playwright Dolores Prida and performances by Latino musical stars, such as Denise de Kalafe and Ruben Blades, have been canceled in Miami because these individuals have visited or performed in Cuba.

The Cuban community's anticommunism is an important factor in explaining the community's alliance with the Republican party, which has a hard-line foreign policy rhetoric (see Table 8.5).

While preoccupation with Latin American Communism generally and the Castro regime specifically still stands as a core political issue in the community, it is no longer the singular Cuban issue it once was. For example, survey data shows

Table 8.5
Party Loyalty by National Origin (percentages)

	Mexican	Puerto Rican	Cuban	Anglo
Always Republican	13.4	13.3	63.4	24.8
Former Republican	1.9	3.8	0.7	4.4
Always Democrat	77.3	79.5	22.2	57.3
Former Democrat	7.3	3.4	13.7	13.7

Source: Latino National Political Survey, in de la Garza et al. 1992: 127.

that over three fourths of Cuban Americans are concerned with politics more in the United States than in Cuba. Only 4 percent of Cubans identify more with homeland politics than with U.S. politics, and 20 percent are equally concerned with both Cuban and U.S. politics.

Cuban voting patterns and loyalties to the Republicans are contingent not only on an anti-Castro foreign policy or the enormous popularity of Ronald Reagan, but also on the Republican party's ability and willingness to address other political, social, and economic needs of the Cuban community.

Cuban American politics can no longer be solely understood in terms of militant exile politics. A more traditional brand of American ethnic politics now emerges. The significance and force of anti-Castro symbolism is still alive, but it has been combined with more mundane concerns for jobs, domestic social services, and other substantive policy concerns.

Not only are Cuban Americans interested in electing staunch anticommunists; they also expect their elected officials to serve the interests of their community. This tension between the old politics of exile and the new ethnic politics has created a two-dimensional voting pattern among Cubans. For offices that have great symbolic power, such as president and U.S. Senator, exile politics is still quite evident. For many state and local offices, however, ethnic politics and concern with servicing the community become dominant. Although this metaphor of a dual political identity within the community is admittedly too neat to apply literally, it does help to explain why Cubans do not vote uniformly Republican in all elections. Below the presidential level, especially in congressional elections, where local issues begin to take precedent over foreign policy issues, some Democratic candidates have demonstrated an ability to attract Cuban support.

THE CUBAN MODEL

The Cuban experience in Miami is unique. The Cuban political model has been shaped by the demographic and geographic conditions of Dade County. The Cuban economic enclave would have been extremely difficult to establish without access to Latin American capital. Moreover, the rapidity and large numbers of the Cuban migration to the United States, combined with their concentration in Dade County, made them politically relevant in a short time. Similarly, tripartite politics and the anticommunist ideology of the Cuban exile community have created an extremely cohesive political community.

REFERENCES

America's Watch. 1992. Dangerous dialogue: Attacks on freedom of expression in Miami's Cuban exile community. America's Watch 4, no. 7 (August): 2.

Boswell, Thomas D. 1994. A demographic profile of Cuban Americans. Miami: Cuban American National Council.

Browning, Rufus, Dale Rogers Marshall, and David Tabb. 1984. Protest is not enough. Berkeley: University of California Press.

————, eds. 1990. *Racial politics in American cities*. New York: Longman.

Dade County School Board. 1991. *Annual report 1991*. Miami: Dade County Public Schools.

de la Garza, Rodolfo O., Louis DeSipio, F. Chris Garcia, John A. Garcia, and Angelo Falcón. 1992. *Latino voice: Mexican, Puerto Rican, and Cuban perspectives on American politics*. Boulder, CO: Westview Press.

DeQuine, Jeanne. 1990. Diverse ethnic groups remain enemies in Miami. Reuters news service, 3 July.

Fagen, Richard R., Richard A. Brody, and Thomas J. O'Leary. 1968. *Cubans in exile: Disaffection and the revolution*. Stanford: Stanford University Press.

Florida International University. 1991–1993. Florida Poll, July 1993 and March 1991.

Garcia, Chris, and Rodolfo O. de la Garza. 1977. *The Chicano political experience*. North Scituate, MA: Duxbury Press.

Grenier, Guillermo. 1992. The Cuban-American labor movement in Dade County: An emerging immigrant working class. In *Miami now! Immigration, ethnicity, and social change*, edited by Guillermo Grenier and Alex Stepick. Gainesville: University of Florida Press.

————, eds. 1990. *Racial politics in American cities*. New York: Longman.

Hero, Rodney. 1992. *Latinos and the U.S. political system: Two-tiered pluralism*. Philadelphia: Temple University Press.

Hollman, Lurie. 1987a. Miami moving to a Latin beat. *St. Petersburg Times*, 19 July, 3A.

————. 1987b. Taking sides in politics: Ethnic loyalty shapes government in Miami. *St. Petersburg Times*, 19 July.

Miami Herald. 1989. Miami Herald-Channel 6 Poll, 27 February.

Morris, Milton. 1975. *The politics of black America*. New York: Harper & Row.

O'Hare, William. 1987. Best metros for Hispanic businesses. *American Demographic* (November): 33.

Perez, Lisandro. 1992. Cuban Miami. In *Miami now! Immigration, ethnicity, and social change*, edited by Guillermo Grenier and Alex Stepick. Gainesville: University of Florida Press.

Philips, Michael M. 1991. Minority businesses flourish in south Florida. *San Diego Union Tribune*, 8 October, 5A.

Portes, Alejandro. 1982. Immigrants' attainment: An analysis of occupation and earnings among Cuban exiles in the United States. In *Social structure and behavior: Essays in honor of William Hamilton Sewell*, edited by R. M. Hauser, 91–111. New York: Academic Press.

Portes, Alejandro, and Robert L. Bach. 1985. *Latin journey: Cuban and Mexican immigrants in the United States*. Berkeley: University of California Press.

Portes, Alejandro, and Alex Stepick. 1993. *City on the edge: The transformation of Miami*. Berkeley: University of California Press.

Rieff, David. 1987. *Going to Miami*. Boston: Little Brown.

Rother, Larry. 1992. A black-Hispanic struggle over Florida redistricting. *New York Times*, 30 May, 4A.

Sewell, Dan. 1990. Cubans have transformed Miami into an island of opportunity. *Los Angeles Times*, 23 December, sec. A, p. 2.

Sharp, Deborah. 1993. For Cubans, success, conflict. *USA Today*, 15 July, 8A.

Shorris, Earl. 1992. *Latinos: A biography of the people*. New York: W. W. Norton.

Stack, John F., and Christopher Warren. 1990. Ethnicity and politics of symbolism in Miami's Cuban community. *Cuban Studies* 20: 11–29.

Torres, Maria. 1986. Cuban exiles are not a bit golden. *Chicago Tribune*, 15 November, C11.
U.S. Census Bureau. 1993. *Hispanics in America*. Washington, DC: Government Printing
Office.

9

The Effects of Primordial Claims, Immigration, and the Voting Rights Act on Mexican American Sociopolitical Incorporation

Rodolfo O. de la Garza

This chapter proposes a new framework for analyzing how that part of the United States population with Mexican origins is incorporating itself into the larger society and its social polity. The political significance of this incorporation is evidenced by an alarm with which contemporary American racial and ethnic politics are being described (Schlesinger 1992). As the nation's second largest minority, Latinos are increasingly the focus of this debate. The theoretical importance of the issue is manifested in the intensity with which the major paradigms used to analyze Mexican incorporation are critiqued (Chavez 1991; Skerry 1993). This analysis has many implications for urban politics in that the issues that most affect Hispanics, an overwhelmingly urban population, are manifested primarily in our cities.

I focus on this population because the experiences of native-born and immigrant Mexicans are fundamental to any attempt to explain how the nation's Hispanics relate to the American polity. Because almost two thirds of the nation's Hispanic population are Mexicans deeply rooted in American society, the experiences of this group define the model for the evolving relationships between Latinos and the society at large. That is, even though the factors that explain the establishment of other Hispanic communities in the United States differ from those that explain the Mexican-origin experience, once such communities are established, their relationship is strongly affected by the space that the Mexican-origin population occupies in the nation's social and political processes.

The Mexican-origin population consists of immigrants and native-born citizens. I use the term "Mexican Americans" when referring to those who are born in the United States, and distinguish them from Mexican immigrants, foreign-born residents, and naturalized citizens. The term "Mexicans" will be used to designate the combined population.

THEORETICAL MODELS OF INCORPORATION

At present, two theoretical models dominate the debate regarding the social and political incorporation of Mexicans into the United States. The first, based on the experience of European immigrants, has been recently resurrected by neoconservative analysts (Chavez 1991; Skerry 1993) even though specialists on Mexicans have long questioned its utility. The second, which was central to the internal colonialism model, equates the experience of Mexicans and other Latinos with that of African Americans (Acuña 1972). The most recent academic version of this argument, albeit in somewhat modified form, is that offered by Rodney Hero (1992) in his *Latinos and the U.S. Political System.* Policy advocates such as the National Council de la Raza also implicitly employ it over the objections of neoconservative analysts (Kamaski and Yzaguirre 1991; Chavez 1991; Skerry 1993).

At first glance, both models seem valid because Mexicans in the United States share some of the same experiences that both European immigrants and African Americans have had: Like African Americans, Mexicans have been the victims of racial discrimination, and like, for example, the Italians and Irish, most come from immigrant stock. Closer inspection, however, indicates that the similarities Mexicans share with European immigrants or African Americans, are more superficial than substantive.

In comparison to African Americans, for example, the racial status of Mexicans has never been clear (San Miguel 1987). There is no doubt that Mexicans have experienced intense and widespread racially based discrimination. It is equally clear, however, that this discrimination has varied greatly because of many factors including class and religion (Moore 1970; Acuña 1972). Thus, even in Texas where anti-Mexican sentiment was most virulent, Mexicans did not experience the virtually universal discrimination African Americans have experienced. For example, as measured by indicators such as residential segregation, Mexicans are much less isolated from mainstream society than African Americans (Massey and Denton 1993). Furthermore, the most segregated Mexican neighborhoods are populated by immigrants, whereas according to the Latino National Public Survey, second- and third-generation Mexican Americans are much more likely to reside in mixed neighborhoods. Mexican American political disenfranchisement has also been significantly less severe and extensive (de la Garza and DeSipio 1993).

The comparison between Mexican immigrants and those from European countries is equally fallacious for several reasons. First, the presence of Mexicans in American society precedes immigration. Even though Mexicans numbered fewer than 100,000 when what is now the Southwest became American territory, the region is defined by an indelible Mexican culture. This has allowed Mexican immigrants, whether they came in 1850 or 1994, to join the heirs of Mexicans who lived in the region prior to 1848 in making what is in effect a primordial claim on the Southwest. Participating in this claim allows Mexican immigrants to develop a unique psychological relationship to American society, one which no other immigrants can share. This claim, it must be emphasized, is not irredentist (de la Garza and Vargas 1992). It is, instead, a claim about the inherent right to participate fully in American society while retaining the right to maintain Mexican cultural practices. It should be noted that this right may be exercised less vigorously than it is defended (Grebler, Moore, and Guzman 1970; de la Garza et al. 1992).

Second, European immigrants came in one major wave, whereas Mexican immigration has been continuous during the twentieth century. Third, prior to the 1970s, when the civil rights movement took hold in the Southwest, anti-Mexican discrimination was so pervasive and institutionalized that Mexicans experienced virtually none of the intergenerational mobility that characterized the experience of the European immigrants (Fuchs 1990; Grebler, Moore, and Guzman 1970). Although the Irish had taken over Tammany Hall after fifty years and were moving up the economic ladder as well, seventy-five years after the signing of the Treaty of Guadeloupe Hidalgo, the killing of Mexicans in Texas was so commonplace as not to arouse attention (Skerry 1993: 22). Thus, while European immigrants experienced upward mobility, Mexican economic and political elites were displaced, and Mexicans as a group experienced downward mobility. This discrimination began to change after 1970 when barriers preventing Mexican mobility fell under heavy assault. The 1975 extension of the Voting Rights Act (VRA) to the Southwest, for example, dramatically increased the opportunity for Mexicans to enjoy greater social and political mobility.

In addition to overstating the historical similarities between Mexicans and either African Americans or European immigrants, the currently dominant models used to analyze Mexican incorporation ignore the extent to which social and political relationships between Mexicans and society and the polity have been fundamentally altered since 1975. The remainder of this chapter examines the factors that distinguish the Mexican experience in the pre- and post-VRA periods.

THE MEXICAN EXPERIENCE IN THE PRE- AND POST-VRA PERIOD

The VRA changed the rules of society and politics in the Southwest. It helped to institutionalize a new generation of Mexican American organizations—the Mexican American Legal Defense and Education Fund (MALDEF), the Southwest Voter Registration and Education Fund (SVRP), and the Southwest Council of La Raza (which would later become the National Council de la Raza). Not only have these and other organizations blossomed since 1975, but they have also been instrumental in creating the climate that led to the 1975 VRA extension.

More significantly, institutions such as these have used the VRA and related legislation and judicial decisions—for example, *Lau vs. Nichols* (414 U.S. 563 [1974]), *Keyes vs. School District No. 1, Denver* (Colorado 462 F.2d 1058, 1060 [1973]), and *Plyler vs. Doe* (458 U.S. 1131 [1982])—to expand the opportunities available to all Mexicans. This has been accomplished in two steps. Thanks directly to the VRA, the number and autonomy of Mexican American voters increased substantially, and this increase has resulted in a sharp rise in the number of Mexican Americans elected or appointed to office. Also, working under the cover of VRA-era policies and supported by a mobilized and growing Mexican American electorate, these new officials used their positions to defend Mexican American interests (Polinard and Wrinkle 1988). Their efforts have significantly reduced the systemic discrimination against Mexicans and expanded dramatically the educational, employment, and political opportunities available to them.

As this more open environment evolved, the most recent and perhaps most prolonged wave of immigration began. Between 1970 and 1980, the Mexican population increased by 3,510,000, 38 percent of whom were immigrants. Between 1980 and 1990, immigrants contributed 34 percent of the increase of 4,755,000. From 1970 until 1980, the foreign-born share of the Mexican population increased from 18 to 26 percent; between 1980 and 1990, it increased to 32 percent. Moreover, the overall contribution of this wave of immigrants to the growth of the Mexican population is substantially greater than these numbers suggest because many of these immigrants had children after they entered the United States. The National Latino Immigrant Survey (NLIS) found that 94 percent of the households of legal resident Mexican immigrants include children born in the United States (Pachon and DeSipio 1994).

In addition to increasing the nation's Mexican population, these immigrants altered its composition. However motivated and industrious they may have been, they came with little education and low job skills. NLIS found that 67 percent of legal resident Mexican immigrants had less than a high school education, and 55.2 percent had less than eight years of school. Not surprisingly, almost 60 percent became laborers or service providers in their first jobs (Pachon and DeSipio 1994). This wave of immigrants greatly expanded that segment of the Mexican population which was the least prepared to take advantage of new opportunities resulting from the combination of changing attitudes (as evidenced by the enactment of new legislation) and the increased capabilities of Mexicans to combat discrimination. Additionally, these immigrants also were unprepared for the accelerated restructuring of the labor market of the 1980s (Blank 1994).

Prior to this period, immigration had a much different impact. Before the VRA was enacted, anti-Mexican discrimination was so pervasive that there was little intergenerational mobility either between the first and second generation, or between the second and subsequent generations. Thus, comparing data from 1970 and 1980, one researcher concluded that the results of his analysis do not

> support the argument that the low socioeconomic status of the Hispanic population is a reflection of Hispanic immigrant socioeconomic status. Instead, they support the argument that the Hispanic native-born and immigrant are relatively the same. The similarities between these two groups suggest that native-born Hispanics, and children of both native born Hispanics and immigrants, are not undergoing the process of incorporation. (Valenzuela 1990–1991: 65)

As is shown, this pattern changes in the post-VRA period. Not all Mexicans are equally situated to take advantage of the changes effected in the post-VRA period. Those who have benefited least are those who, regardless of citizenship, were of such an age that they had already had their life's chances impaired by low education attainment. That includes Mexican Americans born before 1950 who were the victims of pervasive discrimination in education and employment. It also includes Mexican immigrants of any age who came and continue to come as poorly educated teenagers and adults.

Those who benefited most are those Mexican Americans young enough to partake in the new opportunities that began to become available in the late 1970s, especially those who came as children and completed their precollegiate schooling after 1975. Older Mexican immigrants, those who came as adults with little education, found fewer opportunities of personal consequence. In all cases, of course, the extent to which any Mexican children benefited from these changes also varied as a function of familial socioeconomic characteristics. Because education is the best predictor of an individual's income, social status, and rates of political participation, the changes in Mexican American education attainment realized in the post-VRA period are therefore particularly significant (see Table 9.1).

Data from the Latino National Political Survey illustrate dramatic differences for older groups regardless of nativity. Mexicans sixty-five and over, whether immigrants or third generation, were uneducated. Even though Mexican Americans were somewhat more educated than immigrants, over 60 percent of second- and third-generation Mexican Americans had fewer than eight years of school. Twenty-five percent of whites in this age group were similarly educated. This pattern suggests the extent to which anti-Mexican discrimination historically did not differentiate between Mexican immigrants and Mexican Americans.

This similarity across generations regardless of nativity decreases with age, however. Second- and third-generation Mexican Americans in the age bracket 41–64 are much more educated than Mexican immigrants. Yet, relative to whites in this age group, they remain undereducated. Twenty percent of Anglos in this cohort had less than twelve years of school, compared to 51 and 63 percent, respectively, of second- and third-generation Mexicans. This pattern indicates that while they were developing into socially distinct groups, the gap between Mexican Americans and Mexicans remained rather constant.

More significant, however, and illustrative of how the VRA has affected Mexican American education opportunities, is the difference between VRA age cohorts, pre-VRA cohorts and whites. The VRA cohorts, those in the age brackets 18–24 and 25–40, in both the second and third generations, are much more educated than the pre-VRA cohorts; indeed, those 18–24 are less likely to have 0–8 years of school than whites of the same age. Whites between 18–40, however, are much more likely to have post–high school education than Mexican Americans of this age. Nonetheless, second- and third-generation Mexican Americans in the 25–40 cohort are 1.82 and 2.75 times, respectively, more likely than the 41–64 pre-VRA cohort to have post-high school education. Because of the small number of second generation VRA cohort cases, however, these percentages should be cautiously interpreted.

This pattern is also evident regarding occupational status (see Table 9.2). While approximately 50 percent of the VRA age cohorts of the second and third

Table 9.1
Education by Ethnicity, VRA Cohorts, Age, and Nativity

VRA Cohorts	Age	Grades 0–8	Grades 9–12	High School Graduates	Post High School	No.
Mexicans	18–24	36.5%	15.5%	42.6%	5.4%	148
1st generation	25–40	58.7%	9.0%	25.4%	7.0%	402
	41–65	79.9%	6.3%	12.1%	1.7%	147
	66+					
Mexicans						
2nd generation	18–24	2.6%	28.2%	61.5%	7.7%	39
VRA cohorts	25–40	15.4%	21.2%	42.3%	21.2%	52
pre-VRA	41–65	49.2%	14.3%	28.6%	7.9%	63
cohorts	66+	62.5%	21.9%	12.5%	3.1%	32
Mexicans						
3rd generation	18–24	3.5%	32.7%	60.2%	3.5%	113
VRA cohorts	25–40	7.1%	24.8%	53.0%	15.0%	266
pre-VRA	41–65	29.5%	21.2%	41.1%	8.2%	146
cohorts	66+	64.7%	20.6%	11.8%	2.9%	34
Anglos	18–24	6.5%	21.7%	65.2%	6.5%	46
non-VRA	25–40	0.0%	11.6%	55.5%	32.9%	146
cohorts	41–65	7.1%	12.9%	52.1%	27.9%	140
	66+	25.0%	17.0%	50.0%	8.0%	112

Source: Latino National Political Survey 1989; 1990

generations hold the highest status, only 24 and 39 percent, respectively, of the second and third generation pre-VRA cohorts hold these positions. Whites 18–24 are slightly less likely to hold the highest status jobs than comparably aimed Mexican Americans, while those between 25 and 40 are somewhat more likely to hold such positions. Again, the difference in job categories of white and Mexican Americans between 41 and 64 years old is particularly notable. Immigrants between 18 and 64 are unlikely to hold these high status jobs.

Congressional Acknowledgment of Discrimination

The VRA changes resulted when Congress acknowledged the systematic discrimination Mexicans had experienced since 1848, the impact of which was exacerbated by the primordial claim that Mexican Americans as a people had rights emanating from their having established a society in the Southwest that was incorporated into the United States as a result of the United States–Mexico War. Those rights included not only all the rights of citizens but also other rights as codified in the Treaty of Guadelupe Hidalgo. The violation of these rights was

Table 9.2
Occupation by Ethnicity, VRA Cohorts, Age, and Nativity

VRA Cohorts	Age	Manager Tech.	Services	Farm/ Forestry	Precision Operators	Un-employed	No.
Mexicans	18–24	15.8%	14.9%	11.4%	50.9%	7.0%	114
1st	25–40	14.1%	23.2%	9.5%	51.6%	1.6%	306
generation	41–65	16.5%	17.3%	12.6%	51.2%	2.4%	127
	66+	33.3%	33.3%	0.0%	0.0%	33.3%	3
Mexicans 2nd generation							
VRA	18–24	50.0%	12.5%	3.1%	25.0%	9.4%	32
cohorts	25–40	50.0%	4.5%	0.0%	36.4%	9.1%	44
non-VRA	41–65	24.3%	21.6%	0.0%	45.9%	8.1%	37
cohorts	66+	0.0%	33.3%	16.7%	50.0%	0.0%	6
Mexicans 3rd generation							
VRA	18–24	52.8%	15.7%	1.1%	21.3%	9.0%	89
cohorts	25–40	48.5%	16.5%	1.7%	29.2%	4.2%	237
non-VRA	41–65	38.8%	19.4%	4.9%	30.1%	6.8%	103
cohorts	66+	33.3%	44.4%	11.1%	0.0%	11.1%	9
Anglos	18–24	48.5%	12.1%	3.0%	30.3%	6.1%	33
non-VRA	25–40	58.0%	10.7%	0.8%	27.5%	3.1%	131
cohorts	41–65	58.8%	8.8%	2.6%	21.9%	7.9%	114
	66+	46.7%	21.0%	0.0%	13.3%	20.0%	15

Source: Latino National Political Survey 1989; 1990

sufficient argument to extend the VRA to the Southwest (de la Garza and DeSipio 1993).

Mexican Americans had been originally excluded from the VRA and related legislation including affirmative action policies even though they were poor. Additionally, these protections were not meant to protect them because they were immigrants. Indeed, Congress rejected efforts to extend such protections to European immigrant groups because there was no basis for immigrants to demand such protections (DeSipio and de la Garza 1992). These protections were later extended to Mexican Americans because the nation had systematically violated both their rights as Americans and the rights inherent in the primordial claims they made on the Southwest.

The intensity of Mexican American demands for incorporation thus stems from anger over historic discrimination that is rooted in a primordial foundation which, in the most fundamental sense, is independent of immigration. Nonetheless, protests against abuse were made more urgent as immigration increased the population. Moreover, once the claim gained standing and Mexican Americans came under VRA coverage, there can be no doubt that immigrants have fueled many of the political gains made since 1975. The number of elected officials has increased significantly as a result of VRA-mandated redistricting, especially where population growth has been the strongest because of the rise in immigration.

Thus, for the first time in the history of the Mexican population in the United States, intergenerational economic and political mobility exists although it is not easily detectable for several reasons. First, it is so recent that many Mexican Americans were too old to benefit from the new opportunities created in the post-VRA period. Instead, only a small segment of Mexican Americans benefited from these new opportunities in ways that are measurable by aggregate data sets. Second, until now no one has conceptualized the Mexican experience in ways that account for the separate effects of the VRA and continuous immigration. Thus, even if the data had been available, no one has analyzed it this way. Third, most Mexican immigrants who have arrived since 1970 have come as adults without the skills or education to benefit from societal changes. By expanding the lower ranks of the Mexican population, they conceal mobility among VRA cohorts. Fourth, because of their low education attainment and limited job skills, these immigrants now rear their children under conditions unlikely to generate high intergenerational mobility. It must be emphasized that any children, regardless of race or ethnicity, raised in households where parents have less than eight years of school and are employed in the least rewarding and most unstable jobs, would be unlikely to experience high mobility.

EFFECTS OF CONTINUOUS IMMIGRATION

In time, a larger proportion of Mexican Americans will experience economic mobility because of VRA-generated opportunities. However, even as that develops, it will not be easily discerned. Instead, the overall education and economic attainment of Mexicans may show only slight increases, remain flat, or even decrease because of continuous immigration. In other words, the new generation of Mexican immigrants may increase the ranks of Mexicans who have low education and limited job skills more rapidly than the new generation of Mexican Americans enjoying mobility will deplete them. This is especially likely given that the new immigrants are establishing families under conditions that have little likelihood of producing high mobility for their children.

The proportion of Mexican adults today with less than a high school education and low job skills substantially exceeds those with at least a high school education and higher status jobs. This situation has at least two major causes: the great majority of older Mexican adults were reared in a hostile environment that effectively denied them education and the opportunity to develop rewarding job skills; in addition, the number of immigrants with little schooling and few job skills has increased. Furthermore, even as new generations of Mexican Americans benefit from the post-VRA environment, this educational mix may not change substantially in the foreseeable future because the older, less educated generations are being replaced by two groups: (1) the VRA generations and (2) relatively uneducated and low-skilled immigrants. As of 1990, among those in the age bracket 18–40, the latter exceeded the former. Among Mexicans overall, therefore, there is likely to be modest changes in education attainment even while there is substantial improvement in education among the native born.

This population mix affects Mexican political incorporation similarly. The presence of Mexican immigrants, who are ineligible to vote unless they are naturalized, greatly inflates the proportion of Mexicans who neither register nor vote (de la Garza and DeSipio 1992). Furthermore, the recent influx of immigrants has been so substantial that the number of adult noncitizens exceeds the number of Mexican American voters (Pachon et al. 1992).

A major consequence of this comingling of populations is a reduction in the interest that parties and candidates have in the Mexican American vote (Pachon and Arguelles with Gonzales 1994). The largest Mexican neighborhoods are home to immigrants and citizens alike. When candidates, however, recognize that these areas have few voters, they are disinclined to invest scarce resources in campaigning there. Thus, it is reasonable to assume that citizens in these neighborhoods are extremely unlikely to register and vote. In other words, even with the opportunities afforded by the VRA, Mexican American electoral participation will continue to be damped down by age, education, and the like. It is, therefore, not surprising that VRA cohorts do not participate at greater rates than older cohorts (see Table 9.3).

Political Representation and Primordial Claims

As has been noted, because of their population increases between 1970 and 1980, Mexican Americans were able to take advantage of the political opportunities created by the VRA (de la Garza and DeSipio 1992). Combined with the number of children born to immigrants, immigration affected population growth similarly between 1980 and 1990. This growth, in turn, affected the 1982 and 1992 redistricting and reapportionment that resulted in dramatic increases in the number of Mexican American officials elected since 1970.

Adding irony to the political equation is the fact that immigration also intensifies protests over underrepresentation. In other words, even with VRA provisions, immigrants increase the population of any given jurisdiction more quickly than the electoral system can be redesigned to insure a current proportional representation. Before 1970, electoral systems were rigged against Mexican Americans. Thanks to the VRA, redistricting based on the 1980 census sought to correct that historical exclusion by designing districts that were heavily populated by recent immigrants, that is, those individuals who had no history of historical exclusion. By 1990, Mexican Americans were again underrepresented relative to their population, chiefly because immigration had once more swelled the numbers of Mexicans. Further complicating this adjustment is that in cities with a high immigrant to Mexican American ratio such as Los Angeles, Houston, and Dallas, it is difficult to design districts that meet VRA requirements. Such cities have few

Table 9.3
Mexican Voting Activities by VRA Cohorts, Age, and Nativity

VRA Cohorts	Age	Registered Voters	Voted in 1988	No.
Mexicans	18–24	45.5%	36.4%	11
1st generation	25–40	70.5%	45.5%	44
	41–65	65.7%	51.4%	35
	66+	89.5%	73.7%	19
Mexicans				
2nd generation	18–24	56.4%	25.6%	39
VRA cohorts	25–40	68.9%	54.9%	51
non-VRA cohorts	41–65	87.3%	69.9%	63
	66+	93.8%	78.1%	32
Mexicans				
3rd generation	18–24	56.6%	31.0%	113
VRA cohorts	25–40	79.6%	46.1%	269
non-VRA cohorts	41–65	93.8%	66.4%	146
	66+	97.1%	57.1%	35
Anglos	18–24	39.5%	63.9%	44
non-VRA cohorts	25–40	61.3%	86.6%	142
	41–65	77.7%	94.2%	139
	66+	83.0%	98.2%	112

Source: Latino National Political Survey 1989; 1990

Mexican American voters. Given this ratio, electoral officials have tried to satisfy VRA representational requirements by designing districts with very few voters, but this solution has had negative implications for Mexican American political efforts in general and for the individuals elected from such districts. For example, because of the mix of citizens and noncitizens in their districts, several Mexican American elected officials in southern California are elected with substantially fewer votes than their white counterparts. It is reasonable to expect that this may diminish their influence and their ability to rise on the political ladder.

The intent of redistricting and reapportionment is to enable jurisdictions to be sensitive to population movements, including increases resulting from immigration. What makes the Mexican case distinctive is the VRA requirement for proportional representation. That is, reapportionment does more than redistribute electoral seats based on population shifts; it must also reallocate those seats in ways that protect the right of Mexican Americans to have an equal opportunity to elect representatives they choose, usually Mexican American candidates. This right, as was noted previously, is based on the VRA's recognition of historical discrimination. The intensity with which Mexican Americans continue to press their demands reflects the primordial claims they make on American society.

Clearly, the demands for redistricting and reapportionment illustrate how that primordial claim includes populations who have no right to make it. For example, by what right do Mexican immigrants who arrived in 1980 participate in VRA protections? In my judgment, similar questions could be asked about all immigrants who arrived after the 1970s, when the barriers to Mexican American incorporation begin coming down. Although others may disagree with the date, it is indisputable that this distinction becomes real at some point around 1970. Therefore, it is important to ask by what logic are those immigrants after 1970 included in the population on whose behalf primordial claims are made?

The primordial claims, it should also be noted, are also invoked to protest low economic and education attainments among Mexicans. Thanks to the VRA, an increasing number of Mexican American officials can make these protests meaningful. Many of these claims are being made on behalf of populations who have not been historically deprived but who nonetheless participate in the primordial claim. Mexican immigrants, who came as uneducated adults, in other words, cannot blame their lack of schooling or their limited job prospects on American education and employment discrimination. Nor can it be asserted that because of the nation's historical obligation to Mexican Americans, the primordial claim, the nation has a particular obligation to such Mexican immigrants. This claim, however, is made when aggregate statistics that do not desegregate the native- and foreign-born populations are used to describe the status of Mexicans in the United States and to justify remedial policies to benefit Mexicans.

CONCLUSIONS

What, then, are the implications of these changes for Mexican social, economic, and political life? First, at the most general level, they indicate that Mexicans now occupy a broader space in American society. For the first time, there is clear intergenerational mobility, and Mexican Americans now have the institutional and political strength to insure its continuance. Second, Mexican immigrants increasingly constitute a distinct segment of the Mexican population. Third, the education, political, and economic openings created in the post-VRA era offer a wide range of opportunities to all Mexicans. However—and this is a crucial point—not all Mexicans are equally situated to take advantage of those opportunities.

Mexican Americans and Mexican immigrants have and will continue to benefit differently from the opportunities that have become available since the mid-1970s. The children of second- and third-generation VRA-cohort Mexican Americans who have already benefited from societal changes have far more opportunities than do second-generation children reared in low-income households where parents have less than a high school education. Unfortunately, this is the case with the majority of Mexican immigrant households. Thus, the possibility now exists that the Mexican population will bifurcate even more dramatically than African

Americans have, that is, one segment of Mexican Americans will incorporate fully into the middle and higher strata of American society, while another is channeled into a virtually inescapable cycle of poverty. Those in the bottom track will be there primarily not because of anti-Mexican discrimination but because of the inability of this nation, given its current economic conditions, to incorporate large numbers of uneducated and unskilled immigrants. Even if they were whites, such individuals would have few options.

This bifurcation may result in sharp divisions even within second- and third-generation VRA cohorts. The successful group will be made up primarily of the children of the VRA cohorts who are already benefiting from societal changes. The unsuccessful group will consist of the children and grandchildren of the immigrant households described in the preceding paragraph. It is an American tragedy that, given extant social policy, few children reared in households with these characteristics located within deteriorating or deteriorated neighborhoods experience substantial social mobility. This is as true for whites as for Mexicans. However, a greater proportion of Mexicans match this profile. Even if certain individual Mexican Americans and whites experience comparable life chances, the percentage of Mexican Americans who remain in poverty will greatly exceed the percentage of poor whites. This pattern will maintain even though, thanks to affirmative action, some Mexican Americans may have a better opportunity to receive financial aid to attend college and escape poverty than would a comparably deserving white student.

Politically, the implications of this analysis are equally clear. The VRA has effectively eliminated the obstacles that historically diminished Mexican American electoral participation. Thus, Mexican American representation is greatly increasing even though voting rates have remained rather constant. Furthermore, any existing underrepresentation more likely results from the influx of immigrants rather than from any denial of Mexican Americans' equal access to the electoral process. This completely reverses the pattern in pre-VRA periods when Mexican American underrepresentation was caused by discrimination.

Despite these changes, the population patterns described previously will continue to generate demands for more political representation and improved services. As has already occurred in cities such as Houston and Los Angeles, pursuing these objectives will worsen relations with African Americans who consider these demands less deserving than their own. Mexicans will continue to appeal to the primordial claim, thus increasing the levels of urban conflict.

It is impossible to understand the historical relationship Mexicans have had with American society without considering the claim to primordial rights and the effects of continuous immigration. Equally invalid is any analysis of that relationship in its current and future forms without accounting for how those two factors interact with the VRA. Without this analysis, we cannot measure Mexican social and political experiences, and thus we cannot know what our problems are and how to address them.

Future analysts who do not desegregate the Mexican population into the components I have presented here, or into appropriate variations, will be challenged to explain why they have not done so. Others may be prompted to use this formulation to explain the basis of the claims that other Latino groups (and other immigrant groups as well) make on U.S. society. If recent Mexican immigrants have no legitimate basis for participating in programs designed to compensate Mexican Americans for violations of their primordial claims, on what basis do Cuban and Dominicans participate in such programs, especially if their participation displaces that of African Americans?

The present study suggests that Mexican Americans are not incorporating into mainstream society as European immigrants did. Whereas it took Europeans three generations, over 150 years passed before the process began in earnest for Mexican Americans. Moreover, while Europeans expressed appreciation for the opportunities this society offered them, Mexican Americans have and will continue to protest their historical losses. The primordial claims of Mexican Americans guarantees, in other words, that Mexican American politics will never be the politics of gratitude.

REFERENCES

Acuña, Rodolfo. 1972. *Occupied America: The Chicano struggle toward liberation*. San Francisco: Canfield Press.
———. 1988. *Occupied America: A history of Chicanos*. New York: Harper and Row.
Blank, Rebecca M. 1994. Outlook for the U.S. labor market and prospects for low-wage entry jobs. Paper presented at the Urban Institute Conference, March.
Chavez, Linda. 1991. *Out of the barrio: Toward a new politics of Hispanic assimilation*. New York: Basic Books.
de la Garza, Rodolfo O., and Louis DeSipio. 1992. *From rhetoric to reality*. Boulder, CO: Westview Press.
———. 1993. Save the baby, change the bathwater, and scrub the tub: Latino electoral participation after seventeen years of Voting Rights Act coverage. *Texas Law Review* 71, no. 7 (June): 1479–1539.
de la Garza, Rodolfo O., and Claudio Vargas. 1992. The Mexican-origin population of the United States as a political force in the borderlands: From paisanos to pochos to potential political allies. In *Changing boundaries in the Americas*, edited by Lawrence A. Herzog, 89–112. San Diego, CA: Center for U.S.–Mexican Studies.
de la Garza, Rodolfo O., Louis DeSipio, F. Chris Garcia, John A. Garcia, and Angelo Falcón. 1992. *Latino voices: Mexican, Puerto Rican, and Cuban perspectives on American politics*. Boulder, CO: Westview Press.
DeSipio, Louis, and Rodolfo O. de la Garza. 1992. Making them us: The link between immigration policy and voting rights policy. In *Nations of immigrants: Australia, the United States, and international migration*, edited by Gary Freeman and James Jupp. Melbourne: Oxford University Press.
Fuchs, Lawrence H. 1990. *The American kaleidoscope: Race, ethnicity, and the civic culture*. Hanover, NH: University Press of New England.
Grebler, Leo, Joan W. Moore, and Ralph C. Guzman. 1970. *The Mexican-American people: The nation's second largest minority*. New York: Free Press.
Hero, Rodney E. 1992. *Latinos and the U.S. political system: Two-tiered pluralism*. Philadelphia: Temple University Press.

Kamaski, Charles, and Raul Yzaguirre. 1991. Black-Hispanic tensions: One perspective. Paper presented at APSA, September.

Marquez, Benjamin. 1993. *LULAC: The evolution of a Mexican American political organization*. Austin: University of Texas Press.

Massey, Douglas S., and Nancy A. Denton. 1993. *American apartheid: Segregation and the making of the underclass*. Cambridge, MA: Harvard University Press.

Moore, Joan. 1970. Colonialism: The case of the Mexican Americans. *Social Problems* 17: 463–471.

Pachon, Harry, and Lourdes Arguelles, with Rafael Gonzales. 1994. Grass-roots politics in an East Los Angeles barrio: A political ethnography of the 1990 general election. In *Barrio ballots*, edited by Martha Menchaco and Louis DeSipio. Boulder, CO: Westview Press.

Pachon, Harry, and Louis DeSipio. 1994. *New Americans by choice*. Boulder, CO: Westview Press.

Pachon, Harry, Louis DeSipio, Juan-Carlos Alegre, and Mark Magna. 1992. *The Latino vote in 1992*. Washington, DC: NALEO Educational Fund.

Polinard, Jerry L., and Robert D. Wrinkle. 1988. *The politics and policies of district representation: The Mexican American experience*. Working paper #4. New directions for Latino public policy research. IUP/SSRC Committee for Public Policy Research on Contemporary Hispanic Issues. Austin: Center for Mexican American Studies, University of Texas.

San Miguel, Guadalupe. 1987. *Let all of them take heed*. Austin: University of Texas Press.

Schlesinger, Arthur M., Jr. 1992. *The disuniting of America*. New York: W. W. Norton.

Skerry, Peter. 1993. *Mexican Americans: The ambivalent minority*. New York: Free Press.

Valenzuela, Abel, Jr. 1990–1991. Hispanic poverty: Is it an immigrant problem? *Journal of Hispanic Policy* 5: 59–84.

Weber, David J. 1973. *Foreigners in their native land: Historical roots of the Mexican Americans*. Albuquerque: University of New Mexico Press.

10

More Than the Sum of Its Parts:
The Building Blocks of a
Pan-Ethnic Latino Identity

Louis DeSipio

Recent scholarship on Latino populations nationwide has emphasized the distinct-ness of the Latino national-origin populations. Mexican Americans, Cuban Americans, and Puerto Ricans, as well as the emerging Latino populations from other countries in the Caribbean, Central America, and South America have been shown to have little contact with each other and, as a result, little affect for each other (Bean and Tienda 1990; de la Garza et al. 1992; Shorris 1993; Pachon and DeSipio 1994). Ethnicity, however, is a dynamic process (Smith 1981; Padilla 1985; Keefe and Padilla 1987). As a result, findings such as these of Latino ethnicity—which is better understood in terms of a collection of distinct national-origin based ethnicities—could well become dated, whether by the time of their publication or in the near future. By the same measure, the dynamism of ethnicity could assure that the current low level of pan-ethnic Latino identity could come to disappear over time.

In this chapter, I assess potential foundations for a pan-ethnic Latino identity. I look at five factors that facilitate the development of this pan-ethnic identity: (1) common cultural characteristics, (2) mandated common ethnicity and statutory recognition of Latino rather than national-origin based ethnicity, (3) the role of Mexican American, Cuban American, Puerto Rican, and other Latino elites in shaping a common identity, (4) the common public policy needs and concerns of the Latino communities, and (5) increasing contact between Latino populations with various ancestries. As I indicate, none of these factors operates in isolation. Instead, they are mutually reinforcing in the process of building a Latino ethnic identity.

DEFINING A POPULATION

The first difficulty in talking about a pan-ethnic Latino identity is the multiple terms available to identify this population. Although analysts often use Latino and

Hispanic interchangeably (as I do in this chapter), many who identify as Latino or Hispanic not only prefer one term, but also object to the other. Even if that problem could be overcome, Latino and Hispanic are not the only identity terms used. Hispano, Spanish, and Latin are used by some. The government has used the rather cumbersome and bureaucratic-sounding term "Spanish-origin population." Thus, to the extent that a common identity is in the process of developing, it is unclear what it should be called. This is more than simply an issue of names. Instead, the inability to define a single term to identify this population, between Latino or Hispanic, on the one hand, and the more cumbersome, but probably more technically accurate Spanish-origin population, on the other, gives rise to questions about the validity of the whole enterprise.

Even if Latinos could agree on a single term, there is no consensus on its application. Some who use this term mean people who can trace their ancestry to the Spanish-speaking regions of Latin America and the Caribbean. Others extend coverage to all Spanish-speaking regions of the world, including Spain. Others extend the definition beyond the Spanish-speaking world to include Brazil and Portugal and, perhaps, some Filipinos. There is no definitive answer, then, as to who is Latino. As a result, it is important when examining analyses of this population to see who the analyst includes. In this essay, I define Latinos as residents of the United States who can trace their ancestry to the Spanish-speaking regions of Latin America and the Caribbean. Similarly, I use the terms "Latino communities" and "Latino populations" to reflect the self-perceived distinctness of the national-origin populations—for example, Mexican American, Puerto Rican, and Cuban American—that constitute the U.S. Latino population. As I suggest, to the extent that a pan-ethnic Latino identity exists, it is in the process of being shaped. So the answers to these questions of who Latinos are and what they should be called will emerge over the coming years.

CULTURAL AND ECONOMIC LINKAGES

Cultural and economic factors have long facilitated the idea that there are commonalities among the various populations who trace their ancestry to Latin America and the Caribbean. These include three attributes from Latin America that help shape the Latino experience: (1) language, (2) ethnic and racial intermixture, and (3) political socialization under corporatist governments. In addition, there are three commonalities shaped by U.S. experiences: (1) ties to immigration, (2) discrimination, and (3) high shares of the population with lower than average levels of formal education, low earnings, and occupations at the lower skill levels. In other words, Latinos are more likely than other populations to have low socioeconomic status (SES) indicators.

Language

Undoubtedly, the most important among these cultural linkages is language. By the way that I have defined the population I am concerned with—common ancestry in the Spanish-speaking regions of Latin America and the Caribbean—I have linked all Latinos to areas where the dominant language is Spanish. Thus, in terms of origin, Spanish is a link between various Latino populations. The link, however, goes deeper. At one level, language links immigrants from various parts of Latin America. It would be a mistake, however, to see all Latinos as Spanish speakers. Instead, most second-generation and beyond Latinos are English-dominant, and many speak no Spanish at all (de la Garza et al. 1992: Tables 2.28 and 2.29). For these native-born, non–Spanish-dominant Latinos, Spanish offers a different sort of cultural link—the experience with language-based discrimination is a part of the Latino experience in the United States.

As I have indicated, the language-based cultural link works at two levels. First, among immigrants, Spanish is overwhelmingly the dominant language. Among Mexican Americans and Cuban Americans, for example, the majority speak Spanish exclusively at home. Among all of the Latino national-origin groups, immigrants (and, in the case of the Puerto Rican population, migrants) make up a large share of the population. More than one third (35.1 percent) of Latinos counted in the 1990 census were born abroad (U.S. Bureau of the Census 1991a; 1993). Among adults, first-generation immigrants make up an even larger share of the Latino population: 37.7 percent in 1990, increasing to 43.8 percent by 1994 (U.S. Bureau of the Census 1991b; 1995). The language patterns of these immigrants drive popular perceptions that Latinos universally speak Spanish.

As large as the share of the foreign-born is, the native-born make up a larger share. Survey evidence indicates that few native-born Latinos are Spanish dominant. Of the remainder the majority are English dominant. Though not Spanish speakers, I would argue that the native-born also share in the common culture based on language. Exclusion from the dominant society based on their use of Spanish or their ancestors' use is a part of the Latino experience. Sensitivity, then, to the needs of non-English speakers is the second linkage across Latino populations.

This cultural attachment to a non-English language is born out by survey data. Although Latinos (citizens and noncitizens alike) overwhelmingly supported the proposition that U.S. citizens and residents should learn English, they also believed that social services should be provided to non-English speakers and that people should be taxed to pay for bilingual education (de la Garza et al. 1992: Tables 7.15–21, 10.52, and 10.54).

Thus, across the Latino populations, language serves as a cultural and symbolic link, which not only connects Latinos of various ancestries and various periods of immigration, but also serves to distinguish Latinos from other U.S. populations.

Ethnic-Racial Intermixture

A second legacy of Latin America for many Latinos is the result of the ethnic mixture of the native populations with Spaniards and other Europeans. In some regions of Latin America, this mixture also includes the descendants of Africans and Asians who migrated to Latin America after colonization. The result for some in the Latino community is a wide range of phenotypes. In many cases, this legacy distinguishes the appearance of Latinos from those of the non-Hispanic populations in the United States.

Beyond the range of phenotypes, the ethnic mixing of Latin America leads to another potentially unifying force for Latinos. They challenge the dominant society's polar understandings of race in terms of just white and black. Throughout U.S. history, this ongoing effort to limit the conception of race to white and black has led to the classification of Mexican Americans and then other Latinos as white (in re *Rodriguez*, District Court, Western District of Texas, 3 May 1897; *Mendez vs. Westminster School District*, 161 F. 2nd. 774, 1947). More recently, this national conundrum about Latinos and race resulted in the Census Bureau's decision to classify Latinos both in racial and ethnic terms (popularizing the term "Hispanic" in the process). As a result, government data on whites and blacks fails to disaggregate Hispanic whites and Hispanic blacks, muddying the picture of the socioeconomic conditions of all three populations.

Increasingly, Latinos are defying this bipolar understanding of race and identifying in racial terms with some reference to Latin America or to a pan-ethnic Latino identity. Respondents to the Latino National Political Survey demonstrated this attachment to a pan-ethnic racial identity. Respondents of Mexican ancestry were slightly more likely to use a Latino referent to identify their race than they were to use white, though citizens were more likely to see themselves as white. Puerto Ricans were slightly more likely to say they were white, though a substantial minority identified racially in pan-ethnic Latino terms. Few Cuban Americans identified racially with a Latino referent (de la Garza et al. 1992: Tables 2.2 and 10.2). This effort among some in the Latino communities to distinguish themselves from the dominant society's bipolar notion of race offers a second cultural link for a national Latino ethnic identity.

Political Socialization in Latin America

Along with language and ethnic mixture, the political heritage of Latin America offers a third possible cultural link for Latinos. This Latin American political culture is not universal, but for many includes a common experience with totalitarian corporatist governments and highly inarticulated class systems (in contrast to the "liberal" individualist values of the American system). Analysts who focus on the legacy of Latin America on Latinos see political commonalties stretching from Mexico to Cuba and Puerto Rico and throughout the region. The legacy of the Latin American experience is, according to some analysts, a failure among many Latinos, particularly Mexicans and Puerto Ricans, to take advantage of the liberal political system and instead to accept some form of machine or boss rule (Anders 1979).

Survey data from the Latino National Political Survey indicate that there may be some validity in this approach. Latinos reported a preference for larger government, involved in a wider range of policy areas, and were willing to pay taxes to receive these added services (de la Garza et al. 1992: Tables 7.3, 7.4, and 10.40). As these findings can also be explained in terms of the class positions of many Latinos, the potential impact on the development of a Latino ethnic identity of the legacy of political socialization in Latin America should be interpreted with some caution.

Immigration

A second set of common cultural experiences emerges from Latino experiences in the United States. The first of these is an experience with or a direct connection to immigration. Not all Latinos trace their ancestry to immigrants to the United States. At the time of the ratification of the Treaty of Guadelupe Hidalgo, approximately 100,000 former Mexican subjects resided in the United States. These Latinos with a territorial connection to what is today the southwestern United States are the exception. Most Latinos, like most people in the United States, trace their ancestry to immigrants. The Latino experience is different than that of most Americans, however, in two ways. First, immigration from the Americas has been an ongoing element in the immigrant stream. Second, it makes up the largest share of contemporary immigration (DeSipio 1995).

The earliest Latino migrants to the United States were mainly surplus laborers seeking employment in the United States. Clearly, this experience was not unlike those of many European immigrants of the same period. The large waves of immigration from Mexico and the Caribbean, however, began after the peak periods of European immigration, just after the cutback in European immigration in the 1920s. Increasingly these Mexican- and Caribbean-origin immigrants were joined by immigrants from other parts of Latin America. In the 1960s, these economic refugees were joined by two other types of immigrants. With the enactment of the 1965 Immigration Act, family members of immigrants began to migrate in large numbers. Also beginning in the 1960s, political refugees joined the flow, particularly Cuban Americans. Today, approximately 200,000 Latinos immigrate each year for permanent residence, and an unknown number enter in an undocumented status.

Although the foreign born make up a minority of the Latino population, one of the impacts of this immigration is to provide a linkage among Latinos of various ancestries. Almost all have themselves or have ancestors who immigrated. As I have suggested, this does not make them unique. What does, however, is that with the large levels of contemporary immigration, the ill treatment that many first-generation immigrants experience reinforces the distinctness felt by many Latinos, even those who are second- and third-generation Americans. In a personal conversation with Professor Walter Dean Burnham of the University of Texas, he said, "the discrimination experienced by each new immigrant reinforces the feeling of a primordial connection to the country of origin among the native born."

Discrimination

The second of the U.S. experiences that lead to the potential for Latino unity is a common experience with discrimination. This experience is not always direct;

instead, it is the perception that Latinos face disproportionate levels of discrimination in U.S. society.

The historical record is replete with evidence of discrimination against the Mexican Americans and Puerto Ricans. This experience in the electoral arena led to the passage of the Voting Rights Act discussed later (de la Garza and DeSipio 1993), in the educational arena it generated the federal mandate of bilingual education (San Miguel 1987), and in the labor market it assured inclusion of Latinos under various civil rights acts. It is important to note that the remedies to this pattern of discrimination have been to craft solutions that treat all Latinos as equally entitled to the remedy, regardless of the degree to which they or their conationals actually experienced the discrimination.

This highlights a contradiction in Latinos' perceptions of discrimination. According to the Latino National Political Survey, the majority of Latinos believed that Mexican Americans, Puerto Ricans, and Cuban Americans (the groups discussed in the survey) face "a lot" or "some" discrimination. These levels of perceived discrimination were higher than those of perceived discrimination against other groups in U.S. society except for African Americans. Despite these high levels, only a minority believed that they themselves had been discriminated against based on their ethnicity. Non-U.S. citizens were even less likely to perceive personal discrimination than were citizens (de la Garza et al. 1992: Tables 7.5, 7.8–14, 10.41, 10.44–50). Thus, discrimination offers another link across Latino communities, although not perhaps in the expected way. Instead, it is the perception of discrimination rather than a direct experience that can serve to connect the political agendas of the Latino communities.

Socioeconomic Class

Overall, Latinos earn less, have less formal education, and have lower prestige jobs than do non-Hispanic whites (Anglos); their family incomes are, on average, seven to eight thousand dollars less per year than those of Anglo families (Cuban American family incomes are comparable to those of Anglo families). Other socioeconomic indicators reinforce the notion that Latinos share a common disadvantage in the American society. The average number of years of education is less (ten versus twelve years) and labor force participation (though higher due to the relative youth of the population) tends to be concentrated at the low paying end of the spectrum. Poverty in the Latino communities, particularly child poverty, is closer to that for African Americans than for Anglo Americans. Unlike poverty in the African American community, however, Latino children in poverty are more likely to have two parents present in the household; thus, Latinos are more likely to be classified as the working poor. As Rodolfo de la Garza points out in his essay for this book, the experiences of the native born should be distinguished from those of the foreign born. Nonetheless, the class position of the majority of Latinos offers another linkage across which a pan-ethnic Latino identity can be built.

MANDATED COMMON ETHNICITY AND STATUTORY ROLE FOR ETHNICITY

These common cultural characteristics provide a basis for potential ethnic unity, but certainly offer no guarantee that a common identity will emerge. American history is full of examples both of U.S. ethnic identities that have emerged, such as Italian American, and those that have not, such as the regional national identities of Italy. Latinos, however, have an added inducement that earlier immigrant populations either did not have or had only informally from local governments: statutory recognition by the federal government, state and local governments, and many public and private sector programs of a single ethnic identity.

There are several results of this mandated common ethnicity. First, it reduces the likelihood of the development of an ethnic movement around one of the national-origin groups. Second, it expands the coverage of policy programs designed to meet the needs of some Latinos (for example, Mexican Americans) to all Latinos. Finally, it offers a link that Latino ethnic leaders can use to build a pan-ethnic identity.

Statutory Role for a Pan-Ethnic Latino Ethnicity

The decision to recognize these national-origin groups under a pan-ethnic rubric went hand in hand with the development of federal programs that targeted specific public policy needs. The most important of these was the extension of the Voting Rights Act (VRA) to the Spanish-origin population in 1975 (de la Garza and DeSipio 1993). The results of the VRA indicate how federal programs can miss their intended beneficiaries and reduce the overall effectiveness of the program. They also demonstrate, however, that this statutory role for a pan-ethnic Latino ethnicity can serve as an inducement to create or strengthen that ethnicity.

Congress originally enacted the Voting Rights Act in 1965 to guarantee African Americans access to the polls in the southern states where they faced the highest levels of intimidation and exclusion (Davidson and Grofman 1994). When the legislation came up for renewal in 1975, Mexican American leaders and a representative from one Puerto Rican organization convinced Congress that state efforts to exclude Mexican Americans and Puerto Ricans were comparable to those that kept blacks from the polling places in the South. With little debate, Congress extended the key provisions to the Spanish-origin population and created several new protections for Latinos who resided in areas with concentrations of 5 percent Latino or greater—most importantly bilingual election materials and protections during the redistricting process.

The Mexican American and Puerto Rican leaders who testified in 1975 argued that the exclusion that Mexican Americans experienced in the Southwest was comparable to that experienced by blacks in the South. As a result, they argued, similar protections needed to be provided. Although their examples did not present the full panorama of voter exclusion and manipulation experienced in the Southwest (and virtually nothing on the manipulation of the Puerto Rican vote in New York), Congress extended the protections already being offered to African Americans to the Spanish origin and other specified language minorities (Asians, Native Americans, and Alaskan Natives) as well as providing bilingual election materials. There was little justification offered; the rationale for bilingual ballots was to provide a remedy for U.S. citizens among the language minorities who had not been educated in English and, as a result, could not participate in the political process.

The blanket coverage of the Spanish-origin population created an entitlement to voting protections not just for those who had experienced discrimination, but also for those who joined these language minority communities after the enactment of the law. Among these subsequent additions were new immigrants. Thus, bilingual ballots came to be perceived as a tool to speed the political entry of immigrants. Redistricting protections also extended beyond the original beneficiaries creating the potential for conflict between protected communities made up mostly of immigrants and other communities (either with or without protection). This situation has led to conflict in Miami between the largely immigrant Cuban community and the native white and black communities.

In this same period, Congress passed legislation requiring the provision of bilingual education to Spanish-dominant children. Again, this legislation attempted to redress the historical discrimination against Mexican Americans, particularly in Texas, but was extended to all Latinos, regardless of national origin or nativity. Federal as well as state affirmative action and minority preference legislation quickly expanded from the black community to Latinos in this period as well.

Each of these programs created the impetus for new coalitions to protect their benefits and to fight for their expansion or protection. Thus, they offer an inducement for ethnic leaders to identify and behave as Latinos instead of as Mexican Americans, Puerto Ricans, or Cuban Americans.

Elite Efforts to Build a Latino Identity

The potential emergence of a Latino ethnicity depends also on the role of elites in promoting a pan-ethnic identity. Just as legislation targeting Latinos as a group began to emerge in the mid-1970s, so did organizations attempting to speak for these groups and elected officials speaking to the national-origin community, as well as the pan-ethnic community. Among the organizations that formed in this era were the Congressional Hispanic Caucus, the National Association of Latino Elected Officials (NALEO), and the National Hispanic Chamber of Commerce. Other organizations, more closely tied to one of the Latino national-origin groups—such as the Mexican American Legal Defense and Education Fund (MALDEF), the National Council of La Raza (NCLR), the League of United Latin American Citizens (LULAC, despite its name, has traditionally been a Mexican American organization), and ASPIRA, a Puerto Rican organization focusing on education issues—diversified their research and advocacy agendas to focus broadly on Latino issues as well as on national-origin based issues. Their boards of directors and memberships now include people of various ancestries. In the 1980s, a network of regional organizations with a Latino focus emerged to supplement these national organizations including the Latino Institute in Chicago, the Tomas Rivera Center in southern California and Texas, and the Hispanic Federation in New York.

These organizations representing the multiple roots of the Latino community reflect a conscious, nonexclusive effort by elites to craft a pan-ethnic identity. Each organization seeks to address the national-origin basis of defining ethnicity while it seeks to identify pan-ethnic issues. Over the past twenty years, the efforts of these organizations have been supplemented by a growing pool of Latinos at all levels of elective office. Currently, for example, there are sixteen Latino members of Congress. Two members of the president's cabinet are Latino, one of whom, Henry Cisneros, was considered as a Democratic vice-presidential nominee in 1984. Nationally, over 6,000 Latinos serve in elective office. While some of these officeholders identify as Latino and some identify with their national origins or view themselves in nonethnic terms, these officials supplement the efforts of Latino organizations to bring Latino issues to national prominence.

The efforts to create an organizational infrastructure to support a pan-ethnic identity have met with mixed success. Latino organizations do not depend on their memberships for support, and none has many active members. Instead, each relies to varying degrees on philanthropic, corporate, and government support to survive. In addition to small memberships, the organizations are not very well known to Latinos; accordingly, efforts to link Latinos organizationally have been more the work of elites than the masses. The eventual success of these organizations will depend on the degree to which they can extend their reach beyond community elites.

Common Public Policy Needs and Concerns

The experience of the Latino organizations formed over the past twenty years shows the fourth element that can link the Latino populations. As identified by Latino organizations, common public policy needs are felt by all Latinos: political empowerment, naturalization and immigrant settlement assistance, primary and secondary education, access to higher education, job training, social service delivery, child poverty, housing, and crime prevention. These issues transcend national-origin based needs and offer the foundation for a Latino political agenda.

That said, the needs vary somewhat by region of the country and by national-origin group. Naturalization and immigrant settlement policy do not directly concern Puerto Ricans, who are U.S. citizens by birth. Yet, the ability of the Puerto Rican community to influence New York politics depends in part upon settlement and naturalization of Dominicans and other Latino populations in the city or state. Similarly, empowerment strategies might seem to be of less concern to the Cuban American community who have been very successful in shaping Miami politics (see Moreno, Chapter 8). Again, however, their continued influence locally and their increased influence nationally will depend on their ability to maintain high levels of activism in the future.

Latinos of various ancestries expressed wide agreement on many domestic issues (de la Garza et al. 1992). Despite reporting that they were ideologically conserva-tive, they called for expanded government social services (for which they were willing to pay extra taxes), and increased efforts by the government to assist with the settlement of immigrants (although many thought that there were too many immigrants). In addition, while opposing the proposition that English should be the official language of the United States, they argued that all citizens and residents should learn English. They supported capital punishment, and although more evenly divided than on other issues, they opposed abortion. This agreement on public policy issues should assist organizational and elite efforts to shape a Latino identity around a common set of concerns.

Geographic Overlap

The fifth condition uniting the Latino national-origin groups into a pan-ethnic identity is the increasing geographic overlap among them. Traditionally, Latino populations had very little contact with each other. Mexican Americans resided primarily in the Southwest; Cuban Americans, in Florida; and Puerto Ricans, in New York and the Northeast. Until recently, the primary area of contact between two of these national-origin groups was Chicago where Mexican Americans and Puerto Ricans have resided in large numbers since the 1950s (Padilla 1985). Over the past twenty years, however, there has been wide representation of nations of origin in the Latino community (U.S. Bureau of the Census 1993).

Equally important, this diversification has led to a geographic concentration of Latinos of various national origins in major U.S. cities. New York has become home to many Dominicans and Colombians as well as to Puerto Ricans; Los Angeles, to many Salvadorans and Guatemalans as well as Mexican Americans (DeSipio et al. 1994; Torres 1995). In Miami, the Latino population has diversified to include not just Cuban Americans, but also Latinos from throughout the Caribbean, Central America, and South America (Grenier and Stepick 1992). Other cities with pre-viously dominant Latino populations including Houston, San Francisco, and Boston have also seen increasing diversification in the origins of their Latino populations.

This emerging geographic diversity both promotes and dampens Latino unity. Now that Latinos have moved beyond their areas of initial residence in the United States, the multiple residence promotes unity in that it assures greater contact between Latino populations and allows them to understand the cultural and other linkages that I have outlined in this chapter. More important, the geographic contiguity of populations in major cities creates the foundation for coalition politics. Thus, Latinos who do not initially see their needs as being served by pan-ethnic efforts can come to see that their needs are better served by the larger numbers offered by Latino community-wide political efforts.

This discussion is not meant to suggest that the diversification of the origins of the Latino population is a panacea for the development of a Latino ethnic identity.

Multiple Latino populations can lead to conflict just as easily as it can lead to cooperation. Yet, the common public policy needs and the group-based delivery of services in many cities raise the likelihood that cooperation will occur more frequently than conflict, particularly when community elites are seeking to develop a broader identity.

CONCLUSION

While the effort to develop a national Latino ethnic identity may seem a recent phenomenon, the effort has been going on for most of this century. Local accounts from as early as the 1920s indicate efforts to unite the various Latin American-origin populations in New York into cultural and political coalitions (Sánchez Korrol 1983). The first national effort occurred in the late 1930s when unionists formed the Congress of Spanish Speaking Peoples and held a national meeting in 1939 in Los Angeles which included Mexican Americans, Puerto Ricans, and Cuban Americans (Sánchez 1993). The legacy of these early efforts should not be lost in the current efforts to forge a Latino pan-ethnic identity. These early pan-ethnic organizational efforts were quickly overpowered by efforts to organize around nation-origin lines.

Clearly, the efforts in the period since 1975 have been much more comprehensive and much more successful than these early endeavors. Nationally recognized organizations and national leaders speak of Latino concerns and needs; the activities of these organizations and leaders shape national and state policy, and the leaders and organizations are sought out as participants in the national political process. What, then, has changed to make contemporary efforts at the development of Latino ethnic identity more successful than earlier efforts?

The first factor is demographic. Due in large part to immigration over the past twenty years, the Latino population is both large (nearly 10 percent of the national population), growing rapidly, and, due to its concentration, particularly large in key metropolitan areas. Demographics alone do not guarantee the success of these efforts at identity building. The second factor has to do with ethnic leadership. Latino leaders of all ancestries have sought to identify common ground on which to build a national Latino agenda. While not always successful, these coalition efforts have reached a point where they no longer present themselves as coalitions, but instead as representing a people. These efforts may well have moved ahead of the community that the leaders represent. But, according to theories of ethnic and group leadership, it is the role of leaders to move those they represent in directions the leaders feel to be in their mutual interest. When they lose this connection to the led, they will no longer be recognized as leaders. A final factor is the receptivity of the host society. Over the past thirty years, the United States has been open to group-based policies and group-based remedies for past discrimination. While this is clearly changing in the mid-1990s, the centrality of the Latino community to national policy making is unlikely to change.

This leaves one final question: Will Latino come to be the primary ethnic identity held by people who can trace their ancestry to the Spanish-speaking regions of Latin America and the Caribbean? As I have suggested, this question cannot be so easily answered. Ethnicity is dynamic and unpredictable. At present, Latinos do not use a pan-ethnic identity as their primary ethnic identification. The use of the pan-ethnic identifier increases among the native born, suggesting that identity as a Latino may be a part of immigrant acculturation. Yet, its use varies between national-origin groups (with Mexican Americans the most likely to use Latino or Hispanic). This would suggest that if immigration were to slow or stop, the population would increasingly see itself in pan-ethnic terms. Accompanying the increased use of pan-ethnic identifiers, however, is a move away from ethnic identifiers completely to identify as American without a connection to a Latino identity at all. Thus, the process of ethnic identification has an unclear end with a pan-ethnic Latino identity being just one possibility. Here the role of leadership will play a particularly important role. Ethnic leaders can shape an identity that resonates with Latinos. The society can reward or discourage ethnic identity in general. Only the future will show how these are used.

REFERENCES

Anders, Evan. 1979. *Boss rule in south Texas: The progressive era*. Austin: University of Texas Press.

Bean, Frank, and Marta Tienda. 1990. *The Hispanic population in the United States*. New York: Russell Sage Foundation.

Davidson, Chandler, and Bernard Grofman, eds. 1994. *Quiet revolution in the South: The impact of the Voting Rights Act 1965–1990*. Princeton: Princeton University Press.

de la Garza, Rodolfo O., and Louis DeSipio. 1993. Save the baby, change the bathwater, and scrub the tub: Latino electoral participation after seventeen years of Voting Rights Act coverage. *Texas Law Review* 71, no. 7 (June): 1479–1539.

de la Garza, Rodolfo O., Louis DeSipio, F. Chris Garcia, John A. Garcia, and Angelo Falcón. 1992. *Latino voices: Mexican, Puerto Rican, and Cuban perspectives on American politics*. Boulder, CO: Westview Press.

DeSipio, Louis. 1995. Immigrants, denizens, and citizens: Latin American immigration and settlement in the 1990s. *Current World Leaders International Issues* 38, no. 2 (April): 63–87.

DeSipio, Louis, Harry Pachon, Sonia Ospina, and Eric Popkin. 1994. The political incorporation of "new" Latino immigrant populations: The Dominicans, Colombians, Salvadorans, and Guatemalans. Paper prepared for presentation at the American Political Science Association, New York City.

Grenier, Guillermo, and Alex Stepick. 1992. *Miami now! Immigration, ethnicity, and social change*. Gainesville: University Press of Florida.

Keefe, Susan E., and Amado Padilla. 1987. *Chicano ethnicity*. Albuquerque: University of New Mexico Press.

Pachon, Harry, and Louis DeSipio. 1994. *New Americans by choice: Political perspectives of Latino immigrants*. Boulder, CO: Westview Press.

Padilla, Felix. 1985. *Latino ethnic consciousness: The case of Mexican Americans and Puerto Ricans in Chicago*. South Bend, IN: University of Notre Dame Press.

San Miguel, Guadalupe, Jr. 1987. *"Let all of them take heed": Mexican Americans and the campaign for educational equality in Texas, 1910–1981.* Austin: University of Texas Press.

Sánchez, George J. 1993. *Becoming Mexican American: Ethnicity, culture, and identity in Chicano Los Angeles, 1900–1945.* New York: Oxford University Press.

Sánchez Korrol, Virginia. 1983. *From Colonia to Community: The history of Puerto Ricans in New York City, 1917–1948.* Westport, CT: Greenwood Press.

Shorris, Earl. 1993. *Latinos: Biography of a people.* New York: Macmillan.

Smith, Anthony. 1981. *The ethnic revival.* New York: Cambridge University Press.

Torres, Andrés. 1995. *Between melting pot and mosaic: African Americans and Puerto Ricans in the New York political economy.* Philadelphia: Temple University Press.

U.S. Bureau of the Census. 1991a. Race and Hispanic origin. *1990 Census Profile 2* (June). Washington, DC: Government Printing Office.

———. 1991b. Voting and registration in the election of November 1990. *Current population reports, population characteristics,* series P-20, no. 453. Washington, DC: Government Printing Office.

———. 1993. *1990: The foreign-born population by race, Hispanic origin, and citizenship for the United States and states.* CPH-L134. Washington, DC: U.S. Bureau of the Census, Ethnic and Hispanic Branch, Population Division.

———. 1995. Reported voting and registration, by race, Hispanic origin, and age, for states: November 1994. Unpublished data.

Part IV

Jews and American Politics

11
American Jews and
Their Liberal Political Behavior

Lana Stein

The word "liberal" has taken on a pejorative connotation in American politics over the past decade. In the Reagan-Bush years, liberals seemed to include those in favor of civil liberties, redistributive policies, and active civil rights enforcement. Liberals also were viewed as being weak on defense and timorous regarding the maintenance of traditional family and religious values.

This description, with slight modifications, fits the political inclinations of most American Jews. Compared with any other grouping of whites in the United States, Jews give a higher proportion of their vote to Democratic presidential candidates and contribute up to half the funds received by the standard bearer's campaign (Cohen 1989: 1). They also have participated in numbers disproportionate to their presence in the population in liberal and radical organizations, ranging from the old Socialist Party to Americans for Democratic Action, from the civil rights movement to Students for a Democratic Society.

A number of writers, many of them Jewish, have attempted to analyze this phenomenon. It is a puzzle in many ways. Jews have succeeded in American economic and political life to a degree unmatched in European countries. Although anti-Semitism has been ever present in the United States, its more virulent manifestations have receded since World War II, and limitations on access, particularly to higher education, ended in the mid-1960s. Jews as a group enjoy a very high median family income, are well represented in the professions, and hold many political offices. Today, ten U.S. senators are Jewish.

Despite material success and expanded opportunities, Jews remain largely in the Democratic Party and still are active in liberal causes. In this chapter, I attempt to chronicle the extent of Jewish liberal participation and the reasons for it, as well as the exceptions to this norm. My conclusions are forged by various readings as well as my own Jewish upbringing. As the daughter of immigrants from eastern

Europe, I could observe at close range the political prognostications of former socialists and anarchists who became Democrats and Zionists. Kristol (1990: 112) notes that Jewish immigrants "naturally brought with them their political beliefs," which still influence Jewish political thinking today.

THE ROOTS OF JEWISH LIBERALISM

The largest group of Jewish immigrants came to the United States from eastern Europe between 1880 and 1920. In their native lands, they often lived in ghettoes locked at nightfall or in small villages, or shtetls. Their economic lives were closely circumscribed, and pogroms periodically threatened their physical safety. The possibility of induction into the armed forces for a lengthy tenure hastened the departure of many. There was no vestige of democratic government in eastern Europe then, and some explored radical alternatives to the autocracy and the inequality they experienced.

Thus, some Jews brought their radical ideas with them to the United States. At the same time, many of the immigrants had been reared in orthodox religious households. Critical to the belief system, the idea of tzedukah, or charity, is one of the threefold obligations of the High Holy Day period. Lipset (1990: 21) highlights "the norms underlying tzedukah: the obligations on the fortunate, the well-to-do to help individuals and communities in difficulty." In either case, an emphasis on societal betterment is a natural product of these radical or religious beliefs. In fact, several centuries ago, Moses Maimonides, a seminal Jewish thinker, specified that the highest form of charity is giving someone a job.

The arrival in the new world for many immigrants often meant residing in squalid tenements and working long hours in sweatshops or in small businesses. The streets were not initially paved with gold for these or other new settlers. A number of Jews continued to look to radical alternatives as a means to a better life. In fact, New York City's garment industry became "one of the great centers of American socialism" (Scholnick 1990: 9). Jewish unions in the needle trades and in other industries formed the United Hebrew Trades, which backed the Socialist Party (Lipset 1990: 17). Both the Forward, the Yiddish daily newspaper, and the Workmen's Circle (Arbeiter Ring), the largest immigrant-based fraternal organization, were socialist.

Howe (1976: 322–323) notes that although socialism did not become a mass movement in the United States, a number of its "social proposals" later were enacted as domestic policy. He argues that "Jewish socialism transformed the conscience of Jews" by "creating a new type of person: combative, worldly, spirited and intent upon sharing the future of industrial society with the rest of the world." Over time, Jewish socialists and garment workers had to moderate their political ideas "as they found themselves gradually being absorbed into American society."

Its status as a distinct religious minority also led the Jewish community to focus on church-state issues as well as concerns about equal access to opportunities. By the 1930s, the B'nai Brith emerged as the largest Jewish secular organization (Sachar 1993: 410–411), and its Anti-Defamation League led legal and political battles against discrimination. The convergence of political and religious strains of influence on Jewish thought can be seen in the agenda of Stephen Wise, a leading figure in the reform movement and president of the American Jewish Congress. In 1922, Wise's agenda focused on a "program of civil rights for all Americans . . . Negro civil rights, employment discrimination, church-state relations—as well as issues of anti-Semitism and Zionism" (Sachar 1993: 410).

Some Jews may have been initially hesitant to enter the traditional two-party system in the United States because of the domination of the political machines at the local level. Scholnick (1990: 10) speaks of "rising Jewish-Irish friction" in northern cities, which "worked to minimize the number of Jewish votes an Irish-based Democratic Party could expect to gain." Yet, it was Tammany's Al Smith who helped lead Jewish voters to the Democratic lever. As governor of New York, Smith sponsored numerous social welfare measures. He was ably assisted by Belle Moskowitz, a Jewish social worker (see, for example, Caro 1975). Further, Smith's 1928 campaign for the presidency was marred by religious bigotry. This campaign "made American Jewry's shift to the Democrats . . . an accomplished fact" (Scholnick 1990: 11).

Despite this shift, a number of Jews remained with and gave their votes to the Socialist Party in 1932 and 1936. It was not until 1940 that the Workmen's Circle, the *Forward*, and the clothing workers came to strongly endorse Roosevelt (Scholnick 1990: 175). In addition, although the clear majority of Jews did not identify with the Communist Party, "a large proportion of American Communist Party members in the 1930s were of Jewish origin" (Scholnick 1990: 18).

Most Jewish Americans found a home in the Democratic Party during the New Deal, though, and they have never abandoned it. The New Deal's programs provided at least a partial answer to concerns of *tzedukah* and of more radical sentiments. However, it is important to remember that the New Deal and later Democratic/liberal policies also answered other fundamental Jewish needs. As Ginsberg (1993: 140) trenchantly notes, "in the face of social discrimination they found protection and opportunity as members of a political coalition organized . . . around a liberal and social agenda. . . . The liberal Democratic coalition also promoted and continues to promote principles of civil rights that serve the interests of Jews."

Jewish Attitudes and Political Behavior

Jews came to the United States as a persecuted minority, and they continued to experience stereotyping and various forms of discrimination. Their political affiliations had and continue to have at their core a fear of discrimination and attachments to policies that lessen such discrimination for themselves as well as others. To that end Jews looked to the Democratic Party, played an active role in many facets of the civil rights movement, and supported the American Civil Liberties Union (ACLU).

Jews have played important leadership roles in the ACLU, and its membership is predominantly Jewish (Ginsberg 1993: 1–2). As core elements of its agenda, the ACLU promotes separation of church and state and opposes prayer in the schools. Jewish organizations such as the American Jewish Congress, the American Jewish

Committee, and the Anti-Defamation League took part in the litigation to block school prayer (Ginsberg 1993: 100).

Americans for Democratic Action (ADA), formed just after World War II as a liberal alternative to communist-dominated labor groups, has a strong Jewish component. In fact, Gillon (1987: 23) describes "the type of person the ADA attracted" as a Jewish man, "somewhat under forty years of age, a professional holding a Bachelor's degree." The ADA platform endorses civil rights that benefit Jews as well as a liberal social agenda.

Cohen (1989: 11) published the results of a survey demonstrating that the Jewish population in America is liberal in thought and that at least some of the roots of that liberalism lie in the memory of historical discrimination against Jews:

> Jews in the United States retain images of widespread and potentially dangerous anti-Semitism. These images, in turn, influence the process whereby Jews make political decisions, either individually or collectively. . . . Much of the political debate within Jewish organizations and in Jewish periodicals centers on the question of which candidate, party or political campaign is most hospitable or antagonistic to Jews and their communal interests.

Although many believe that anti-Semitism is a relatively minor problem in the United States today, a substantial number of Jews do not. Cohen (1989: 11) found that 65 percent of the Jews polled "thought that some influential positions were closed to Jews," while 76 percent believed that "American anti-Semitism was currently a serious problem."

Compared with other whites, Jews were much more favorably inclined toward the American Civil Liberties Union, the National Association for the Advancement of Colored People (NAACP), and the National Organization for Women (NOW) (Cohen 1989: 13). Cohen (1989: 13) found that liberalism among Jews is highly linked with education and, interestingly, that Jews are twice as likely as other whites to send their children to college.

For Jewish Americans, historical tradition and a philosophical predisposition lead them to liberal political behavior and liberal coalitions. Yet, this liberalism is based in group self-interest as much or more than it is in altruistic tradition. To fight second-class status and poverty, Jews turned first to socialism and then to the Democratic Party. They supported civil liberties and civil rights for their own protection as well as that of others. Their participation in liberal groups reflected an assessment of self-need as well as a desire for general societal improvement.

In those instances when perceived Jewish interest differs from the aims of a liberal coalition there is a weakening of traditional ties. The memory of discrimination overrides basic liberal values.

Conflicts with the Liberal Agenda

Most Jews advocate the separation of church and state, and they play significant roles as members and leaders of the American Civil Liberties Union. However, not all Jews joined in the ACLU's defense of free speech or freedom of assembly. Going back to the early 1920s, Jewish friends of the ACLU objected to its defense of anti-Semites (Walker 1990: 61). The American Jewish Congress, however, a more liberal organization of Jews of eastern European origin, did join with the ACLU in 1937 in arguing against a New York law that "prohibited speech advocating hatred" (Walker 1990: 117).

Even before World War II, not all Jews would stand up for civil liberties when cases involved intolerance directed against them. That point certainly came home in 1977 when a group of American Nazis wanted to march in Skokie, a Chicago suburb that was home to many Jews of whom between 800 and 1,200 were concentration camp survivors. Walker (1990: 324) sums up the sentiment in this way: "The 1967 Six-Day War in the Mideast had sparked a revival of Jewish self-consciousness, and the memory of the Holocaust, support for Soviet Jews, and support for Israel became important political rallying cries. In this atmosphere, Jewish community leaders felt constrained to defend the survivors." Jews throughout the country deplored the intended march and some canceled their ACLU memberships in protest of that organization's defense of the right of the Nazis to assemble.

In a similar vein, Jewish organizations broke with the ACLU and civil rights organizations over the issue of affirmative action. Cohen (1989: 25) found Jews to be largely unsympathetic to affirmative action, and their views were actually very similar to those of other whites. Jews had supported and participated in the civil rights movement out of proportion to their numbers in the population. On the issue of affirmative action, however, many Jewish organizations broke rank. They rejected this remedy to employment and education discrimination because they found it emblematic of the quotas that had kept many of them from prestigious universities and professions in years past. However well intended, any system employing numeric set-asides could limit Jewish accomplishment. After all, Jews today are represented in law and in higher education at levels higher than their proportion in the population.

The creation of the state of Israel in 1948 gave a new focus to American Jewish politics. Prior to the Holocaust, Zionist sentiment was not shared by all elements in the Jewish community. Socialists as well as many of the orthodox did not sanction efforts to achieve a homeland. Such divided sentiments are less common now. Lipset (1990: 19) agrees that today "Israel has become the religion of the American Jews. It is the center of Jewish life, the cause to which more Jews are dedicated than any other." Jews in America have, on occasion, equated attacks on Israel with anti-Semitism and have defended practices by the Israeli government that their liberal tradition would deplore at home. This attachment to Israel has led to breaks with some liberal allies and has contributed to tensions with various African American leaders and their organizations. It also has led to divisions among Jews themselves with some, at times with a New Left background, decrying Zionism and separating themselves from Jewish institutions.

Jews opposed the war in Vietnam in large numbers (Ginsburg 1993: 130). Winston (1978: 207) found that, as early as 1965, "opposition to the war was rooted in several major organizations, in general those with a reform theology." Rabbi Abraham Heschel of the Jewish Theological Seminary, the bulwark of conservative Judaism, worked with Clergy and Laity Concerned about Vietnam, and partici-pated in a two-day organizational meeting in Washington, D.C. in February 1968 (Zaroulis and Sullivan 1984: 157). He was one of many Jews to work with this antiwar group. The American Jewish Congress declared its opposition to the war in 1966 (Winston 1978: 192).

Other Jewish leaders, however, kept silent or gave some support to the war in Southeast Asia. They followed the direction of "the Israeli government [which] suggested that American Jews use restraint before criticizing the war efforts" (Winston 1978: 207); criticism of the war by prominent Jewish groups might damage American political and military support of Israel.

In addition, American Jews gave less support to the Democratic ticket in 1972 than at any time since the New Deal. Some Jewish leaders felt that George McGovern's views on Israel indicated that he would provide only tepid support to that country (Isaacs 1974: 1–5). Diminished support, however, meant that only two thirds of Jews voted for the Democratic standard bearer instead of the usual almost eight out of ten.

In short, segments of liberal American Jewry are willing to sever ties with liberal organizations when they feel their own interests are threatened. Jews' perception of themselves as a marginal group thus can either buttress or undermine their normally liberal political behavior.

ARE JEWS TODAY AS LIBERAL AS BEFORE?

About one fifth to one quarter of the Jewish population is conservative and votes Republican in many elections. There are identifiable Jewish champions of the conservative cause: Norman Podhoretz, Irving Kristol and his son William, and others identified with Commentary, Public Interest, and now the New Republic. Though quite vocal and visible, they are not yet part of a majority. Yet Lipset (1990: 23) reports that "younger Jews are more likely to vote Republican than older cohorts, by 10 to 15 percent." To date, this increasing Republican sentiment has not shown up clearly in the presidential returns.

Irving Howe (1976: 628) also believes that historical Jewish liberalism in the United States has been tempered in the postwar era and that the impact of the authority of Israel "upon American Jews was necessarily conservative." The com-mitment to liberalism remains among many American Jews, but the "intensity in which it [is] held and the readiness to expend energy and accept inconvenience in its behalf may slowly have declined" (1976: 625).

Nonetheless, Jews continue their support of the Democratic Party. They are more likely to vote Democratic than any other white group. Ginsberg (1993: 142) concludes that the party is "the backbone of the liberal political camp, and, thus of Jewish power in American politics." Various white ethnic groups in urban areas, largely Catholic, have clearly moved away from the Democratic Party, first in the Nixon years and decidedly under Reagan and Bush. Yet, in the 1980s and again in

1992, Jews remained in the fold although their incomes might indicate that they would do otherwise.

The reasons for this allegiance are complex. A partial explanation lies in the prominence of the Christian right in the Republican Party, a perception that keeps some Jews tied to their traditional partisan allies. Their marginal status can be reawakened by arguments that prayer be required in the schools, that reproductive rights be limited, and that a Christian America be promoted. Marginality and the old fears can outweigh the pull of economic benefits brought by tax cuts and other Reagan policies.

Ginsberg argues that Jews differ from other whites more in their voting behavior and political activity than in their attitudes. Their attitudes, however, remain dissimilar on "such issues as church-state relations and on social issues where their own marginal or minority status gives Jews a stake in cultural pluralism and protection for behavior that the majority regards as deviant and nonconformist" (1993: 142). Ginsberg joins the group highlighting the perception that Jewish marginality influences the environment in which political decision-making takes place.

Isaacs (1974: 21–22) echoes these sentiments. He finds that "in the case of the Jews, unique factors inherent in the religion and culture have combined with the anti-Semitism to produce a particularly Jewish attitude toward government and politics." Despite considerable success in the United States, Jews generally consider themselves threatened. Hence, it is logical for them to identify with liberal positions regarding social welfare and civil liberties. Yet, some—and in certain cases, most— will deviate from their support of liberal candidates, causes, and organizations. When they perceive their own needs to be in conflict with the positions of their liberal allies, they cease their support. Self-preservation is the prism through which they filter various policies. Scholars agree that Jews' early radicalism, as well as the idea of *tzedukah*, keeps them in the liberal camp and that their marginal status or the perception of that status is the ultimate arbiter of their political behavior.

Evidence presents contrary signals to those who might prognosticate about Jewish political behavior. Its remarkable consistency suggests that any change will likely be gradual. However, generational replacement could hold the key. For Jewish children growing up in the United States today, the idea of marginal status may be more remote than it was for their grandparents. Depending on others' actions, the sense of being threatened may not reappear among those coming of age. This could be what we see among those now voting Republican in higher percentages than their elders. Jews have been liberals because they have a strong sense of being underdogs. They have joined many liberal groups fighting for the underdog. Some, however, always leave if such groups back policies contrary to Jews' self-interest. If the sense of being an underdog fades, Jews may not get involved as they traditionally have done. Finally, the emergence of the Jewish state has generated considerable nationalism, which is rarely the friend of liberalism.

REFERENCES

Caro, Robert. 1975. *The power broker*. New York: Random House.

Cohen, Steven M. 1989. *The dimensions of American Jewish liberalism*. New York: American Jewish Committee.

Gillon, Steven M. 1987. *Politics and vision: The ADA and American liberalism, 1947–1985*. New York: Oxford University Press.

Ginsberg, Benjamin. 1993. *The fatal embrace: Jews and the state*. Chicago: University of Chicago Press.

Howe, Irving. 1976. *World of our fathers*. New York: Touchstone.

Isaacs, Stephen D. 1974. *Jews and American politics*. New York: Doubleday.

Kristol, Irving. 1990. The liberal tradition of American Jews. In *American pluralism and the Jewish Community*, edited by Seymour Martin Lipset. New Brunswick, NJ: Transaction.

Lipset, Seymour Martin. 1990. A unique people in an exceptional country. In *American pluralism and the Jewish community*, edited by Seymour Martin Lipset. New Brunswick, NJ: Transaction.

Sachar, Howard M. 1993. *A history of the Jews in America*. New York: Vintage.

Scholnick, Myron I. 1990. *The New Deal and anti-Semitism in America*. New York: Garland.

Walker, Samuel. 1990. *In defense of American liberties*. New York: Oxford.

Winston, Diane. 1978. Vietnam and the Jews. In *The sociology of American Jews*, edited by Jack Nusan Porter. Boston: University Press of America.

Zaroulis, Nancy, and Gerald Sullivan. 1984. *Who spoke up?* Garden City, NJ: Doubleday.

12
The Impact of Demographic and Social Change on the Jewish Political Agenda in the 1990s

Terri Susan Fine

Several conflicting elements—demographic and sociological—serve both to unify and to diffuse the Jewish American community, affecting political attitudes and support for a number of social policies. Chiefly these changes have occurred in the religious, historical, and social foundations that underlie Jewish political attitudes. Jewish partisanship differs significantly from that of non-Jews, and manifests its political attitudes within various social and foreign policy arenas. Reflecting Jewish voting behavior, several demographic and social trends—particularly in friendly associations, marital patterns, and ethnic identity—point to changes in Jewish political attitudes and political behavior. This political environment both fosters and hinders the Jewish political agenda from being a priority among American Jews.

HISTORICAL FOUNDATIONS

Jews in America constitute both a religious and an ethnic minority. Differences in religious observances, beliefs, and cultural values associated with being immigrants constitute the basis for dual minority status. Most Jews, of course, do not hold Christians' belief that Jesus was the Messiah, and many continue to observe religious rituals and festivals that the majority of the American population knows little about. Moreover, social traditions associated with Jewish ethnicity differ from those of mainstream American culture: learning and speaking other languages such as Hebrew and Yiddish, as well as preserving various Eastern European and Middle Eastern cultural traditions involving music, art, cuisine, literature, dance, and manner of dress.

Ethnic and religious minorities share in their ancestral immigrant experience. Jews emigrated to the United States in order to escape the pogroms created by autocratic regimes such as the one in Russia in the early twentieth century. Upon coming to this country, they experienced both economic and religious discrimination and suffered from social ostracism (Steinberg 1989). Significant disparities between mainstream Christian religions and the Jewish faith created a separateness between the two cultures. Manner of dress, rules regarding food preparation and eating, as well as the preclusion to working on Saturdays contributed to the notion that Jews could not and would not assimilate to traditional American values and social customs. At the same time, Jews promoted education as the means to advance social mobility, whereas other immigrant groups settled for skilled and unskilled trades (Steinberg 1989: 137). Jews, then, did not join forces with other immigrant populations as readily as other groups did with one another, and their assimilation did not occur so smoothly.

This early immigrant experience and a long tradition of social justice led to greater support for a democratic political system and respect for divergent political views. At the same time, Jews tend to be attentive to and to question the wisdom of government decisions that serve to limit rather than broaden the rights of others. This holds true even if, on religious grounds, Jews disagree with those choices. This paradox stems from Jewish immigrant experiences and religious teachings: on one hand, the opportunity to escape religious persecution, emigrate to the United States, and pursue educational opportunities fostered support for the political system; on the other hand, the discrimination convinced many that the system did not function to their advantage. Their views of the political world changed accordingly.

POLITICAL IDEOLOGY AND PARTISANSHIP

Like many other minorities, Jews express tolerance for other minority groups and seek to promote a political agenda that advances the inclusion of all, or most, groups in mainstream society. Jews took an active role, for instance, in early efforts by blacks to guarantee civil rights protection and promote legislation that forbade economic and educational discrimination. Involvement in the civil rights movement served a dual purpose for Jews. First, those same protections from discrimination that had been accorded blacks would also benefit them. Second, working toward civil rights for blacks also served a moral imperative found in religious teachings oriented toward a strong sense of social justice (Ginsberg 1993: 146). The Democratic Party's efforts to create a New Deal coalition by reaching out to those facing economic hardship during the Great Depression included both Jews and blacks. Consequently, political activism among blacks and Jews was promulgated by participation in Democratic Party politics that has continued to the present day.

Jews are also far more likely than Protestants or Catholics to support equal rights for women and a feminist policy agenda. For instance, they were more inclined than the general population to favor the Equal Rights Amendment (Waxman 1983: 149). Political activism among Jewish women is also stronger than among non-Jewish women because of the religious orientation that fosters communal connectedness. Social changes instituted by the women's movement coupled with high levels of community volunteerism have subsequently led to greater political activism for liberal causes among Jewish women (Umansky 1995).

Nearly one half of Jewish Americans are self-identified liberals. They support the separation of church and state, reproductive choice, and other such issues. This liberal ideology stems from their immigrant roots and minority experience. Another thirty percent identify themselves as moderates. By contrast, one fifth of American Protestants and one fourth of those who are Catholic identify themselves as liberals.

At the same time most Jews tend to hold conservative views on economic policy and fiscal matters (Erikson and Tedin 1995: 198), conditioned by their early success in corporate America. About one fourth of Jewish Americans call themselves conservatives on social issues, and this ranks them among the lowest proportion of conservatives. Ideological differences are greatest between Jews and Protestants rather than Catholics (Erikson and Tedin 1995). As a large proportion of American Catholics have immigrant roots, their closer ideological proximity to Jews is expected.

Furthermore, over one half of Jews identify themselves with the Democratic Party whereas less than one fifth call themselves Republican (Erikson and Tedin 1995: 180). These findings are consistent with their immigrant origins and minority religious position and were reinforced by early Democratic Party efforts to bring Jews into its New Deal coalition. Protestants favor the Republican Party, whereas Catholics are evenly split between Democrats and Independents, and one fifth are Republican identifiers.

Jewish liberalism is reflected in policy support, particularly in those arenas where one's minority religious position may cause one to question whether a political system dominated by one particular faith adheres to and respects the separation of religious and political institutions. Questions of religious practices (e.g., school prayer) and policy questions connected to religious doctrine (e.g., abortion) exhibit the greatest religious differences among Jews, Protestants, and Catholics.

Jews are far more inclined than Catholics or Protestants to support abortion rights. While approximately 40 percent of both Protestants and Catholics take the prochoice position, nearly 90 percent of Jews do. Prayer in public schools also receives similarly disparate support levels. Nearly two thirds of Protestants and Catholics favor prayer in public schools, whereas less than one fifth of Jews are supportive (Erikson and Tedin 1995).

Jewish liberalism is also reflected in a feminist political orientation. While traditional Jewish doctrine is not feminist (only the more liberal denominations of Judaism allow women to hold positions of authority and to participate in religious observances traditionally granted to men), Jews are far more likely than Protestants or Catholics to agree that men and women are equally suited for politics (Erikson and Tedin 1995), an argument that grows out of minority status and immigrant roots rather than religious doctrine. Jews also tend to demonstrate high levels of political tolerance. Atheists, homosexuals, and communists are far more acceptable to Jews than to most Protestants or Catholics (Erikson and Tedin 1995).

These findings indicate the liberal orientation that stems from the immigrant experience and a history of discrimination. In general, Jewish Americans support advancement of greater rather than fewer individual choices, especially those that are inconsistent with mainstream views derived from traditional Christian sentiments. Others argue that religious and ethnic minority status does not lead to Jewish political views significantly differing from those positions held by other religious and ethnic majorities. These political views exhibit greater consistency with mainstream American conservatism than the minority status of Jews would suggest. While Jews, for example, took an active role in the civil rights movement and enjoy the benefits of antidiscrimination policy, they have not supported affirmative action remedies (Ginsberg 1993: 147), chiefly because Jews do not constitute one of those groups targeted by such programs. Additionally, economic mobility and educational advancement have led to an overrepresentation of Jews in some institutions where blacks are underrepresented, given their relative proportions in the general population. Consequently, Jews in corporate and academic positions often consider affirmative action efforts for other minorities, especially black Americans, as a threat to their economic power (Ginsberg 1993: 152).

When compared with Protestants and Catholics, Jews have profited from acculturation, assimilation, and the work ethic in that a larger proportion of them have achieved a higher socioeconomic status. While they comprise only 3 percent of the U.S. population, a far greater percentage of Jews is found among the economically advantaged and more prestigious occupations such as law, medicine, business, and the academy.

Generally speaking, most Americans support broad economic opportunity and oppose initiatives that obstruct that opportunity. Support for equal opportunity is also far greater than are efforts aimed at achieving that goal in practice. For example, opposition to affirmative action quotas in employment far exceeds opposition to quotas in higher education (Fine 1992).

Jews and Economics

Government efforts to restrict one's ability to climb the corporate ladder, through levying additional taxes or by giving opportunities that are not based on merit, tend to earn more negative public sentiment, especially from those who believe they will most likely suffer as a consequence of such actions. Therefore, those who have higher incomes tend to oppose increased social welfare spending. Higher income cohorts are also more inclined to oppose a guaranteed job and minimum standard of living (Erikson and Tedin 1995). Economic views among Jews tend to reflect American public opinion toward economic opportunity.

Jews tend to be more economically conservative than one would expect in light of their ideological and partisan orientations. When compared to Protestants and Catholics, for example, Jews are least likely to support the government's role in reducing income differentials. Almost one half of Catholics support this proposition, whereas less than 40 percent of Jews do. One fourth of Jews believe that government should improve the standard of living, whereas one third of Catholics do (Erikson and Tedin 1995). Here we see how minority religious and ethnic status does not achieve similar effect in two religious minorities. At the same time, a recent survey by the American Jewish Congress finds that 80 percent of Jews support the use of public funds to stimulate the economy (Hockbaum 1993), thereby bolstering the argument that the government should play a role in determining individual prosperity. Economic considerations dominate policy views among people of various faiths (Sigelman 1991).

This paradox may signal changing Jewish political attitudes. Many of the liberal attitudes expressed by Jews are also shared by those in the socioeconomic elite, the group to which an above average proportion of Jews belongs. Those without a college education tend to be more conservative than those who have completed a baccalaureate degree or some graduate work (Erikson and Tedin 1995). While the foundation for many policy views originally was based on one's ancestral immigrant experience, the trend now seems to be moving toward economic and educational experiences. Consequently, generational considerations and opportunities associated with academic achievement may have fostered a growing conservatism in Jewish political attitudes.

Those issues particularly salient to American Jews also wield the greatest attention from policy makers, even if these issues are not salient to other religious groups (Repass 1971). Thus, they achieve a greater impact on political involvement such as voting, party activism, and donor behavior.

Jews and Foreign Policy

Because of the high priority they place on maintaining the existence and safety of Israel, American Jews have a far greater tendency to pay attention to U.S. foreign policy with Israel and other Middle Eastern countries than do Christians (Hockbaum 1993). Accordingly, they are concerned with the Arab-Israeli peace process, the implications for Jewish political power, and other territorial issues.

Furthermore, American Jews pay close attention to how the U.S. government is responding to Israel's requests for financial assistance as more Jewish emigrants from the former Soviet Union are absorbed. In 1990, two phenomena facilitating mass emigration to Israel by Soviet Jews occurred: Soviet policies allowing Jews to emigrate to Israel were substantially relaxed, and the United States capped the total number of Soviet Jews allowed to immigrate at 50,000 per year, an almost insignificant number given that as many as one million Jews were now free to leave the Soviet Union. Given these projections, the Israeli government asked the United States to provide a $400 million loan guarantee enabling Israel to borrow money from commercial banks at reasonable interest rates. The Bush administration responded that the guarantee would be provided on the condition that the Israeli government stop expanding settlements. Arab factions expressed concern that if emigrating Soviet Jews settled in the territories, they would crowd out the Palestinians. The Bush administration defended its position on the grounds that, even if the money was not spent in the territories, the guarantee would free other Israeli funds to be spent on settlements. As a result, emigration of Soviet Jews to

Israel became tied to controversial territorial considerations (Singer and Seldin 1992).

Furthermore, policy makers often find it difficult to oppose certain politically charged issues and fear electoral reprisals (Erikson and Tedin 1995). Politicians know that Jews will oppose efforts aimed both at weakening Israel's political and military strength and at disregarding Russian Jewish immigrants. If American Jews do not like what they see, their voting behavior, contribution activities, and lobbying efforts will reflect their disapproval.

The Jewish political agenda is also advantaged because it exists primarily within the realm of foreign rather than domestic or economic policy, in which the public at large holds relatively greater interest (Miller et al. 1976). The public generally remains ignorant of major turns in foreign policy, which undergoes rapid fluctuations. Consequently, politicians may be more inclined to respond to these foreign policy issues than they would otherwise. High voter turnout among American Jews, along with their attentiveness to issues that are not a dominant force in the general electorate's voting behavior, suggests that their minority status is compensated for by these forces. When seeking the Jewish vote, therefore, candidates may be more likely to take a pro-Israel stance on issues mentioned above. As a large proportion of their constituency is inattentive to those issues, candidates are less likely to offend non-Jews.

At the same time, the public views the presidency as the institution chiefly responsible for the conduct of U.S. foreign policy (Erikson and Tedin 1995). Presidential candidates may, then, be more sensitive than congressional candidates when addressing these issues over the course of their campaigns. Foreign policy actions at the presidential level hold greater public attention than do congressional actions. American Jews, as an electoral force, become highly motivated for pro-Israel candidates, and they take a critical interest in their policies.

JEWISH POLITICAL BEHAVIOR

Many scholars note that education is a key force driving voting behavior (Neuman 1986). As education increases, so does political involvement, particularly voting. Because Jews are, as a group, better educated than non-Jews, they are more likely to vote. Coupling Jewish immigrant roots with the liberalizing effect on political attitudes of educational advancement means that most Jews are politically socialized as Democrats and vote accordingly, a pattern confirmed by their vote in the 1992 presidential election. Specifically, a survey sponsored by the American Jewish Congress found that 86 percent of Jewish voters backed Bill Clinton, whereas only 10 percent supported George Bush and even fewer, 4 percent, voted for Ross Perot. By contrast, 44 percent of Catholics voted for Clinton as did 33 percent of Protestants (Hockbaum 1993). Modest fluctuation did occur within certain demographic subgroups of American Jews. For instance, more Jewish women than men voted for Clinton, and younger Jews were more likely to cast their vote for either Bush or Perot than did their senior counterparts over the age of sixty.

Jews also voted in a manner inconsistent with the rest of the American public because economic circumstances and education levels did not affect how Jews voted. Lower-, middle-, and upper-class Jews supported Clinton in the same proportions. Jewish high school graduates and those who completed graduate or professional school also granted him similar levels of support. Those forces that tend to cause fluctuating vote patterns did not achieve differentiation among American Jews in the 1992 presidential election.

Several forces contributed to this agreement among Jewish voters: habit, ideology, political socialization, and issue salience. While most Jews identified with the Democratic Party in 1992, changing demographic conditions may lead to a realignment of affiliations (Hockbaum 1993). The same forces that provided a catalyst to Jewish social, economic, and political differentiation no longer provide the immediacy they once did. The generations of Holocaust survivors, the immigrants of the 1940s and later, and those who witnessed the founding of the state of Israel are dying. They leave children and grandchildren who now compose the greater proportion of American Jews, people who have assimilated into mainstream America more so than previous cohorts. Those factors that promulgated liberal ideological leanings and strong ties to the Democratic Party may be weakening.

These dynamics might suggest that the Republican Party's approach to economic and foreign policy are consistent with the Jewish political agenda and that individuals whose religious and ethnic ties are weaker than those of their parents and grandparents might find the Republicans more appealing. The expectation has not yet materialized, however, that American Jews are ready to shift allegiance to the Republicans despite their commitment to economic conservatism, their opposition to affirmative action, and their perception that the Republican Party staunchly supports Israel (Ginsberg 1993). Demographic and sociological changes that might otherwise foster weaker commitments to both ethnic and religious ties and ritualistic observance resulting in greater Republican identification and voting patterns have been impeded by a strong pro-Israel commitment among Jews of all denominations (Glazer 1995). Consequently, the economic conservatism being put forth by the Republican Party that third- and fourth-generation Jews find appealing has not yet created a Republican block within this cohort.

Demographic and Sociological Change

Many demographic and social forces affect Jewish political attitudes and behavior. Higher than average education levels, income, and social class among Jews have contributed to a deconcentration of Jews in urban areas and an increase in the number of Jews living in suburbia. One consequence of suburban living is the interaction between Jews and non-Jews that may not otherwise occur in urban centers and ethnic neighborhoods. This interaction increases the likelihood that Jews and non-Jews will develop friendships and intimate relationships that they otherwise would not.

Increased mobility exposes one to mainstream cultural norms and lower levels of Jewish population concentration. As a result, interfaith marriage among Jews is higher than among Protestants and Catholics. According to the National Jewish Population Survey, the percentage of Jews marrying non-Jews has increased from 8 percent in 1970 to 31 percent in 1990, a four-fold increase. Seventy-five percent of the children born of these unions are not being reared as Jews and often without any religious identity. Intermarriage is most likely to occur in the Midwest and the West, two regions of the country lacking large urban centers with a high concentration of Jews. Additionally, younger Jews tend to have more gentile friends than their parents did and to express less opposition to interfaith dating (Singer and Seldin 1992).

Children of both interfaith and conversionary marriages are more favorably disposed to the Jewish people than they are to feeling a psychic connection with the Jewish community (Mayer 1983). Furthermore, although children of both marital types express great pride in Israel, they are uncertain about supporting political candidates simply because these politicians are favorable to Jewish concerns. It appears that the increase in interfaith marriages and the geographical dispersion of Jews have led to a weakened connection between ethnic and religious ties to the political process (Mayer 1983; Cohen 1995).

In addition, the growth of the suburbs as a haven for the middle and upper classes, the two economic groups to which most Jews belong, has meant that interaction among Jews is reduced. As their percentage of the total population becomes less, Jews experience lower levels of interaction. Accordingly, the number of interfaith relationships, whether casual or intimate, is increasing (Singer and Seldin 1992).

The assimilation of Jews into mainstream society and the increase in the number of Jews who seek to further their education have had an effect on the numbers of marriages and newborn children. Non-Jewish women between twenty-five and twenty-nine have, on average, twice as many children as Jewish women in the same age group. Women with advanced degrees tend to delay childbirth until they have either completed their education or entered their professions. At that point, birthrates tend to decline as a consequence of advancing age, and women who delay bearing children have fewer children than women who do not (Singer and Seldin 1992). In short, there are fewer Jews being born, either because of the declining birthrates or because of the increasing number of interfaith marriages.

This comprehensive picture suggests that those factors that make Jews distinctive both socially and politically paradoxically contribute to the potential decline of Jewish political influence at the mass level. Public opinion analysts note that the family is the greatest source of political socialization. The family provides the earliest, most ingrained, and most trusted source of any type of information including that geared toward government and the political process. Intermarriage and delayed age at first marriage have resulted in fewer Jews receiving a Jewish education and developing the requisite Jewish identity that fosters the political opinion and behavioral dynamics traditionally associated with American Jews.

As American-born Jews have more children and as the older generations die, the collective memory of persecutions under the Nazis or in the Russian pogroms fades. These cultural changes will have wide-ranging effects on the Jewish political agenda. Many of the forces that have advanced Jewish success and survival in American society now suggest that the Jewish political agenda is less important to policy makers as well as to Jews themselves. At the same time changes are occurring in American public opinion which favor the Jewish political agenda. These are found in the role that public opinion plays in American political life and the extent to which issues of political importance garner public attention and reaction.

A corollary exists in the African American community. Older blacks are far more likely to call themselves Democrats and express strong support for civil rights policies than do younger blacks (Fine 1993). Younger blacks enjoy greater access to economic, educational, social, and political power than their parents and grandparents whose opportunities were impeded. Lacking the degree of firsthand exposure experienced by older generations has caused a generational difference in the perception that government intervention is warranted on behalf of blacks. In the case of Jews, combining generational effects with the increased mobility that is a consequence of advanced education means that socializing Jewish children to U.S. foreign policy with Israel and the Middle East will less likely occur in present and future generations than in the past.

THE FUTURE OF THE JEWISH POLITICAL AGENDA

A shift in the Jewish political agenda and its impact on elite behavior has occurred. Contradictory indications as to how those changes will evolve in the future are also apparent. The advantages stem from the nature of the issues at hand as well as the high levels of participation among Jews that are fostered by their strong political orientations. Because the Jewish political agenda includes issues that have not achieved high levels of salience and attention by the American public, the strength of pro-Israel lobbying efforts is not likely to diminish.

At the same time, the increase in suburbanization and mobility has achieved negative political results. Representative democracy is based on majority rule. As the Jewish population itself has dispersed, so too has the political clout that accompanies a high concentration of Jewish voters in certain geographic locations. At the presidential level, opposition to the Republican administration's response to Israel did not produce the same political punch that it otherwise might have, if the Jewish population had been more geographically concentrated.

One prime example of population dispersal is found in metropolitan New York City. The aging Jewish population that sustained a strong political voice there is moving to southern Florida en masse. As a result, Jewish political influence is on the decline in New York City, whereas it is increasing in southern Florida. The proportion of Jews who are members of Florida's state legislature and U.S. Congressional delegation are increasing, particularly among those representing southern Florida and the Gold Coast regions of that state. At the same time, the concentration of Jews in southern Florida, as opposed to a more general population dispersion in the South, has not stemmed the growing Republicanism of that region.

The population shift and accompanying change in Jewish political influence are also tempered by generational factors. Older women vote less often than men in the same generational cohort. Being socialized to the political process when it was not considered appropriate for them to participate means that older women are less politically active than older men.

Several additional factors will have a negative effect on the strength of the Jewish political agenda. Among these are increasing intermarriage rates and decreasing birthrates among Jews and the number of children receiving a Jewish education, either formally through educational institutions or informally through family socialization. A Jewish religious identity fosters a Jewish political identity. The forces contributing to the development of that identity are on the decline.

Despite these trends, Jews are distinctive in their deep commitment to a dynamic often referred to as symbolic ethnicity (Gans 1979). This commitment is coupled with religious teachings fostering a strong defensive reaction whenever they feel threatened. As Jewish political attitudes and social behaviors become more similar to those of mainstream Christian culture, the manifestation of those attitudes in behavior may not change. Shifting Jewish political attitudes may not achieve the impact that one would otherwise anticipate.

REFERENCES

Cohen, Stephen M. 1995. Jewish continuity over Judaic content: The moderately affiliated American Jew. In *The Americanization of the Jews*, edited by Robert M. Seltzer and Norman J. Cohen. New York: New York University Press.

Erikson, Robert, and Kent L. Tedin. 1995. *American public opinion: Its origins, content, and impact*. 5th ed. Needham Heights, MA: Allyn and Bacon.

Fine, Terri Susan. 1992. The impact of issue framing on support for affirmative action programs. *Social Science Journal* 29, no. 3: 323–334.

———. 1993. Public opinion toward equal opportunity issues: The role of attitudinal and demographic forces among African Americans. *Sociological Perspectives* 35, no. 4: 705–720.

Gans, Herbert. 1979. Symbolic ethnicity: The future of ethnic groups and cultures in America. *Ethnic and Racial Studies* 2: 1–18.

Ginsberg, Benjamin. 1993. *The fatal embrace: Jews and the state*. Chicago: University of Chicago Press.

Glazer, Nathan. 1995. The anomalous liberalism of American Jews. In *The Americanization of the Jews*, edited by Robert M. Seltzer and Norman J. Cohen. New York: New York University Press.

Hockbaum, Martin. 1993. *The Jewish vote in the 1992 presidential election*. New York: American Jewish Congress.

Mayer, Egon. 1983. *Children of intermarriage: A study in patterns of identification and family life*. New York: American Jewish Committee.

Miller, Arthur H., Warren W. Miller, Alden S. Raine, and Thad A. Brown. 1976. A majority party in disarray: Policy polarization in the 1972 elections. *American Political Science Review* 70: 753–778.

Neuman, W. Russell. 1986. *The paradox of mass politics knowledge and opinion in the American electorate*. Cambridge, MA: Harvard University Press.

Repass, David. 1971. Issue salience and party choice. *American Political Science Review* 65: 389–400.

Sigelman, Lee. 1991. If you prick us, do we not bleed? If you tickle us, do we not laugh? Jews and pocketbook voting. *Journal of Politics* 53, no. 4: 977–992.

Singer, David, and Ruth R. Seldin, eds. 1992. *American Jewish year book 1992*. Philadelphia: Jewish Publication Society.

Steinberg, Stephen. 1989. *The ethnic myth: Race, ethnicity, and class in America*. Boston: Beacon Press.

Umansky, Ellen M. 1995. Feminism and American reform Judaism. In *The Americanization of the Jews*, edited by Robert M. Seltzer and Norman J. Cohen. New York: New York University Press.

Waxman, Chaim I. 1983. *America's Jews in transition*. Philadelphia: Temple University Press.

Part V

Native Americans and the
Challenge of Urban Life

13
Coalitions and Alliances: The Case of Indigenous Resistance to the Columbian Quincentenary

Glenn T. Morris

For indigenous peoples (including American Indians, Alaskan Natives, and Native Hawaiians) within the boundaries of the contemporary United States, a persistent dilemma arises regarding the need and advisability of forming alliances with those other peoples and organizations with similar yet distinct purposes and objectives. Since the nadir of indigenous demographics in the late nineteenth century, placing the indigenous (American Indian) population in the United States at approximately 240,000, it has been abundantly clear that the force of indigenous claims against the United States, or against any entity seeking to deny indigenous rights, such as transnational corporations, would not be appreciated solely through the mobilization of the individual or collective populations of indigenous nations. Indigenous peoples—with a few exceptions in Arizona, New Mexico, Oklahoma, and the Dakotas—do not generally represent significant electoral or other demographic blocs that can fundamentally affect the direction of local, state, or regional politics.

Even if indigenous voting strength could be unified and mobilized, the effectiveness of indigenous participation in U.S. pluralist politics to address such critical issues as treaty rights, natural resource rights, and the exercise of the right of political and economic self-determination, is remote. Indigenous electoral "victories" have been limited primarily to relatively superficial advances, such as securing a few seats on school boards or, at best, attaining a seat in a state legislature.

The ability to confront, through electoral politics, the structural obstacles posed by the settler state to indigenous self-determination presents not only a formidable practical problem, but also an inherent contradiction between expressions of independent indigenous sovereignty and indigenous participation in the system of the colonizing settler state. This contradiction exposes the fundamental difference between indigenous peoples in the United States and other interest groups—be they civil rights organizations, human rights groups, or environmental organizations. However, even given the differences resulting from the electoral marginalization of indigenous peoples in the United States, the question of political alliances with nonindigenous peoples and groups becomes especially salient.

Despite continuing attempts by the government to categorize indigenous peoples in the same manner as other "minority" groups, there is no escaping the historical reality that interactions between indigenous peoples and the United States are rooted in a nation-to-nation relationship, negotiated through treaties and based in language that revolves around basic international issues of territory, jurisdiction, and sovereignty. No other group or people in the United States, whether voluntary or involuntary immigrants, has a relationship with the U.S. government defined through such conditions and semantics. The closest is that of Puerto Ricans in Puerto Rico and some Pacific Islanders whose relationship to the United States is, at least theoretically, defined according to international legal principles of decolonization.

Accordingly, the goals and aspirations of indigenous liberation are found at odds not only with the dominant culture, but also frequently with organizations and movements generally considered to be natural allies of indigenous peoples. Recently, several instances of environmental groups purporting to represent the interests of indigenous peoples have suffered the wrath of those same indigenous peoples when the environmental organizations struck deals, in the "best interests" of the indigenous peoples, with transnational corporations over the taking of natural resources in indigenous territories (Kane 1993; Meeker-Lowry 1993). Similar conflicts have occurred over issues of seal hunting or whaling in the Arctic and over spiritual use of traditional territories by indigenous nations, with environmental groups asserting that indigenous peoples possess insufficient environmental consciousness or political competence to insure protection of the environment (Mander 1991: 387; Wuerthner 1987).

The antagonisms between some environmental organizations and indigenous peoples are sometimes attributed to racism in the environmental movement. Yet, even in coalitions with people of color, indigenous peoples often find sympathetic ears, but shallow understanding of the goals of the indigenous rights movement. While many civil rights groups struggle for greater economic opportunity within the dominating system, for greater suffrage and electoral representation, or for wider access to state and federal services, indigenous peoples are often struggling for a return of territory and for a recognition of authority over it. Civil rights groups appear to coalesce with indigenous peoples in an attempt to wrap their movement or issues with the moral authority of Indian grievances, but without a full appreciation of indigenous aspirations.

This is nowhere clearer than with the issue of mascots for professional sports teams, such as the Washington Redskins, the Atlanta Braves, and the Cleveland Indians (Churchill 1994). In the abstract, most people of color pledge their support to indigenous rights. On the question of team mascots, however, not only do the majority of players, many of whom are African Americans, raise no objection to the continuing racist depiction of Indians as mascots, but many fans who are people of color see no offense in the Braves' "Tomahawk Chop" or the Washington Redskins' "war cry." This lack of solidarity with American Indian people over relatively simple issues reveals the potential for even greater divisions when more complex questions of territory, forced relocation, and the recognition of natural resource rights arise.

One explanation for the difference between indigenous claims and traditional civil rights agendas is found in the nature of the claims themselves and in the nature of the remedies sought. The civil rights movements have been rooted in the notion that rights inure to individuals and that the exercise of rights is essentially an individual act like voting or purchasing a home in a non-discriminatory environment. Indigenous rights claims, however, often implicate group rights, such as the right of an indigenous nation to be recognized as a separate and distinct people, the right to have its jurisdiction and authority recognized in its territory, and the right to be free from policies that threaten the survival of the collective (genocide/ethnocide).

Those who hope for coalitions with indigenous peoples or organizations often fail to recognize this fundamental difference. They assume that a common definition of justice or a common appreciation for how claims will be addressed is present, when often a profound ignorance of one another persists. Consequently, the building of alliances and coalitions between indigenous peoples and other movements raises complex questions that require a patient parsing of issues and tactics.

Although examples of conflict and misunderstanding abound in the area of indigenous peoples' rights, the enormity of the crises facing indigenous peoples requires the construction of alliances with sympathetic movements and organizations. What may appear as deep social, political, or economic problems in other communities can accurately be described as destructive to the point of genocide in indigenous contexts (Churchill 1992). The imperative to resolve conflicts between the dominating society and indigenous peoples often creates an immediate, practical need for indigenous peoples to form alliances with anyone who seems sensitive, willing, and able to form such an alliance. Defining the conditions of such alliances will be crucial for the advancement of an indigenous rights agenda.

ALLIANCES VS. COALITIONS

There are three distinct categories of organizational interaction with indigenous peoples: unilateral assimilations, coalitions, and alliances. The first category includes primarily those organizations in the nineteenth and early twentieth centuries that viewed their role in indigenous affairs as a paternalistic, assimilationist mission. The second category, coalitions, views indigenous peoples as distinct (albeit usually subordinate) actors in wider movements for social change. This type of coalition, which was usually assumed to be of semipermanent duration, was generally found during the civil rights movement of the 1960s, but remnants can be found in more contemporary expressions, such as Jesse Jackson's Rainbow Coalition. The third category, alliances, has evolved from the lessons learned from earlier coalitions and is characterized by ad hoc organizations. The term alliance, as opposed to coalition, was adopted by the American Indian Movement of Colorado to describe its relationship to other movements and organizations in organizing around the Columbus Quincentenary in 1992; its alliances were based on three fundamental understandings:

1. The operative term in the relationship is "ally," i.e., that there exists a political, social, economic, environmental, and perhaps spiritual commonality between members of the alliance, that is formally articulated and recognized, and that binds members of the alliance together.

2. The alliance is devoid of hierarchy, and each member of the alliance participates on a co-equal basis; there is no coercion to be brought to bear on any alliance participant and no expectation exists for any alliance member to agree with or to participate in every decision or action of the alliance. There is a basic expectation that alliance members will recognize a loyalty to the broad purposes for which the alliance was formed, and that at any time that they no longer agree with those purposes, will leave the alliance.

3. The alliance is rooted in the principle of mutual respect, i.e., no alliance member has the right to interfere in the internal affairs of another organization, and no alliance member is expected to subscribe to an alliance decision that would put it at odds with the principles of its own organization. Participation in the alliance should in no way impair the autonomy or independence of any organization to address its own constituency or its own issues.

For centuries, indigenous peoples in North America have formed alliances with other peoples and nations, most notably among the six nations of the Iroquois Confederacy (Grinde and Johansen 1991) and with other indigenous nations across the continent (O'Brien 1989). Such alliances were sometimes for defense, but more often were used to strengthen economic, cultural, and social bonds between peoples.

After European powers invaded indigenous territories, native nations were often forced by circumstance to ally themselves with one or more of the primary colonizing powers. Regardless of the choice made, the overall welfare of the indigenous peoples suffered (Debo 1970). This result is the first indication of the profound paradigmatic difference between indigenous peoples and the Europeans who would seek coalitions or alliances with them. In some instances, the failure of the initial arrangements between indigenous and non-indigenous peoples continues to hamper relations with fear, suspicion, and mistrust.

Conversely, the relationship between indigenous peoples and escaped African slaves was marked by a much greater respect, understanding, and eventually, symbiosis. Many escaped slaves were taken into indigenous societies; as a result, many African Americans today can claim American Indian heritage (Forbes

1988). Similar relations can be found in the history between indigenous peoples and Chicanos in the American Southwest. Today, these historical realities forge closer links between indigenous movements and other communities of color.

For many decades, indigenous peoples in North America have been befriended by groups and organizations, primarily Euro-American, wanting to "help" the Indian. Much of the help was quickly translated into unilateral, paternalistic policies of private organizations and federal legislation designed to transform indigenous peoples into the image and likeness of those who were purporting to "help." The collusion of missionaries, politicians, and the U.S. military in an overt policy of assimilation was reflected in the late 1800s through groups such as the Boston Indian Citizenship Committee, the Women's National Indian Association, and the Indian Rights Association. These groups organized to "help" Indian peoples by advocating the dissolution of tribal relations and reservations and the conversion of Indians into Christian capitalists, by bestowing U.S. citizenship on all Indians, and by instituting a universal government operated school system for the "education" of all Indian children (Prucha 1973: 49).

The result of this help from Euro-American "allies" was the passage of the Dawes Severalty Act, arguably the most destructive piece of federal legislation ever passed in the area of Indian affairs. The act led to the loss of 90 million acres of Indian territory and to the destruction of Indian systems of governance and social-cultural cohesion.

By 1923, a group of reformers, led by John Collier and representing themselves as the "real friends of the Indians," formed the American Indian Defense Association (AIDA), for the purpose of defeating the policy of assimilation represented by the Dawes Act. Although commendable for its opposition to assimilation policy and its attendant ethnocide, AIDA possessed its own streak of paternalism that would be found in the Indian Reorganization Act of 1934, which it advanced (Kelly 1983). Through this law, sovereign Indian governments were transformed into the image and likeness of the U.S. system, a condition that destroyed indigenous models of governance and undermined the confidence of American Indian peoples in their own political traditions; a consequence continuing to the present (Robbins 1992: 94–112).

These two examples justify the skepticism about alliances with non-indigenous groups and organizations. The examples also reveal tendencies among groups that would coalesce with indigenous peoples to control the agenda of any coalition and to control the strategy and tactics of the movement for indigenous rights. These tendencies are explained by Trask (1993) in the context of the Native Hawaiian sovereignty movement:

[Euro-American] fear of Native issues often masks fear of losing control over the coalition. This fear exacerbates the already haole [Euro-American] cultural trait of being aggressive and dominating in meetings. In turn, this familiar behavior angers Hawaiians and makes us feel increasingly distant and sullen. . . . [Haoles] want to be both one of the group while also dominating the group. That is to say, haoles tend to take command almost without thinking about whether they should and they tend not to doubt their correctness when confronted by opposing cultural arguments which, in any event, they don't recognize as cultural behavior. (250–252)

Unfortunately for many indigenous organizations, the coalitions spawned with other peoples of color by the civil rights movement of the 1960s also reflected an ignorance of American Indians and their aspirations. Some of the same myths held by Euro-Americans, ranging from the "noble savage" to the "vanquished people," colored how African Americans, Asians, and Latinos viewed Indians. In the civil rights marches, tent cities, and other campaigns, it was always important to have a few Indians in the mix, especially in buckskins and feathers, but very few were in positions of leadership, or in visible public positions when it came time for speeches, pronouncements, or policy making (Deloria 1973: 169–195; 1971: 59–63; Steiner 1968).

Again, part of the explanation for that treatment is a generalized racism against indigenous peoples that labels them as backward, primitive, and lacking civilization (Wilmer 1993: 95–126). A broad tenet of socialization in the dominating culture, this attitude is transferred to and often absorbed by other peripheral groups in U.S. society. Consequently, even though African Americans, Latinos, and Asians often had more in common with American Indians than with the dominating society, the attitudes of the dominating society were still defining the relations between different communities of color in the 1960s and 1970s.

In addition, the goals and aspirations of the respective organizations and movements are substantially dissimilar. While Martin Luther King, Jr. was marching for desegregated lunch counters, the Oglala Lakota were fighting for a return of the Black Hills; while Cesar Chavez was fighting for better conditions for farm workers, the Nisqually were demanding that their international fishing treaties with the United States be respected. Those aspirations and demands are viewed differently not only by the advocates, but also by the political and economic system that is confronted by the demand. The first aspiration calls for integration and acceptance into the system; the second may ultimately call for the right to a separate and independent existence from the system.

Despite these historical differences between movements of peoples of color, Trask's warning about the pitfalls of coalition building between indigenous and nonindigenous organizations rings familiar to many people of color in similar circumstances. It should be remembered, however, that some alliances in the American Indian context have been constructed between indigenous and nonindigenous groups with extremely powerful and beneficial results.

As Indian militancy rose—for example, the American Indian Movement (AIM) in the early 1970s, which experienced a violent response by the U.S. government—a number of alliances with nonindigenous peoples were constructed. One of the first was the Wounded Knee Legal Defense/Offense Committee (WKLDOC), a consortium of mainly non-Indian attorneys committed to the legal defense of AIM members who were prosecuted as a result of the seventy-one-day occupation of the community of Wounded Knee in 1973. WKLDOC worked tirelessly on the hundreds of cases emanating from Wounded Knee, and became an important pool of legal expertise for AIM, even to the present (Mathiessen 1983: 72).

Subsequent to Wounded Knee, a South Dakota–based alliance of indigenous peoples, environmentalists, and ranchers formed the Black Hills Alliance (BHA) to address issues of environmental degradation, treaty rights, and the destruction of family farms. BHA attempted to expose the structural similarities of the issues that concerned the diverse members of the alliance, and to construct long-term solutions based on mutual respect and understanding (Mathiessen 1983).

One of BHA's greatest successes was the 1980 Black Hills Survival gathering, attended by thousands of people determined to stop the destruction of the Black Hills and to advance the cause of indigenous rights. A highlight of the gathering was a landmark speech given by Dakota AIM leader Russell Means, in which he critiqued the European worldview regarding the environment, technology, and development. On the question of alliances he said,

> When I use the term "European," I'm not referring to a skin color or a particular genetic structure. What I'm referring to is a mind set, a world view which is the product of the development of European culture. People are not genetically encoded to hold this outlook, they are acculturated to hold it.
>
> What I'm putting out here is not a racial proposition, but a cultural proposition. Those who ultimately advocate and defend the realities of European culture and its industrialism are my enemies. Those who resist it, who struggle against it, are my allies, the allies of American Indian people. And I don't give a damn what their skin color happens to be. Caucasian is the white term for the white race; European is an outlook I oppose.
>
> I trust the community/culturally based vision of all the races which naturally resist industrialization and human extinction. Clearly individual whites can share in this, given only that they have reached the awareness that continuation of the industrial imperatives of Europe is not a vision, but species suicide. White is one of the sacred colors of the Lakota people: red, yellow, white and black. The four directions, the four seasons, the four periods of life and aging, four races of humanity. (1982: 30–31)

Means's speech, however, did not ignore the need for a regular separation of issues and for a mutual respect for separate and co-equal identities within alliances. Reminiscent of Malcolm X's message that "whites who are sincere don't accomplish anything by joining Negro organizations and making them integrated. Whites who are sincere should organize among themselves and figure out some strategy to break down the prejudice that exists in white communities. This is where they can function more intelligently and more effectively, in the white community itself, and this has never been done," (Malcolm X 1991: 90), Means said,

> I work with my own people, with my own community. Other people who hold non-European perspectives should do the same. I do not proclaim

myself able to effectively deal with the struggles of the Black community in Watts or Newark. And I don't expect a Black activist from those communities to be particularly effective in the day-to-day struggles of the Lakota people. Each cultural group can and must build upon the basis of its own cultural integrity. This is our strength and the source of our vision, a vision which compels us to resist the industrialization of European culture. It is the sort of vision which allows us to come together, to ally with one another, to pool our strength and resources and to resist Europe's death culture while retaining our own identities as human beings. (1982: 31)

Within struggles for indigenous peoples' rights in recent years, a number of other alliances and coalitions have been formed, with varying degrees of success. Among the more successful have been the Big Mountain Support Groups, focusing international attention on the relocation of traditional Diné people from their homeland in northern Arizona (Kammer 1980), the Western Shoshone Defense Council, to defend the rights of the Western Shoshone Nation under the provisions of the 1863 Treaty of Ruby Valley (Mander 1991: 303–318), and the Leonard Peltier Defense Committee, an extremely effective international network to publicize the case of the famous political prisoner, Leonard Peltier (Mathiessen 1983).

Some of the deepest understanding and respect between indigenous peoples and Euro-Americans emerged in the context of the Wisconsin fishing rights struggle in the late 1980s and early 1990s. As a result of federal court decisions recognizing expanded treaty hunting and fishing rights for the Anishinabe peoples in what is now Wisconsin, a severe backlash developed from conservative Euro-American hunting and fishing interests. As the Anishinabe fishers tried to exercise their treaty-guaranteed rights, groups of disgruntled Euro-Americans engaged in violence and other obstruction toward the Indians. In response, several Euro-American groups organized to assist the Anishinabe, among them the Wisconsin Greens and Honor Our Neighbors' Origins and Rights (HONOR) (Gedicks 1993: 163–185). These alliances continue today and have taken up other issues such as mining and toxic pollution.

More recently, an informal coalition of people of color has been formed by such notables as Ben Chavis of the NAACP and indigenous activists such as JoAnn Tall of Native Action and Tom Goldtooth of the Indigenous Environmental Network. This coalition seeks to publicize the similar hazards faced by communities of color from environmental pollution and to develop a collective strategy to combat the future poisoning of communities of color by industry and government (Bullard 1993; Taliman 1994). Against this backdrop the American Indian Movement of Colorado began to organize for the 500th anniversary of Christopher Columbus's arrival.

INDIGENOUS PEOPLES' REACTIONS TO THE COLUMBIAN QUINCENTENARY

The quincentenary of Christopher Columbus provided indigenous peoples throughout the Americas with an educating and political organizing opportunity of unequal proportion. With this momentous anniversary came an opportunity to give voice to the indigenous perspective of the Columbian legacy—the "view from the shore," as opposed to from the ship, if you will. (South and Meso American Indian Information Center 1991; Barriero 1992). The year 1992 provided a chance for indigenous peoples to expose the common political, legal, religious, and economic threads that have run from 12 October 1492 to the relocation, killings, and continuous denial of indigenous peoples' rights (AIM of Colorado 1991).

For many indigenous groups, the quincentenary was a classic occasion to lay bare the essential truths of colonialism and survival as indigenous peoples have experienced, and continue to experience, them. It was an opportunity to enter educational institutions from kindergartens to graduate schools in order to provoke a re-examination of the history of the Americas and to analyze the Columbus story from beginning to present. It was also an opportunity to draw important connections between the socialization of students and other citizens and continuing government policies that subordinate indigenous peoples (Wilmer 1993).

A number of books and publications emerged in the years immediately preceding the quincentenary, setting the stage for the debate (Barriero 1992; Sale 1990; Jaimes 1992; Rethinking Schools 1991). For the quincentenary, there were plans across the continent to bring attention to indigenous viewpoints on the "discovery" of the Americas, and to the continuing efforts at survival and resurgence by the various indigenous nations throughout the hemisphere (South and Meso American Indian Information Center 1990, 1991, 1992).

The Columbus Day holiday officially began as a state celebration in Colorado in 1907. Prior to that date, there were periodic proclamations and ad hoc recognitions of the date or of Columbus, but there was no official designation of a holiday to honor Columbus. In fact, Columbus Day did not become a national holiday until 1971, after being signed into law by Lyndon Johnson in 1968 (Sale 1991: 350–364).

Because of the genesis of Columbus Day as an officially sanctioned state celebration, the American Indian Movement of Colorado (Colorado AIM) adopted the position that it had a particular responsibility to use the quincentenary as a focal point for changing attitudes and policy regarding the celebration of Columbus Day (American Indian Movement of Colorado 1991). Commencing in 1989, the Colorado AIM began a four-year educational and organizing campaign to alter public perceptions, education curricula, and public policy with regard to the celebration of Columbus. It initiated a series of public demonstrations and print and speaking campaigns to provoke debate and discussion of the quincentenary.

In October 1989, the Colorado AIM held its first public demonstration on the Columbus theme. In organizing for the demonstration, AIM contacted its traditional allies within the American Indian community of Denver and Colorado, such as the Denver Indian Center and other local Indian organizations, Euro-American support groups such as the Big Mountain Support Group, and environmental organizations with whom AIM had worked in the past, such as Greenpeace and Earth First!

In communities of color, AIM relied on its traditionally friendly relations with like-minded liberation organizations. During Wounded Knee, the Denver-based

Crusade for Justice, a Chicano resistance organization led by Rudolfo "Corky" Gonzales, helped to supply arms and food to the besieged AIM forces inside Wounded Knee. That support created an alliance that has continued through the Columbus Day campaign to the present.

From the beginning, an activist Asian American organization, Making Waves: Asians in Action, and its primarily woman-led leadership, stood in complete solidarity with AIM, and worked to raise the consciousness of the generally conservative Asian American community of Denver.

In the beginning, the only two African American organizations that participated in the alliance with AIM were the Nation of Islam and the All-African Peoples' Revolutionary Party (AAPRP). Their participation was as much a reflection of the personal relationships between the local leadership of the organizations as it was the organizational relations between the groups.

In 1989, approximately 200 people participated in the counter-Columbus rally on the steps of the state capitol. After a short march to a local statue honoring Columbus, which AIM had demanded the city remove, AIM leader Russell Means poured blood on the statue and was arrested (*Rocky Mountain News* 1989). The criminal charges were later dismissed on First Amendment grounds.

AIM's willingness to confront its perception of an overtly racist and anti-Indian system, combined with the willingness of AIM's members to risk arrest and physical injury in pursuit of their articulated principles, proved to be most advantageous in building alliances. In each year of the campaign, the stakes were raised higher, and with the raising of the stakes, the counter-Columbus alliance swelled.

The Columbus Day Parades

In 1990, the Federation of Italian American Organizations (FIAO) revived its Columbus Day parade, which had been dormant for nearly three decades. Immediately upon learning of the revival, Colorado AIM contacted the federation and requested that the parade not be revived under the theme of Columbus as a hero. Instead, AIM suggested that the parade be held as a general celebration of Italian American heritage and culture. The FIAO rejected AIM's request and proceeded with plans for a celebratory Columbus Day parade, but invited various American Indian organizations to participate (*Rocky Mountain News* 1990).

In response, AIM announced that it would stop the parade, through civil disobedience if necessary. Although AIM formally requested that it be allowed to march in the parade, its application was denied because parade organizers were convinced that AIM was planning to disrupt the parade internally. No other Indian organizations accepted the invitation to march in the parade.

On the day of the parade, AIM and approximately 300 allies met on the steps of the state capitol in anticipation of blocking the parade. The allied organizations from the previous year, plus a few new peace and justice organizations and additional Chicano student organizations, joined with AIM in the protest. At the eleventh hour, the FIAO requested that AIM lead the parade, with its protest and anti-Columbus banners. AIM agreed to do so on the condition that the FIAO would enter into serious negotiations designed to transform Columbus Day into a multiracial celebration of diversity in the Americas. Although this agreement was widely reported, the condition for negotiations was not. Consequently, many groups and organizations, which originally were sympathetic to AIM's position, concluded that AIM had abandoned its strong counter-Columbus position (*Denver Post* 1990).

Although initial AIM-FIAO negotiations were scheduled, FIAO canceled them, and would not reschedule. One week prior to the 1991 parade, FIAO contacted AIM to attempt an accommodation, but AIM rejected the overture, saying that FIAO had wasted an entire year and had violated the agreement from the previous year. In the meantime, AIM representatives had been visiting organizations, churches, and schools to organize around the issue of the quincentenary, but one event made AIM's organizing job much easier: In April 1991, the Ku Klux Klan, having decided that Colorado was prime recruitment territory, scheduled a public rally at the state capitol. In response, an alliance of approximately one dozen community organizations, including AIM, posed a counterpresence at the Klan rally. When the Klan attempted to march into downtown Denver, the rally turned violent, and the Klan was dispersed. Despite the violence, AIM's leadership role in containing the violence was key to forging stronger relations with diverse community organizations, especially in communities of color. A second Klan rally in July 1991 further solidified AIM's leadership role when it was announced that Colorado AIM led the list of the Klan's enemies.

By October 1991 AIM had secured the support of dozens of community-based organizations in its counter-Columbus effort. Part of its effectiveness was the promise that the parade would not proceed this year. As the parade approached, tensions mounted, but the unity of the alliance was apparent. AIM sponsored potluck dinners and discussion sessions that allowed representatives from various organizations and movements to express their own issues, while AIM attempted to tie them back to the quincentenary.

On 12 October 1991, over 1,000 activists from nearly two dozen organizations, from as far away as Kansas and South Dakota, had gathered at the state capitol to protest the parade. As the parade proceeded in front of the capitol, Russell Means delivered a fiery speech about the Columbus legacy and the responsibility of the crowd to advance a new truth about the history of the hemisphere, for the sake of the next generation. One sign in the crowd crystallized the sentiment: "Lies written in ink will never disguise facts written in blood."

At the conclusion of his speech, Means led the alliance to the parade route, and approximately 200 people blocked the parade, fully aware that they would be arrested. Hundreds of other protesters lined the parade route with banners and signs; fake blood was poured in the street to represent the millions of indigenous peoples' lives lost since 1492 from warfare, massacre, and disease.

The parade was blockaded for over an hour, but by negotiation, only four of the main organizers of the protest, Means and three other AIM leaders, were arrested (*Rocky Mountain News* 1991; *Denver Post* 1991). The parade essentially broke apart in confusion, and AIM considered the blockade and the arrests to be an essential

building block toward organizing a massive counterforce to any Columbus celebra-
tions in the quincentennial year. Unlike the previous year when AIM tried to
accommodate the FIAO, AIM proved in 1991 that it was prepared to advance its
principles even if it meant going to jail.

Immediately after the 1991 parade, AIM began organizing for 1992. It sent
information flyers to organizations, schools, and churches. It visited the regular
meetings of organizations and talked about the common ground between them.
The organizing strategy for 1992 targeted specific groups with specific themes.

African Americans

The lack of African American participation in past years was troubling to AIM,
which clearly had not effectively communicated what it considered to be the racist
nature of the Columbus holiday to the African American community. Throughout
1992, AIM representatives visited African American organizations and schools,
relating the history of Columbus as an African slave trader prior to his arrival in the
Americas. AIM emphasized the link between Columbus and the Caribbean slave
trade, and reminded African Americans of the historical link between escaped slaves
in the South and the indigenous nations that harbored them, a practice that
precipitated the Seminole Wars in Florida. AIM raised the issue of the Columbus
statue in Denver's preeminent park, and asked if African Americans would stand for
a similar statue of a Nightrider or of a statue to a famous slave trader.

By mid-1992, AIM had secured the support of its traditional allies in the Nation
of Islam and AAPRP, but also had the support of the NAACP, the Rainbow
Coalition, the Urban League of Denver, all of the Black Student Alliance groups
from local college campuses, and the major black ministerial organizations in the
city. However, AIM did not get the support of the African American mayor of
Denver, Wellington Webb.

Chicano/Latinos

The alliance between AIM and Chicano groups, especially the Crusade for
Justice, was strong, although relations with these groups had strained when
Colorado AIM took a position in support of the Miskito, Sumo, and Rama Indians
in their opposition to Nicaraguan Indian policy in the mid 1980s. Over the years,
however, with continuing dialogue, and with the open, public positions of AIM
against such propositions as English Only in Colorado, whatever rifts had developed had been bridged.

AIM's organizing in the Chicano community was relatively easy: it simply
focused on the common heritage of both Indians and Chicanos, emphasized that
it was the colonial systems of both the United States and Mexico that kept
Chicanos and Indians separated from one another and prevented the respective
communities from recognizing their common points of unity. At the Klan rallies
earlier, the AIM security unit had joined forces with other security units of Chicano
organizations, and a cordial and trusting relationship developed. By late summer
1992, the major Chicano organizations of Denver—the Crusade, the student
organizations MeCHA and United Mexican-American Students, Organization of

Latin Americans, Hispanics of Colorado, and Chicano organizations from across Colorado—had endorsed the October action.

Asian Americans

Although some Asian organizations (Making Waves) had been active in the counter-Columbus movement from the beginning, overall interest in the Asian community was not strong. Making Waves attempted, in a rather light-hearted way, to remind the Asian community that it should thank American Indians for stopping Columbus, because, after all, he was headed for Asia, and the cataclysm that befell the Indians of the Americas might have been visited instead on Asia.

Each year, Asian representation in the protest grew, albeit not enormously given the relative size of the Asian American population in Denver. There were, however, Asian contingents led by Making Waves and populated by Asian students, many of them Southeast Asian immigrants standing in solidarity with AIM.

At one point in 1992, a division within the Asian community developed when the Asian American Advisory Council to the mayor asked AIM to commit to nonviolence and peace in the October 1992 demonstrations. Because AIM had always committed itself to nonviolence except in defense of its members if attacked, it was puzzled by the request. Some members of the advisory council thought that the communiqué was inappropriate and represented pressure by the city to temper AIM's position, since no similar letter was sent to the Italian federation.

Arabs and Jews

From the beginning of the campaign in 1989, AIM had received the support of the New Jewish Agenda (NJA), a progressive, anti-Zionist, organization with which Colorado AIM had a long and mutually respectful relationship. In addition, many Jews, participating in a number of organizations ranging from the National Lawyers' Guild to the Denver Region Greens, were active and vocal in their support of AIM. Although NJA attempted to help AIM to organize a broader base of support for the counter-Columbus actions in the mainstream Jewish community and in synagogues, it was generally unsuccessful. One reason was that the local leadership of the Anti-Defamation League of B'nai Brith had pegged AIM as anti-Semitic because of AIM's strong support of Palestinian rights, and because of AIM's cordial relations with the Nation of Islam. Nonetheless, NJA's support of AIM was unflagging, and Jewish support of the actions was strong. NJA was particularly effective in reminding Jews of the connection of the commencement of the Columbus voyage and the expulsion of Jews from Spain on the same day. They pointed to the evidence that Columbus's voyage might very well have been financed through the confiscated wealth of expelled Spanish Jews.

Despite a relatively small Arab American community in Denver, AIM had developed a good relationship with local Arabs, especially the local chapter of the Arab American Anti-Discrimination Committee. It had been vocal in its opposition to the Persian Gulf War, and the Arab community remembered that when requested to support the Columbus campaign.

Other Alliances

The coalition to stop the Columbus Day parade was truly a multiracial and multicultural alliance. Among the most important alliances were those with the peace and justice groups in Denver, including the progressive Euro-American churches and the Colorado Council of Churches. AIM articulated its message on the quincentenary from dozens of pulpits around the state. It also allied with other organizations devoted to peace and justice questions such as the Boulder Peace Center, the Denver Region Greens, Big Mountain Support Group, and the National Lawyers Guild.

The gay and lesbian community also gave significant support to AIM's work, partially in response to AIM's active opposition to Amendment 2, an anti-gay/lesbian constitutional amendment initiative. Similar support came from environmental groups in the region, which have recognized the connection between the destruction of the environment and the plight of indigenous peoples.

Not all of the progressive community supported AIM or its tactics. Those in the ACLU camp thought that AIM was too heavy-handed in its tactics and that it was actually infringing on the constitutional rights of the FIAO to hold its parade. AIM responded that the parade represented a continuing pattern of genocide and ethnocide against indigenous peoples and that it advocated a racist ideology that results in the ongoing destruction of Indian peoples, cultures, and societies. Because of the genocidal nature of the message of the parade and the degree of state support that the parade received (e.g., closing downtown Denver and providing police protection), AIM argued that the parade was not protected by the First Amendment (American Indian Movement of Colorado 1991).

The result of all of this coalition building was that on 10 October 1992, nearly 3,000 people from as far away as California, Montana, and New York, from fifty-four local and regional organizations, came together to stop, if necessary with their bodies, the Columbus Day parade in Denver (Lippard 1993). Nearly 1,200 police, the Denver SWAT team, canine corps, and paramedics had been mobilized. AIM had organized a legal team of forty lawyers and eighty legal observers. It had a thirty-member medic team to deal with tear gas or club wounds, and it had arranged an elaborate system of food and housing to sustain over a thousand people for several days.

Fifteen minutes prior to the parade's scheduled commencement, the police and organizers canceled the parade (Rocky Mountain News 1992). Print and television media around the world reported the cancellation, but failed to mention the alliance responsible. Instead, the blame was placed on AIM and "Indians" (Billings Gazette 1992). On 10 October 1992, Colorado AIM and its allies sent a message about Columbus as a divisive and racist icon to the city of Denver, to the state of Colorado, and to the United States government. AIM declared that as long as there was a day honoring Columbus, AIM would oppose it. Apparently, the parade organizers received that message; the parade has not returned.

CONCLUSIONS

The Columbian Quincentenary in 1992 provided Colorado AIM with an opportunity to disseminate an indigenous peoples' perspective on the arrival of Columbus and its impact on indigenous peoples and societies. It also provided an opportunity for empowerment of the American Indian community of Denver, of Colorado, and of the country. Almost without intention or design, a consequence of the Columbus Day action was the coalescing of one of the most diverse and broad-based alliances that had been seen in Denver in recent memory.

One question was whether AIM should disband this alliance or whether it had the responsibility to maintain the vitality of the alliance beyond the quincentenary. Since 1992, Colorado AIM has been able to maintain its relations with members of the alliance, although in a rather amorphous and fluid condition. In 1993, when the FIAO decided not to hold a parade, AIM sponsored a multiracial celebration, focusing on the contributions of all peoples to the construction of the contemporary Americas. AIM also dedicated seven aspen trees to the city of Denver as a living memorial to the Indian ancestors who had been sacrificed in the "American Holocaust" (Stannard 1992). Hundreds from the 1992 alliance returned for the next year's celebration (*Rocky Mountain News* 1993), helped to plant the trees, and committed themselves to a permanent future celebration of multiracial respect to replace the Columbus Day parade in Denver (Noel 1993). Consequently, the current status of the alliance rests somewhere in between Trask's fear of permanent coalitions controlled by pushy and culturally insensitive nonindigenous peoples or groups that she eschews, and the limited, ad hoc coalitions that she advocates (1993: 255–259).

The alliance in Denver flew in the face of the traditional models of interest group pluralism that are supposed to comprise conventional political coalitions and alliances in the United States (Dahl 1956; Lowi 1979: 50–61; Mansbridge 1990: 3–22). Instead, the alliance was formed on the basis, not of quid pro quo, but of finding a common ground against racism, and to reconstruct a sense of community on that common ground. This alliance confirmed the notion that political alliances need not be rooted entirely, or even primarily in the realm of self-interest, but can be guided by adherence to a shared altruism, with self-interest simply as a backdrop (Mansbridge 1990: 133–143).

Lasch (1984: 94) describes the growth of political cynicism and isolation as a process leading to the destruction of community because "men and women have no confidence in the possibility of cooperative political action—no hope of reducing the dangers that surround them." The alliance provided evidence that the atomization created through the operation of self-interested pluralism can be defeated by a common interest in the restoration of broad notions of racial justice and multiethnic mutual respect. The alliance proved that cooperative, altruistic, political action not only can attain positive political results, but can instill a sense of political purpose into a jaded political environment.

REFERENCES

American Indian Movement of Colorado. 1991. Why we oppose Columbus Day and Columbus Day Parades. Reprinted in the *Denver Post*, 12 October.

Barreiro, José, ed. 1992. *View from the shore: American Indian perspectives on the quincentenary*. Ithaca, NY: Akwekon Press.

Billings Gazette. 1992. Columbus parade canceled after Indian activists' threats. 11 October, 6-A.

Bullard, Robert D. 1993. *Confronting environmental racism: Voices from the grassroots*. Boston: South End Press.

Churchill, Ward. 1994. Crimes against humanity. *Cultural Survival Quarterly* (winter): 36–39.

——— . 1992. *Struggle for the land: Indigenous resistance to genocide, ecocide, and expropriation in contemporary North America*. Monroe, ME: Common Courage Press.

Dahl, Robert. 1956. *A preface to democratic theory*. Chicago: University of Chicago Press.

Debo, Angie. 1970. *A history of the Indians of the United States*. Norman: University of Oklahoma Press.

Deloria, Vine, Jr. 1969. *Custer died for your sins*. New York: Avon Books.

——— . 1973. *God is red*. New York: Dell Publishing.

Denver Post. 1990. Indians lead parade, 10 October, 1.

——— . 1991. Indian leaders block parade, 13 October, C-1.

Forbes, Jack. 1988. *Black Africans and Native Americans: Race, color and caste in the evolution of red-black people*. New York: Oxford University Press.

Gedicks, Al. 1993. *The new resource wars: Native and environmental struggles against multinational corporations*. Boston: South End Press.

Grinde, Donald A., and Bruce E. Johansen. 1991. *Exemplar of liberty: Native America and the evolution of democracy*. Los Angeles: UCLA American Studies Program.

Jaimes, M. Annette, ed. 1992. *The state of native America: Genocide, colonization and resistance*. Boston: South End Press.

Kammer, Jerry. 1980. *The second long walk: The Navajo-Hopi land dispute*. Albuquerque: University of New Mexico Press.

Kane, Joe. 1993. With spears from all sides. *New Yorker*, 27 September, 54–79.

Kelly, Lawrence C. 1983. *The assault on assimilation: John Collier and the origins of Indian policy reform*. Albuquerque: University of New Mexico Press.

Lasch, Christopher. 1984. *The minimal self: Psychic survival in troubled times*. New York: W. W. Norton.

Lippard, Lucy. 1993. Folding the tents. *Z Magazine*, May, 53–56.

Lowi, Theodore J. 1979. *The end of liberalism: The second republic of the United States*. New York: W. W. Norton.

Malcolm X. 1991. *Malcolm X talks to young people: Speeches in the U.S., Britain, and Africa*. New York: Pathfinder.

Mander, Jerry. 1991. *In the absence of the sacred: The failure of technology and the survival of Indian nations*. San Francisco: Sierra Club Books.

Mansbridge, Jane J., ed. 1990. *Beyond self-interest*. Chicago: University of Chicago Press.

Mathiessen, Peter. 1983. *In the spirit of Crazy Horse*. New York: Viking Press.

Means, Russell. 1982. The same old song. In *Marxism and native Americans*, edited by Ward Churchill. Boston: South End Press.

Meeker-Lowry, Susan. 1993. Killing them softly: The rainforest harvest. *Z Magazine*, July–August, 41–47.

Noel, Tom. 1993. AIM aims to end Columbus Day, clashes with Aspen in civic center. *Denver Post*, 16 October, B-11.

O'Brien, Sharon. 1989. *American Indian tribal governments*. Norman: University of Oklahoma Press.

Prucha, Francis Paul. 1973. *Americanizing the American Indians: Writings by the "friends of the Indian," 1880–1900*. Cambridge, MA: Harvard University Press.

Rethinking Schools. 1991. *Rethinking Columbus: Teaching about the 500th anniversary of Columbus' arrival in America*. Milwaukee, WI: Rethinking Schools.

Robbins, Rebecca. 1992. Self-determination and subordination: The past, present, and future of American Indian governance. In *The state of native America*, edited by M. Annette Jaimes. Boston: South End Press.

Rocky Mountain News. 1989. Indians protest Columbus Day, 11 October, 5.

——. 1990. Indians target Columbus Day, 20 September, 20.

——. 1991. Indians halt parade in protest, 13 October, 4.

——. 1992. Protesters succeed in shutting down parade, 11 October, 6.

——. 1993. Multicultural rally celebrates diversity, 11 October, A-4.

Sale, Kirkpatrick. 1990. *Conquest of paradise: Christopher Columbus and the Columbian legacy*. New York: Alfred Knopf.

South and Meso American Indian Information Center. 1990. Indigenous alliance of the Americas on 500 years of resistance: Resolutions from the first continental conference on 500 years of Indian resistance, *SAIIC*, 17–21 July.

——. 1991. *SAIIC Newsletter* 6, nos. 1–2 (spring/summer).

——. 1992. *SAIIC Newsletter* 6, no. 3 (spring/summer).

Stannard, David. 1992. *The American holocaust: Columbus and the conquest of the new world*. London and New York: Oxford University Press.

Steiner, Stan. 1968. *The new Indians*. New York: Delta Books.

Taliman, Valerie. 1994. Right to clean environment fundamental. *News from Indian Country* (newsletter), March.

Trask, Haunani Kay. 1993. *From a native daughter: Colonialism and sovereignty in Hawai'i*. Monroe, ME: Common Courage Press.

Wilmer, Franke. 1993. *The indigenous voice in world politics*. Newbury Park, CA: Sage.

Wuerthner, George. 1987. An ecological view of the Indian. *Earth First!* 7, no. 7 (August): 20–22, 34.

14
Politics in the Mainstream: Native Americans as the Invisible Minority

Walter C. Fleming

Today American Indian people are often asked, particularly by European visitors, why Native people do not unite against the American government, state governments, or whatever institution these international observers feel Indians ought to be uniting against. These individuals fail to understand that this is not as easily accomplished as it might seem nor is unity necessarily desirable (see Cornell 1988). There is an assumption that, given a common history and their relatively small numbers, Indian people ought to be a perfect model for some type of coalition building. These same visitors express disappointment that Native Americans cannot or do not exert more political pressure to achieve some ends which no one can agree on in the first place. These perceptions are based upon two common misconceptions about American Indians: (1) that there exists a people called "American Indians" and (2) that American Indians can unite to be an effective lobby for their causes. Each of these assumptions deserves close scrutiny.

In 1984, 283 federally recognized tribes existed throughout the United States, including nearly 200 Alaskan villages, each as a unique political entity. Some 317 federal reservations and 21 state reservations cover vast territories across the continent (Waldman 1985: 198). Of the approximately 2,200 distinct Indian languages once spoken in the Americas, perhaps as many as 300 are found in North America. Over 100 survive in the United States and are spoken by Indians today. It is estimated that approximately one third of all Native Americans still speak their native language (Waldman 1985: 65–67).

A Native person will first identify himself or herself as a member of a tribe, then as an American Indian. Even though the Crow and Northern Cheyenne reservations share a contiguous border, a Crow will not presume to speak to the aspirations of a Cheyenne. Tribal allegiances thus override the larger ethnic identity, and Indian people do not share the same wants and desires, or concur on the same issues.

Unlike other minority groups, Native Americans do not represent a large enough segment in American society to feel they can be an effective participant in mainstream politics. One of the fundamental differences between Native American people and other minority groups in the United States is that Indian people, in the main, do not feel that they are a part of the mainstream, nor do they necessarily wish to be. This is, in part, because American Indians were for the most part, unwillingly consumed by American society.

HISTORICAL ANTECEDENTS

Not without just cause, American Indians have a general mistrust of the American political process. Federal Indian policy has, until recently, been designed to alienate Indians from the land and force Indians to assimilate into American mainstream society. Thus, mainstream politics, at the local, state, and federal levels, has sought to destroy the cultures and peoples who once called the Americas their own.

American Indians have been separated from the American political process, either by choice or by design, since the formation of the Republic. In those formative years, American Indian tribes were considered sovereign nations, and the political process originally reflected that of nation to nation, as evidenced by the fact that the United States government signed over 650 treaties with Indian nations between 1776 and 1871 (Cohan 1982). The history of federal Indian policy has been a chronicle of attempts to incorporate Indians forcibly into American society. The reservation system was designed to isolate them where the government could exert its control over their lives under the guise of "civilizing" them. Thus, American Indians became wards of the federal government, subject to the will of the Great White Father.

The reservation system, which began in the 1850s, the General Allotment Act (1887–1934), and the Termination Era of the 1950s are all policies promulgated by the federal government to the detriment of Indian people. While the entire history of the federal government's policy is too complex to discuss here (see Prucha 1984), it is important to note that no consent was sought and none was given. Native people had no voice in those decisions.

Today, as American Indians lack direct representation in Congress, they have to depend upon non-Indian friends to represent their interests at the national level, and for the most part these lawmakers do act in their best interests. This has not always been the case, however. American history is filled with instances when elected representatives, who, in the name of advocacy on behalf of Indian people, promulgated policy and legislation that ultimately proved detrimental to Indians. One of the best examples is Senator Henry Dawes of Massachusetts, who, in 1887, assumed leadership in the passage of the General Allotment Act (25, sec. 331). The Dawes Act, as it was commonly called, authorized the allotment of reservation land to individual Indians to be held in trust for twenty-five years, after which the individual received a free and clear title to it. In the interim these Indians were to learn the "civilized" art of agriculture.

Underlying this policy is the assumption that the American Indians wanted to become farmers. Most were unwilling to abandon their communal lifestyle or lacked the training and experience to farm. They were unable to make a living as farmers and, therefore, after the trust period ended, many lost their land due to nonpayment of taxes or were forced to sell their allotments to non-Indians. As a result, Indian landholdings were reduced from 138 million acres in 1887 to 48 million in 1934 (Collier 1934: 16).

Although this policy was disastrous to Indian culture and livelihood, it was supported by many Indian advocacy organizations such as the Friends of the Indian (Prucha 1973). Reflecting the standard line of government thinking, Senator Dawes firmly believed that he was acting in the best interest of Indian people. Indeed, for decades government policies regarding the Indian people promoted this so-called benevolent attitude, but without consultation with them and usually without their consent.

More recently, however, those who have worked on behalf of Indians and Indian issues have done so with the approval and assistance of Indian people. Senator Robert Kennedy and Presidents John F. Kennedy and Richard Nixon were noted advocates for Indian education and tribal sovereignty. At present, Senator Daniel Inouye of Hawaii, the chairman of the Senate Committee on Indian Affairs, has been a tireless proponent for Indians. Had they been able to participate fully in the democratic process from the beginning, American Indians would not have had to depend upon the benevolence of America's national leaders.

American Indian Citizenship

American Indians were prevented from taking part in the mainstream political process for the simple reason that they were not citizens of the United States until the Citizenship Act of 1924 [8, sec. 1401[a][2]). The citizenship question reached a climax with *Elk vs. Wilkins* (1884) when the Supreme Court held that John Elk, an Omaha Indian, could not assume the rights as an American citizen and exercise his voting privileges, even though he had abandoned his tribal membership. The Omaha, Nebraska voter registrar, Charles Wilkins, refused to register Elk as a voter because, as Wilkins argued, Elk was an Indian, not an American citizen (*Elk vs. Wilkins*, 122 U.S. 94 [1884]; see also Smith 1970: 25–35). Thus, as noncitizens, American Indians were denied the right to vote or hold public office, basic rights taken for granted by most Americans, including African Americans, who were granted formal U.S. citizenship in 1870 by the Fourteenth Amendment to the Constitution. To be sure, having the right to vote and being able to vote are two very different things; yet it was well into the twentieth century before American Indians were granted the same recognition in the very country they were born in.

The Citizenship Act of 1924 naturalized "Indians born within the territorial limits of the United States." The statute stipulated that "all non-citizen Indians born within the territorial limits of the United States be, and they are hereby, declared to be citizens of the United States: Provided, That the granting of such citizenship shall not in any manner impair or otherwise affect the right of any

Indian to tribal or other property" (sec. 1401[a][2]). Despite this promise, Indians were denied access to alcohol until 1953, and their free exercise to practice religion was not affirmed until the passage of the American Indian Religious Freedom Act in 1978.

The driving force behind the citizenship legislation was Charles Curtis, a Kaw-Osage from Oklahoma, who had served in the House of Representatives before closing his career as vice president under Herbert Hoover. This legislation was passed largely to reward the many noncitizen American Indians who served in the U.S. military during World War I, defending a nation to which they owed so little.

Prior to this legislation, many Indians had been made citizens by treaties and federal statutes, many of which were provisional and required eligible Indians to abandon traditional ways of life and to adopt the customs of American society. American citizenship was thought to be inconsistent with continued participation in tribal government or with the practice of tribal culture. Even as Indians were denied participation in the so-called American democratic process, some traditional tribal governments extended to women voting rights, granted former slaves full tribal privileges, and had clearly understood rules developed by consensus.

In one sense, the acquisition of United States citizenship further eroded American Indian sovereignty. Some traditional American Indians still reject U.S. citizenship in the belief that to do otherwise allows the government to regulate their lives completely. Thus, they assert only tribal citizenship, despite the federal government's insistence that all Indians are now American citizens. While allowed dual citizenship (tribal enrollment and membership), American Indians today are still bound to the absolute authority of the federal government of which they are a reluctant part.

It is no wonder that with such a history of oppression and cultural genocide, American Indians view the federal government's political process with suspicion. Presidents, congressmen, governors, and legislators—all elected by due political process—have, time and time again, exercised their authority as representatives of their constituents (which never include Native Americans) to the detriment of Indian rights, lands, and culture.

Institutional Racism and Discrimination

Even though some American Indians may wish to participate in mainstream politics, they are often prevented from doing so by racism and fear. The confirmation of citizenship in 1924 theoretically granted Indians the right to vote; however, there existed no protection under federal statutes if states wished to prevent them from doing so. In fact, several states—for example, North Dakota, Arizona, Maine, and Minnesota—as late as 1957 successfully prevented Native Americans from voting, contending that the Fifteenth Amendment did not apply because Indians, as wards of the federal government, did not pay state taxes, and that Indians lived on federal, not state lands (see Deloria and Lytle 1983: 222–227). For twenty years Arizona prevented American Indians from voting by citing a state law that declared Indians to be "persons under disability," solely because of the federal trust relationship. Deloria and Lytle note that "in 1948 in *Harrison vs. Laveen*, 67 Ariz., 337, 196 P.2d 456, the state supreme court reversed itself and Indians gained the franchise permanently" (1983: 222).

One might jump to the conclusion that, following the turbulent battles in the streets and courtrooms during the 1950s and 1960s which culminated with the passage of the 1965 Voting Rights Act, those barriers preventing minorities from taking full advantage of their constitutionally guaranteed right to vote would have been successfully eliminated. The political record states the contrary. In 1968, Congress passed a controversial law known as the Indian Civil Rights Act (ICRA), which essentially does two things: it confers specific civil rights on all persons subject to the jurisdiction of a tribal government; and it authorizes the federal courts to enforce these rights (25, secs. 1301–1341). The ICRA is the only law ever passed by Congress which expressly limits the power of tribes to regulate their internal affairs. As finally enacted, the ICRA confers all of the fundamental rights in the U.S. Constitution to Indian people, except five: It does not prohibit tribes from (1) establishing a religion or (2) from discriminating in voting on account of race, tribes are not required (3) to convene a jury in civil trials or, (4) in criminal matters, to issue grand jury indictments or (5) appoint counsel for indigent defendants.

The Indian Civil Rights Act sought to protect American Indians from any infringement upon civil rights by tribal government. A more serious issue was the preservation of the rights of Indian people as American citizens. One significant threat to the right of American Indians to participate in the electoral process came in Big Horn County, Montana. In 1986 Windy Boy and others filed suit against Big Horn County, challenging the at-large system of voting for board of commissioners and school board. Their claims arose under Section 2 of the Voting Rights Act 42 U.S.C. § 1973, the Fourteenth and Fifteenth Amendments to the Constitution, and 42 U.S.C. § 1983. The plaintiffs claimed that at-large voting denied them equal opportunity to participate in the political process and to elect representatives of their choice.

Big Horn County, Montana is 5,023 square miles, larger than Connecticut. According to the 1980 census, 11,096 people lived in the county, of whom 52.1 percent were white, 46.2 percent were American Indian, and 1.7 percent belonged to other races. There were 7,308 residents of voting age, of whom 59 percent were white and 41 percent American Indian, members of the Crow and Northern Cheyenne tribes (the majority of the county lies within the Crow reservation and partially within the Northern Cheyenne Reservation).

In the long history of this county, no American Indian had ever been elected to the board of commissioners, and only one tribal member had ever been elected to a school board seat. Plaintiffs argued that Indian candidates were prevented from ever being elected because of official discrimination, racially polarized voting, and election practices. A key factor that the court considered was the extent that official discrimination in Big Horn County touched on the rights of Indians to vote or participate in elections. Indians who registered to vote were removed from voting lists, whereas others, who had voted in primary elections, had their names removed before the general elections for no apparent reason.

Other evidence of official discrimination was confirmed. The election administrator, for example, gave the Indians numbered cards and told them that they could not get more until the cards were returned. No such requirements were in force for non-Indian voters. In one instance, an Indian requested voter registration cards and was given only a few, with the explanation that supplies were limited. His wife, a non-Indian, then went back to the county building and requested cards. She was given fifty cards more than her husband and was told to return as many times as she needed to. If Indian voters were successful at all in obtaining registration cards, the election administrator disqualified many registrations because of minor errors. These same standards were not applied to white voters.

Discrimination was also evident in the county's failure to make official appointments of Indians to county boards and commissions. Often stepping stones to elected public offices, there have been only fourteen appointments of Indians, since 1924, out of several hundred made. One county commissioner testified that he had nominated Indians for positions only to have the nomination die for lack of a second. Perhaps more difficult to prove, the charge of "racially polarized voting" occurs when race or ethnicity is a "determinant of voting preference." The Supreme Court had commented, "Voting along racial lines allows those elected to ignore [minority] interests without fear of political consequences, and without bloc voting the minority candidates would not lose elections solely because of their race" (*Rogers vs. Lodge*, 102 S.Ct. 3272, 3279 [1882]).

Clearly, there is a strong correlation between the race of the voter and the race of the candidate for which a voter casts a ballot. In Big Horn County, Indians vote for Indians; whites, for whites. The defendants suggested that partisanship, not race, explained the voting patterns of the county. The county generally tends to vote Democratic—and Indian precincts overwhelmingly vote Democratic—but this pattern in itself does not negate race as a factor.

Courts look to evidence beyond statistical correlation to determine whether politics is race conscious. Certainly the statistical evidence in *Windy Boy* (*Windy Boy vs. Big Horn County*, 647 F.Supp. 1002 [1986]) supports the contention that race was an issue. In Big Horn County, Indians were more likely to cross over to vote for non-Indian candidates than whites would vote for Indians, but even with this pattern, there must exist corroborating evidence.

In the 1982 primary election, the success of several Indian and pro-Indian candidates prompted a strong reaction among white voters, whose turnout in the subsequent general election was ten percent higher than two years earlier. Registration among whites rose from approximately 75 percent at the time of the primary to 91 percent at the time of the general election. A bipartisan campaign committee was formed to support those candidates who opposed Indian and pro-Indian candidates, and its write-in candidate was nearly elected. This strong reaction among white voters to the candidacy of Indians and pro-Indians provides further proof that race conscious politics existed in Big Horn County. Election procedures made it extremely difficult—evidently impossible—for an Indian candidate to win in board of commissioners elections. Terms were staggered so that one vacancy occurred each year; thus, it seemed more likely that head-to-head contests would take place, in which Indian candidates, being in the minority, were sure to lose.

The court examined other factors, such as the size of the voting district, the slating process, and the lingering effects of discrimination, before it determined that at-large elections in Big Horn County (1986) did, in fact, violate Section 2 of the Voting Rights Act. The court therefore ordered that a new system of elections be adopted. This case was finally resolved by realigning the county into three districts, one of which is in the south end where American Indians constitute the majority. In the northern part of the county whites predominate, and the middle district is composed of roughly equal numbers of Indians and non-Indians.

Such issues are bound to be raised more frequently as the American Indian population continues to become an urban population (see Thornton 1987). According to the 1990 Census, 437,431 (or 22 percent) of the total 1,959,234 American Indians, Eskimos, and Aleuts resided on American Indian reservations and trust lands (U.S. Bureau of the Census 1991). As this trend increases, the rights of American Indians will continue to be tested.

AMERICAN INDIANS AS A POLITICAL FORCE

American Indians are the smallest of the major minority groups in the United States. The nearly two million American Indians and Alaskan Natives in the United States represent only 0.8 percent of the total population of the United States. Given this small population, it is highly unlikely that Native Americans can or will have much of an impact on national politics. As shown by the most recent national elections, neither of the two main political parties—despite occasional acknowledgments by presidential candidates who have spoken more out of moral obligation than political purpose—has made significant efforts to develop campaign platforms or focus campaign strategies to garner American Indian support.

Even in the western states, where the majority of reservations are found, the population of American Indians is hardly large enough to make any dramatic impact upon state and local elections (see Table 14.1). With perhaps the exception of Alaska (where Eskimos and Alaskan Natives represent 15.6 percent of the state's population), no state has a Native population significant enough to form a viable lobby or voting bloc.

In a few western states—notably South Dakota, North Dakota, and Montana—the American Indian population represents the largest minority group in the state. Given the historical and cultural importance of those tribes, one would expect that the support of Native Americans would be sought. That is not the case, however. In those states, largely carved out of former Indian land, most of the people hold their Indian neighbors in low esteem.

That viewpoint results from many misconceptions. Many non-Indians resent what they view as the "special privileges" they believe Indian people receive from the federal government: free housing, education, medical care, and financial

Table 14.1
States with Significant Indian Populations

State	Total Population	American Indians, Eskimos, and Aleuts	Percent of Total
Alaska	550,043	85,698	15.6
New Mexico	1,515,069	134,355	8.9
Oklahoma	3,145,585	252,420	8.0
South Dakota	696,004	50,575	7.3
Montana	799,065	47,679	6.0
Arizona	3,665,228	203,527	5.6
North Dakota	638,800	25,917	4.1
Wyoming	433,588	9,479	2.1
Washington	4,866,692	81,483	1.7

Source: U.S. Bureau of the Census 1991.

support. They resent that they, as taxpayers, must foot the bill. Many believe Indian people receive money simply because they are Indian. Most non-Indians do not know (and perhaps do not care) that such "privileges" as medical care and education are rights received by Indian people in exchange for the millions of acres they ceded to the federal government. Thus, those "privileges" have been bought and paid for at an enormous price.

The common complaint uttered by non-Indians in states with large Indian populations that Indians pay no taxes, yet benefit from taxes paid by others, is a misconception based on a half-truth. Indeed, there are taxes that some Indians do not pay because of the nature of the reservation system. A reservation is defined as "land that has been set aside by the federal government for the use, possession, and benefit of an Indian tribe or group of Indians" (Pevar 1983: 17). While states have the right to regulate all persons within their borders, the one notable exception is Indians. Article 1 of the U.S. Constitution gives Congress exclusive authority over Indian affairs; thus, American Indians who live on reservations (federal lands) do not live within the jurisdiction of the state and are exempt from state taxes. They are still responsible, however, for federal taxes such as income taxes and gasoline taxes. But because the majority of non-Indians do not understand the history, policies, and workings of their own government, they view Indians as enjoying the benefits of representation without taxation.

It is therefore unlikely that Native Americans will ever be able to make inroads in state politics although they have had limited success at the local level. Since they constitute such a small percentage of the national population, the opportunities to elect representatives to Congress are few. Thus, American Indians have to take their successes when they get them.

The Only Indian in Congress

Certainly, as the original inhabitants of this country and as citizens, American Indians have the right to representation at the national level. Yet, only a handful of Indians have served in the United States Congress—six in the House and three in the Senate. Currently, the only American Indian in the Senate is Ben Nighthorse Campbell from Colorado, who is of Northern Cheyenne descent. (Although not enrolled as a member of the Northern Cheyenne tribe of Montana, Campbell has been selected to the Cheyenne Council of Chiefs and the Northern Cheyenne have embraced him as one of their own.)

Campbell's story is unique in American political history. A competitor in judo at the Olympic games held in Japan and as a nationally known artist and silversmith, Campbell served several terms in the Colorado legislature. With his pony tail and bolo ties, Campbell captured the attention of the country when he ran for the Senate seat. Viola (1993: 257) notes that "Ben Nighthorse Campbell occupied a unique niche in the U. S. Congress. As the representative from the Third District of Colorado, the state's enormous Western Slope, he was responsible for the needs and interests of a widespread and diverse constituency, few of whom were Indian. As the only American Indian in Congress, he also found himself, de facto, the representative of all Indians throughout the United States." When Indian leaders from across the country went to Washington, D.C., they usually included on their agenda a stop at Campbell's office.

While serving in the Colorado legislature, Campbell was not considered a representative of his Indian constituents, nor did he necessarily consider himself as such: "Indian people knew I was in office, but for the most part they left me alone, not because they didn't like me, but because Indian people historically have not been very active in the political process." Even when he sought their backing, it was given gladly but cautiously. When campaigning among the Southern Utes, for example, he was told by an elderly woman, "You know, Ben, if Indian people help you too much we're going to hurt you." "I didn't quite understand her then," Campbell admits, "but as I spent more time in politics I began to recognize the racial prejudice and bigotry that sometimes lies just under the surface. I always had a couple of strikes against me. I was an Indian in an area that did not have very many Indian voters, and I had long hair" (Viola 1993: 215).

His Colorado campaigns and elections did not go unnoticed, and he rose quickly to be the representative in Congress of virtually all American Indians. Campbell was reminded of this distinction one day in Montana, on the Northern Cheyenne Reservation, when he was made a chief in the Cheyenne tribe. At one point in his remarks, Two Moons, a Cheyenne elder turned to Campbell and said, "You, too, are now a Cheyenne chief. Because you are a chief and because of where you are, in Washington, D.C., you are now the leader of our people, and we all follow you. You have to stand up for our rights. You have to speak out for your people. You are in a position to help us, and we are grateful for your help" (Viola 1993: 134). Viola observes that "Campbell, of course, was not 'their' congressman, but this mattered little to the Indians who came to him with problems. To them ethnicity transcends legal boundaries. Campbell is 'one of the People,' and they believed he would do for them what he could" (1993: 230).

Campbell's election to the U.S. Senate is significant because it has an impact beyond the borders of Colorado. A committee called American Indians for Ben Nighthorse Campbell for Congress enlisted the support of such Native American notables as Olympic gold medalist Billy Mills and actor Will Sampson, famous for his role in the award-winning movie *One Flew Over the Cuckoo's Nest*. This effort proves that American Indians can band together nationwide to help a candidate (Viola 1993: 230). In a recent development Campbell renounced his affiliation with the Democratic Party and became a Republican, but his support among Native Americans has not wavered, an indication that perhaps American Indians consider national politics outside their influence or interest.

The Indian Lobby

American Indians have been most successful in generating political strength and achieving their goals when they have had a specific flag to rally around. The American Indian Movement (AIM), for example, gained recognition in Minneapolis, Minnesota when it sought to counter police abuse of Native American citizens in that community. AIM has expanded its concern and activity to include tribal and national Indian issues.

A number of significant national organizations emerged in the 1960s and 1970s to advocate for Indian causes. Among the more influential are the Coalition of Indian-Controlled School Boards, the American Indian Higher Education Consortium, the National Congress of American Indians, the National Tribal Chairman's Association, the Native American Rights Fund, and the Council of Energy Resource Tribes. As Cornell (1988) has argued, the existence of such organizations does not constitute a united front; indeed, one wit once observed that being Indian means having the opportunity to join forty or fifty Indian unity organizations. Still, these organizations have successfully lobbied for legislation to advance tribal schools and colleges, to increase funding for social services, and for direct control of tribal resources. Most recently, Indian lobbyists rallied to pass the National Museum of the American Indian Act (S. 978, 101st Congress 1st Session) and the American Indian Graves and Repatriation Act.

There is a growing interest among American Indians in international political movements. American Indian participation in such organizations as the World Council of Indigenous Peoples, and their participation in the most recent Earth Day Summit in Brazil, demonstrates an expanding concern for international political, social, and environmental issues. Such victories point to a great potential to influence the decision-making process globally. This awakening of interest and power, albeit limited, is a product of Native American recognition of the political process as well as, perhaps, an indication of demographic shifts of the American Indian population.

Outside Alliances

It is said that powerless people need powerful friends. American Indians have been fairly successful in gaining such friends, usually on an ad-hoc basis, as their alliance with environmentalists illustrates. Such organizations as the Friends of the Earth have worked with tribes to protect wilderness areas and sacred lands. These alliances have been strained sometimes by differences in perceptions about what exactly constitutes protection: conservationists opposed the restoration of Havasupi lands on the rim of the Grand Canyon on the grounds that Indians were incapable of managing a "wilderness" area (Cornell 1988: 171). To the Havasupi, these lands are not wild but sacred; thus, they are to be utilized for religious expression. Periodically, however, such organizations have successfully staved off attempts to develop lands considered both sacred sites and wilderness, but the goal is the same: to prevent the exploitation of land.

Pan-Indianism

In the 1950s the American Indian population began a dramatic shift from a reservation-based people to an urban populace. This is a product not only of migration but of direct federal government action, ingrained in such policies as Termination and, more directly, Indian Relocation. In 1940, only 8.1 percent of all Native Americans lived in an urban setting (Cornell 1988: 132), whereas in 1990, the U.S. Census reported that only 23 percent of all American Indians lived on a reservation (U.S. Census 1990; see also Cornell 1988: 132). An obvious product of this migration to the cities is the evolution or development of pan-Indianism, a transitional stage between assimilation and tribalism, or cultural synthesis. As typically characterized, pan-Indianism is a process wherein individual Indians retain cultural identity in a generic sense while specific tribal identities, or "culture," are de-emphasized.

Cornell states that "[u]rban supratribalism [pan-Indian] has emerged as a political response to particular characteristics of the contemporary Indian situation." He contends that "urbanization did not bring politics into Indian lives; it brought Indians into new politics" (1988: 133, 136). Many of the leaders of national Native American organizations, such as the American Indian Movement, for example, are products of the Relocation era. So, too, are many tribal leaders. Perhaps the most notable urban Indian to return home to lead at the tribal level is Wilma Mankiller, former principal chief of the Cherokee Nation, one of the largest tribes in the United States. These individuals contribute a global awareness of the mainstream political process.

CHALLENGES AND SOLUTIONS

Either as a result of institutional racism or by their own choice, Native Americans have not had total and unrestricted access to the mainstream political process. There is, however, a growing recognition among American Indians that they have more opportunities, albeit formative, to participate more fully in national politics. For example, there were fifty-one American Indian delegates at the 1988 Democratic National Convention in Atlanta, where an American Indian caucus was formed as an official body within the Democratic Party. Similar activity is not yet evidenced in the Republican Party, understandable as most Native Americans who indicate party preference identify themselves as Democrats.

Because of their small population, American Indians are unlikely to make significant advances into mainstream politics, although white Americans are on their way to becoming a minority. By 2050 it is projected that African Americans, Hispanics, and Asians will constitute 53 percent of the U. S. population (see Table 14.2).

In 1993, the non-Hispanic white population represented 76 percent of the U.S. population. The Census Bureau estimates that this percentage will decrease to 68 percent in the year 2010. Estimates of the American Indian population for the year 2050 show little apparent growth, at least as measured by the percentage of American Indians in the general population. However, the Census Bureau projects that the Native American population will double from 2.1 million people in 1995 to 4.3 million in 2050.

Even if the projections are accurate and the Native American population does reach four million, American Indians will remain the smallest "major" minority group in the United States in the twenty-first century. That status suggests that American Indians must consider other avenues by which their voice can be better heard. Since the nonwhite population in the United States is growing at such a significant rate, coalition building among minority groups offers nonwhites an opportunity to influence national policy in meaningful ways. While, in theory, this opportunity sounds promising, American Indians are not terribly optimistic that their circumstances will change as a result. One barrier toward coalition building is the lack of a unifying organization or leadership class among Indian people. Most federally recognized tribes belong to the National Tribal Chairman's Association, but not all American Indians are enrolled. Leaders such as LaDonna Harris, chair

Table 14.2
Percentage of United States Population by Race

Race	1995	2050
Asian	3.5	9.7
Hispanic	10.2	22.5
Black	12.0	14.4
White	73.7	52.5
American Indian	0.7	0.9

Source: U.S. Bureau of the Census 1992.

of the Commission on Urban Indians, Wilma Mankiller, former chief of the Cherokee nation, and Vine Deloria, Jr., Lakota scholar, are influential, but speak only on behalf of their own organizations or tribes. Who represents American Indians?

Native Americans share with other minority groups a deep concern about unemployment, underemployment, inadequate health care, and the lack of educational opportunities. Although these issues can unite minorities in efforts toward solutions, some issues specific to Native Americans need to be addressed. Some past successes can serve as the foundation for building coalitions with African Americans, Hispanics, and others. During the 500th anniversary of Columbus's "discovery," for example, African Americans joined with Native Americans and others to reflect on the legacy of this event. Although their agreements in this case do not guarantee full agreement on all issues—for example, the offensive use of American Indian nicknames and mascots for sports teams—there is room for hope (Giago 1994: 187–190).

The desire by Native Americans to retain their cultural identities is strong. Despite 500 years of attempts to assimilate the Indian into the "dominant society," Native American cultures remain active, but they need to be assured that political and cultural autonomy for Indian nations will remain a plank in the political agenda of any minority coalition. Certainly the success of recent movies such as *Thunderheart*, *Dances with Wolves*, and Disney's animated cartoon *Pocahontas*, indicates interest in, if not sympathy for, American Indians and their cultures. Although often romanticized, these images help bridge the chasm between Native Americans and others in modern society, so long as the image does not become a stereotype. By becoming more knowledgeable about the rich cultures of American Indians, other minority groups and organizations can recognize the desires of Indian people without presuming to speak on their behalf. Together, minorities must be willing to join in the fight to rectify past wrongs.

REFERENCES

Citizenship Act. 1924. 43 Stat. 253, *U.S. Code.* Vol. 8, sec. 1401(a)(2).

Cohan, Felix S. 1982. *Handbook of federal Indian law.* Charlottesville: Bobbs-Merrill.

Cornell, Stephen. 1988. *Return of the native.* New York: Oxford University Press.

Deloria, Vine, Jr., and Clifford M. Lytle. 1983. *American Indians, American justice.* Austin: University of Texas Press.

General Allotment Act. 1887. *U.S. Code.* Vol. 25, sec. 331.

Giago, Tim. 1994. Notes from Indian country: Mascots. In *Visions of an enduring people*, edited by Walter C. Fleming and John G. Watts. Dubuque, IA: Kendall/Hunt Publishing.

Indian Civil Rights Act. 1968. *U.S. Code.* Vol. 25, secs. 1301–1341.

Pevar, Stephen L. 1983. *The rights of Indians and tribes.* New York: Bantum Books.

Prucha, Francis Paul, ed. 1973. *Americanization of the American Indians: Writings by the "friends of the Indian," 1880–1900.* Cambridge, MA: Harvard University Press.

———. 1984. *The great father: The United States government and the American Indian.* Lincoln: University of Nebraska Press.

Smith, Michael T. 1970. The history of Indian citizenship. *Great Plains Journal* 10 (fall): 25–35.

Thornton, Russell. 1987. *American Indian holocaust and survival.* Norman: University of Oklahoma Press.

U.S. Bureau of the Census. 1990. *Census of the population, 1990.* Vol. 2: *Characteristics of the population.* Part 1, *U.S. Summary.*

——— . 1991. Total and American Indian, Eskimo, or Aleut persons for American Indian reservations and trust lands, 1990. *American Indian and Alaska native areas, 1990.*

——— . 1992. *Population projections of the United States by age, sex, race, and Hispanic origin, 1993–2050.* Report P25, #1104, September.

U.S. House of Representatives. 1934. *Memorandum hearings on H.R. 7902 before the Homage Committee on Indian affairs.* 73rd Congress, 2d session.

Viola, Herman J. 1993. *Ben Nighthorse Campbell: An American warrior.* New York: Orion Books.

Voting Rights Act. 1973. *U.S. Code.* Vol. 42, sec. 2.

Waldman, Carl. 1985. *Atlas of the North American Indian.* New York: Facts on File Publications.

Part VI

Arab Americans and Political Images

15
Arabs and Muslims in American Society

Mohammad T. Mehdi

America has been the land of opportunities, but also the land of prejudice and racism. The first group to land on these shores considered itself the "original" inhabitants—the native peoples notwithstanding—and felt that the next group were intruders, not as good or as qualified as they!

Mainly white Anglo-Saxon Protestants, this first group preceded the Catholics, the southern Europeans, and the Hispanics, who were perceived as second- and third-class citizens in the society. Then appeared on the scene those who were neither Protestants nor Catholics, not even Europeans. At various periods and under different circumstances there were the blacks, the Jews, the Chinese, the Japanese, and the Vietnamese, to name a few.

One of the last groups to come to the American shores, the Arabs and Muslims began their immigration at the end of the nineteenth century in several waves from Syria and Lebanon. They were called Turkos because Syria and Lebanon were under the rule of the Ottoman Empire. Other waves followed, including Palestinians after 1948, Egyptians after President Nasser nationalized much of Egypt's feudal landholdings, and Iraqis after the persecutions ordered by Saddam Hussein.

Larger waves of Muslims came to the American shores, particularly from the Indian subcontinent, so that by the 1940s the second mosque in America was built in Sacramento, the first mosque having been built by Syrian-Lebanese Muslims in 1932 in Cedar Rapids, Iowa. At present, huge numbers of Muslims from India, Pakistan, and Bangladesh make up approximately 60 percent of the immigrant Muslims in America.

Not all Arabs are Muslims, nor are all Muslims Arabs. Islam, as a universalistic religion, embraces people of many ethnic, national, and racial backgrounds and has nearly 1.5 billion adherents throughout the world. As a linguistic group the Arabs number about 200 million, and 94 percent of them are Muslims.

Islam is not a new religion. With its compelling universality, it maintains that it is the continuation of Judaism and Christianity. A Muslim is not a Muslim if he or she does not believe in the messages of Moses, Jesus, all other prophets, and Mohammad (peace be upon them all!). Under the old Jewish tradition, the story goes that all the people rejected God's message, except for the Jews who were chosen to carry it.

Under Islam, the story is completely different. The Qur'an maintains that God submitted the message to the Heavens and Earth (everybody), and all rejected it—all except for the humankind under Islam, whatever nationality, religion, color, or continent is chosen. This broad and logical approach of Islam appeals to millions of people. In America, accordingly, the number of adherents to Islam is growing everyday. These new converts to Islam are sources of strength which will add to the political power of the Arabs and Muslims on the American national scene.

The Arabs and Muslims have been subjected to more than traditional prejudice against new arrivals to the American shores. General prejudice against Islam has existed in the West from the days of the Crusades. Broadly, the Western image of Arabs and Muslims revolves around camels, harems, terrorism, Khomeini, and enmity and hatred toward the Christians and Jews. In addition, the effort of the Jewish lobby and publicists in Washington, D.C., New York, Chicago, and every large city across the continent has misrepresented the Muslims and Arabs, creating the image of the ugly Arab and ugly Muslim. For the uglier the Arab and Muslim image, the brighter the image of Israel, it is thought.

And then, there is the general American need to pick on a foreign villain. In the recent past there were Ortega, Noriega, Gaddafi, Khomeini, the "Evil Empire," and regretfully all these have disappeared. It seems that Islam and Islamic fundamentalism are the new candidates to satisfy the American need for a foreign villain.

THE HISTORICAL SETTING

To appreciate the position of Arabs and Muslims as a minority in American polity, one must understand the history behind modern Western civilization and modern Arab and Muslim relationships.

Modern Western civilization starts with the fourteenth-century renaissance in Western Europe and, earlier, the Magna Carta in England, which was signed in 1215. During this period, the West experienced the Renaissance, the Reformation during the sixteenth century, the Industrial Revolution, a political revolution (the American Revolution), a social revolution (the French Revolution), capitalism (an economic revolution), and the computer and sexual revolutions of recent years. These great events took place over 500 years which included bloody revolutions and warfare, gradual evolution, and peaceful settlement of disputes.

By contrast modern Arab and Muslim history begins about the time of World War I. In modern terms the Arabs and Muslims are seventy or eighty years old, whereas the West is over 500 years old. The Muslims have not had their wars of reformation, nor their political and social revolutions. The open society in the modern West is the result of long years of revolutions and evolution. The East is now experiencing what the West experienced two or three hundred years ago. The individual has not been emancipated from the traditional society in the East, as yet.

Therefore the Arab and Muslim communities, transplanted to America, have their psychological roots in the closed societies of the Middle East and South Asian countries, which, politically, are roughly in the seventeenth-, eighteenth-, or nineteenth-century periods. Similar to the governments in the West in those centuries, Arab and Muslim governments are oppressive regimes, and the society is fearful of the government. The Arabs and Muslims come to America with the heavy baggage of suspicion and fear of politics. Their participation in the political process is at the lowest level, and their concerns with working hard, making money, and minding their own private business at the highest. "You should not criticize America; it has been good to us!" Arab and Muslim parents usually advise their American-born children.

As in the post-Reformation period in the West, Muslims direct their efforts to building mosques, religious schools, and centers. The number of mosques has increased across America from four or five in the early 1950s to more than 1,200 by the 1990s.

Adapting to an Open Society

In the main, American Arabs and Muslims are a society in transition between commitment to religion as the center of life to a community in which secularization and participation in the political process are primary forces in the society. If Arabs and Muslims are to participate in the political process, they need first to emancipate themselves from the old-country baggage. But there are additional problems for them in the American society, chiefly their being associated with terrorism abroad and in the United States. Thus they are put on the defensive in their relationship to fellow Americans.

Most Arabs and Muslims feel ill at ease at the exercise of their First Amendment rights of freedom of speech, press, and assembly. Even the first clause of the First Amendment concerning freedom of religion is not a source of comfort because many of them, afraid to identify themselves as Muslims, suffer the consequences of their silence. As American society has experienced many horrors against the minorities and the new arrivals in the past, Arabs and Muslims, being the last groups on the scene, will withstand the waves of prejudice as others did in the past. They will be subjected, however, to an extended period of prejudice and discrimination as long as the Palestinian problem continues unresolved and the pro-Israel lobby in Washington, D.C. has greater strength than the disorganized Muslims and Arabs.

The three million Arabs and ten million Muslims are products of the old life in which politics was a taboo and people were afraid of the government. Having little appreciation of the nature of an open society and their rights under the Constitution, they are not politically active. Second- and third-generation Arabs, however, will be fully American and fully appreciative of their social and political opportunities. The Arab and Muslim minorities today are engaged in all aspects of American life except the political field. They are doctors, dentists, lawyers, mechanics, university professors, scientists, surgeons, ditch diggers, carpenters, grocery store owners, and businessmen throughout the United States. Arab and Muslim women, for the most part, continue in traditional patterns by accepting their role as docile homemakers, but there are conspicuous exceptions, leading women toward emancipation. Arab and Muslim radio and television programs reach an audience of thousands. In addition, there are newspapers and magazines which carry news of the old country as well as news of concern to Arabs and Muslims as Americans.

Another important development in establishing the identity of Arabs and Muslims and ultimately their political role in the American society is the effort in New York to have the banks, major department stores, schools, and restaurants, for example, decorate their facilities with the Crescent and Star during December as they are decorated with Christmas trees and the Hanukkah menorahs. Chase Manhattan Bank recently decorated the entrance of its headquarters with a big Crescent and Star. The Christmas tree and the Jewish menorah were, of course, also in place. Gradually, it is expected that all facilities which now decorate with Christmas trees and Hanukkah menorahs will decorate with the Crescent and Star also, as establishments seek to comply with the provisions of the Civil Rights Act of 1964. In one sense, Arabs and Muslims are integrated into the American society except for political participation, which is, after all, the distinguishing feature of the open society and the sign of full and meaningful integration.

While there may be an excellent Arab physician and a first-rate Muslim chemist by twentieth-century standards, they may, in their psychological approach to life as individuals, have an eighteenth- or nineteenth-century outlook. A clear example of this kind of dual personality can be seen in the following case. One luminary was asked to contribute to the campaign of an Arab running for a political office. After thoroughly thinking about the pluses and minuses of the contribution, he decided not to contribute to the campaign: "My contribution to the campaign will not be useful as our candidate's chances to win are limited. But if I contribute to the building of a mosque, my rewards from Allah/God are assured."

When the mosques, which are purely religious institutions, become political community centers as well, the Arabs and Muslims will become a more meaningful part of American society. There have been more denunciations of the Serbs killing and raping Muslim women in Bosnia and denunciations of the terrorist who killed Muslim worshippers in their sanctuary in Hebron in the churches and synagogues than in the mosques! The politicization of the mosques is on the agenda of some Arab and Muslim reformers.

RELATIONS TO OTHER COMMUNITIES

As a new group with heavy baggage brought from centuries past, Arabs and Muslims enter the American political scene as a politically disorganized group, resisting participation in the political process. Its relations to other groups, accordingly, begin with severe problems beyond those of typical relations in America. Group relationships—racial, religious, or cultural—in America have from the beginning encountered prejudice against the new arrivals because they are different. There has been always the fear that the new arrivals with their strange faces would compete with those in the established society for jobs. Certainly, the usually liberal labor movement opposes immigration because of this fear, which has been in the background of all group relationships in the country, putting aside the prejudice of being against the blacks simply because they are blacks or against the Jews simply because they are Jews.

Fear and group interests create alliances or oppositions. The so-called Jewish support of blacks in the 1960s was successful because it was in the mutual interest of both groups. American Jews were as much subject to discriminatory laws and practices as black Americans. Civil rights legislation eventually prohibited discrimination against Jews, blacks, Hispanics, Arabs, and the Fiji Islanders. When affirmative action legislation provided more opportunity for less advantaged blacks, many Jewish organizations appealed to the courts. The *Bakke vs. Board of Regents* case (438 U.S. 265 [1978]) was one of the first to challenge affirmative action for blacks and other less fortunate minorities to attain equal opportunities. When Jewish groups asked for the support of blacks to help Israel occupy Palestine, blacks resisted and later resented being called upon to support the Jews who they thought were doing something wrong, occupying another people's land.

PROBLEMS OF POLITICAL PARTICIPATION

The Arab and Muslim minorities face one big political problem: tensions between the Arab-Muslim community and the Jewish community. It is feared that the relation which presently ranges between "cool" to "correct" may deteriorate and become as ugly as or even uglier than the black-Jewish relations. Islam, which is the second largest religion in America, has been attacked by the highly powerful Jewish lobby. "Muslim terrorism" was the talk of the town and the headline of most New York papers after the explosion in the World Trade Center. The media had convicted the suspects as terrorists, and the ABC television network affiliate in New York had sent its senior reporter to what it called the cradle of terrorism, Egypt.

Even though the conflict in Palestine is political, not racial or religious, the media has made it a religious conflict between Arab and Muslim terrorists and the Jews. The prevention of a violent outbreak in America between the two communities should be the goal of all concerned. On 7 March 1994, Arab and Muslim community leaders in New York City met with rabbis and other Jewish leaders in Brooklyn to begin a political dialogue. In contrast to various interfaith meetings, they discussed the hard questions of Palestine. This political dialogue was one in which Muslims, Christians, and Jews called upon the parties to "be good boys and good girls" as if the problem would disappear when they concluded by saying Amen!

The political dialogues dealt with the heart of the issues and made the parties aware of each other's concerns, pains, and potentials. "Only if we can share each other's pain! When a Jewish student is shot on the Brooklyn Bridge and dies, we feel sorry and share the agony with his family and with the Jewish community," said an Arab spokesman at the dialogue. "But we hope Jews would also share the pain of the Palestinian families who were killed in their mosques in Hebron or [who are] being killed by the Israeli paratroopers every day," he added.

The cooperation and alliance of Arab organizations with other minorities is therefore related to the political positions of these organizations and not to the ethnicity of the groups. Of course within the black and Latino communities, similar subdivisions exist, and ultimately the cooperation will be not among ethnic groupings, but among political and ideological groups.

It stands to reason that the Arabs and Muslims should establish alliances with other minorities who have been subjected to the same kind of discrimination by the earlier settlers and established groups! Arab-black and Arab-Hispanic alliances are ready to be established and to cooperate and coordinate their activities toward, possibly, the establishment of a third political party. There are many problems confronting such developments. On the Arab and Muslim side, the "poor" appreciation of the political process and the failure to contribute money to that end are two of the basic problems. No organization or alliance can be established without money.

Arab and Muslim participation in American political life has been very limited, and their cooperation with other minorities even more so. At least forty members of Arab and Muslim background have held seats in various state assemblies and senates. The U.S. Congress has had at least ten members of Arab origin. The Senate has had two or possibly three Arab American senators, but most of these have been politically inactive on Arab issues, and their Arabism has been expressed in enjoying delicious Arab cuisine, listening to Arab music, and speaking a few words of broken Arabic with a heavy accent.

To illustrate the difficulties of getting Arabs and Muslims to participate in the political process, consider the case of Mohammad Medhi, the only candidate for the U.S. Senate who has an Arab and Muslim background. In the 1992 elections he spoke openly on Arab American issues and received 56,000 votes in the state of New York, whereas his opponent, Alfonse D'Amato, received 3 million votes. The Arab candidate spent $3,000 while D'Amato spent $10 million! Why did the Arab-Muslim candidate spend a meager $3,000 running for the U.S. Senate? Although at least one million Arabs and Muslims live in New York state, they are not politically aware and hardly ever contribute money to political activities because to do so has never been a part of their experience.

To raise the $3,000, the candidate had many embarrassing occasions. In a mosque in Brooklyn, attended primarily by Palestinians (Palestine is the major Arab American political issue about which the candidate was speaking on radio and television), the Muslim congregation of more than 100 worshippers contributed the total sum of only $29. On a campaign trip to Buffalo, this candidate was received by an audience of six individuals in a mosque. Happily, his press conference on the steps of city hall was attended by almost all news media representatives in the area. The news media appreciated his newsworthiness as the first Arab-Muslim candidate for the U.S. Senate even if the Arab-Muslim community was puzzled as to why an Arab-Muslim should run for the Senate and waste all that money.

As another example that illustrates the problem of transition from earlier centuries to the twentieth century, one Arab-Muslim organization felt that it was in order for American Muslims to meet and pay a visit to Pope John Paul II when he visited the United States. Well-to-do and intellectual Muslims and Arabs objected to meeting with the pope. They would say, "You will never be able to convert him to Islam . . . so what is the use of . . . meeting with him?" Lack of financial contributions to political activities further hinder Arab and Muslim organizations to become effective instruments on the American scene. Yet there have been occasional successes, despite the inhibition.

The American Arab Institute, based in Washington, D.C., was able to establish contacts with Rev. Jesse Jackson and support his Rainbow Coalition in 1988. It also managed to get the Democratic National Convention to allow them a few minutes to speak to the convention, but its talk was limited politically; hence, no discussion of the Palestine question or any support for the Palestinian human rights was allowed while Jewish and other ethnic politicians expressed their support for Israel.

All Arab and Muslim organizations in Washington, D.C. have difficulties in raising funds from local sources; some receive a few "pennies" from abroad, either from Arab and Muslim governments or from rich Arab oil millionaires. These small contributions inhibit the freedom of these organizations in America and make them, in the main, follow the policies of their benefactors.

The contributions are small because benefactors think about America in the same terms that they use to think about their homeland. If in an Arab country $100,000 is allocated for publicity and information, that amount reaches the whole country, particularly because the several radio and television stations are owned by the government. But $100,000 and even several million dollars spent in huge America with its multiple media outlets will hardly scratch the surface of American society. Presently, the Arab and Muslim organizations in America are divided between those that follow the status quo and those critical of existing Arab governments and State Department policy in support of those regimes. When an Arab government spends $20 billion to purchase Phantom jets or when Yasir Arafat shakes the hand of Yitzak Rabin at the White House with the blessing of the U.S. government and news media, some Arab American organizations supported the purchase and the handshake. Others denounced the purchase as the waste of good money for a not-so-good purpose and called the handshake a charade and a sellout of Palestine to the occupiers of the Holy Land.

Nevertheless, because America is an "open society" Arabs and Muslims are having an impact on the American social, cultural, and political scene. The reason for their success is not due to their political participation or the money they contribute to the parties. However, politics draws the reluctant Arabs and Muslims in its powerful waves and embraces them despite their resistance and refusal.

America is moving toward a cultural pluralism that makes it a richer land. Instead of being confined to a Judeo-Christian tradition or being an Anglo-Saxon fiefdom, it seeks to be pluralistic in every field. It is today based on a Judeo-Christian-Islamic tradition and heritage, Anglo-Saxon–Latino–Afro–Asian, multira-cial and ethnicity and multilingual and indeed multieverything. This is wholesome despite the reluctance of the established groups to appreciate the new progressive, universalistic development which seeks to remake America as the world, rather than a mere portion thereof.

THE IMPACT ON AMERICA

Some Islamic principles can help the American society today. For example, Islam forbids the consumption of alcohol and the use of drugs; it is a strong advocate of family ties. Were its principles adopted, Islam could have powerful effects on Americans of all faiths. But its most significant impact is in the field of race relations. Islam is a color-blind religion. The Qur'an stresses that all people are equal regardless of their race, nationality, color, and even religion. They are judged by God not on the basis of their color or creed, but rather on their deeds. Prophet Mohammad states that there is no difference between whites and blacks, between Arabs and non-Arabs, except in their behavior toward fellow human beings.

This Islamic opposition to racism can have a wholesome impact on a racist society. It teaches that the individual, regardless of race or class, has human worth equal to that of any other individual. In the various mosques and Muslim centers, the attendants and worshippers are of all colors and nationalities. This, one hopes, will be the face of America tomorrow.

Within twenty years, Arabs and Muslims will be properly politicized and part of the American community. Alliances will be established with blacks, Hispanics, and other minorities. With that development, the balance of power in America will begin shifting away from the obsession with mother Europe toward the two thirds of humankind in Asia, Africa, and Latin America. The new America will be opposed to racism, economic exploitation, and colonialism. The billions of dollars America is wasting on the unproductive arms industry will be directed to the elimination of poverty, hunger, and disease in this country and throughout the world. Israel will become similar to Formosa in the Far East. Without American subsidies amounting to $6 billion a year, people may know that Israel is there somewhere, but nobody will take notice of that fact. The Palestinians will have been recognized in their own land of Palestine.

Within twenty years, thanks to the Arab and Muslim political emancipation and alliance with blacks, Hispanics, and other minorities, America will not have to assume the burden of the claim of being the leader of the world. It will simply be first among equals, a status which is more logical, universalistic, and admirable.

16
The Arab Lobby:
Political Identity and Participation

Ayad Al-Qazzaz

Arab American organized political activities—here referred to as the Arab lobby—are somewhat new on the American political landscape, having a history of only about thirty years in this country. Prior to about 1965, the Arab community in the United States was considered politically passive and generally uninterested in political matters except for a few occasions (Sulieman 1994). There is very little research on this subject, and most of what is available has been published recently, the most prominent being Baha Abu-Laban and Michael Sulieman's edition, *Arab Americans: Continuity and Change* (1989) and Yvonne Y. Haddad's edited book, *The Muslims of America* (1991). The third section of Abu-Laban and Sulieman's book is especially important because it focuses on the political activism of the Arab American community on the national level. Haddad's book contains several chapters that deal with organizations and the political activities of Muslim Americans, including Arab Americans.

On the other side are works written by adversaries who seek to weaken and undermine the Arab lobby. The Anti-Defamation League (ADL), a pro-Israeli lobby, for example, published *Pro-Arab Propaganda in America: Vehicles and Voices* (1983), and the American Israeli Public Affairs Committee (AIPAC) published *The Campaign to Discredit Israel* (1983).

For the purpose of this chapter, the Arab lobby is defined to include the following organized activities: first, those with the purpose of informing and educating the American public about the history, culture, and religion of Arabs and Arab Americans; second, activities designed to protect and defend the interests of Arabs and Arab Americans against negative images and stereotypes; and third, any activities designed to encourage the U.S. government to pursue a balanced and evenhanded policy toward Arab issues and concerns, particularly the Palestinian-Israeli conflict.

Using this definition, four major interest groups that promote the objectives and goals of the Arab lobby are delineated. First, American corporations, which export billions of dollars of American goods and services every year to the Arab world, occasionally sponsor or finance programs, seminars, or projects on the people and culture of the Arab world. For example: Standard Oil has produced several films on Islam; Mobil Oil Corporation sponsors and supports many of the outreach programs organized by the various Middle East centers throughout the United States; ARAMCO sponsors educational programs and publishes *ARAMCO World*, which prints cultural articles on the Arab world and Arab Americans. Second, Arab governments on many occasions hire lobbyists to promote their own interests and sponsor cultural activities or exhibits on their country's behalf. Third, the activities of the emerging lobby of American Muslims can be considered part of the organized activities of the Arab lobby. Many of the activities of the American Muslim community, numbering between three and four million, overlap or are similar due to the fact that many members of the Muslim lobby are of Arab origin. The issues that concern the Arab Muslim community are similar to those of the Arab lobby, and the two groups share similar views (Haddad 1991: 217–235). Fourth, organizations made up mainly of people of Arab American origin such as the Arab American University Graduates (AAUG), the National Association of Arab Americans (NAAA), Arab American Anti-Discrimination Committee (ADC), and Arab American Institute (AAI) promote the objectives of the Arab lobby.

The primary focus of this chapter is to discuss and analyze the organizations made up of people of Arab American heritage that represent the main body of the Arab lobby. Despite the large number of Arab Americans who are of the Islamic faith, the terms "Arab" and "Muslim" are not to be considered synonyms. The term "Arab" is a cultural term, not a religious or a racial one. It refers to a group of people who share a common language, geographical region, and set of customs and traditions. There is a sizable Christian community in the Arab world, and about half of the Arab American community is Christian. The Muslim community, however, comprises all who accept and follow the Islamic faith, irrespective of nationality, race, or ethnicity.

THE ARAB AMERICAN COMMUNITY: DEFINTION AND OUTLINE

The term "Arab American" refers to all the people who trace their origin to one of the following countries that belong to the Arab League: Algeria, Bahrain, Djibouti, Egypt, Iraq, Jordan, Kuwait, Lebanon, Libya, Mauritania, Morocco, Oman, Palestine (PLO), Qatar, Saudi Arabia, Somalia, Sudan, Syria, Tunisia, United Arab Emirates, and Yemen. Even though the Palestine Liberation Organization (PLO) is not officially a country, it is a political entity recognized by the United Nations as representing the interests of the majority of Palestinians. Excluded from this designation are the people from the major ethnic groups who have been living in these countries for centuries, such as Kurds, Assyrians, and the

Armenians. The term "Arab American" itself gained currency in the late 1960s and started to replace other designations based on the city or country of origin and faith. On occasion the term is used along with designations of the country of origin.

The size of the Arab American community is approximately three million, including people born overseas and their offspring. The major concentrations of Arab Americans live in Michigan, California, New York, Massachusetts, Illinois, and Texas. Smaller communities are found throughout the Northwest and Midwest. Detroit, with over 250,000 people of Arab origin, has the largest concentration of Arab Americans. Next is Los Angeles, which claims to have more than 100,000 people of Arab origin.

Arab Americans came to the United States in several waves, reflecting changes in American immigration policies as well as social, economic, and political conditions of the Arab countries of origin. Arab immigration can be divided into two major categories: the early immigrants, who came to this country during the period 1875–1945, and the recent immigrants, who came after 1945. Although arbitrary, this definition brings into focus the differences between the two Arab immigrant groups.

Motivated by economic factors, the majority of the early immigrants came from Lebanon. Most of them were Christian, uneducated, and unskilled people who spoke little or no English. For these people peddling and low-paying jobs were the springboards to attaining better jobs, professional positions, and to becoming successful entrepreneurs. A large number came to enjoy the benefits of large urban centers, but all sought to better their lives, to stay long enough to accumulate enough wealth, and then to return home. However, in time, most of them decided to settle in America permanently and to bring their families and relatives to join them (Al-Qazzaz 1979).

The early Arab immigrants' experiences were much like those of other immigrants in that they assimilated to the new society and placed assimilation above ethnic identifications (Huseby-Darvas 1994: 9–21). There are several identifiable factors that accelerated the process of assimilation among the early Arab immigrants. First, their numbers were small compared to those of other groups in the United States at the time: the Arab American community was less than half a million. Second, the melting pot atmosphere encouraged ethnic groups to de-emphasize their distinctiveness. Third, patriotic pressures increased during World War II. Fourth, the costs and difficulties of transportation made it impossible in those days to have continuous contacts with the home country (Yinger 1981; Nader 1991).

As can be expected, the children and grandchildren of the early Arab immigrants are well represented in mainstream American society. Many of these have achieved a significant degree of fame and influence in this society: Donna Shalala, the current Secretary of Health and Human Services; Candy Lightner, founder of Mothers against Drunk Drivers (MADD); Paul Anka and Paula Abdul, popular singers; Casey Kasem, spokesman for the American Top 40; the Farrah Brothers, founders of the Farrah Company for men's and women's slacks; Paul Orfalea, owner of Kinko's, the biggest chain of copying services; John Sununu, former chief of staff for President Bush and governor of New Hampshire and currently a CNN commentator. Other examples of influential Arab Americans are listed in the *Arab Almanac* (Haiek 1992) and in Casey Kasem's article in *Parade* (1994).

The recent immigrants or the second wave came from all over the Arab world, including Iraq, Egypt, Palestine, North Africa, and the Gulf countries. They are evenly divided between Muslim and Christian. Many of the recent immigrants are literate, highly qualified professionals with advanced degrees that put them in favorable bargaining positions to obtain good jobs in the competitive market (Zogby 1990). Many of the new arrivals are students who came here not just to study but to remain. As with the first wave of Arab immigrants, economic and political reasons motivated many in the second wave. The 1967 and 1973 Wars, the 1979 civil war in Lebanon, the Iran-Iraq War of 1980–1988, the Israeli invasion of Lebanon in 1982, and the Gulf War have all played significant roles in this immigration.

Recent immigrants, as compared to early immigrants, are more ethnically conscious and less assimilated into mainstream American society. They continue to keep their ethnicity and culture alive in this country in various forms and shapes. Several factors contribute to the ethnic preservation of the new Arab immigrants. First, many of the new immigrants are Muslims and highly protective of their religious identity. Second, many believe that adopting the American way of life could undermine their family and social values. Third, the negative political environment of stereotypes exacerbates problems of assimilation and further excludes them from becoming Americans (Nader 1991). Fourth, the continuous flow of immigrants and information from the Arab world as a result of new technologies makes it much easier for the new immigrants to be in contact with their country of origin. Fifth, the new climate of multiculturalism that has prevailed in the United States since the late 1960s encourages all groups to embrace their ethnic identity and preserve their cultural heritage. Whereas the social tendency during the first wave of Arab immigration was to encourage ethnic groups to assimilate and hide their identity—for example, by changing one's name (Yousif to Joseph, Mohammed to Mike, Farid to Fred, Haddad to Smith)—immigration in the 1960s and 1970s represents a radical departure from this pressure. The new trend encourages individuals to be proud of their ethnic heritage. Now it is accepted to be "hyphenated" (Arab-American) and called by one's ethnic name. Furthermore, multiculturalism considers diversity a healthy, productive, and positive force that enriches the community and enhances the quality of life.

THE BIRTH OF THE ARAB LOBBY

The Arab lobby in the United States can be seen as the product of several factors. First, the 1967 War, with its defeat and humiliation, was probably the most important catalyst that brought about organized activity by the Arab American community. The hostile environment in the aftermath of the war and the barrage of negative images and stereotypes of Arabs shocked and traumatized the Arab American community. The war produced a lot of soul-searching, the beginning of a new consciousness, and an awakening of Arab Americans. The war forced and galvanized Arab Americans into organized action, which did not exist before 1967, to defend themselves against the hostile environment and to provide the public with an alternative source of information on issues of concern to the Arab community. The recent immigrants, especially those of Palestinian origin, reacted more sharply than others, in part because they have been so politicized at home and are versed in the history and heritage of their countries of origin. Many of them are products of the revolutionary period and pan-Arab nationalism under the leadership of Abdel Nasser of Egypt, who advocated abolishing artificial boundaries between Arab countries and creating a unified political entity with greater strength and cohesion.

Second, in the aftermath of the killing of Israeli athletes at the Munich Airport during the 1972 Olympics, the Nixon administration formed a special cabinet committee in charge of combatting terrorism in this country. Comprising representatives from the FBI, the CIA, the Attorney General's office, the Departments of State, Defense, Treasury, and Transportation, "Operation Boulder" caused an increase in organized political activity among Arab Americans. Major targets of this committee were people of Arab origin and others who supported them. The policy intended to restrict entry of persons of Arab origin, to collect data on persons of Arab origin, and to compile dossiers on leaders and organizations of people of Arab origin applying for permanent residency or citizenship. This vicious and racially discriminatory campaign against persons of Arab origin offended the dignity and pride of many Arab Americans, particularly those of Syrian and Lebanese origin who view themselves as loyal and law abiding Americans. This policy generated among many Arab Americans the feeling of need for organizations to defend and protect their interests. The National Association of Arab Americans (NAAA), organized in 1972, was born out of this environment.

Third, Arab governments abroad—including Egypt, Syria, Iraq, the Gulf countries, and the PLO—on numerous occasions openly or covertly sent feelers to the United States. Their mission was to encourage some Arab Americans to form their own organizations in order to counter the Israeli lobby. In addition, they sought to provide the American public, as well as the policy makers, with alternative viewpoints and sources of information.

Fourth, the political realization that swept the United States in the second part of this century saw the advantages of ethnicity in the struggle for power, income, and status. This environment encouraged ethnic groups, including Arab Americans, to organize in order to promote their interests and culture within a society that viewed them in a negative and stereotypic fashion.

Activities and Accomplishments of the Arab Lobby

Among the various Arab American organizations now operating in the United States (Haiek 1992), four merit special attention for their activities, the scope of their accomplishments, and their effectiveness in raising the political conscience of Arab Americans as well as educating the general public about mutual concerns.

Founded in 1967, the Association of Arab American University Graduates (AAUG) leads the education efforts of the Arab lobby. Its membership comprises university professors, lawyers, and physicians, many of whom are veterans of the Organization of Arab Students (OAS). It has published over seventy books and pamphlets dealing with the Arab world, its history, its people, and its culture, including *Arabs in America: Myth and Realities* (1975), *Arab Americans: Continuity and Change* (1989), *Arabic Speaking Community in American Cities* (1974), and *The Arab American: Studies in Assimilation* (1969). It also publishes the *Arab Quarterly Journal*, an outlet for controversial viewpoints. Among the first organizations to study the Arab American communality, the AAUG is particularly concerned with Palestinian issues and occasionally sends delegations to the Arab world on fact-finding missions. In the late 1980s and early 1990s the organization experienced a decline in membership and fewer financial resources chiefly because of its left-of-center position on Arab issues and the emergence of competing organizations.

Founded by Americans mainly of Lebanese and Syrian origin, the NAAA seeks to accommodate Arab Americans who are unable to identify with the liberal or left Arab American organizations. Openly modeled after the pro-Israeli lobby, the American Israeli Public Affairs Committee (AIPAC), the NAAA promotes its objectives by meeting with officials, appearing before Congress, conducting workshops on lobbying, and educating Arab Americans on the political process. It holds annual conventions in which government officials and representatives are invited to discuss Middle East policy, to meet with Arab officials abroad, and to educate them about Arab views and perspectives. It also publishes occasional surveys and monitors the voting behavior of the members of Congress. In addition, the NAAA recognizes Israel and encourages the U.S. government to pursue evenhanded policies.

Modeled after the Anti-Defamation League (ADL), the Arab American Anti-Discrimination Committee (ADC) was established in 1980 to fight racism, prejudice, and discrimination against Arabs and Arab Americans, and to monitor foreign policy in the Middle East. Its founder was the former senator from South Dakota, James G. Aburezk, who had extensive experience in the American political process. Unlike other Arab American organizations, the ADC is a grassroots organization with chapters and committees throughout the United States that monitor acts of discrimination, incidents of violence, and slurs or stereotypes against members of the Arab American community. ADC claims a membership of 25,000, although, independent resources think these figures are exaggerated. The actual number may be closer to 5,000.

Since its inception, the ADC has fought many battles. For example, it is responsible for changing the content of screenplays as in the case of *Aladdin*, and demanding apologies from CBS anchor Dan Rather and former Secretary of State Henry Kissinger for ethnic slurs or prejudiced remarks. Furthermore, the ADC has filed legal actions and has taken companies to court in order to stop certain advertisements in which a stereotyped image of the Arab has been used. With as many as 3,000 people attending, the annual ADC conventions are lively occasions where Arab American issues are discussed. The ADC also publishes a newsletter and occasional papers, and has printed several books on Arab Americans. During the Gulf crisis, the ADC criticized both Iraq's invasion of Kuwait and U.S. military action in the area, whereas other Arab organizations like the NAAA and the Arab American Institute (AAI) damaged their credibility because they tried to support both the Gulf countries and the American military policy.

Established in 1984 after its founder Jim Zogby clashed with the ADC chief, James Aburezk, the Arab American Institute (AAI) seeks to encourage Arab Americans to be active in the political system through voter registration and nominations of Arab Americans for local, state, and national offices. The institute strongly encourages the formation of Republican and Democratic Arab American clubs within the Republican and Democratic parties. To this end, the AAI has organized several leadership conferences where people of Arab origin meet officials with the purpose of learning how to influence the political process. The institute took a very active part in Jesse Jackson's 1988 presidential campaign. The president of the institute, Jim Zogby, was appointed as national cochair of the campaign with specific responsibilities for finance and delegate tracking. He and other Arab Americans were able to collect $700,000 for Jackson (Samhan 1989: 227–251).

Problems and Difficulties

The problems and difficulties experienced by the Arab lobby can be attributed to myriad causes. First, the size of the Arab American community is small, not exceeding three million, which is about one percent of the total U.S. population. Second, the Arab American lobby lacks cohesiveness and unity (Jabara 1989: 201–206) because the Arab American community is heterogeneous and made up of many subcommunities identified with country of origin, religion or sect, and political ideology. Other sources of disunity in the Arab American community may stem from the fact that some Arab Americans are born in this country, whereas others are born overseas. All of these factors have produced hundreds of organizations, each with its own leaders and agenda.

Arab Americans born overseas lack the experience of being actively involved in politics. Many of them come from countries with a low level of civic responsibility. Arab governments have discouraged the development of a civic society and its manifestations—political parties, voluntary organizations, trade unions, professional organizations, media, and other interest groups—which act as intermediaries between individuals and the government, as instruments to articulate people's views and concerns, and to create a balance between the governed and the government, bolstering the system's capabilities in conflict management. These instruments were either discouraged, censored, or created by the state to reflect the state's views rather than the individual's (Aruri 1989). Thus when Arab Americans come to this country, they are bewildered with the complexities of the political system. Furthermore, while coping with a new complex economic system, they spend countless hours at work, trying to improve their standard of living; thus they have little time to devote to political issues that do not bring them immediate benefits. Also some Arab Americans born overseas fear the consequences of their political involvement on their businesses—a backlash of the Jews and the wrath of the Israeli lobby.

Moreover, Arab Americans have not yet mastered the art of coalition politics, the dominant feature of American politics. While coalition politics does not guarantee success, it definitely increases its chances. What complicates this situation further for Arab Americans, particularly those born overseas, is that they are not active in issues other than Arab issues. To succeed in building a coalition, one must show interest in issues of concern to other groups. Arab Americans are still considered by many as a lobby with a single issue: the Arab-Israel conflict. Consequently, Arab American groups find it difficult to strike a coalition with mainstream groups. Many of these groups shun Arab American groups and do not solicit their cooperation either because they consider them insignificant or a liability. Furthermore, a coalition with the Arab lobby may antagonize the Jewish element in an organization. In 1972, presidential candidate George McGovern, for example, turned down an Arab American endorsement for fear of alienating Jewish support. Similarly, in the 1984 presidential election Walter Mondale rejected $5,000 in contributions from small businessmen in Chicago.

Several Arab American organizations, however, are moving in the direction of coalition politics. The ADC and AAI have worked with mainstream organizations, as demonstrated by their contributions to Jesse Jackson's 1988 presidential campaign, an effort that helped teach them the process of building coalitions. This process was motivated in part because both groups were able to understand each other's political position and were able to find common ground (Samhan 1989: 227–251).

The turmoil in the Arab world has also affected deeply the unity, effectiveness, and operations of the Arab lobby: the civil war in Lebanon (1979–1990), the signing of the Camp David Accords (1979), the Iran-Iraq War, and the Iraqi invasion of Kuwait (1990). These conflicts split the lobby into factions and crippled its operations. For example, all these events negatively affected the membership of the AAUG. The civil war in Lebanon led some Lebanese members to reject the organization because of its siding with the Palestinians against the Maronite Lebanese. Likewise, some Egyptians left the AAUG after the signing of the Camp David Accords because the organization was critical of the agreement. The Iraqi invasion of Kuwait threw the Arab American lobby in disarray and caused many setbacks. Some Arab organizations who opposed not the Iraqi invasion but also the way the United States handled it, lost some of the financial support they received from Gulf countries. Others, who sided with the Gulf countries and approved of the way the United States handled the invasion, lost many of their members out of disagreement with the organization's position. The invasion tore the Arab American community apart. Some members turned to Islam, an alternative to overcome the alienation experienced in the United States. The invasion diverted the Arab lobby's attention from the main issue, the Palestinian issue, and made it difficult to defend. Furthermore, the invasion increased the negative coverage of the Arab and Islam in the U.S. mass media, including TV programs, popular novels, news broadcasts, and movies.

The lack of financial resources has also contributed to the problems and difficulties faced by the Arab lobby, which works on a shoestring budget. Arab Americans earn above-average incomes, but many are reluctant to make generous political contributions partly because they are not accustomed to doing so in their home countries, out of fear of repercussions or lack of commitment to the recipient of their contributions. In addition, on numerous occasions Arab governments have attempted to pressure Arab organizations to promote one agenda at the expense of others. These manipulations may take different forms, such as financial contributions directly or indirectly to advance certain goals.

Another difficulty facing the Arab lobby is the Israeli lobby—an efficient, resourceful, and highly organized opponent which knows well the rules of the game and plays by them. Furthermore, the Israeli lobby is successful in part because many of its members are active in many non-Jewish issues. Many take leading roles and hold high positions in organizations that appeal to many ethnic groups. Thus they are able to establish coalitions and steer other organizations to their side of the issues. Individuals are then more willing to contribute financially to their own causes as well as those of others.

One should be careful, however, not to exaggerate the power of the Israeli lobby. Some Arab Americans have a tendency to do that, asserting that the Israeli lobby has hijacked the American government and subverted it to Israeli interests (Haddad 1991). Such exaggeration is both misleading and dangerous. It is misleading because it does not give us a true picture of American foreign policy, which, in its historical and global context, is almost the same the world over, whether in Latin America, Central America, Africa, or the Middle East, and if there are differences, they are in details, not in the composite picture. U.S. policy has little to do with fostering freedom and democracy in the world. It is much more concerned with establishing a world order conducive to profits for U.S. enterprises and corporations (Abraham 1989: 17–43). It is also dangerous to exaggerate the posture of the Israeli lobby because this perception will discourage Arab Americans from getting involved in the political process and will paralyze them on the ground, making them believe that nothing can be done and that all work and contributions are a waste of time and resources.

The Arab lobby suffers from its narrow agenda. The primary focus on the Palestinian issue and its related matters has caused the Arab lobby to neglect or subordinate other domestic and international issues, thereby impeding the building of coalitions. The lobby has difficulty adjusting or reacting when other issues emerge which may be politically relevant to their causes. For example, the Iran-Iraq War was hardly treated or mentioned in lobby publications. These organizations neglected the war despite the fact it was tragic and lasted for eight years with one million dead and a cost of $450 billion dollars. Other issues besides the Palestinians were avoided either because they were divisive or because many of the leaders of the organizations are Palestinians and do not want new issues to divert the attention from the main issue of Palestine, or perhaps they just don't know how to deal with it effectively.

THE PEACE PROCESS BETWEEN THE ARABS AND ISRAEL

The Madrid Conference of 1991 represented a major change in the relationship between the Arabs and Israelis. It may lead to a resolution of the conflict or reduce its intensity and importance. The conference has already led to the signing of the Declaration of Principles between the Palestinians and Israelis on 12 September 1994, and to the peace treaty between Jordan and Israel in October 1994. While it is too early to evaluate the impact of the peace process on the Arab lobby, it is possible to make some preliminary observations about the positive and negative impacts it will have. On one hand, the peace process could promote the disunity and incohesiveness of the Arab lobby and thus reduce its participation in the political process. A hostile environment, fear, discrimination, and violence often encourages ethnic groups to become mobilized to work together in order to defend themselves and protect their interests. Once the reason for solidarity is changed or disappears, the organization is often weakened to the point of extinction.

On the other hand, the peace process may help reduce negative stereotyping and the hostile environment of harassment, racism, and discrimination. This new climate can encourage people of Arab origin to be more active in the political process and devote more time and money to these activities. Furthermore, the peace process may shift the Arab lobby's focus from the Palestinian-Israeli conflict to important domestic issues such as affirmative action, racism, discrimination, hate crimes, education, and taxes. Finally, the peace process will encourage more coalition politics between Arab American organizations and others. As Arab American organizations shift their focus to domestic issues, they will find it much easier to work not only with marginalized groups but also with those in the mainstream.

CONCLUSION

The size of the Arab American community will continue to increase as waves of new immigrants continue to arrive in America to seek better opportunity to improve their lives and to escape from political persecution. The numbers of Arab immigrants will depend both on the political instability and lack of economic development in the Arab world, and on U.S. foreign policy, immigration laws, and economic opportunities. These factors will, of course, be influenced by the atmosphere toward ethnic groups in the United States. The Arab lobby has achieved a limited degree of maturity and sophistication as can be seen in public meetings, seminars, news conferences, congressional hearings, formation of clubs within the Democratic and Republican parties, books, articles, and newsletters. Arab Americans have begun to understand that in order to make a difference and to exert their influence, they must get involved in the legislative process and be active participants. Despite its advances, the Arab lobby is still a minor player in a major struggle, and it faces numerous problems and difficulties. Its future will depend on how successful it is in overcoming these difficulties.

REFERENCES

Abraham, Nabeel. 1989. Arab American marginality: Myths and praxis. In *Arab Americans: Continuity and change*, edited by Baha Abu-Laban and Michael Sulieman. Belmont, MA.: Association of Arab American University Graduates.

Abu-Laban, Baha, and Michael W. Sulieman, eds. 1989. *Arab Americans: Continuity and change*. Belmont, MA: Association of Arab American University Graduates.

Abu-Laban, Baha, and Faith Zeady. 1975. *Arabs in America: Myth and realities*. Evanston, IL: University Press International.

Al-Qazzaz, Ayad. 1979. *Transitional links between the Arab community in the U.S. and the Arab world*. Sacramento, CA: Cal Central.

American Israeli Public Affairs Committee. 1983. *The campaign to discredit Israel*. Washington, DC: AIPAC.

Anti-Defamation League. 1983. *Pro-Arab propaganda in America: Vehicles and voices*. New York: ADL.

Aruri, Nassir. 1989. The recolonization of the Arab world. In *Arab Americans: Continuity and change*, edited by Baha Abu-Laban and Michael Sulieman. Belmont, MA: Association of Arab American University Graduates.

Haddad, Yvonne Y., ed. 1991. *The Muslims of America*. New York: Oxford University Press.

Haiek, Joseph, ed. 1992. *Arab American almanac*. 4th ed. Glendale, CA: New Circle.

Huseby-Darvas, Eva Veronika. 1994. Coming to America: Dilemmas of ethnic groups since the 1880s. In *The development of Arab American identity*, edited by E. McCarus. Ann Arbor: University of Michigan Press.

Jabara, Abdeen M. 1989. A strategy for political effectiveness. In *Arab Americans: Continuity and change*, edited by Baha Abu-Laban and Michael Sulieman. Belmont, MA: Association of Arab American University Graduates.

Kasem, Casey. 1994. We're proud of our heritage. *Parade*, 16 January, 4–6.

Nader, Jean A. 1991. An Arab American domestic agenda for the 1990s. Working paper prepared by the Arab American Institute, Washington, D.C.

Samhan, Helen H. 1989. Arab Americans and the elections of 1988: A constituency come of age. In *Arab Americans: Continuity and change*, edited by Baha Abu-Laban and Michael Sulieman. Belmont, MA: Association of Arab American University Graduates.

Sulieman, Michael W. 1994. Arab Americans and the political process. In *The development of Arab American identity*, edited by E. McCarus. Ann Arbor: University of Michigan Press.

Yinger, J. M. 1981. Toward a theory of assimilation and dissimilation. *Ethnic and Racial Studies* 4, no. 3: 249–264.

Zogby, John. 1990. *A demographic profile of Arab Americans*. Washington, DC: Arab American Institute.

Index

About the Contributors

AYAD AL-QAZZAZ is a professor of sociology at California State University, Sacramento. He is the author of several books, including *The Arab World: A Handbook for Teachers; Women in the Middle East and North Africa: An Annotated Bibliography; Transitional Links between the Arab Community in the U.S. and the Arab World;* and, most recently, *The Arab World Notebooks.*

YONG HYO CHO is a professor of public administration and director of the Masters in Public Administration Program at San Francisco State University. His most recent publications include *The Real Predicaments of Declining Cities* and *The Cultural Roots of Entrepreneurial Bureaucracy.*

RODOLFO O. DE LA GARZA is vice president of the Tomás Rivera Center and Mike Hogg Professor of Community Affairs in the Department of Government at the University of Texas in Austin. His most recent publication includes *Ethnic Ironies: Latinos and 1992 Elections.*

LOUIS DESIPIO is an assistant professor in the Department of Political Science at the University of Illinois. Dr. DeSipio is also a social science research associate at the National Association of Latino Elected and Appointed Officials Education Fund in Washington, D.C. and Los Angeles.

TERRI SUSAN FINE is an associate professor in the Department of Political Science at the University of Central Florida. She has published articles in such journals as *Presidential Studies Quarterly, Women and Politics, Social Science Journal,* and *Sociological Perspectives.*

WALTER C. FLEMING is an assistant professor with the Center for Native American Studies at Montana State University. Mr. Fleming has worked for the Bureau of Indian Affairs and the Bureau of Reclamation.

MARTIN L. KILSON is professor of government at Harvard University. He is currently working on *Politics of African Populism*; *Politics of Inclusion: Blacks in American Political Culture*; and *Black Politics in Cleveland 1967-1990s*. Also forthcoming are *African Autocracy: Political Development in Third World States* and *Neither Insiders nor Outsiders: Blacks in White America*.

PAN SUK KIM is currently chairman of the Department of Public Administration at the University of Inchon in South Korea. He was previously an assistant professor in the Department of Urban Studies and Public Administration at Old Dominion University in Virginia.

PAULA D. MCCLAIN is a professor of government and incoming chair of the Woodrow Wilson Department of Government and Foreign Affairs at the University of Virginia. Dr. McClain's most recent book is an edited volume, *Minority Group Influence: Agenda Setting, Formulation, and Public Policy*.

MOHAMMAD T. MEHDI is president of the American Arab Relations Committee and Secretary General of the National Council on Islamic Affairs. He has written many books on American relations with the Arab and Muslim worlds, among which are *Constitutionalism: Western and Middle Eastern*; *Nations of Lions Chained*; *Terrorism: Why America is the Target*; and *Islam and Intolerance: A Reply to Salman Rushdie*.

DARIO MORENO is an associate professor of political science at Florida International University. His areas of research and teaching are Cuban American politics and U.S.–Latin American relations. He has published two books, *U.S. Policy in Central America: The Endless Debate* and *The Struggle for Peace in Central America*.

GLENN T. MORRIS is an associate professor of political science and director of the Fourth World Center for the Study of Indigenous Law and Politics at the University of Colorado at Denver.

DON TOSHIAKI NAKANISHI is a professor in the Graduate School of Education and director of the Asian American Studies Center at the University of California, Los Angeles. Dr. Nakanishi is on the editorial boards of *American Journal* and the University Press of Virginia, Race and Ethnicity in Urban Politics Series.

ARATI RAO is an assistant professor of political science at Wellesley College where she teaches courses on feminist political theory, politics of race and ethnicity, human rights, and the politics of identity.

WILBUR C. RICH is a professor of political science at Wellesley College. His most recent book is *Black Mayors and School Politics: The Failure of Reform in Detroit, Gary, and Newark.*

LANA STEIN is an associate professor of political science and public policy administration and a research associate with the public policy centers at the University of Missouri–St. Louis. Dr. Stein is the author of *Holding Bureaucrats Accountable: Politicians and Professionals in St. Louis.*

L. LING-CHI WANG is an associate professor of Asian American studies in the Department of Ethnic Studies at the University of California, Berkeley. Professor Wang lectures and writes on Asian American history and civil rights and education issues affecting Asians in the United States.

JERRY GAFIO WATTS is currently associate professor of American studies at Trinity College, Hartford, Connecticut. His most recent book is *Heroism and the Black Intellectual: Reflections on Ralph Ellison, Politics, and Afro-American Intellectual Life.*